Qualitative Research in Psychology

Qualitative Research in Psychology

Expanding Perspectives in Methodology and Design

Edited by
Paul M. Camic
Jean E. Rhodes
Lucy Yardley

Foreword by Michael Bamberg

American Psychological Association, Washington, DC

First Printing January 2003
Second Printing August 2003
Third Printing January 2004
Fourth Printing February 2007
Fifth Printing June 2009

Published by
American Psychological Association
750 First Street, NE
Washington, DC 20002
www.apa.org

To order
APA Order Department
P.O. Box 92984
Washington, DC 20090-2984
Tel: (800) 374-2721
Direct: (202) 336-5510
Fax: (202) 336-5502
TDD/TTY: (202) 336-6123
Online: www.apa.org/books/
Email: order@apa.org

In the U.K., Europe, Africa, and the Middle East, copies may be ordered from
American Psychological Association
3 Henrietta Street
Covent Garden, London
WC2E 8LU England

Typeset in Century Schoolbook by World Composition Services, Inc., Sterling, VA

Printer: Data Reproductions, Auburn Hills, MI
Cover Designer: Michael Hentges Design, Alexandria, VA
Project Manager: Debbie Hardin, Carlsbad, CA

Library of Congress Cataloging-in-Publication Data

Qualitative research in psychology : expanding perspectives in methodology and design / edited by Paul M. Camic, Jean E. Rhodes, Lucy Yardley.-- 1st ed.
p. cm.
Includes bibliographical references and index.
ISBN 1-55798-979-6 (alk. paper)
1. Psychology--Research--Methodology. 2. Qualitative research. I. Camic, Paul Marc, 1955- II. Rhodes, Jean E. III. Yardley Lucy, 1961-

BF76.5.Q338 2003
150′.7′2--dc21 2002033220

British Library Cataloguing-in-Publication Data
A CIP record is available from the British Library.

Printed in the United States of America

Contents

Contributors

Michael Bamberg, Clark University, Worcester, MA
Tatiana Bertsch, New York University, New York
Kathy Boudin, Bedford Hills, NY
Iris Bowen, Albion, NY
Paul M. Camic, Columbia College Chicago, Chicago, IL
Judith Clark, Bedford Hills, NY
Jessica Hoffmann Davis, Harvard University, Cambridge, MA
Elliot W. Eisner, Stanford University, Stanford, CA
Michelle Fine, City University of New York, New York
Carol Gilligan, New York University, New York
Amedeo P. Giorgi, Saybrook Graduate School, San Francisco, CA
Barbro M. Giorgi, John F. Kennedy University, Orinda, CA
Julie A. Hengst, University of Illinois, Urbana–Champaign
Karen Henwood, University of East Anglia, Norwich, UK
Donna Hylton, Bedford Hills, NY
Bettina Johnson, Market Insite Group, Ft. Worth, TX
Steinar Kvale, University of Aarhus, Rissokov, Denmark
Jeanne Marecek, Swarthmore College, Swarthmore, PA
Migdalia Martinez, Bedford, NY
Joseph E. McGrath, University of Illinois, Urbana–Champaign
Peggy J. Miller, University of Illinois, Urbana–Champaign
Missy, Bedford Hills, NY
Michael Murray, Memorial University of Newfoundland, St. Johns, Newfoundland, Canada
Nick Pidgeon, University of East Anglia, Norwich, UK
Jonathan Potter, Loughborough University, Leicestershire, UK
Donald Ratcliff, Biola University, La Mirada, CA
Jean E. Rhodes, University of Massachusetts, Boston
Rosemarie A. Roberts, New York City
Pamela Smart, Bedford Hills, NY
Renée Spencer, Boston University, Boston, MA
María Elena Torre, City University of New York, New York
Debora Upegui, New York City
Su-hua Wang, Urbana–Champaign, IL
M. Katherine Weinberg, Harvard University, Cambridge, MA
Lucy Yardley, University of Southampton, Southampton, UK

Foreword

Michael Bamberg

Every newly established research tradition has its own way of coming into being, and qualitative research is no exception. With regard to my own initial involvement with what later became established as *qualitative research*—or, as I call it when presenting it to my students, *qualitative inquiry*—it is hard to pinpoint when and how it all began. I do not think that there was a particular event or a sudden insight that can be woven into my academic life story and labeled as my "turning point." It simply happened. However, I clearly recall many events over 8 to 10 years (in the late 1970s and early 1980s) at different places (Berkeley, San Diego, Nijmegen, Berlin) and involving friends and colleagues around the same age cohort though from quite different disciplines (sociology, anthropology, linguistics, education, political science, comparative literature, health sciences and nursing studies, psychology). These events consisted of meetings in which my colleagues and I discussed transcripts of interviews, observational records, or papers we had come across before they were published. During them something took place that contributed to my slow and gradual turn to qualitative methods as the preferred inquiry method in psychology. Although these meetings often had some flavor of subversiveness and conspiracy, taking place most often outside the institutions where we were doing our research and teaching, they were not governed by an anti-institutional stance but, as strange as this may sound, by work with actual data. These data came from real people with real lives; people who were sharing aspects of their subjective, experiential life-worlds—including their emotions, desires, and moral values. We, as investigators, were bystanders, allowed to catch a glimpse of who these people were, how they wanted to be understood, or how they made sense of others and themselves, including their own experiences and their lives.

What stood out most for us at that time was our interest in singular cases and discursive processes that seemed to represent the individuality and subjectivity of experiences of our research participants—something that thus far had not been central to the social and humanistic sciences, not even in psychology. In contrast to our traditional endeavors to generalize across individual cases, to discover patterns, laying out "underlying" structures or systems that seemed to govern particular actions or events, possibly even as an attempt to uncover underlying universals, it was the unique that aroused our interest.

Explanatory approaches that had been developed and worked up within the hypothetico–deductive model of knowledge as something that was out there to be conquered were out. *Observing, describing,* and *understanding* became the new key terms, and the new business was knowledge building and knowledge generation rather than affirmation or falsification of some previously established hypotheses. To seek and to understand what was subjective in the experience and lives from the point of view of our research participants became the primary task—asking to be empathic with regard to the subjectivity and experience of our participants, particularly of those who were vulnerable, disadvantaged, or opening their wounds from social or personal maltreatments. In sum, the original but initially relatively unreflected turn to make the individual participants with their unique experiences more central to the research process gave birth to a redefinition of the role of the researcher and his or her relationship to what now became the "research participant" and consequently to what could count as knowledge, the status of data, and the status of interpretation and analysis.

Reflecting on a time before the debates between quantitative versus qualitative and between explanatory versus interpretive methods, I do not think that any of us had in mind that what we were doing could become codified, canonized, and handed down to new students of psychology in the form of a systematic methodology. The idea that this type of working with observational data and recorded conversations could possibly be integrated back into the disciplines that we were representing, particularly into the discipline of psychology, was foreign to us back then. But exactly this has happened in the course of the past 15 or so years—again, as a slow and gradual process, resulting in quite a number of, at first, self-designed courses and quite a number of textbooks, handbooks, and cookbooks for how to better understand and how to carry out qualitative research across the disciplines. It is interesting to note that psychology lagged considerably behind in this development.

This volume is one of the first books to appear in psychology that substantially addresses the importance of qualitative inquiry as a vital means of approaching the problems studied by psychologists. Paul M. Camic, Jean E. Rhodes, and Lucy Yardley have chosen some of the best minds in the field to produce an eloquent volume that will have great appeal to graduate students and seasoned researchers alike. This book is organized and written in a way that invites readers to come along for an adventure of discovery that enlivens the essence of research in the field.

The first part of the book, which acts as a cornerstone of qualitative inquiry for psychologists, does not get bogged down by epistemological and ontological foundational debates that often turn young students of qualitative data more off than on. These first four chapters provide an excellent introduction to qualitative methodology within the context of existing and emerging social sciences research. The second part goes on to introduce 10 different methods used in qualitative research. Each chapter reveals and develops its stance with regard to the connection between theory and (moral and political) practice and communicates effectively where and how to apply (and not to apply) the suggested methodological exigencies. Each chapter is thoughtfully laid out as an apprenticeship to a field of study on its own, exemplifying the methods and applying them. At the same time all chapters leave considerable space for students of qualitative data to try out their own ambitions and to explore their own questions and interests in novel ways, taking what has been offered in this book as stepping stones into a deeper involvement—not just with methodological approaches but with psychology as a whole.

I am confident that the collection presented in this book will help overcome old rifts and controversies and contribute to the development of a much more inclusive psychology—one that clearly sees the challenges qualitative research brings to the discipline—but also one that is no longer threatened but willing and able to integrate the world of subjective experience and the processes of its construction as central.

Preface

Perhaps one of the most striking features of this volume is that it is one of the first books on qualitative methods to be published by the American Psychological Association (APA). Although other disciplines (i.e., anthropology, sociology, education, marketing, program evaluation) have vigorously incorporated qualitative methods for a number of years, most of academic psychology has had an ambivalent relationship with qualitative methods. Psychology's strong preference for quantitative approaches is reflected in undergraduate and graduate course requirements, the composition of journal editorial boards, and the APA *Publication Manual,* which makes no mention of protocol for presenting qualitative findings. Although relatively late in coming (particularly compared with the European psychological traditions), this book represents an important step toward the greater integration of qualitative methods into academic and applied psychology.

In editing this volume, our goal was to bring together experts from across a broad range of psychological perspectives (e.g., social, developmental, clinical, community, environmental, personality, educational, psychodynamic, phenomenological, feminist, and health psychology), all of whom have been contributing to research using established and emerging qualitative methods. By drawing from a wide spectrum of fields, we hope to provide researchers with a theoretically informed and practically applicable basis for comparing the relative benefits and limitations of each approach as it bears on their particular research topic. Our target audience ranges from advanced undergraduate and graduate students to established researchers from within the boundaries of psychology. A closely allied secondary audience is students and researchers in cultural studies and cultural policy, education, anthropology, sociology, and social work. This book is also likely to have appeal to practitioners in hospitals, clinics, schools, cultural institutions, and business organizations where a portion of their job responsibilities are research related. We have developed this book with all of these readers in mind.

What is also significant about this volume and what makes it unique is that it addresses issues that are of primary concern to psychologists. The vast majority of textbooks previously published in qualitative research has been in other disciplines such as anthropology, education, nursing, and sociology. Moreover, unlike most previous volumes, this book provides readers with detailed descriptions of the actual procedures that are used in carrying out specific research methods.

Of course, no book can fully capture the complexity, nuances, and techniques embedded in each approach. Nor can it provide complete coverage of the full range of qualitative methods that are available to researchers. Space limitations prevent us from including such approaches as the research case study method, protocol analysis, and biographical and historical analysis. These omissions do not imply their lack of importance and, in fact, we hope to explore these and other promising approaches in subsequent work to be published in the future.

The book is organized into two major parts. The first part includes chapters that introduce readers to issues of epistemology, ontology, and the place of qualitative research within psychology both as an alternative approach to research methodology and as a complementary one, used in conjunction with quantitative approaches. A pressing question addressed by all seven authors of this part is, "What counts as knowledge?"

Paul M. Camic, Jean E. Rhodes, and Lucy Yardley (chapter 1) argue for the value and validity of qualitative work, present some of the conflicts surrounding qualitative methods, discuss the manners in which qualitative approaches relate to quantitative research, and highlight the merits and uses of qualitative methods for various purposes relevant to the work of psychology. Elliot W. Eisner (chapter 2) examines the root of the term *qualitative* in the social sciences and relates it to the contemporary conduct of the art and science of qualitative research in psychology. He examines the distinctions between qualitative and quantitative work and provides examples of arts-based qualitative research while asking researchers to reflect on artistry as a process that researchers would do well to emulate.

Joseph E. McGrath and Bettina A. Johnson (chapter 3) discuss some of the crucial epistemological and methodological issues that beset both qualitative and quantitative research in psychology. Some of these are at a paradigmatic level, including questions about reality and how we can know it, about objectivity, about causality, and about the role of temporal and contextual factors. Other issues they discuss are those at an operational level and have to do with how empirical evidence is collected, aggregated, analyzed, and interpreted. Jeanne Marecek (chapter 4) presents what is shared by qualitative and quantitative approaches and what is not, which helps us to arrive at a fuller understanding of both. She challenges some of the misconceptions of both qualitative and quantitative work by examining considerations of generality, validity, reliability, objectivity, and subjectivity. She also addresses the false dichotomy that has emerged between quantitative research as deductive and qualitative research as inductive.

The second part presents several major qualitative research methodologies, each contained within a separate chapter. The psychologists who developed the methods themselves wrote several of the chapters in this section, and all of the authors invited to contribute are actively engaged researchers and well-known experts in their respective research domains. These chapters follow a parallel organization that includes (a) specific and detailed information about the applications of the methodology; (b) subsections addressing issues in design, sampling, data collection, data analysis, and interpretation; and (c) a research case example illustrating the methodology presented in the chapter.

Jonathan Potter (chapter 5) presents a thorough introduction to discourse analysis and discursive psychology using a study of AIDS counseling as a research example of how to use this approach. Michael Murray (chapter 6) examines narrative psychology and narrative analysis by first reviewing the theoretical foundation of this approach, discussing the various forms of narrative psychology, and concluding with a research example based on a series of interviews with patients with chronic pain. Donald Ratcliff (chapter 7) presents a discussion of the use of video recordings as qualitative video research, an emerging research tool, carefully discussing methods of data collection and analysis. His use of children's social interactions and rituals in a school hallway is an example of how these methods can be adapted and applied to a specific context.

Karen Henwood and Nick Pidgeon (chapter 8) chart and debate the rationale for doing psychological research using grounded theory, one of the most well-known qualitative research methods. Looking at grounded theory not as a unitary method but as a node around which useful discussions of epistemology, ethics, and validity can occur, these authors examine an extensive corps of discussion data from focus groups about the importance and value attached to woodlands and trees by the British public. Carol Gilligan, Renée Spencer, M. Katherine Weinberg, and Tatiana Bertsch introduce the *Listening Guide* method (chapter 9), which provides researchers with a way of attending to human conversation. This method, introduced in detail for the first time, involves a series of focused readings of texts, each designed to bring the researcher into relationship with a person's distinct and multilayered voice by focusing on, or listening to, a particular aspect of the narrative. Michelle Fine and associates (chapter 10) explore the history, method, opportunities, and challenges of participatory action research with a close look at a research project conducted by a team of university-based researchers and women inmates in a maximum security prison. These researchers analyze the relationships of insider–outsider researchers and the differential epistemologies, knowledge, vulnerabilities, and responsibilities both groups bring to the task as they take readers through the design, data collection, analysis, and interpretive phases of the study.

Jessica Hoffmann Davis (chapter 11) presents an emerging qualitative method, portraiture as methodology, which examines the research portrait as a written narrative that seeks to balance elements of context, thematic structure, relationship, and voice into an aesthetic whole to provide a carefully constructed cohesive interpretation of data. Drawing on the author's work at a community art center that creates a supportive and high-expectation environment for African American artists, this chapter focuses on the collection of data through observation, interview, and review of visual materials and the production of a narrative portrait. Peggy J. Miller, Julie A. Hengst, and Su-hua Wang (chapter 12) provide a brief history of ethnographic methods in anthropology and its more recent history within psychology. Through the use of a case study in developmental cultural psychology, readers are guided through the characteristics of ethnographic inquiry, which includes hypothesis development, data collection, analysis, and interpretation of data and the use of writing to describe one's findings. Specific attention is paid to the ethnographic interview, participant observation, artifacts as data, archival data, and ethical concerns. Amedeo P. and Barbro M. Giorgi (chapter 13) provide a clear demarcation of the descriptive phenomenological method from other types of phenomenology. Phenomenological methods are compared and contrasted with the traditional scientific method to provide a framework from which to better understand descriptive phenomenology. They present a demonstrative example using a research participant's internalized homophobia, showing in detail how the method is applied. Finally, Steinar Kvale (chapter 14) outlines psychoanalytical qualitative research. Drawing on postmodern conceptions of science, the causistic, relational, constructive, and pragmatic aspects of knowledge are outlined, and the strength and weakness of psychoanalytical knowledge production are discussed. Kvale emphasizes seven key aspects useful in the psychoanalytical research interview (case study, open mode of interviewing, interpretation of meaning, historical dimension, human interaction, pathology as topic of investigation, and instigation of change) and concludes the chapter with an example of such an interview.

* * *

The idea for this book came after teaching qualitative methods for a number of years to graduate students in psychology. Although there were several textbooks available for graduate-level instruction, none adequately addressed the research training needs specific to psychologists interested in qualitative research methods. Concurrently with our work with graduate students, an increasing number of colleagues inquired about incorporating qualitative methods in their research. The final shove to develop such a book came after Paul Camic, at an annual meeting of the APA, presented a paper that incorporated qualitative methods in its design. The overwhelmingly strong and supportive audience response to the qualitative methodology—at an APA paper session—was the impetus to begin this volume.

In addition to our students and APA audience members, we are also very grateful to Lansing Hays of the APA, who sponsored and guided this work from its inception. We especially want to thank Lansing for his enthusiasm, challenging questions, and deadpan humor, which helped carry us through the two years of writing and editing this volume. It is an honor for all of us to be publishing this work with the APA. We would also like to thank Lawrence Wilson and Andrew Causey for their helpful comments about several chapters in this volume and our reviewers at the APA—both anonymous and known—for their extremely helpful suggestions.

Part I

Ways of Looking at the World: Epistemological Issues in Qualitative Research

1

Naming the Stars: Integrating Qualitative Methods Into Psychological Research

Paul M. Camic, Jean E. Rhodes, and Lucy Yardley

In *The Phantom Tollbooth,* Norton Juster tells the story of two brothers, King Azaz and the Mathemagician, who inherited their father's kingdom of Wisdom.

> They were by nature very suspicious and jealous. Each one tried to outdo the other . . . King Azaz insisted that words were far more significant than numbers and hence his kingdom was truly the greater, and the Mathemagician claimed that numbers were much more important than words and hence his kingdom was supreme. They discussed and debated and raved and ranted until they were on the verge of blows when it was decided to submit the question to arbitration by the princesses Rhyme and Reason. After days of careful consideration in which all the evidence was weighted and all the witnesses heard, they made their decision: "Words and numbers are of equal value, for, in the cloak of knowledge, one is warp and the other woof. It is no more important to count the sands than it is to name the stars. Therefore, let both kingdoms live in peace. (Juster, 1965, pp. 74–75)

Unfortunately, Rhyme and Reason's exquisite logic fell on deaf ears. The princesses were banished from the kingdom, and the full breadth of knowledge remained elusive for many years. A similar fate appears to have beset the kingdom of psychology, where quantitative and qualitative methodologists have met each other with resistance and skepticism. Rather than finding a common ground, numbers have prevailed and qualitative approaches to understanding the human experience have been relegated to an ancillary role. This overreliance on positivism and the experimental method throughout the 20th century has hampered inventiveness, restricting the very nature of the questions that have been asked and the sources of data that have been considered legitimate.

As in the *Phantom Tollbooth,* where the princesses were ultimately rescued and their recommendations heeded, a momentum from the muted corners within and surrounding psychology is gradually restoring qualitative methods to their rightful place in the field. We hope that this volume helps to build on this momentum—nudging psychological researchers toward greater inclusiveness and the full acceptance of qualitative methods.

Background: The Fundamental Questions

In his attempt to rescue Rhyme and Reason, the protagonist in the *Phantom Tollbooth,* Milo, journeys through the kingdom of numbers, Digitopolis. There a man who poses a series of problems, including one about a 68-foot-long beaver, confronts him.

> "That's absurd," objected Milo, whose head was spinning from all the numbers and questions. "That may be true," he acknowledged, "but it's completely accurate, and as long as the answer is right, who cares if the question is wrong? If you want sense, you'll have to make it yourself" (Juster, 1965, p. 175).

Psychologists, perhaps more than any other social scientists, have been prone to privileging methods and procedures over research questions (Gergen, 1985). Putting the methodological cart before the horse has constrained our full understanding of psychological processes. Moreover, basic ontological, epistemological, and methodological questions, such as "What is real?" "Who knows what is real?" and "How do you know what is real?" are asked and answered in ways that implicitly privilege the experimental method. Fully addressing these questions is critical, however, because their answers form the very foundation of inquiry in the social sciences. In deciding what is real, and for whom it is real, a pluralistic approach to research might encourage both skepticism and innovation, be a little subversive, take on new topics and questions, but remain rigorous, thorough, and useful. Shweder (1996), in an important essay about the differences between *quanta* and *qualia,* suggests that we "put our metaphysical cards on the table (our assumptions about the underlying nature of social reality)" (p. 175), thereby revealing what research is all about.

Those "cards" vary, of course, among the contributors to this volume. What is perhaps a common core to all the chapters, however, is a discarding of the notion that what separates quantitative and qualitative approaches to research is whether to count or not count, measure or not measure, sample or not sample, administer a questionnaire or conduct an interview. Because all social science research counts and measures in some way or another, the true difference is in what to count and measure and what one discovers when doing so (Shweder, 1996, p. 179). Stated another way, the questions become, "to count or to discover the name," "to measure or to listen and observe," or "to administer a questionnaire or talk with someone." Qualitative research questions whether an objective conception of reality can truly exist and suggests that other forms of investigation are necessary to increase our understanding of the thing we are studying (Cafasso, Camic, & Rhodes, 2001). Humans, not the gods, created all forms of inquiry, and we can and should modify them as needed to make inquiry relevant to our work as psychologists, social scientists, and educators. We may not find *the* answer to what is real, but the richness within the different realities may provide us with a better answer.

"What is real?" evokes the issue that divided the brothers in the Kingdom of Wisdom. As a profession, psychology has generally decided that numbers are more real than words and responses on paper-and-pencil tests more real (and valid) than interviews, conversations, and other complex forms of representation. However, "How do you know what is real?" is perhaps the question that best defines empiricism and provides a substantial foundation for a qualitative psychology. Of course, we *all* know what is real—but our realities may be different, depending on our cultural background, our gender, sexual orientation, our race, or age. Each of us—and certainly each and every research participant in our respective studies—possesses "an alternative symbolic universe (which) poses a threat because its existence demonstrates empirically that one's own universe is less than inevitable" (Berger & Luckmann, 1966, p. 108). However, to make psychology more than empirical—to make it scientific—most of our research paradigms and methods deny the existence of an alternative symbolic universe (Tashakkori & Teddlie, 1998).

Among other problems, the assumption that it is primarily scientists who know what is real becomes a denial of the experience of research participants as a valid source of knowledge. This is really not an issue for biologists or chemists, because their "subject" may be a diseased cell or a chemical interaction. When doing research involving people a de facto hermeneutic relationship develops in that the researcher and the participant are affected by each other and modify their responses, behaviors, and perceptions based on that interaction, and of course on events and histories before the interaction. This is the case whether one uses an interview or a psychometric instrument to collect data. Yet in most of psychological research the psychologist–scientist controls the definition of reality and "the threat to the social definitions of reality is neutralized by assigning an inferior ontological status, and thereby not to be taken seriously cognitive status, to all definitions existing outside the social universe" (Berger & Luckmann, 1966, p. 115). Those representations of research that exist outside of positivism and the experimental method are looked on as inferior and are not taken as seriously by journal editors, funding sources, doctoral dissertation committees, or faculty in psychology departments.

Related to this issue is the question of "Who is to judge what is real?" In *The Phantom Tollbooth,* Rhyme and Reason, as a collaborative pair, were the judges of what was real. They carefully evaluated the worth and importance of words and numbers within the context of their society and could see that both brothers' perceptions of number and narrative had merit. The same holds true with psychological methods. No particular paradigm or method that is represented in this or other volumes can or should be privileged above all others. Rather, they should be subject to questions about validity, rigor, usefulness, and applicability, as well as to questions about who controls the data and from whose perspective the data are interpreted (Newman & Benz, 1998).

Validity and Objectivity in Qualitative and Quantitative Research

Two of the most frequently cited differences between qualitative and quantitative approaches to research are their methods of inquiry and the degree of control that each purports is necessary within the research setting. This often amounts to whether the research takes place in a naturalistic context or in a regulated laboratory-like setting (Hoshmand, 1999; McGartland & Polgar, 1994), suggesting that there is greater validity in the latter venue. We believe there are several problems with this conceptualization, which overly dichotomizes and overly simplifies the issue of validity by creating artificial boundaries and falsities. First, this conceptualization begs the definition of "naturalistic," because there is nothing naturalistic about a psychiatric hospital, outpatient counseling service, chronic pain clinic, cancer treatment program, large corporation, or school, all settings in which qualitative studies have taken place. Second, there is little naturalistic about the *actions* of observing or interviewing someone in any of these settings. Third, elevating the laboratory and the experimental method—and all that that image entails—onto a "pure" and objective plane where the values and biases of the researcher are supposedly left at the door and where statistical control ensures validity and objectivity is highly problematic. Fourth, "objectivity," as taught in many psychology textbooks and classrooms, is a myth. No experiment, no research question, and certainly no interpretation of data can possibly be truly objective. The types of problems we are interested in, the questions we ask, the kind of data we collect, and the analyses we undertake all emanate from some context, be it socioeconomic, political, cultural, or personal.

Moving beyond these artificial boundaries and falsities and expanding the paradigms and methods psychologists use to study the human experience, as Rhyme and Reason urge, puts more information and experience—about ourselves as researchers and the people we study as participants—all under the cloak of knowledge.

The chapters in the first section of this book delve into these issues and conflicts, describing points of both reconciliation and debate. Eisner (chapter 2) argues that all forms of inquiry, like all forms of representation, have their own advantages, limitations, and biases. Methods have the effect of constraining what one looks for—as he puts it, "nothing is as selective as perception." Nonetheless, qualitative methods can yield rich, generalizable, and valid research. To this end, he suggests strategies for strengthening and evaluating the merits of qualitative methods. McGrath and Johnson (chapter 3) make similar points—that both approaches involve assumptions that shape and restrict the conclusions that can be drawn from the data. Rather than arguing the merits of any particular approach, they take a more ecumenical approach to the research endeavor. Because different methods pose different, complementary strengths and weaknesses, they ponder, why not make use of as wide a range of methods as possible at each level of the research process? However, Marecek (chapter 4) rightly cautions that mixing methods is not straightforward. She notes that qualitative methods are often treated as subsidiaries to quantitative work, an approach that is unable to maximize their potential. Moreover, quantitative and qualitative methods often are premised on divergent epistemological bases and may produce contradictory sets of outcomes. As such, we should tread carefully on this path of inclusiveness. Nevertheless, inclusion within a single study of both qualitative and quantitative methods can be justified on the grounds that interlacing methods, even when they yield disparate findings, enrich our understanding of human behavior (Rabinowitz & Weseen, 2001). By touching on different aspects of the same phenomena, the two methodological approaches yield a more complete story.

If qualitative and quantitative research have some similar goals and characteristics, but also some essential differences, then we must ask if there are any shared criteria that can be used to judge their validity. Certainly some criteria are especially or even uniquely relevant to particular methods, although their relevance is not necessarily defined by whether the methods are qualitative or quantitative. For example, sample size is crucially relevant to statistical power but has minimal relevance to case-study analysis, and attention to the structure and sociolinguistic functions of a verbal account is a fundamental requirement for discourse analysis but is not a necessary part of a phenomenological analysis of the content of the account. As a consequence, it is not possible to specify clear-cut common procedures for ensuring validity, and the rapidly proliferating checklists for evaluating the validity of qualitative studies risk limiting the methods used and questions asked (Barbour, 2001), just as the positivist criteria for quantitative research have done. Nonetheless, there are higher order criteria that are relevant to all forms of rigorous empirical research, whether qualitative or quantitative, and can be satisfied in very different ways by each different piece of research (Yardley, 2000). First, to qualify as empirical—in some way corresponding to what is real—research must be shown to be well-grounded in some kind of data. This grounding must permit the object to object, as Kvale puts it (chapter 14); in other words, the outcome of the research must be demonstrably shaped by the process of eliciting data, whether this is achieved by means of experimental hypothesis testing, participant input, or inductive theory building. To qualify as good quality research, rather than casual description or uninformed interpretation, the researcher(s) must also display thoroughness; expertise in the application of the method selected; and awareness of the relevant theoretical, historical, sociocultural, and interpersonal context of the research. To demonstrate the preceding qualities, the methods used and conclusions drawn must be clearly described and carefully justified. A final pragmatic criterion for good research is that it should be meaningful and useful to at least some people, for some purposes.

John Dewey, a pioneer of psychology and "pragmatic" philosophy, suggested that all inquiry and evaluation, whether scientific, moral, or common sense, is ultimately concerned with the question of what things are good for. This question is undoubtedly of central importance to our inquiry into how the methods that are used by psychologists might profitably be expanded by the adoption of qualitative methods. Because we have suggested that qualitative methods may offer different benefits and insights from the quantitative methods traditionally used by psychologists, the following section considers what qualitative methods are particularly good for, illustrating these merits by reference to the wide range of very different approaches to qualitative research presented in the second section of this book.

What Is Qualitative Research Good For?

In keeping with the tradition of qualitative research, to address this question we will offer a personal, selective interpretation of some of the themes that recur across several different methods. However, this analysis is far from exhaustive or definitive, not least because, as the title of this book suggests, many of these methodological features of qualitative psychological research are innovative and evolving.

Exploration and Theory Development

A valuable use for qualitative research, of which most quantitative researchers are aware, is as a tool for exploring a topic or problem that has not previously been researched. The logic of experimental or questionnaire research demands that the relevant variables are predefined and outcomes predicted a priori on the basis of theory. In contrast, more inductive methods such as grounded theory (Henwood and Pidgeon, chapter 8) and ethnography (Miller, Hengst, and Wang, chapter 12) encourage the researcher to approach a topic without firm preconceptions about what variables will be important or how they will be related and to gradually build a theory to explain the data that are collected. Similarly, the phenomenological psychological method (Giorgi and Giorgi, chapter 13) is a method for *discovering* psychological meanings by identifying the essential psychological constituents or structure of an interviewee's description of an experience. However, qualitative researchers do not view such exploration as an attempt to produce an "objective" description of a phenomenon, because they assign a vital role to the researcher in constructing the analytical interpretation, whether through imaginative transcendence of "taken-for-granted" meanings (Giorgi, 1970) or by applying disciplinary knowledge and theoretical sensitivity to the topic (Henwood & Pidgeon, 1994).

Situated Analysis

As all of the authors in the first section point out, it is impossible to seek to maximize simultaneously both external validity (representativeness of real-world contexts) and internal validity (precision and control). Although it is misleading to make an absolute distinction between "naturalistic" and "scientific" research, it is clear that experimental research usually requires a degree of artificial manipulation or control of the key variables, whereas qualitative research typically seeks to maximize the ecological validity of the data by gathering it in real-world contexts. This latter approach permits analysis of the way in which these real-world contexts affect the phenomenon under investigation. For example, awareness of the fundamental influence of social context on what people say has led discourse analysts (see Potter, chapter 5) to focus their attention on naturally occurring talk, because the discursive resources and strategies people use are often quite different in everyday conversation than when speaking to a research interviewer. Similarly, Ratcliff (chapter 7) was able to capture on video an aspect of children's behavior that was unique to the specific context of the school corridor, because this represented a social space mid-way between the schoolroom and playground. To gain a deeper understanding of the influence of context, some researchers find it helpful to immerse themselves for a prolonged period in the personal, sociocultural, or historical context of the topic they are studying (Miller, Hengst, & Wang, chapter 12).

Holistic Analysis of Complex, Dynamic, and Exceptional Phenomena

Qualities are emergent properties arising from the configuration of elements in a whole. Hence qualitative research is necessarily holistic; microanalysis of parts is always undertaken in the context of a larger whole. For example, the illustration of ethnography provided by Miller, Hengst, and Wang analyzes in detail a single example of an American mother's account of her child's misdemeanor. However, this account has meaning only in relationship to the broader cultural context, and derives its particular analytical significance precisely because it *deviates* from the normative cultural pattern observed in their study—that American mothers typically do not talk at all about their children's misdemeanors.

In qualitative research, collection of very detailed data about just a few examples of a phenomenon—even a single case—permits analysis of multiple aspects of a topic. A period of observation or series of interviews typically yields an intimidatingly vast repository of data about a multitude of interacting elements and aspects of the topic studied. Inevitably, qualitative researchers must be selective in their analysis, but freedom from the restrictive constraints of meeting statistical assumptions (see McGrath and Johnson, chapter 3) permits consideration of fine distinctions, exceptions, and complex patterns of interrelationships. Qualitative data also allow researchers to develop multilayered interpretations by returning to the data to carry out multiple analyses of different aspects of the topics, which can be contextualized by the other analyses. For example, Ratcliff initially used grounded theory to develop an explanatory classification of his entire corpus of video data on children's behavior in school hallways, then carried out secondary microanalysis of particular video sequences to examine the nature, patterning, and meaning of ritual behavior more closely, and later invited independent student researchers to jointly develop a taxonomy of hallway rituals. Moreover, even the analysis of deviation, inconsistency, and omission can be undertaken. Whereas in quantitative research inconsistency is treated as error and nonresponse as missing data, in discourse analysis (Potter) and psychoanalytical analysis (Kvale, 1996) the internal contradictions, pauses, and absences in people's talk are valuable pointers to important areas of tension, difficulty, or conflict, whereas deviations from typical or "normal" behavior provide particularly useful information about cultural norms and the reasons for and consequences of transgressing these.

The dynamic complexity added by the dimension of temporal change is also fundamental to many forms of qualitative research. Murray (chapter 6) explains how people's narratives embody the dynamics of their identity by simultaneously shaping the past and projecting into the future; hence, narrative analysis provides an intrinsically chronological perspective on the lives of narrators. Kvale notes that the psychoanalytical approach of conducting multiple interviews over an extended time period not only builds up a very rich biographical context for analytical interpretation and creates a relationship of trust that encourages greater self-disclosure but also allows the analyst and the patient to test the value of an interpretation pragmatically, by observing its effects on the patient's reactions over time.

Analysis of Subjective Meaning

One way of thinking about the difference—and complementarity—between quantitative and qualitative research is to consider quantitative research as the process of producing a map of a place and qualitative research as the process of producing a video of that place. A map is extremely useful; it conveys with economy and precision the location of a place and its relationship to other places in terms of proximity and direction. However, even the most detailed map is unable to convey an understanding of what it is like to be at that place. In contrast, a video conveys in vivid detail the constantly changing perspective of the observer. Although this perspective is selective and could not easily be used for navigation, it is able to communicate something of the subjective experience of being there. This capacity of qualitative research to gain partial access to the subjective perspectives of others therefore makes it an ideal method for research into subjective meaning, whether this consists of abstracting the psychological core of an experience (Giorgi and Giorgi, chapter 13); recording the many inner voices that compose personal identity and experience (Gilligan and Spencer, chapter 9); or following a tortuous trail of symbols, associations, and inconsistencies to uncover latent meanings that may be irrational, ambiguous, or suppressed (Kvale, chapter 14).

Just as making a video is not a matter of random or neutral recording but rather of aesthetically framing a sequence of scenes to convey a particular impression to a viewer, the analysis of subjective meaning contains aesthetic and interpersonal dimensions (discussed later) that are largely absent—indeed, excluded—from the process of map-making, or quantitative research.

Analysis of the Aesthetic Dimension of Experience

As a scientific discipline, psychology has tended to deny the aesthetic dimension of research and to ignore the aesthetic dimension of human experience, because this cannot be meaningfully reduced to quantities (see Eisner, chapter 2). But as Dewey (1934) has noted, science itself can be regarded as an extension of art—in other words, the technology of using the accumulated culture of generations to create and comprehend a perceptual–motor experience in the here and now. Many of the authors of the chapters in this book note that qualitative research is a skill or craft, akin to that of an artist. Some of the methods used draw explicitly on the arts. Davis (chapter 11) uses the art of portraiture as an extended metaphor throughout her chapter to illustrate how creating a case study involves aesthetic skills such as selecting the elements that form the dominant themes and the background context, achieving balance and coherence of the whole image, and giving voice to the unique perspective and insights of the author(s) of the work. Similarly, Gilligan and Spencer (chapter 9) use music as an extended metaphor for their method of listening to narratives to identify the distinctive rhythms, signatures, and tonalities of each person's multiple voices and the counterpoints, harmonies, and dissonances they compose. She also highlights the intrinsically poetic quality of narrative, evocatively conveyed by the "I-poem" of isolation, which was revealed by the simple but innovative method of juxtaposing all the self-referent expressions in the narrative of a depressed woman.

Relational Analysis and Reflexivity

Undertaking situated, holistic analysis of meaning does not simply entail considering multiple aspects of a phenomenon and contextual influences; rather, it implies a fundamentally relational approach to the topic and to research itself. Qualitative research therefore requires an appreciation of the relationships of all participants in the research with each other and with the wider society in which they are embedded. For example, Miller, Hengst, and Wang (chapter 12) explain how ethnography always entails at least double vision, because the process of trying to understand another culture inevitably involves contrasting it with one's own culture, so that insight is gained simultaneously into the taken-for-granted assumptions and interpretive frameworks of both cultures.

Discourse analysis is another form of qualitative research, which is founded on relational analysis. Discourse can be analyzed relationally in several ways (e.g., Wetherell, Taylor, & Yates, 2000). First, the intrinsically relational nature of linguistic meaning can be a focus for study; for example, how terms such as "abnormal" or "male" take their meaning from their relation to the terms "normal" and "female." Second, discourse can be analyzed as dialogue or social interaction. Discursive psychology (Potter, chapter 5) examines the ways in which meanings and effects are coproduced in interactions, playing close attention to how this process of coconstruction is influenced by the context of the setting in which the dialogue takes place. For example, an account of a malfunctioning car could take the meaning and have the effect of an excuse for lateness if offered in the context of arriving late at a meeting and if those who arrived earlier politely sympathized with the mishap, thus helping to construct the latecomer as blameless. A third implicit context for all discourse is the wider sociocultural and rhetorical context in which such coconstructions take place. For example, the account is more likely to be successful in constructing the individual as blameless if he or she is relatively powerful, or a core group member, than if he or she is a low-status outsider—and if the account can draw on effective rhetorical resources (for example, humorously depicting the event as an unusual and entirely unforeseeable quirk of fate—"of course, the one time I really need it the car breaks down"). Murray (chapter 6) notes that the influence of sociocultural context on apparently personal narratives is so profound that it shapes our identity and consciousness, furnishing the roles and plot lines that we use to live in a way that makes coherent sense to ourselves and to those with whom we interact. For example, a participatory action research collective of female researchers and inmates at a New York state prison (see Fine et al., chapter 10) showed how inmates' narratives depicting themselves as dual personalities—the "old, bad" and "new, transformed" selves—did not simply reproduce negative social stereotypes of criminals but facilitated the development of a reflective agency that allowed the women to condemn the crimes they had committed in the past while articulating a positive identity for the present and future.

Awareness of the constructive nature of talk is most explicit in forms of discourse analysis, but has much wider relevance. All psychological studies involve humans who are speaking and acting in a social and linguistic context, and so qualitative researchers whose interest is not solely in language nevertheless find it useful to consider the sociolinguistic processes influencing the talk and action they are studying. For example, Henwood and Pidgeon (chapter 8) enriched their grounded theory analysis with consideration of different interpretative perspectives on the themes that had emerged, including perspectives that analyzed these themes as discursive practices. This allowed them to consider participants' statements about "valuing trees" not simply as expressing personal opinions about vegetation but as tapping into and constructing systems of symbolic and social value in which trees were associated with life and health.

For many qualitative researchers, awareness of sociocultural context and interpersonal relations necessarily extends to a reflexive consideration of the role of the researcher, the relationship between researcher and participants, and the influence of the researcher on the research process. Indeed, the first analytical step in the *Listening Guide* method (Gilligan and Spencer, chapter 9) requires the analyst to attend to his or her own responses to the interviewee's narrative—partly to ensure that the voice of the interviewee is not distorted or submerged by the emotional response of the analyst, but also because, as in psychoanalysis, the analyst's reactions provide a valuable empathic link to the subjective experience of the interviewee. Kvale (chapter 14) highlights additional features of the psychoanalytical relationship from which researchers might profit, suggesting that the close, embodied interaction between analyst and patient fosters intuitive and bodily modes of knowing and provides a wealth of information that is absent from the "psychology of strangers" constructed from single "snapshot" encounters with research participants. Both Kvale and Murray welcome the opportunity provided by narrative and interview methods for interviewees to exert control and influence, setting the agenda and entering into dialogue with the interviewer to reject interpretations that do not make sense to them.

The relationship between research participants is most thoroughly addressed by methods such as participatory action research, which attempts to give all participants the opportunity to contribute to the construction of practical knowledge within a democratic research community. Fine and her coparticipants (chapter 10) describe the advantages and challenges of carrying out this kind of research in the setting of a prison. Those with "inside" knowledge were not only able to provide insights into formal and informal practices and connections that no outsider could have obtained, but were also in a position to critically evaluate and challenge the accounts offered by other insiders. However, research contributions had to be carefully tailored to an environment in which the researchers could not meet freely and were constantly obliged to consider what information could be safely disclosed to whom. Nevertheless, the participants felt that the research process not only effected constructive changes for them personally—in terms of academic and personal growth and achievement—but also engaged with the wider community, positively influencing the prison climate, the attitudes of other inmates and correction officers, and relations with family and friends.

As this section has made abundantly clear, qualitative research methods can be extraordinarily useful, providing unique access into our understanding of the human experience. In a sense, the chapters in this volume enable psychologists to circle above the patch worked landscape of various qualitative approaches, noting their different hues and shared boundaries. It is only when researchers are on the ground and meaningfully using the methods, however, that they can fully experience their texture, affordances, and constraints. Moving from the negative stereotypes of qualitative research current in psychology to a more balanced approach will require a sea change in the field. Perhaps most important, students need exposure to qualitative methods alongside quantitative methods so that they can better appreciate their relative strengths and limits. To this end, psychology departments need to incorporate a series of qualitative methods courses that provide the same meticulous level of detail as the courses that are typically offered in quantitative methods. The final section of this chapter offers a call to action to encourage academic psychology to take up this challenge.

Teaching Qualitative Research

Few psychology departments in North America and Europe teach qualitative research as a significant part of their usual curriculum in research methods. Ignoring methodology that does not fall under the umbrella of positivism is *the* most significant barrier that impedes new generations of psychologists from understanding and appreciating different ways to examine the phenomena most often studied by psychology. At the undergraduate and graduate levels, room can be made in the curriculum to incorporate the study of different paradigms and research traditions. The result of this curriculum expansion will be a richer and more substantially encompassing profession, better able to respond to the increasing complex questions of the 21st century. This volume is one example of resources available to help the graduate school instructor, as well as the practicing research psychologist, to better understand, appreciate, and make use of the broad range of qualitative methods for research in psychology.

Starting at the undergraduate level, an introductory research methods class could begin with an examination of the assumptions of positivist, postpositivist, constructivist, and interpretive paradigms, as discussed in chapters 2 to 4. Using the tenets of problem-based learning, a specific problem (such as assessing psychotherapy outcome, determining employee satisfaction, or evaluating psychology trauma services) could be used to engage the class in discussion about how best to research these situations. Each paradigm could be treated as a separate "case" that students could decipher and debate. From this comparative beginning, the class could then go on to discover some of the research methods emanating from each paradigm. This would entail examining the questions that each method can and cannot answer. Rather than teaching just one methodological paradigm or world view, this approach encourages students to think more critically about why and how one specific method is chosen over another. We believe this pedagogical approach also encourages students to think about the questions to be asked before considering the design and method(s) of the study. Considering time and content limitations in undergraduate education, this may be as far as the presentation of qualitative methods advances. It is, however, a very different beginning to understanding research than is presently available in most psychology departments.

In graduate education, one master's level course could provide more in-depth information about several of the qualitative methods presented in chapters 5 to 14 and allow students to obtain some hands-on experience in data collection and analysis in one or two of those methods. On the doctoral level a two-course sequence that integrates quantitative and qualitative methods could begin a student's research training, followed by two additional research methods classes focused on more advanced methods of design and analysis, in either qualitative or quantitative approaches. A fifth research class, which is common in many doctoral programs, could act as an integrative seminar experience where studies are examined and conducted that incorporate both qualitative and quantitative designs. Graduate students could then truly develop an integrative perspective about research methods and leave their doctoral program with a wider range of intellectual tools, and perhaps with some of the wisdom of princesses Rhyme and Reason, realizing the folly of adhering to a methodological hierarchy that prevents a richer understanding of human beings.

References

Barbour, R. S. (2001). Checklists for improving rigor in qualitative research: A case of the tail wagging the dog? *British Medical Journal, 322,* 1115–1117.

Berger, P. L., & Luckmann, T. (1996). *The social construction of reality.* New York: Doubleday.

Cafasso, L. L., Camic, P. M., & Rhodes, J. E. (2001, Nov.). *Middle school climate examined and altered by teacher-directed intervention assessed through qualitative and quantitative methodologies.* Paper presented at the annual meeting of the National Middle School Association, Washington, DC.

Dewey, J. (1934). *Art as experience.* New York: Perigee.

Gergen, K. J. (1985). The social constructionist movement in modern psychology. *American Psychologist, 40,* 266–275.

Giorgi, A. (1970). *Psychology as a human science.* New York: Harper & Row.

Henwood, K., & Pidgeon, N. (1994). Beyond the qualitative paradigm: A framework for introducing diversity within qualitative psychology. *Journal of Community and Applied Social Psychology, 4,* 225–238.

Hoshmand, L. T. (1999). Locating the qualitative research genre. In M. Kopala & L. A. Suzuki (Eds.), *Using qualitative methods in psychology* (pp. 15–24). Thousand Oaks, CA: Sage.
Juster, N. (1965). *The phantom tollbooth.* New York: Random House.
Kvale, S. (1996). *InterViews: An introduction to qualitative research interviewing.* Thousand Oaks, CA: Sage.
McGartland, M., & Polgar, S. (1994). Paradigm collapse in psychology: The necessity for a "two" methods approach. *Australian Psychologist, 29,* 21–28.
Newman, I., & Benz, C. R. (1998). *Qualitative–quantitative research methodology.* Carbondale: Southern Illinois University Press.
Rabinowitz, V. C., & Weseen, S. (2001). Power, politics, and the qualitative/quantitative debates in psychology. In D. L. Tolman & B.-M. Miller (Eds.), *From subjects to subjectivities: A handbook of interpretive and participatory methods. Qualitative studies in psychology* (pp. 12–28). New York: New York University Press.
Shweder, R. A. (1996). Quanta and qualia: What is the "object" of ethnographic research? In R. Jessor, A. Colby, & R. A. Shweder (Eds.), *Ethnography and human development: Context and meaning in social inquiry* (pp. 175–182). Chicago: University of Chicago Press.
Tashakkori, A., & Teddlie, C. (1998). *Mixed methodology: Combining qualitative and quantitative approaches, second edition.* Thousand Oaks, CA: Sage
Wetherell, M., Taylor, S., & Yates, S. J. (2001). *Discourse as data: A guide for analysis.* Thousand Oaks, CA: Sage.
Yardley, L. (2000). Dilemmas in qualitative health research. *Psychology and Health, 15,* 215–228.

2

On the Art and Science of Qualitative Research in Psychology

Elliot W. Eisner

Research in psychology, like research in other fields, is shaped by ideas and ideals regarding matters of method. By *ideas* and *ideals* I mean beliefs about what is legitimate to study and how such study should be done. Psychologists, like others, embrace "religions" that they believe define the right way to do things. The power—and the conflicts—among these religions is nowhere more apparent than in debates about the legitimacy of qualitative research in psychology, a field that has struggled so desperately to be regarded as a science. And the science that has historically been most appealing to psychologists has been physics, by consensus the most rigorous and fundamental of all the sciences. Hence it is understandable that when a vision of a scientific psychology developed in the mid-19th century, psychophysics was the conception that served as its model.

Psychophysics came to the fore when there was interest in establishing psychology as an experimental science. It was in 1858 that Wundt first established his laboratory in Heidelberg and two decades later created another in Leipzig. During the same period Helmholtz began his scientific studies of perception, and Fechner was doing experiments in psychophysics, the results of which were published in his important work, *Elements of Psychophysics* (1889/1966). The German orientation to psychological research was influenced by the backgrounds that people such as Helmholtz brought with them; Helmholtz was "by interest and temperament a physicist" (Boring, 1929, p. 288), Wundt a physiologist, and Fechner a physicist and philosopher. Americans like G. Stanley Hall and William James traveled to Europe to study with these German giants, and they returned to the United States armed with methods they were eager to use and, more important, with beliefs about what a science of psychology required. Of course they gave what they learned an American twist, but the influence of their experience in Europe was unmistakable.

The late 19th century was a watershed for American psychology; it defined a set of ideas and ideals that is still with us. These ideas were further strengthened by the influence in the first half of the 20th century of logical positivism, operationism, and American behaviorism. For psychology to be a science, empiricists argued, it was necessary to use publicly replicable procedures and to use methods of description that were "objective"—that is, methods that provided little or no space for the exercise of personal judgment. To meet this criterion the phenomena psychologists examined needed to be measurable. This, of course, imposed constraints on the problems that could be studied; measurability defined what was legitimate to research. Mind was not a good candidate for research. Behavior was.

What American psychology fielded during the first 50 years of the 20th century was a stable of powerful, empirically oriented psychologists, men such as E. L. Thorndike, James Cattell, John Watson, Clark Hull, and Edward Chase Tolman. In addition, there were others outside of psychology who provided comfort and support for the quantification of psychology. These others were a cadre of German philosophers, members of the Vienna circle, people such as Otto Von Neurath, Hans Reichenbach, Rudolf Carnap, and Herbert Feigel, individuals who wanted to cleanse philosophy of the florid excesses of philosophical language, its obscurantism, and the imprecision of metaphysics. Their aim was to develop a unified theory of science with physics at its core and mathematics as its language.

The desire to develop a science of nature did not start in the 19th century, however. It started, if one can claim start dates in human history, with the Enlightenment. For convenience, we may say it started with Galileo and Descartes and their interest in the measurement of relations. Toulmin described the impact of Galileo's and Descartes' work this way.

> The intellectual revolution was launched by Galileo Galilei, and by René Descartes. It had two aspects: it was a scientific revolution, because it led to striking innovations in physics and astronomy, and it was the birth of a new method in philosophy, since it established a research tradition in theory of knowledge and philosophy of mind that has lasted right up to our own times. (1990, p. 14)

John Dewey makes similar observations regarding the impact of Galileo's work:

> The work of Galileo was not a development but a revolution. It marked a change from the qualitative to the quantitative or metric; from the heterogeneous to the homogeneous; from intrinsic forms to relations; from esthetic harmonies to mathematical formulae; from contemplative enjoyment to active manipulation and control; from rest to change; from eternal objects to temporal sequence (Dewey, 1929, pp. 94–95).

It is significant that both Toulmin and Dewey describe the shift that Galileo stimulated as a revolution. It represented in Thomas Kuhn's terms a paradigm shift, a new way of seeing and understanding nature (1996). The Enlightenment was predicated on humanity's capacity to reason and on human perfectibility. It embraced the view that nature was orderly and that with human reason and proper methods its order could be discovered and understood. Scientific method was the key to discovery and quantification was its prime element. This shift from attention to quale—that is, the qualitative features of experience, to attention to quanta, matters of magnitude—was a revolution.

In its particulars, according to Toulmin (1990), the revolution that was the Enlightenment was also represented by a shift in emphasis from the oral to the written, from attention to the local to attention to the general, from the timely to the timeless, and from the particular to the universal. Each shift in emphasis was an effort to move to abstraction, to get the personal and the subjective out of the process, and to discover those regularities that constituted the natural order that scientists cared about. The particular was considered noise in the system. What one wanted was a display of the anatomy of nature, not its individual countenance. The climate had changed. New ideas and new ideals emerged. These new ideas and ideals function today as the epistemological foundations of most contemporary research in psychology.

Emerging Methodological Tensions

Traditions constitute the glue of culture. They hold things together and are hard to change. Thus, it is understandable that a field that prides itself on its scientific respectability should be skeptical about research efforts that are guided by criteria and methods that differ from the ones that have for so long prevailed. Galileo's influence shifted the mode of description from quale to quanta, the ramifications of which altered our conception of method. Objectivity, as I have indicated, required procedures that precluded or severely diminished the need for judgment; it regarded the presence of judgment as a failing, a source of error, the location of bias, and the seat of obfuscation. Like the scoring of ballots, the standards were to be uniform and universal. Judgments about how a ballot had to be counted were not permissible. What was wanted was the ability to see things as they really are. The correspondence theory of truth prevailed. According to Richard Rorty, philosophers and scientists wanted to hold up a mirror to nature (1979).

In addition to the foregoing desiderata, the experiment became the methodological ideal in doing research. Never mind issues of external validity; experiments made it possible to locate causes if the experimental conditions were sufficiently controlled. These beliefs represented a kind of methodological catechism that was to be learned by aspiring researchers seeking tenure and needing to do really "rigorous" research. Even as late as the 1950s qualitative research was not an issue; for some it was an oxymoron.

Doing qualitative research became an issue during the late 1960s and early 1970s with the growing interest in pluralism: methodological, cultural, and epistemological and with the discontent with research in the social sciences that often failed to address the everyday realities of ordinary men and women. For many scholars who felt a need to get close to the phenomena of interest in their context, the laboratory was not necessarily the best location. If one wanted to understand how people felt and behaved, one needed to study people in their natural habitats. Another research perspective was needed, one in which judgment might not be all that bad.

This shift in cultural climate provided the conditions for what we now call qualitative research. But although the term "qualitative research" has great currency, its meaning is not altogether clear. Just what makes a study qualitative and in what sense is it research?

First it should be recognized that all experience is in some way qualitative; qualities are the sources our sensory system picks up as we have intercourse with the environment. In this sense qualities make consciousness possible. But if this is so, can there be empirical research that is not qualitative? My answer is no. The term *empirical* comes from the Latin *empiria,* which means to experience. Empirical research always refers to phenomena that can be experienced, and to be experienced the senses must be engaged with qualities, even when the qualities in question are imaginative. The study of imaginative content results in claims about qualities whose conclusions can in some way be inspected, inferred, or examined.

If this is so what is the difference between qualitative studies and nonqualitative studies? The difference is not that one addresses and describes qualities whereas the other does not. Both quantitative and qualitative research address and describe qualities; the difference between the two resides in the forms used to represent them—that is, in the means researchers use to describe what they have studied. Quantification, the hallmark of scientific method, describes with respect to magnitude. Qualification describes qualities through the use of descriptive language and the meanings associated with such language. For example, consider the difference between heat and temperature. To describe heat is to describe the experience one is likely to have if something is, say, touched. Temperature, however, is a measure of heat. To describe heat qualitatively is to use words to engender imaginative experience. To describe heat quantitatively is to measure its magnitude with respect to a scale. Similarly, anxiety can be measured and it can also be described linguistically, but the two forms of representation provide different information. When the language used to describe the outcomes of qualitative research are artfully crafted it allows someone to feel the heat.

Let me also point out that a researcher may obtain a wide variety of quantitative data but choose to portray his or her results qualitatively rather than quantitatively. For example, a researcher might want to study tensions between a couple and decides to count the incidence of negative comments they make to each other over three therapeutic sessions. Clearly the researcher could report the incidence of such comments, but might choose instead to construct a narrative in which the character and quality of those comments were conveyed to a reader.

To experience life in a concentration camp and decide to make its features public one might want to use statistical charts, but in the end one might want to tell a story or make a film. The data collected do not prescribe the form the disclosure can take. For example, William Foote Whyte's *Street Corner Society* (1993), a sociological study of Italian life in the North End of Boston, could have been a film—a different work to be sure—if Whyte had film-making skills and the desire to do so.

I have been discussing the descriptive features of qualitative research largely with respect to language use. But language has more than one form.

Consider the description of wine, or the description of a professional football game by a skilled radio announcer. In the former, metaphors are used to render qualities of experience generated by the qualities of the wine. A wine critic may talk about the wine's nose or its finish or its roundness or buttery character. The wine critic's task is to say the unsayable by using language evocatively. The football announcer also uses language evocatively and like the wine critic also possesses a complex lexicon of technical terms to describe what is going on. What we have in both cases are individuals who can "read" phenomena in their respective fields and who use language to render the qualities they have experienced.

The use of evocative language is a means through which the describer attempts to help a reader or listener secure an image of and feel for the situation or qualities being described. The more evocation is engendered through language, the closer the description comes to being an art form. The most refined manifestation of language being used as an art form is found in poetry and literature. When we read literature we secure a grasp of the contexts, situations, crises, and resolutions that the writer invents for us. Through that invention we are able to participate imaginatively in other worlds. Description need not be linguistic. Description can be visual, as in film or videography. There is more than one way or means for describing, and each conceals as well as reveals. Quantification is one, but only one, form of representation. Each form of representation has, one might say, its own bias.

Bias comes from many sources. One source, as I have already indicated, is the form of representation one chooses to use. Some things need to be seen to be known—or believed. Bias also comes from the fact that the form of representation one elects to use influences, but does not determine, what one looks for. To paraphrase Abraham Maslow, if the only tool you have is a hammer, you treat everything as if it were a nail. We tend to look for what we know how to see or render with the tools we know how to use. Bias also emerges from the theoretical frame of reference we apply to the phenomena we address. Freudians and Hullians see different worlds (Bronfenbrenner, 1970). Another source of bias comes from the purposes we have; nothing is as selective as perception, and what we are interested in learning affects what we are likely to look for.

Sources of Meaning in Qualitative Research

The point of the foregoing is to underscore the idea that all forms of inquiry, like all forms of representation, have their own constraints and provide their own affordances, including the constraints and affordances of quantification and experimentation. Mind cannot be uncoupled from matter. The methodological question for researchers is not answered by discovering how to secure a view of the world from the knee of God or how to achieve an ontologically objective perspective; all perspectives are framed. The question is, what can we learn from the perspective we take? What we call qualitative research provides a perspective.

I already alluded to the evocative character of literary and poetic language. Evocation is largely a function of the way language is shaped—that is, the form that is conferred on it by the researcher. Those who know how to craft language (or image if the medium is film) function as artists when they do so. The crafting of form is an artistic activity that requires an idea worth expressing, the imagination needed to envision a means for doing so, the technical skills needed to realize in a material the form envisioned, and the sensibility needed to determine if the form created is likely to be instrumental to the meanings one wants to convey. Such achievements are formidable, yet that is what the work of art requires.

To illustrate how form affects meaning, consider the difference between notational and analog systems of representation. In a notational system—arithmetic, for example—substitutability among the elements is possible with no alteration or loss of meaning. "4 + 4 = 8" can be expressed in an infinite number of ways: "IV + IV," "VIII, "9 – 1," and even, if one wants to quip, "ate." With notational systems, meaning remains constant even when the form changes. In analog systems, painting or writing, for example, a change in a part or section alters one's experience and hence the meaning of the piece. Change a section of a painting from red to blue and the experience of the painting is changed. Alter a paragraph or a word in a paragraph and its meaning, if ever so slightly, is altered. Those who do qualitative research must make judgments about such highly nuanced qualitative relationships, and in making such judgments, somatic forms of knowing come into play. There is no algorithm one can appeal to in order to decide what changes might be made in an analogue system.

The absence of algorithms in qualitative research means that the process of composing must rely on sensibility and seek coherence to achieve credibility. Language needs not only to be evocative or expressive; its elements need to be aesthetically composed. To be aesthetically composed the researcher needs to be a writer. Writing well is an art. It is important to remember that the crafting of language so that it evokes experience instrumental to understanding is not a parlor game. Its function is to enlarge understanding by providing the reader with a form that informs. Such renderings of form serve epistemic interests. How such forms inform and issues related to it are addressed in the next section.

The Function of Form in Qualitative Research

Just how does a narrative inform? How does a qualitative case study illuminate the relationships it addresses? How do works like Kozol's *Savage Inequalities* (1991), or Peshkin's *God's Choice* (1986), or Geertz's *The Interpretation of Cultures* (1973) help us understand not only what they address explicitly but what they convey implicitly beyond the case? There are several means used by these scholars to inform about in credible ways the cases about which they write. One of these means is the level of factual detail they use in their writing. Authors of qualitative studies increase their credibility when a reader comes to believe that its author has done the necessary homework to understand the situation addressed. Credibility, in part, is achieved by knowing what is not obvious about the case.

But if facts alone were an adequate criterion to write a credible qualitative case study, the task would not be so demanding. Clearly they are not. What must also be addressed is the sensitivity with which the researcher reads the seen (or scene). One cannot describe or interpret what one has not seen or in some other way experienced. The experience one has comes to life through the frames of reference one uses and the extent to which one's sensibilities in that domain have been honed to pick up what is subtle but significant given some end in view. What I have called connoiseurship in the domain in question is the means through which one makes sense of the phenomena. Good clinicians know how to see and interpret their client's comments and behavior. In this sense, connoiseurship provides the initiating conditions for interpretation, another formidable but fundamental aspect of qualitative research.

Interpretation has to do with sense making. What does a situation mean? What is its significance? What gives rise to it? How can it be explained? What theoretical ideas help us understand the action that has taken place? Are other interpretations possible? Are they competitive? If so can they be resolved or do we live with multiple interpretations?

The ability to provide a credible interpretation requires a grasp of the context in which an action occurs. For example, the meaning of an interchange between a bickering couple may not be understandable without knowing their history. Behavior is always situated; hence a perspective on the situation provides a necessary frame for interpretation. Bickering can be an expression of anger between two people or it can be a way for a couple to remain emotionally in touch with each other.

Although refinement of the sensibilities in a domain is a way to become aware, the meaning of what one has noticed requires a construction on the part of the researcher. This construction is an act of interpretation. It is worth noting that news analysts and political scientists ply their trade trying to make sense of extremely complex and often rapidly changing political panoramas. It is also worth remembering that we seek their comments to better understand what on its face might seem simple, but which may not be. For example, undermining the power of a repressive leader in a foreign country might look good from one angle, but it might destabilize an entire geopolitical area, a disease that could be worse than the cure. Such political ramifications might not be immediately apparent.

What we have in this bare-bones scenario is an example of a nascent form of qualitative research: A situation or an array of situations is examined, the data are likely to be collected from multiple sources, and the task is to determine what the situation means. In this process meanings may be multiple, depending on the population for whom the situation has meaning. In addition, the interpretation of the situation for any one population may be multiple; there is always more than one way to see and interpret something. Sensibility, reference group, context, and theoretical frame are all consequential in the construction of an interpretation. From the examples I have described it should be clear that qualitative research is far more than the creation of a vivid description of a state of affairs; it is an effort to make sense out of it—that is, the aim of qualitative research is not only to give an account, but also to account for.

Let me review the argument so far. It is this. The Enlightenment created an orientation to nature that put scientific rationality on the pedestal of proper method. This orientation to the study and discovery of nature's regularities animated those interested in creating a science of psychology. This science was to be built on a conception of objectivity that was believed to be best realized through the measurement of behavior. Mind was out, behavior was in. The focus and investigatory practices of American psychologists, influenced as they were by their German counterparts, was on the measurement of what was empirical. The conception of method that was and is inherent in this view still dominates and animates American psychology today.

However, in the 1960s interest in what has come to be known as qualitative research began to emerge in American social science. Qualitative research is differentiated from what is commonly referred as quantitative research by its form of disclosure. Qualitative research uses language and image to capture, describe, and interpret what is studied. The language it uses operates on a continuum extending from the literal to the literary, from the factual to the evocative. In expanding the conception of permissible method it challenged the hegemony of quantification and it created a new array of criteria to guide empirical research in psychology. The features of qualitative research and the criteria that can be applied to appraise its quality is what the remainder of this chapter addresses.

Generalizing From Case Studies

One feature of qualitative research pertains to matters of generalization. In conventional forms of statistical research the canons for generalization are comparatively clear. In simplified terms, one needs to identify a population, randomly select a sample from that population, measure two or more variables, and calculate the probability that the relationships one might find among those variables are statistically significant. If the selection of the sample has been random, the relationships one finds among variables are likely to be found, a fortiori, in the population from which it was drawn. But what about single case studies? Can one generalize with a population of $N = 1$? And if one cannot, what is the point of the enterprise?

Generalization comes in several forms. The form I just described is an example of statistical generalization. There are as well naturalistic generalizations. Naturalistic generalizations are like the generalizations we make during the course of ordinary living. None of us randomly select our experiences, yet we learn from those experiences and we use them to influence subsequent choices. We correct decisions we have made in light of subsequent decisions and we extract from those experiences "lessons" that guide our decision making. The lessons we learn represent what we have come to understand. Through a process that might be described as successive approximation we learn to make better judgments when we need to judge or decide. Imagine the limited range of our ability to generalize if the only data we could use to do so were those derived from randomly selected events.

In addition to naturalistic generalizations there are generalizations derived from what might be called canonical events. These events are perhaps best represented in the arts. They are events that are made vivid by a kind of compression that confers on them a power to help us notice what we might otherwise miss seeing. The noticing I speak of pertains not only to the work as rendered but also to that class of objects, situations, and phenomena that the work exemplifies. For example, *One Flew Over the Cuckoo's Nest* (Kesey, 1962) gives us a picture of what life in a mental institution might be like. The story is powerful, and although it makes no claim that it represents all such institutions, it performs a heuristic function by reminding us in vivid terms what Erving Goffman described in his work, "Asylums" (1961). Works of art, whether in literature, the visual arts, or in qualitative research, can provide a structure, a kind of anticipatory schemata, as Neisser (1976) might say, that facilitates our search. In that sense the work constitutes a heuristic that has application beyond the case it addresses. And in that sense it generalizes; it is about more than itself.

We tend to regard generalization as forward-looking—that is, we generalize to anticipate. But generalization can also help us look backward, it can reorder our past. By reordering our past the lessons learned through qualitative case studies may indeed change our interpretation of the events we previously regarded or understood quite differently. Consider revisionist history or the lessons taught to us by feminists who afforded us an entirely different interpretation of the messages in Dick and Jane readers.[1] Of course revising our past, engaging in what I have called retrospective generalization, is not easy; we are all invested in our own stories, but changes in perspective are possible and in this day and age they are not uncommon. The point of these comments is to challenge the belief that $N = 1$ can have no lessons to teach. It can. It can provide a heuristic that increases the efficiency of the search and that can guide decision making. In fact, it is our most common mode of generalizing.

Another concept relevant to the conduct and assessment of qualitative research has to do with matters of validity. Validity is sometimes regarded as an inappropriate criterion in qualitative research. Some believe that its history in statistically driven research and its association with mental testing have conferred on it a coloration that is incongruous with the spirit of qualitative work. I do not agree. The term *valid,* if one compares it to its opposite *invalid,* refers to unimpaired, well-grounded, justified, or strong. We want, insofar as possible, to create work that is unimpaired, well-grounded, justified, or strong (Stake, 1974).

How can we appraise such qualities? Let me suggest some criteria for determining the validity of qualitative research. There are three I want to

[1]Dick and Jane readers were among the most widely used basal readers in American schools during the 1930s, 1940s, and 1950s. They exemplified gender stereotyping in the roles they assigned to men and women in both the text that students read and in the visual images displayed in the basal reader.

advance. First, we can try to determine if the work in question is structurally corroborated. By structural corroboration I mean that there are sufficient "data points" converging on a point or conclusion to support that conclusion. In a sense, structural corroboration is like circumstantial evidence; it allows one to draw a conclusion or, in the case of the law, to determine a verdict by the preponderance of evidence, evidence relevant to the verdict. Structurally corroborated qualitative research confers validity—strength—to the conclusions drawn.

A second criterion for determining validity pertains to referential adequacy. A qualitative study is referentially adequate if the work in question enables a reader to see the qualities described in the work. The function of qualitative research is to enlarge human understanding. The work is a vehicle to that end. It accomplishes that end when what the work describes can be seen by others through the work's capacity to reveal or illuminate. In this sense, the work performs a function similar to a theory; it organizes perception so that awareness and meaning are enhanced. In a sense, the qualitative researcher, like the critic, serves as a mid-wife to perception.

A third criterion for appraising the validity of qualitative research is consensual validation. By consensual validation I mean something like interrater reliability or interjudge agreement. Do two or more qualitative researchers come up with virtually the same conclusions or observations if they study the same phenomena (Eisner, 1998)? Two comments are appropriate. First, examples of what is sometimes called replication is rare in qualitative research, though one example of it is in the independent studies of Highland Park High School by Philip Jackson and Sara Lawrence Lightfoot (1981). These two independent studies do overlap substantially in both their observations and their conclusions. Other examples are, as I said, difficult to find. When studies do overlap, confidence in the observations and conclusions is likely to increase, but there is no guarantee that consensus might not be misleading. Researchers embracing different interpretive frames may see different things or even if they see the same things they might interpret their meaning differently (Eisner, 1993).

This brings us to the second comment. Differences in description and interpretation among two or more qualitative researchers may be a result of the fact that they attend to different phenomena in the "same" situation. The better question to ask is not, in my view, do the researchers issue the same report, but rather what does each report illuminate? What is it that I can do or understand after having read it? Put another way, the question has to with pragmatics: What can I do with the study?

Such a criterion is not without precedent. There are literally thousands of critical reviews of *Macbeth.* We neither calculate an average score among critical appraisals nor do we try to identify the one true critique. We ask what each reveals. Situations like works of art have multiple layers of meaning, and what we would be wise to seek is what the analysis does to sensitize us to those layers.

Asking about the meanings rendered about a qualitative study relates to its generativity. What is generated? Two things. First, the meanings I have just described. Second, fresh concepts that are the products of what the researcher has seen. By fresh concepts I mean terms such as "logofiction," a term invented by Peshkin (1997) to highlight the ways in which anthropologists have distorted so much of Native American culture through the use of the written "logo"—that is, word. Or, to consider another example, the coining of the term "treaty" by Powell, Cohen, and Farrar (1985) to describe a kind of collusion between high school teachers and students wanting to find a way to live with each other over the course of a school year. The point is that the careful and sensitive study of situations cannot only reveal what is distinctive about them, it can also provide the material to bracket phenomena that can be named and used to search and find similar conditions elsewhere.

What all of this leads to is the acknowledgment of nonscientific forms of knowing, a notion advanced by philosophers such as Ernst Cassirer, Susanne Langer, John Dewey, Nelson Goodman, and more recently by social scientists such as Mark Johnson and neuroscientists such as Antonio Damasio. Nonscientific forms of knowing relate to knowing how and to knowing that. Knowing how is related to "know-how"—an action that one knows how to perform without necessarily understanding why what one does works. Knowing how to ride a two-wheel bike while leaning as one makes a turn is one example. Few people can explain the physics of the action.

But nonscientific knowing also pertains to knowing that, and the that that is known can be what a situation feels like or the sense of elation or pride that someone feels. In these matters it is the artistic treatment of form that carries the reader into these forms of understanding. In other words the arts and the artistic treatment of a medium—language and image—provide portals to experience, experience that enlarges comprehension.

The power of the artistic treatment of language to inform was described poignantly by the American writer Wallace Stegner. At the end of a radio interview he was asked what a piece of fiction needed to be to be great. He paused and then said, "For a work of fiction to be great it has to be true."

If artistically crafted work informs, what are the implications for the conduct of research in psychology? One implication stems from the realization that bias is conferred by omission as well as by commission. The absence of arts-based research is an absence of opportunities to learn, which, of course, is the penultimate mission of research. For more than a few the very idea of arts-based research is oxymoronic. Research is a scientific enterprise, or so it seems. But is it? Is it exclusively so? Might it not be the case that science is a species of research rather than research a species of science? If a philosopher explores the construction of meaning in philosophy, is it not research. Is all historical writing scientific? Not according to Isaiah Berlin. When a novelist, such as Berlin, investigates a community to write about it and then experiments with prose to try to get it right, does that not count as research? I cannot see why not. Thus the questions I am raising are intended to problematize the traditional and comfortable notions that became a part of the psychological research traditions since the mid part of the 19th century.

Lest the reader believe me to be Pollyannaish about the usefulness of an arts-based approach to qualitative research, let me recite some of my concerns.

First, attention to the aesthetics of language or image may override fidelity to the situation one describes. The arts and artistic matters have their own compulsions, and these compulsions can lead one to sacrifice "truth" for interest in or satisfaction with form.

Second, there is inherent in the arts what might be called semantic ambiguity. This ambiguity that could serve useful generative purposes might also make artistically rendered material difficult to interpret.

Third, the pursuit of novelty in arts-based approaches to qualitative research might undermine its practical utility. Investigators might become so enamored with pursuit of creativity that the real needs of consumers might be overlooked.

Fourth, the ability to use new media requires as much skill as the ability to write, yet there are very few programs that promote the option of using new forms of representation and that provide the means for students to develop the necessary skills for using them.

Fifth, doctoral faculties may not have on their roster members who know the medium and the art form well enough to offer useful assistance. For doctoral students this is reason enough to abandon novel approaches to research and to stick with the tried and true.

Sixth, there is the matter of publication. Academics have historically occupied a print culture. Where will nonprint material see the light of day? The Internet might provide an answer; we will have to see.

Seventh, there is the matter of the recalcitrance of some faculty to entertain approaches to research that do not echo the faculty member's pet methodological inclinations. Changing such dispositions might be among the most formidable challenges that forward-looking young researchers may face.

In this chapter I have described the ideas and ideals that animated interest in the creation of a science of psychology. These ideas, born in the mid-19th century, have continued to serve as foundational principles for conducting psychological research. But what we also see is the development of other foundational ideas, ideas that rest on different premises. It is not surprising that there should be controversy and at times conflict about competing ideas regarding the conditions of legitimate research, yet despite these conflicts psychologists like other social scientists are using qualitative research to better understand what might be called "the human condition." In this effort the arts have gradually emerged as sources that have the potential to further such understanding. Whether arts-based psychological research becomes a viable option in psychology remains to be seen. What we do know is that it has sharpened our awareness of the varieties of knowledge that humans use to cope with the world they inhabit. The awareness that this examination of the arts has generated is alone a significant contribution to a science of psychology.

References

Boring, E. (1929). *A history of experimental psychology.* New York; London: Century.

Bronfenbrenner, U. (1970). *Two worlds of childhood: U.S. and U.S.S.R.* New York: Russell Sage Foundation.

Bruner, J. (1985). Paradigmatic and narrative ways of knowing. In E. Eisner (Ed.), *Learning and teaching the ways of knowing, Eighty-fourth yearbook of the National Society for the Study of Education.* Chicago: University of Chicago Press.

Dewey, J. (1929). *The quest for certainty.* New York: Minton, Balch.
Dewey, J. (1934). *Art as experience.* New York: Minton, Balch.
Eisner, E. (1993). Forms of Representation and the Future of Educational Research. *Educational Researcher, 22*(7), 5–11.
Eisner, E. (1998). *The enlightened eye: Qualitative inquiry and the enhancement of educational practice.* Englewood Cliffs, NJ: Prentice-Hall.
Fechner, G. T. (1966). *Elements of psychophysics.* New York: Holt, Rinehart and Winston. (Original work published 1889)
Geertz, C. (1973). *The interpretation of cultures.* New York: Basic Books.
Goffman, E. (1961). *Asylums: Essays on the social situation of mental patients and other inmates.* Chicago: Aldine.
Jackson, P., & Lightfoot, S. (1981). Comprehending a well-run comprehensive: A report on a visit to a large suburban high school. *Daedalus, 110,* 81–96.
Kesey, K. (1962). *One flew over the cuckoo's nest.* New York: Viking Press.
Kozol, J. (1991). *Savage inequalities.* New York: Crown.
Kuhn, T. (1996). *The structure of scientific revolutions.* Chicago: University of Chicago Press.
Neisser, U. (1976). *Cognition and reality. Principles and implications of cognitive psychology.* San Francisco: W. H. Freeman.
Peshkin, A. (1986). *God's choice: The total world of a fundamentalist Christian school.* Chicago: University of Chicago Press.
Peshkin, A. (1997). *Places of memory.* Mahwah, NJ: Erlbaum.
Powell, A., Cohen, D., & Farrar, E. (1985). *The shopping mall high school: Winners and losers in the educational marketplace.* Boston: Houghton Mifflin.
Rorty, R. (1979). *Philosophy and the mirror of nature.* Princeton, NJ: Princeton University Press.
Stake, R. (1974). *Program evaluation, particularly responsive evaluation. New Trends in Evaluation* (Report #35). Göteborg, Sweden: Institute of Education, University of Göteborg.
Toulmin, S. E. (1990). *Cosmopolis: The hidden agenda of modernity.* New York: Free Press.
Whyte, W. F. (1993). *Street corner society: The social structure of an Italian slum.* Chicago: University of Chicago Press.

3

Methodology Makes Meaning: How Both Qualitative and Quantitative Paradigms Shape Evidence and Its Interpretation

Joseph E. McGrath and Bettina A. Johnson

Most discussions of qualitative versus quantitative methods are not ultimately about the use or avoidance of numbers and arithmetic per se. Rather, they include a much broader and deeper set of issues involving fundamental features of the paradigm by which we pursue science. Most of the contemporary arguments urging the use of qualitative approaches are thoroughly embedded within a more general critique of the overall scientific paradigm as applied in our field. Telling critiques of that paradigm have been made from several broad perspectives (called such things as contextualism, perspectivism, constructionism, feminism, and several interpretive perspectives; e.g., Denzin & Lincoln, 1994; Kidder, 1981; Lincoln & Guba, 1985; Smith, Harre, & Langenhove, 1995; VanMaanan, 1979; VanMaanen, Dabbs, & Faulkner, 1982). The common issues in these critiques are (a) the faults of the positivist philosophy of science; (b) the faults of laboratory experimentation; (c) the faults of psychology's theory of measurement and error; (d) the sometimes dubious claims regarding the preeminence of objectivity; (e) the reductionistic tendencies to focus on micro-level directional, mechanical–causal hypotheses stated in terms of abstract variables rather than natural, context-situated processes; and (f) the search for predominately linear relations among variables. Critics argue that because of these faults, the current paradigm is providing us with a limited and distorted picture of phenomena involving human behavior.

Critics have also pointed out that the natural sciences, from which we borrowed our current dominant paradigm, have already abandoned it in favor of other perspectives that better deal with time, causality, and a number of other issues. Therefore, they argue that social and behavioral scientists should follow this example and institute what Smith et al. (1995) call a "new paradigm" or what Lincoln and Guba (1985) call a "naturalistic paradigm." In these and other critiques, an emphasis on qualitative rather than quantitative approaches is just one part—although an important part—of their proffered replacement paradigms.

Within these various critiques of positivism there often seems to be an unstated assumption that, because the present positivistic–experimental–reductionistic–analytical–quantitative paradigm is not working, the alternative paradigm that they offer—which is not positivistic, not experimental, not reductionistic, not analytical, and not quantitative—must be better. Our chapter will probably carry some of that flavor as well. We will try, however, not only to point out the ways in which the dominant paradigm, with its strong preference for quantitative evidence, shapes and constrains the empirical evidence that can be obtained by it, but also to point out the parallel ways that exclusive use of alternative paradigms, with equally strong preferences for qualitative evidence, shape and constrain the evidence as well.

We do not offer a totally balanced approach, however. Much of the discussion of this chapter will dwell on the limitations and constraining effects of the set of assumptions that are embedded within the dominant positivistic paradigm and the associated methods such as experimentation. Such discussion is worth presenting, we think, because the premises of that position are so widely taken for granted, not only in our presentations of scientific information but also in our very training in how science is—and ought to be—done. In this chapter, we will have much less to say about the limitations and constraining effects of the assumptions of alternative perspectives underlying qualitative approaches. That is in part because those assumptions are less well-formulated and uniform and in part because the positivist, quantitative assumptions are so embedded in our discourse.

Our position is not that either qualitative or quantitative approaches are good and the other bad. Rather, our position is that all paradigms for obtaining empirical information about the behavior of human systems pose serious epistemological and evidential problems—and that different paradigms pose different, though equally serious, problems. We also believe that the field needs more use of both qualitative and quantitative approaches. They pose different, and complementary, strengths and weaknesses, and, methodologically, we need all the help we can get.

In the rest of this chapter, therefore, we will discuss many of the specific criticisms that have been raised in the qualitative versus quantitative debate, which are part of a much larger set of issues relevant to all research. Many of these issues have to do with basic assumptions and issues at the paradigmatic level, where the appropriate sources of empirical evidence are determined. These are discussed in the first section of the chapter. Other issues deal with approaches in the treatment of empirical evidence at the operational level. This level involves the collection and processing, aggregation, analysis, and interpretation of the empirical evidence that is deemed appropriate under a given paradigm. These are discussed in the latter sections of the chapter. In all sections, our aim is to show that both quantitative and qualitative approaches involve choices and assumptions that constrain data and therefore the conclusions that can be drawn from them. Throughout the chapter, also, we will concentrate on raising and clarifying the epistemological and methodological issues that beset *both* qualitative and quantitative research. We will leave to other chapters of this book the task of proposing and explicating viable and effective strategies for handling these issues within qualitative approaches.

Table 3.1. Assumptions of Positivistic and Alternative Paradigms

Question	Positivist assumption	Alternative assumption
1. Relation of experimenter (E) to "facts"	Facts independent of E	Facts and E interdependent
2. Relation of E to subjects (S)	S independent of E	S interdependent with E
3. Role of context in studies of systems	Can and should extract essence of phenomena from context	Should study systems embedded in context; meaning is situated
4. Science and values	Can and should be value-free	Cannot be value-free; must make values clear
5. Status of E and S as knower and observer	E superior to S as knower and as observer	E and S part of and influenced by same context
6. How to advance knowledge	Use analytical, reductionist approach; seek universal cause–effect laws at microlevels	Use holistic approaches; seek patterns of relations with situated meaning
7. Criteria of progress in science	Predict and control via generic cause–effect relations	Understand patterns of human activity via many forms of causality

Some Basic Issues at the Paradigmatic Level

We start our consideration by presenting a set of seven assumptions that are embedded within psychology's established positivist research paradigm—at least as practiced within quantitatively oriented research in psychology in the latter half of the 20th century. For each, the positivistic assumption is listed in one column of Table 3.1, and the contrasting assumption that is sometimes proposed by various alternative paradigms is listed in another column.

These assumptions are highly intertwined, some of them with layers of sub-assumptions. Moreover, some of them are on the borderline between being logical and necessary assumptions and being strongly preferred practices. The import of these seven assumptions, and their proposed alternatives, can be discussed more cogently by organizing them into three crucial sets of issues: reality and objectivity; forms of causality; and studying phenomena in dynamic context.

Reality and Objectivity

For psychology and other social sciences, the dominant philosophy of science that drives our views of the existence and pursuit of knowledge is positivism. Positivism is committed to the following ideas about the nature of reality: (a) that there is an orderly, material world that is independent of the observer (and of the observed individuals in the case of research on human systems);

(b) that it is in principle knowable, via rational inquiry; and (c) that the knowledge thus gained is (or in principle can be) independent of the observer. This is philosophical realism in undiluted form.

The idea of objectivity plays a pivotal role in our scientific enterprise. The phenomena we study, our procedures, and we as researchers must attain objectivity for the knowledge we obtain to also be objective. Attaining or presupposing objectivity in these different senses requires many different (and sometimes conflicting) assumptions and procedures, all with profound implications for both qualitative and quantitative research. This section discusses some of the issues and problems raised by the pursuit of objective knowledge.

Foremost in positivism is the idea of the existence of an objective world, a single, fixed reality that we can come to know. To gain knowledge, positivism requires the procedures that are called "measurement" in psychology: observing the essential elements of the phenomena in question (i.e., the "essences") and rendering them in systematic and explicit (preferably, mathematical or quantitative) form. Ultimately, there is often the additional assumption that the formulation of findings in mathematical form will in itself give us insight into the nature of reality. That is, we sometimes assume that our mathematical formulations somehow capture the fundamental principles of phenomena in the "real world." It is also assumed that proper application of these scientific procedures yields, if not certain knowledge, then at least knowledge that is very compelling.

Positivism also assumes that these "observables" are different in kind from the metaphysical, and that those differences are obvious and not a function of the observer and his or her definitions. This raises a long-standing epistemological issue dating back at least to the British philosophers of the Enlightenment era: the issue of whether anyone can "know" reality (if indeed there is a single and fixed reality) in the sense of having certain and undistorted representations of it. Critics argue that knowledge of our sensations or sensory experience is not "pure" knowledge at all; we use our values and beliefs to transform sensory experiences into words or other expressions. If all perceptions are in part a function of the perceiver—not only in regard to the limitations of our sensory–perceptual system but also in regard to the impact of values and attitudes on perception (i.e., the notion that to some degree believing is seeing)—then each of us lives in his or her own unique "reality." Ultimately, that view leads to some version of constructionism or social constructionism, which hold that our perceptions of reality are viewed through a lens focused by societal norms and values. Thus, apart from the ontological issue about the nature and even the existence of a fixed, singular, and knowable "reality," there is also the epistemological issue of whether we ever could objectively know/recognize such a reality if it even exists.

Those adhering to the positivistic paradigm deal with many of these issues by seeming to acknowledge that subjects (Ss) cannot be objective viewers of reality, but nevertheless maintaining that experimenters (Es) can be. This essentially treats the scientists who are studying human behavior as having a privileged epistemological status—as somehow being exempt from influence by the very "laws of human behavior" that they are studying. By these assumptions, social and behavioral scientists "at work" are considered not to have any stereotypes, heuristic biases, attribution tendencies, expectancies, forgetting, perceptual distortions, conformity tendencies, or any other "nonrational" tendencies, however human. By maintaining this detachment from the phenomena being studied, the E is supposedly able to avoid affecting the research process or the "objects" under study.

This view also implies that those Es, because they are "detached," thereby have a better understanding of the *meanings* of the phenomena (in the lives of the Ss, in the case of human systems) than do the Ss themselves. In effect, these assumptions presuppose that the E is superior to the S both as a "knower" (that is, in being able to formulate and conceptualize the nature of the phenomena that are being examined) and as an instrument of observation (that is, in being able to observe facts "objectively," without bias).

Critics of this perspective, however, argue that Es are indeed fully "attached" to the research context, whether they wish to be or not. In effect, human scientists are themselves involved in the matters they are trying to ask about, not just detached observers of those matters, whether they wish to be or not (see, e.g., Faulconer & Williams, 1985). There is considerable research evidence in support of the interdependence between E and S. Some research evidence suggests that even relatively static characteristics of an experimenter (e.g., sex or status) can systematically affect the behavior of individuals in an experiment (reviewed in Unger, 1981).

Many qualitative researchers further argue that the desired "detachment" of the E from the context is a disadvantage. Ss often have an especially valuable standpoint for understanding the phenomena that are a part of their lives. In this view, the very detached standpoint that is so prized in the positivistic paradigm may well be a handicap in understanding human behavior in circumstances that are outside the realm of experience of the E. We have long recognized, for example, that many of our theories—and the data of the studies supporting them—carry an ethnocentric bias that imposes the preconceptions of the researcher's or theorist's culture on the phenomena being studied, whether or not that is appropriate in the given case (Jaeger & Rosnow, 1988).

It is ironic that the idea of objectivity often ends up getting "operationally defined" as intersubjective agreement—that is, agreement among researchers (Hyman, 1964; Kaplan, 1964). On this question, Hyman (1964, p. 33) wrote, "The requirements of objectivity and reproducibility are captured in the definition of science as 'the study of those judgments concerning which universal agreement can be obtained,' " which Hyman attributed to N. Campbell (1952). This conception of objectivity is essentially the very opposite of those other meanings of objectivity, all of which pivot on the idea of *facts separate from the human fact gatherers.* Moreover, if agreement is the key to objectivity, then one must ask, "Agreement among whom?" The de facto answer to that question is, "Among the community of legitimate 'knowers,' properly trained and credentialed scientific experts in the area of study." And that answer is a foot in the door that can be used to justify all sorts of nonrational schema (e.g., Prilleltensky, 1989).

In this discussion, we want to acknowledge that many researchers do seriously consider some (but not all) of these issues. Many adhere to Campbell and colleagues' "hypothetical realism" (see various chapters in Brewer & Collins, 1981), in which successive waves of inquiry and interpretation yield formulations that approach the underlying reality in progressively more accurate approximations. Such hypothetical realists assume that a true reality exists, but also assume that the information obtained about this reality through our current methodologies will always reflect it imperfectly. Most researchers would take seriously the possibility of inaccurate assessments of it by any particular observer or instrument and would also assume that some methods of measurement are more accurate—in other words, more objective—than others. Hypothetical realism does not, however, resolve the underlying epistemological problems raised by critics of positivism in regard to realism.

Furthermore, many researchers follow the positivistic belief that quantification truly captures the underlying nature of reality, without considering many of the limitations and constraints that it brings. Quantification imposes a very strong meaning system on the information thus gathered—the meanings that are implicit in various arithmetics and mathematics. This, in turn, imposes many assumptions about substantive elements and relations (e.g., linearity, unidimensionality) that go with that meaning system. Building those assumptions into the evidence "in advance," as it were, tends to hide the arbitrary, value-laden, error-laden nature of the measurement process itself, and of the mapping of observations to conceptions. Furthermore, in the analysis stage, application of quantitative techniques such as inferential statistics and significance testing gives a powerful—but absolutely arbitrary—basis for resolution of issues of interpretation (e.g., is there or is there not a "real" difference?). It thereby hides the issues that are in dispute. We therefore regard quantification as a mixed blessing, and ask, along with constructionists, feminists, and other critics of positivism: Why not both quantitative and qualitative information?

Forms of Causality

By and large, mainstream research in psychology has made use of a very narrow view of causality. Long ago, Aristotle articulated four forms of causality—formal (quality or essence), final (end state or goal), material (physical make-up), and efficient (effects of prior events; i.e., mechanical cause; White, 1990). But classical positivism has focused almost completely on the latter. Moreover, the form of efficient causality that positivistic research tends to emphasize is a reductionistic, directional, linear form. This type of causal relation involves two or a very few micro-level variables, with A causing B, which in turn causes C, and so on, in a chain-like series of reactions.

Critics of positivism have argued that we not only need a more multivariate, bidirectional, and systemic view of efficient causality, but we also need to pursue some of Aristotle's other forms of causality as well. Critics argue that causal relations in human systems operate at multiple levels, with microlevel variables having effects at higher system levels and vice versa. Some also argue that attempts to develop laws within closed systems such as experimental laboratories necessarily yield laws that are too simplistic to explain behavior (Manicas & Secord, 1983). Because causal processes are also often bidirectional (A affects B and B affects A as well), a holistic or systemic view of causal relations advances our understanding more than does the microlevel, chain-like view.

Regarding other forms of causality besides efficient cause: Critics of positivism argue, first, that human behavior is characterized by intentionality, which irrevocably alters the nature of causal relations. Humans, both individually and in various collective-level systems (groups, organizations, communities), set goals and pursue them—often over long periods of time, often via subtle and complex strategies—which amounts to a kind of "final" causality or teleology. Moreover, human systems, at individual and collective levels, exhibit patterns of growth and development that can be understood most clearly in terms of the idea of "formal" cause. There are also some situations in which Aristotle's ideas of material causality apply, as well. (See Arrow, McGrath, & Berdahl, 2000; Brand, 1979; Lincoln & Guba, 1985.)

The quantitative methods that predominate in the positivistic paradigm almost universally adopt this narrow interpretation of efficient cause. The culture of psychological research is biased in favor of experimentation, most often experiments that isolate a few variables in a closed system (the laboratory) and examine their effects. To analyze and interpret data from experiments, we rely almost exclusively on the logic of null-hypothesis significance testing and inferential statistics (see later discussion). We can best test our hypotheses with inferential statistics if: (a) the hypotheses are in the form of directional relations between reliable, valid measures of a small number of unidimensional variables, (b) the experimenter manipulates the causal variable, and (c) *all other variables* are (i) held constant, (ii) equated via statistical controls, or (iii) equally distributed among conditions via random assignment of cases.

This has been and is a powerful technology for investigation of human activity, as it has been for study of other species and of physical systems as well. By adopting a powerful set of assumptions and a strong set of manipulation, control, and measurement operations, the experimental paradigm has allowed us to make tremendous advances in our knowledge over the past century. The trouble is, of course, that what we "know" we know only within the context of those assumptions and tools; and that knowledge is valid only to the extent that all of the underlying assumptions hold. When one considers the assumptions listed for positivism in Table 3.1 (e.g., that E does not affect the behavior of S), we must have reasonable doubt about the validity of evidence gained by experimental means.

There are many situations, of course, for which the strong forms of experimentation are either not possible or unethical. In some situations, where true manipulation of causal variables is impossible (e.g., sex or age), researchers often ignore this impossibility and treat these variables as though they had manipulated them, so that inferential statistics can still be used. For most of these instances, the positivist paradigm as practiced in psychology does allow tests of covariation between measures of two or more variables, though this approach is considered a much weaker form of inquiry. In such correlational analyses, a determination of the direction of causality, if any, is put in abeyance. In general, correlational relations do not permit inferences about causal direction, although time-lagged correlations do allow indirect causal inferences. But correlational studies exhibit all of the other features of the positivistic logic of a narrow efficient causality: They generally deal with two or very few micro-level variables; they take no account of any system-level processes or constraints; they are most often tests of linear relations, and virtually always of monotonic ones; and although they do not formally specify direction they seldom posit bidirectionality. Therefore, correlational methods still incur all of the restrictions and constraints inherent in the efficient cause perspective, without the advantage of strong causal inferences.

Critics of positivism imply that the quantitative nature of our evidence encourages such a limited and narrow view of causality. Our tools for quantitative analysis make the testing of multivariate relations possible but difficult and costly in terms of requirements for numbers of cases that can be "treated as alike." Thus, although multivariate ANOVA and similar techniques extend ANOVA to allow for tests of several dependent variables at once, the number of independent variables that can be examined in any one analysis is still quite limited. Many of those tools require the imposition of some very strong assumptions, such as linearity of relations, unidimensionality of measures, multivariate normal distributions, uncorrelated error components, and homogeneity of variance. Results of statistical analyses have the meanings they purport to have only insofar as both the empirical data and the underlying substantive phenomena actually conform to those assumptions (i.e., relations are actually linear, errors are uncorrelated, and so on, in both the data of the study and the "real world" sourse of those data). Thus, our quantitative analysis tools seriously alter and constrain the meaning of results.

The logic of experimentation, and the most commonly used tools for quantitative analysis, also have additional effects on the kinds of research questions we tend to ask in a quantitatively oriented psychology: For example, they make it very difficult to study processes over time, while at the same time, they provide a number of techniques that encourage the conduct of our studies in the form of one-shot or very short-term before–after designs. Some of these issues are discussed in the next part of this section, which deals with studying phenomena in dynamic context.

Studying Phenomena in Dynamic Context

Positivism's focus on efficient causality has indirectly influenced the way researchers treat the context in which phenomena occur. Psychology's very strong preference for studying human behavior is by extracting variables from the contexts within which they are embedded. In that view, any features other than the specific independent or dependent variables being studied amount to noise. Our logic of inquiry—most notably in its experimental forms—requires that we get rid of such noise through experimental controls or statistical controls. These practices are so deeply embedded in the quantitative paradigm that they function as though they involved underlying and unquestionable axioms.

Critics of the positivist paradigm argue that human behavior is situated—that is, that its very meaning depends on the context within which it occurs (e.g., McGuire, 1989). Many of these critics argue in favor of programs of research that capture many different features of the context affecting the phenomenon of interest, because no one single methodological perspective can capture all this complexity (Jaeger & Rosnow, 1988). They argue that the tendency for researchers to use the same methodologies, operationalizations, and samples restricts researchers' ability to examine the complex relations that exist in the real world (McGuire, 1973). Moreover, focusing on only proximal or immediate causes for behavior can obscure the effects of higher level causes, such as sociological factors (Scarr, 1985). So, from the point of view of all of these critiques, far from being noise the embedding context is a vital part of what we should be studying.

One very special part of context for human behavior is the temporal context(s) within which that behavior occurs. Positivism, as it has been applied in our quantitatively oriented psychology, has treated that temporal context with substantial neglect in several ways (Kelly & McGrath, 1988). First of all, the logic of positivism holds that: (a) effect must not precede cause; (b) all (causal) processes take time to unfold (though, of course, different processes may take different amounts of time); and (c) there can be no action at a temporal distance (that is, the causal process must be temporally connected to the occurrence of the effect, either directly or via intervening subprocesses or subeffects). Though there is usually much concern to take the first assumption into account, the second and third are largely ignored. Virtually no theories in psychology make statements about the time required for given causes to have their effects, much less precise statements about the functional patterns of those cause–effect relations over time. Moreover, most studies that purport to measure (efficient) cause–effect relations are done over relatively short periods of time, if indeed they are not just one-shot studies (i.e., with a single wave of observation or measurement of all variables concurrently). There are, of course, a number of relatively sophisticated approaches to the study of data using measurements over time (e.g., time-series data, growth-curve analysis; see McGrath & Altermatt, 2000, for a discussion of a number of them in relation to the study of human groups). Sadly, the use of such methods, and the collection of data for which they would be useful, is still rare in many areas of psychology.

The positivistic paradigm neglects temporal matters in another way, as well. When variables are measured more than once, it is a common practice to minimize variation over time, by adding and averaging across successive measures of the same variable. The adding and averaging is done to obtain a more reliable (i.e., more unchanging over time) measurement. Doing so presumes that the underlying concept in question is indeed stable over time, and that all variations in a given measure over time amount to error. Critics of positivism argue that many if not all aspects of human behavior and therefore all of our "variables" change over time (at least in principle).

These assumptions can be reasonable or ridiculous, depending on (a) the variable, (b) the context, and (c) the size of the time interval. For example, if the period of time over which the measures are taken extends from the individual's 1st to 30th birthday, it is almost certainly inappropriate to add and average them, regardless of the nature of the variable. In contrast, if the period of time over which the measurements extend is a matter of seconds, it is likely that adding and averaging may be appropriate for a wide range of behavior variables. Most actual cases, of course, lie somewhere in between these two examples, and so the judgment about their temporal patterning is much more equivocal.

One set of critics of positivism (Arrow et al., 2000; Baron, 1994; Latane & Nowak, 1994; Vallacher & Nowak, 1994) go a step further. They argue that a proper logic of inquiry would include or even focus on tracing the patterning of key system variables over time. For example, Gergen (1973) urged psychologists to focus more on cross-cultural research and content analysis of behavioral records from historical periods to determine the contextual scope and temporal durability of conclusions about human behavior. Latane and Nowak (1994) and Baron, Amezeen, and Beek (1994), among others, show how tracing the trajectories of key system variables over time can add to our understanding of how social systems function.

How does adoption of qualitative methods help address these issues? As discussed earlier, the commitment to efficient cause predisposes researchers to experimental methodologies (and vice versa). Isolation of the variables of interest ignores the rich contextual influences on these variables that are not only important in establishing efficient cause but are also important for other types of cause (i.e., formal, final, and material). Many qualitative methodologies (e.g., life narratives, focus groups, case studies) are geared toward identifying and incorporating such contextual influences that would otherwise be disregarded as confounds in quantitatively oriented research.

A commitment to using evidence in many forms can encourage the researcher to think about relations that are *non*linear, or even nonmonotonic in form, as well as about mutual–reciprocal relationships between multiple variables, perhaps at different system levels. Reliance on a limited set of statistical techniques not only constrains data collection procedures but also constrains the ways in which researchers conceptualize phenomena (Gigerenzer, 1991). There is little use in considering such complex relations if your analysis and interpretation technology will not let you examine them systematically. But if the researcher is committed to a technology that provides a more flexible treatment of the forms and patterns of relations that can be explored, then he or she is free to think about more complex features of human systems.

Some Issues in the Processing of Empirical Evidence

Beyond all these paradigmatic issues, questions about qualitative versus quantitative methods also arise in a number of places at the operational level—in the processing of empirical evidence. The use of empirical evidence in psychological research always begins with making a record of some observations of conditions and events in some human systems. We will refer to this as "records of behavior," following Coombs (1964). The underlying conditions and behaviors on which those records are based are always, in principle, qualitative: Something happens or it does not. We introduce "quantification" of the evidence (or we render it in qualitative form) at three distinct places within the research process.

First, we transform such "records of observations of behavior" into data by systematically translating all observations into forms that are in some sense parallel to one another, and therefore can be aggregated or compared. This is the part of the process that we refer to in psychology as measurement, a term that presupposes the quantitative form, but this can be performed in qualitative forms as well. We will call this process "making data from records of observations," again following Coombs (1964).

Often, in psychology, such a transformation to quantitative form is made at the time of the initial recording—as when we ask participants to put check marks on a questionnaire scale that already has a number line imposed on it, or when we ask them to rank order a set of (qualitative) alternatives. Sometimes, the quantification is imposed later by the experimenter—as when we count up the number of "correct answers" and treat that as a numerical score. Sometimes, of course, the records of behavior are left in qualitative form—as, for example, when we transcribe, verbatim, responses from an interview.

At the second and third stages, we then often aggregate multiple observations and apply tools to analyze these aggregated cases. Aggregation can be done in quantitative form, as when a researcher computes the average length of time that given pairs of people make eye contact during a meeting. Or this aggregation can be in qualitative form, as when a researcher pulls together for comparison the self-descriptions of several people who have been diagnosed as schizophrenic. Tools for analysis and comparison, too, can be either quantitative (e.g., ANOVA, structural equation modeling) or qualitative (e.g., Kidder's 1981 use of negative case analysis, as discussed later in the chapter).

At each of these three stages, whether translating the evidence into qualitative or quantitative form, the researcher imposes a number of assumptions and constraints on the empirical evidence. For example, when we transform observed behavior into data in quantitative form, we make strong assumptions about the nature of the variable(s) we think the behavior displays—about their unidimensionality, monotonicity, appropriateness for representation on an interval or ratio scale, and so on. We make similar assumptions, though usually not as strong and constraining, when we render the data in qualitative form. For example, when we code behaviors into one (and only one) of a set of categories, we assume that the categories are independent, mutually exclusive, and collectively exhaustive; and that they together encompass all of the important ways in which the behavior in question can occur. In both cases, there usually are ways to check some, but seldom ways to check all, of these assumptions.

At the second stage, there is a set of assumptions that we necessarily make when we aggregate observations or cases into either quantitative or qualitative aggregates. For example, for the quantitative aggregation case, we make assumptions about the nature and distribution of random errors of measurement. For both the qualitative and quantitative aggregation cases, we make assumptions about the actual extent to which the aggregated cases are "alike" in all important respects.

In the third stage—analysis and interpretation—the quantitative approach most often involves the application of inferential statistics and use of the much emphasized significance testing associated with it. This imposes another array of strong assumptions on the data about the distribution of cases, about the meaning of variations within sets of cases treated alike, about the logic involved in hypothesis testing and significance levels, and so on. The qualitative approach has not as yet developed a "logic-of-inference" that is as well articulated and widely accepted and widely taught as that of probability statistics. But even these less well-formulated qualitative approaches involve assumptions—about meanings, about the relation of the researcher's understandings to those of participants, and so on. (See several relevant chapters in Smith et al., 1995.) For example, Ceballo (1999) discussed how her assumption of consistency and progress in the life of her research participant led her to draw very different conclusions about her participant's life than her participant had drawn. Ceballo discusses how age, social class, and regional norms affected both her own and her participant's assumptions and construction of events.

The underlying point of this discussion is that any approach, quantitative or qualitative, to these transformations of empirical observations require the imposition of some set of assumptions; and those assumptions both shape and constrain the meaning(s) of the evidence. Note that it is not a question of whether one set of assumptions can be shown to be true or false in a given case. Most often the bases on which we decide such matters are relatively ambiguous judgment calls, not matters to which strong logical or mathematical criteria can be applied. What is crucial is consideration of the ways in which the set of assumptions that is applied in a given case alters the meaning of the evidence.

Assessing the Quality of the Evidence

One of the strengths of quantitative approaches is their ability to provide explicit assessments of the quality of the information obtained in a study. Quantitative techniques are often designed to provide definitive, though arbitrary, answers to questions about the *reliability* (that is, repeatability), *validity* (that is, truth value), and *generalizability* (that is, scope and boundaries of applicability) of a study's measures, of its findings, and of its conclusions. By adopting explicit quantitative criteria (e.g., a specific probability [alpha level] for attributing significance), quantitative researchers provide a set of normative standards for a scientific community in a form that permits one researcher to check on the claims of another. This is a valuable tool, because otherwise there is no way to assess the credibility of differing claims.

One of the biggest criticisms of qualitative research is the absence of such a set of techniques to judge the quality of data. However, several researchers have devised ways to provide equivalent criteria of quality of evidence for qualitative studies. Kidder (1981) applied the four main criteria espoused by Cook and Campbell (1979) to qualitative research. Those four criteria are internal validity or the degree to which strong causal inferences can be made from study findings; external validity or the degree to which findings of a given study are likely to apply to studies of other systems and contexts; construct validity or the degree to which the measures of the study map accurately to the underlying concepts about which inferences are to be made; and statistical-conclusion validity or the degree to which findings are quantitatively strong and unconfounded enough to make definitive conclusions possible. Kidder examined how the rich descriptions of good qualitative studies can be used to estimate the likelihood that the various threats to validity (e.g., history, maturation, etc.) were operating to contaminate that body of evidence.

Lincoln and Guba (1985) proposed the concept of "trustworthiness" as the overall criterion for assessing the worth of information from any scientific study. That concept encompasses four main ideas—the truth value or credibility, the applicability, the consistency, and the neutrality of the information—that correspond roughly to the more familiar concepts of internal validity, external validity, reliability, and objectivity. Lincoln and Guba examined a number of techniques by which those criterion concepts can be explored in information from qualitative research. These techniques tend to require much more complicated and time-consuming activities (e.g., having an external agent conduct an inquiry audit) than simply calculating correlation coefficients between variables. And, of course, results of application of those techniques are almost never as definitive as those of quantitative analyses because they do not rest on strong though arbitrary assumptions about probability levels, distribution of error, and so on.

Both Kidder and Lincoln and Guba included "negative case analysis" in their repertoire of useful ways to assess the quality of qualitative evidence, and that technique illustrates both the value and the risks of substituting these qualitative criterion approaches for the more familiar quantitative ones. This "negative case analysis" includes a process by which the study hypothesis is systematically examined and modified, until *all* cases fit the final hypothesis. Doing so can be an aid in examining potential threats to internal and external validity. At the same time, negative case analysis also resolves the question of "statistical conclusion validity" definitively, but in two quite contradictory ways. On the one hand, it makes statistical analysis *moot,* because 100% of the data fit the (modified) hypothesis so there is no need to ask the "statistical significance" question. On the other hand, it makes statistical analysis *illegitimate,* because if one has (inductively) built the modified hypothesis to fit the data, rather than (deductively) gathered data to test a preformulated hypothesis, the assumptions of an inferential statistics test have been violated and a statistical significance test is inappropriate.

Though not dealing specifically with qualitative and quantitative approaches, McGrath and colleagues (Brinberg & McGrath, 1985; McGrath, Kelly, & Rhodes, 1993; McGrath, Martin, & Kulka, 1982; Runkel & McGrath, 1972) offer a complex view of the research process that provides another conception of how various research paradigms and research strategies (including both qualitative and quantitative approaches) relate to one another and to fundamental research issues. They argue that research always entails activities–information relating to three broad domains: conceptual, substantive, and methodological. They also argue that within each of those domains, effective research *requires* maximizing each of three broad criteria, and that these criteria constitute conflicting desiderata that cannot all be maximized simultaneously. These criteria have slightly different forms in each of the three domains. In the methodological domain, for example, they are generalizability, contextual realism, and precision and control. They are conflicting because the actions taken to increase any one of them tends to reduce the other two or minimize one of them. Research strategies can be categorized by the extent to which they can meet the requirements of each of the three criteria. Some research strategies maximize on one of them, some attempt to optimize two, but no research strategy can maximize all three.

Within this conception, there are three general sets of research strategies: naturalistic strategies (e.g., case studies, field experiments); experimental strategies (e.g., laboratory experiments, judgment studies); and theoretical strategies (e.g., mathematical models, computational models). Each group of strategies is designed to fulfill one of the conflicting desiderata well, but each at the same time is thereby limited in the extent to which it can fulfill the other two. For example, experimental approaches (which most often are quantitative approaches) maximize with respect to precision (of measurement) and control (of variables), and thereby potentially puts the researcher in a position to make strong logical inferences. In doing so, such studies often give up considerable contextual realism. Naturalistic approaches, on the other hand (and many qualitative studies would fit this category) maximize contextual realism and thereby puts the researcher in a position to make claims pertaining to the operation of the systems actually studied. In doing so, however, such studies often give up considerable precision and control, hence the ability to make strong causal inferences.

Both experimental studies and naturalistic ones are relatively weak with regard to generalizability. Experimental studies cannot make claims beyond the (artificial) systems included in those studies; and naturalistic studies cannot make claims beyond the (natural) systems included in theirs. Experimental studies try to compensate for this by formulating questions and concepts at very high levels of abstraction—thus exacerbating their already weak position with respect to context realism. Naturalistic studies try to compensate for their weak position on generalizability by formulating evidence in terms of rich descriptions of complex patterns of relations—thus exacerbating their already weak position with respect to precision and control and strong causal inferences.

The essence of this position is that it is not possible, in principle, to satisfy all of the conflicting criteria for meaningful research information, and the very actions that help with regard to one of them undo one or more of the others. Applying that viewpoint to the topic of this chapter, it is clear that neither qualitative nor quantitative approaches are sufficient, and both are necessary, to the systematic exploration of any given substantive research domain. We will comment more in the final section of this chapter on the need for incorporating discrepant if not downright contradictory approaches in our research.

The Need for Multiple Methodologies

Table 3.1 laid out a set of assumptions about reality, causality, and context. Alternative positions on those assumptions differentiate the dominant positivistic paradigm, to which many of the quantitative approaches adhere, from various alternative paradigms (e.g., perspectivism, constructivism, feminism,

Smith's "new paradigm," Lincoln and Guba's "naturalistic paradigm"), to which many of the qualitative approaches subscribe.

The use of qualitative methods and a supporting paradigmatic view has a number of advantages, as we have tried to point out at various points in the chapter. Those advantages, however, are certainly not gained without cost. Essentially, adopting the assumptions of the alternative perspectives lays the researcher open to a whole array of epistemological and methodological issues—many of which are the very problems that the positivistic paradigm was developed, some centuries ago, to overcome.

Consider the position one is in if one adopts all of the alternative assumptions listed in Table 3.1. If E (as well as S) is a part of the phenomena being studied, and if "the facts" are inextricably connected to E (as well as S), and if it is impossible to attain objectivity in the sense that E's biases and values inevitably affect the data collection and interpretation process—then we are in serious danger of lapsing into the most extreme forms of solipsism—namely that each "observer" (each S as well as each E) experiences a different world, a different reality and causal structure. Moreover, if E does not have a special standing, as observer and as interpreter of evidence about the systems he or she wishes to examine, what then is the advantage, or even the point, of "specialists" doing scientific studies of those systems? Furthermore, if human activity can only be understood when viewed holistically in relation to all of its many layers of embedding contexts, then any specific actions at specific times by specific human systems cannot truly be understood *at all*. Finally, if the criterion for progress in our science is "advances in a common understanding of human systems and human actions," and if every E (and every S) is an equally valid interpreter of evidence and equally effective constructor of those understandings, how then can we claim that we are truly dealing in a scientific enterprise (as that term has come to be understood in our culture, albeit within positivitic premises)?

The positivist paradigm in general, and many of the quantitative tools used within it in particular, were invented to get would-be scientists out of the predicaments implicit in the foregoing questions. The strong inferential logic built into that paradigm, exemplified most clearly in the logic of experimentation, is designed to limit the kinds of findings that can be considered as reflecting "causal" processes (following the Humean logic of mechanical causality). The even more constraining logic of inferential statistics is designed to "objectify"—or at least to make totally explicit, hence reproducible—the decision about whether a given result is a meaningful (i.e., repeatable and generalizable) one rather than just a happenstance within a particular set of observations.

It seems clear that the constraining assumptions of the positivist paradigm really do not reflect "reality" as we experience it. In light of much evidence to the contrary, it would be hard to espouse seriously the view that E does not have any effects on S, or on the "facts" that are adduced from a given set of observations, or to hold that a given human system stripped of its embedding contexts functions in the same way as that system would when fully contextually embedded. In short, the assumptions of the positivist position are not really *true*.

On the other hand, the assumptions of the alternative positions, if fully adopted, make a shambles of the usual meanings of the scientific enterprise. Such a potential lapse into a solipsism that denies the value of systematic efforts to understand human behavior—that is the *dark side* of qualitative research.

We have gone a long way in the past century in advancing our understanding of human actions by following the positivistic paradigm more or less exclusively—even though its assumptions are not true. We have acted as if we were using a "hypothetical positivism" (to paraphrase and broaden Campbell's "hypothetical realism"). We have asked questions as if the assumptions of positivism were true, knowing that they were not literally so. That strategy has served us well.

There is good reason to believe that in many substantive areas we may now have reached the limits of what we can learn about human systems by exclusive use of that paradigm. We must find ways to collect evidence, and to examine it, that will let us learn about human systems *even when* the assumptions of positivism do not hold. That is, we must find ways to learn about human systems even when Es do affect the facts and the S's behavior, and even when systems are profoundly affected by their embedding contexts and even when we know that E's values are affecting what we choose to study, how we study it, and what we think we have learned from those studies. What we are urging here is the simultaneous use of dual paradigms, positivistic and "un-positivistic," and complementary use of quantitative and qualitative methods.

How can we do that? Kidder's (1981) and Lincoln and Guba's (1985) treatments of validity issues, discussed briefly earlier in this chapter, offer two good examples of how one can connect the concepts of the two opposing paradigms. Many of the chapters of this volume contain detailed treatments of other ways in which qualitative methods can be put to use—individually and in combination with more traditional quantitative approaches. Only by a deliberate mixing of quantitative and qualitative approaches, we think, and by a deliberate upholding of *both* of the two conflicting paradigms that underpin those two sets of approaches, can psychology avoid both the overconstraining treatment of complex, dynamic human systems characteristic of quantitative approaches and the solipsistic epistemological quagmire implicit in the perspectives that characteristically underpin qualitative approaches. We urge a deliberate adoption of such a seemingly internally contradictory approach.

References

Arrow, H., McGrath, J. E., & Berdahl, J. L. (2000). *Small groups as complex systems.* Thousand Oaks, CA: Sage.

Baron, R. M., Amezeen, P. G., & Beek, P. J. (1994). Local and global dynamics in social relations. In R. R. Vallacher & A. Nowak (Eds.), *Dynamical systems in social psychology* (pp. 111–138). San Diego, CA: Academic Press.

Brand, M. (1979). Causality. In P. D. Asquith & H. B. Kyburg, Jr. (Eds.), *Current research in the philosophy of science: Proceedings of the philosophy of science association* (pp. 252–281). Ann Arbor, MI: Edwards.

Brewer, M. B., & Collins, B. E. (Eds.). (1981). *Scientific inquiry and the social sciences.* San Francisco: Jossey-Bass.

Brinberg, D., & McGrath, J. E. (1985). *Validity and the research process.* Beverly Hills, CA: Sage.

Campbell, N. (1952). *What is science?* New York: Dover.

Ceballo, R. (1999). Negotiating the life narrative: A dialogue with an African American social worker. *Psychology of Women Quarterly, 23*(2), 309–322.

Cook, T. D., & Campbell, D. T. (1979). *Quasi-experimentation: Design and analysis for field settings.* Chicago: Rand-McNally.

Coombs, C. H. (1964). *A theory of data.* New York: John Wiley.

Denzin, N. J., & Lincoln, Y. S. (Eds.). (1994). *Handbook of qualitative research.* Thousand Oaks, CA: Sage.

Faulconer, J. E., & Williams, R. N. (1985). Temporality in human action: An alternative to positivism and historicism. *American Psychologist, 40*(11), 1179–1188.

Gergen, K. (1973). Social psychology as history. *Journal of Personality and Social Psychology, 26,* 309–320.

Gigerenzer, G. (1991). From tools to theories: A heuristic of discovery in cognitive psychology. *Psychological Review, 98*(2), 254–267.

Hyman, R. (1964). *The nature of psychological inquiry.* Englewood Cliffs, NJ: Prentice-Hall.

Jaeger, M. E., & Rosnow, R. L. (1988). Contextualism and its implications for psychological inquiry. *British Journal of Psychology, 79*(1), 63–75.

Kaplan, A. (1964). *The conduct of inquiry: Methodology for behavioral science.* San Francisco: Chandler.

Kelly, J. R., & McGrath, J. E. (1988). *On time and method.* Newbury Park, CA: Sage.

Kidder, L. H. (1981). Qualitative research and quasi-experimental frameworks. In M. B. Brewer & B. E. Collins (Eds.), *Scientific inquiry and the social sciences* (pp. 226–256). San Francisco: Jossey-Bass.

Latane, B., & Nowak, A. (1994). Attitudes as catastrophes: From dimensions to categories with increasing involvement. In R. R. Vallacher & A. Nowak (Eds.), *Dynamical systems in social psychology* (pp. 219–249). San Diego, CA: Academic Press.

Lincoln, Y. S., & Guba, E. G. (1985). *Naturalistic inquiry.* Newbury Park, CA: Sage.

Manicas, P. T., & Secord, P. F. (1983). Implications for psychology of the new philosophy of science. *American Psychologist, 38,* 399–413.

McGrath, J. E., & Altermatt, T. W. (2000). Observation and analysis of group interaction over time: Some methodological and strategic choices. In M. A. Hogg & S. Tindale (Eds.), *Blackwell handbook of social psychology: Group processes* (pp. 525–556). Malden, MA: Blackwell.

McGrath, J. E., Kelly, J. R., & Rhodes, J. E. (1993). A feminist perspective on research methodology: Some metatheoretical issues, contrasts, and choices. In S. Oskamp & M. Costanzo (Eds.), *Gender issues in social psychology: The Claremont symposium on applied social psychology* (pp. 19–37). Newbury Park, CA: Sage.

McGrath, J. E., Martin, J., & Kulka, R. C. (1982). *Judgment calls in research.* Beverly Hills, CA: Sage.

McGuire, W. J. (1973). The yin and yang of progress in social psychology: Seven koan. *Journal of Personality & Social Psychology, 26*(3), 446–456.

McGuire, W. J. (1989). A perspectivist approach to the strategic planning of programmatic scientific research. In B. Gholson, et al. (Eds.), *Psychology of science: Contributions to metascience* (pp. 214–245). Cambridge: Cambridge University Press.

Prilleltensky, I. (1989). Psychology and the status quo. *American Psychologist, 44*(5), 795–802.

Runkel, P. J., & McGrath, J. E. (1972). *Research on human behavior: A systematic guide to method.* New York: Holt, Rinehart, & Winston.

Scarr, S. (1985). Constructing psychology: Making facts and fables for our times. *American Psychologist 40,* 499–512.

Smith, J. A., Harre, R., & von Langenhove, L. (Eds.). (1995). *Rethinking methods in psychology.* London: Sage.

Suppe, F. (1989). *The semantic conception of theories and scientific realism.* Urbana: University of Illinois Press.

Unger, R. K. (1981). Sex as a social reality: Field and laboratory research. *Psychology of Women Quarterly, 5*(4), 645–653.

Vallacher, R. R., & Nowak, A. (Eds.). (1994). *Dynamical systems in social psychology.* New York: Academic Press.

VanMannen, J. (Ed.). (1979). Qualitative methodology [Special issue]. *Administrative Science Quarterly, 24*(4).

VanMaanen, J., Dabbs, J. M., & Faulkner, R. R. (Ed.). (1982). *Varieties of qualitative research.* Beverly Hills, CA: Sage.

White, P. (1990). Ideas about causation in philosophy and psychology. *Psychological Bulletin, 108,* 3–18.

4

Dancing Through Minefields: Toward a Qualitative Stance in Psychology

Jeanne Marecek

Along the borders of psychology, a quiet but steady stream of qualitative research has gradually been gaining momentum. Social psychology, developmental psychology, cultural psychology, psychology of women and gender, clinical and counseling psychology, and personality psychology: In all these fields, psychologists are trying qualitative approaches. The qualitative umbrella is a large one, sheltering many ways of working and many different traditions, lexicons, and pretheoretical assumptions. Qualitative workers value creativity and innovation and so they have embraced novel forms of data, new means of gathering data, experimental forms of writing, and unorthodox and even playful ways of disseminating results. Their stance is a counterpoint to the strict codification (sometimes verging on fetishization) of methods, statistics, and scientific writing that marks mainstream American psychology.

At the heart of the movement toward qualitative inquiry in psychology are three intertwined elements. First, qualitative inquiry embeds the study of psychology in rich contexts of history, society, and culture. Second, it resituates the people whom we study in their life worlds, paying special attention to the social locations they occupy. Third, it regards those whom we study as reflexive, meaning-making, and intentional actors. Qualitative psychology concerns itself with human experience and action. It examines the patterned ways that we have come to think about and act in our life worlds and that sustain the social structure of those worlds (Kleinman, 1984). I use the term qualitative *stance* rather than qualitative *methods* to indicate that qualitative work involves more than different techniques of collecting and analyzing data. A qualitative stance is grounded in a different epistemology.

Qualitative inquiry has a long history in psychology that goes back to Wilhelm Wundt's *Völkerpsychologie*. Drawing on earlier philosophical traditions stretching back to Vico, Wundt (1921) envisioned a system of psychology with two branches. One, familiar to most readers, was devoted to the laboratory

I would like to thank the editors and Eva Magnusson for their thoughtful comments and criticisms.

study of elementary psychological functions, such as the elements of sensation and perception. The other was the study of higher psychological functions, which, in Wundt's view, extended beyond individual consciousness. Studying these higher functions required methods akin to those used in the fields of ethnology, history, and anthropology (Cole, 1996). In the United States, of course, the first branch became the preeminent one; the second was muted. Nonetheless a line of qualitative inquiry threads through the history of psychology, including William James, Gordon Allport, Robert White, Leon Festinger, and Carolyn and Muzafer Sherif, among others. In addition, the case study, a time-honored form of qualitative inquiry, has a long tradition in clinical psychology, both as a pedagogical tool and as a form of scholarly communication through which practice knowledge is shared and cumulated (Bromley, 1986).

Across much of the world (the United Kingdom, continental Europe, Australia, New Zealand, the Nordic countries, Canada), psychologists are engaging qualitative approaches. Indeed, in the United Kingdom, the Economic and Social Research Council, one of the major sources of funds for postgraduate training in psychology, now insists on adequate training in qualitative methods. In much of the world, psychologists' conversations concern how and when (not if) qualitative approaches should be used (e.g., Bannister, Burman, Parker, Taylor, & Tindall, 1994; Henwood & Nicholson, 1995; Richardson, 1996; Tolman & Brydon-Miller, 2001). Time-honored modes of qualitative inquiry—field-based participant observation, open-ended interviewing, focus groups, narrative analysis, case studies—are being extended and refined. New approaches are being developed, including discursive psychology, participatory action research, and visual storytelling (also called photovoice and community photography; cf., Lykes, 1997). The Britain-based journal, *Feminism and Psychology*, routinely publishes articles that use approaches like these, as does the international *Journal of Health Psychology*. In the United States, the *Journal of Social Issues* (Brydon-Miller & Tolman, 1997) and the *Psychology of Women Quarterly* (Crawford & Kimmel, 1999) have had special issues that featured qualitative approaches.

The time has come for psychology in America to reassess old prejudices about the "subjective," "anecdotal," or "unscientific" nature of qualitative work. Too many psychology departments still issue blanket dismissals of qualitative work. Many graduate programs flatly forbid students to undertake qualitative projects for their dissertations. Too many advisors warn students that such a dissertation will spell the death of their careers in the field. Even undergraduate students report that they have come to understand that they must not undertake qualitative work for a senior thesis because it will damage their chances of getting into graduate school.

The habit of dismissing qualitative work out of hand stands in sharp contrast to the meticulous consideration that psychologists usually give to methodology. Indeed, some call psychology's enthronement of methods "methodolatry." Most of us would rap the knuckles of a student who offered flabby arguments such as, "It just doesn't seem like science" or "If it doesn't have numbers, it can't be psychology" or "I can't tell if it's interesting; it doesn't have any statistics." Yet these are verbatim evaluations written by prominent psychologists reviewing qualitative research manuscripts for publication. Most psychologists would probably agree that the choice of a method should depend on the question under investigation. If so, then how can it be justifiable to rule out qualitative approaches even before there is a research question?

Limiting psychologists to a constricted range of acceptable methods has had costs for the field. The constraints have led some psychologists to disaffection and crises of commitment. For example, Sandra Bem, a senior social psychologist, described herself as "feeling theoretically hemmed in." To do meaningful scholarship, she wrote, "I came increasingly to see myself as having abandoned my disciplinary commitment to psychology" (1993, p. 239). Nicola Gavey recalled how discovering "a model of doing psychology differently" enabled her to conceive "the possibility that psychology could be different, palatable, and even exciting" and "the possibility of imagining a future 'in' psychology" (Gavey, in press, p. 1).

Disaffection is a high cost, but it is not the only one. There is an intellectual price to pay for a narrow vision of psychological methods. A method is an interpretation. That is, any method of inquiry entails a number of pretheoretical assumptions about its object of study. It deforms what it observes in characteristic ways and it predetermines the form that the results of the inquiry will take. In recent times, the discipline of psychology, especially its North American variant, has restricted its adherents to a single method of producing knowledge. That method is presented as the sole way that psychologists work—"the" scientific method. As a result, the assumptions underlying this method are taken for granted and its deformations are invisible. Many psychologists swim in the waters of logical positivism, empiricism, realism, and quantification without knowing they are wet. If we bring qualitative approaches forward and place them in full view alongside conventional methods, we will be better able to appreciate and debate the possibilities and limitations of each.

In what follows, I offer my view of qualitative psychology and what qualitative inquiry offers to psychology. I begin in a negative vein, by taking issue with some common stereotypes of qualitative approaches. Next, I describe what I see as some key features of a qualitative stance. Finally, I briefly suggest some issues that qualitative inquiry places on the table for the rest of psychology.

Qualitative Psychology: What It Is Not

Qualitative work is often seen as the polar opposite to quantitative work. Quantitative work is described as rigorous, hardheaded, and scientific; qualitative work seems mushy, soft, and unscientific. Some writers have characterized quantitative work as agentic and masculine; some have characterized qualitative work as relational and feminine. Like most dichotomies, the quantitative/qualitative dichotomy is false; it covers up a more complex reality. Construing quantitative work and qualitative work as opposites ignores the many features common to both. It also ignores the variety within each pole of the dichotomy. Moreover, the quantitative/qualitative dichotomy, like most dichotomies, is not symmetrical; it encodes a clear hierarchy. Depending on the speaker's point of view, one or the other of the pair is the dark twin.

When qualitative inquiry is viewed from the perspective of mainstream psychology, the resulting description of it is not what qualitative workers themselves would provide. To characterize qualitative work using terms and categories derived from quantitative work yields a skewed version. I begin, therefore, with a discussion of some common myths about qualitative work.

Myth #1: Qualitative Psychology and Quantitative Psychology Are "Complementary Methods"

Embedded in this statement are a number of assumptions that need to be examined and challenged. One is the idea that methods are nothing more than neutral technologies. A method, as I noted earlier, is connected to a powerful and far-reaching set of pretheoretical assumptions. To see qualitative psychology as merely offering an additional set of tools for psychology's methodological toolbox conceals the alternate epistemological stance it embodies.

Several qualitative psychologists have emphasized that their approaches should not be misconstrued as analogous to the technologies of conventional psychology. Chris Weedon (1987), in discussing poststructuralist approaches to knowledge, has insisted on using the term "way of working" rather than "method" in an effort to draw this distinction. She resists the idea of a method as a predefined formula that can be applied in a rote fashion to any research question. Jonathan Potter (1996), discussing approaches associated with social constructionist theory, makes the following observation:

> Indeed, it is not clear that there is anything that would correspond to what psychologists traditionally think of as a "method." . . . The lack of a "method," in the sense of some formally specified set of procedures and calculations, does not imply any lack of argument or rigour; nor does it imply that the theoretical system is not guiding analyses on various ways. (pp. 128–129)

Many researchers advocate combining qualitative and quantitative approaches in the same project. But the question of how (and why) approaches can be combined is complex. It is unlikely that the results of the two approaches will converge in any straightforward way. A qualitative stance differs from quantitative research on many dimensions: It emphasizes the subjectivity and agency of research participants; it embraces the diversity of responses, not modal tendencies; conceptions of reliability, validity, and generalization differ. The form of knowledge qualitative workers hope to produce is different and quite possibly they bring to the table a different understanding of "truth."

On a more mundane level, qualitative inquiry and quantitative studies will often produce outcomes that are disparate and sometimes even incommensurate. For example, Al-Krenawi and Wiesel-Lev (1999) studied Bedouin Arab women's attitudes toward female circumcision. Women's responses to close-ended questions on a survey instrument indicated that they accepted genital surgery and did not connect it to negative effects. However, during unstructured interviews, when women were able to speak to interviewers using their own words, they portrayed a far less benign situation and described a number of distressing and disturbing psychological and social consequences of the procedure.

Niva Piran's (2001) studies of young women attending a highly selective dance school afford another example of how quantitative and qualitative approaches can produce disparate outcomes. Piran described two investigations carried out at the dance school where she worked: One, by a well-known expert on clinical eating disorders, used standardized survey instruments to measure levels of preoccupation with body weight and shape. He sought to compare students at the dance school to students in other school settings to test the hypothesis that such preoccupations were socially transmitted. Piran's own research, in contrast, involved long-term, open-ended group meetings with students. Her aim was to elicit and understand connections between concerns about the body and everyday practices and social relations in the school. Her analysis of girls' reflections and experiences yielded a rich network of overarching conceptual categories about embodiment (e.g., prejudicial treatment of female bodies; invasions of bodily privacy; practices that disrupted ownership of their bodies; the sexualization of the female body). The group work enabled the participants to envision and carry out transformations of their own bodily practices and body talk, as well as to insist on changes in the practices of teachers and fellow students.

In my own work, qualitative inquiry has often yielded surprising information about respondents' experiences, information that contrasts with the results of conventional research approaches. For example, my work on suicide and emotion practices in Sri Lanka draws on first-person accounts about individuals who engaged in suicide or self-harm (Marecek & Ratnayeke, 2001). Much of the time, these accounts are permeated with themes of vengeance, humiliated fury, and high indignation, usually focused on a close family member or spouse. Consider these excerpts from my field notes:

- Malini, aged 15, was accused by her mother of associating with a boy on the way home from school. Malini says that the accusation was false. She says, "My head got hot and it felt like it would explode." She then went into the kitchen and poured kerosene over her body. Her mother entered the room and knocked the box of matches out of her hand just as she was ready to set herself on fire.
- Nimal, aged 29, habitually came home drunk. One evening, his wife and his mother scolded him. He flew into a rage, hurled furniture around the house, and stormed out. An hour later, he returned with a small bottle containing highly concentrated insecticide. As he uncorked it, he announced to them, "Now it is finished. You won't have to worry about my drinking anymore." He swallowed what proved to be a lethal dose.

In contrast, a recent study (Weinacker, Schmidtke, & Kerkhof, 2000) gave a battery of standardized paper-and-pencil measures of anger and hostility to patients admitted to a psychiatric hospital in Germany because they had made suicide attempts. The suicide patients' scores did not differ from those of a control group composed of inpatients with "general psychiatric disorders."

Framing their results in universal terms, those researchers concluded that there is no relationship between anger and attempted suicide.

It is not happenstance that qualitative interviews often unearth a different kind of information than that obtained from scales, indexes, and close-ended interviews. Qualitative researchers take seriously what participants say; they leave the way open to hear what they did not expect. They regard people as intentional agents, actively engaged in making sense of their lives. When qualitative inquiry yields a different picture than quantitative data, the question confronting researchers is not simply, "Which is more true?" but a more difficult one: "What kind of truth am I interested in hearing?"

Myth #2: Qualitative Work Is an Adjunct to Quantitative Research

This myth relegates qualitative inquiry to an ancillary position in relation to quantitative research. In one version of this subordinate relationship, qualitative inquiry is useful only for generating hypotheses. Once the hypotheses are devised, the proper business of science—testing those hypotheses—can get under way. In another version, qualitative material—perhaps a few illustrative quotes from a postexperimental interview—is tagged onto a research report to spice up lifeless statistics. Selecting quotes for their spiciness is not the same as conducting a qualitative study. Failing to distinguish the two no doubt has contributed to the notion that qualitative work is "anecdotal." More generally, the myth holds that quantitative methods can stand on their own, but qualitative approaches cannot do the "real" work of science. In this view, qualitative data have limited value, perhaps serving as a source of inspiration or a means of adding cosmetic appeal or rhetorical flourishes to a manuscript.

Myth #3: Qualitative Psychology Is Inductive; Quantitative Psychology Is Deductive

A common dichotomy holds that quantitative research follows the hypothetico–deductive model, and qualitative approaches are inductive. As one psychologist put it, qualitative research "turns the rules of the hypothetico–deductive procedures inside out" (Kidder, 1996). There is more than a grain of truth in this dichotomy; yet it is easy to overstate it. It is true that qualitative workers work inductively. They begin with observations, build a database, and then theorize from it. Working from the ground up, they generate theories, concepts, and categories from data and then continue to revise their theories and their research questions as the data collection proceeds (cf., Becker, 1998). But qualitative workers do not embark on projects without any preconceived theories or ideas about what they are studying. Without such ideas in mind, researchers would have no idea which observations count as data. As Becker wrote, "Everyone knows there is no 'pure' description, that all description, requiring acts of selection and therefore a point of view, is what Thomas Kuhn said it was, 'theory-laden' " (1998, p. 79).

On the other hand, it is also easy to overstate the degree to which hypothesis-testing experiments proceed in strict accord with the rules of the hypothetico–deductive model. This is an idealization that makes the research process appear more orderly, objective, and "pure" than it often is. The American Psychological Association (APA) publication guidelines (American Psychological Association, 2001) instruct writers to report their investigations as an orderly sequence of tasks progressing from hypothesis development to data-gathering to statistical evaluation of the hypothesis. But producing such a smooth story usually requires a good deal of redescription and omission. The actual unfolding of a piece of research is often messy and ragged. It can involve false starts, jiggling with procedures and measures to produce the desired effects, and looping back and forth among possible statistical techniques to bring a significant effect to light. Experimenters not infrequently reformulate the research hypotheses after preliminary analyses of the data (Katzko, 2002). Thus, hypothesis-testing research, though deductive in its intent, often has inductive and deductive elements.

Myth #4: Qualitative Approaches Guarantee Progressive Outcomes

Some feminists who favor qualitative research have claimed that qualitative approaches like interviews are more egalitarian and more liberatory (Stanley & Wise, 1983). Contrary to these claims, Anne Peplau and Eva Conrad (1989) argued against categorizing a research method as feminist or not according to whether it is "agentic" or "communal," whether it is quantitative or qualitative, or whether it involves experimentation or not. "Any research method," they noted, "can be used in sexist ways and no method comes with a feminist guarantee" (p. 395). In the similar vein, Bernice Lott (1981) argued that what distinguishes research as progressive or not is not a particular strategy of inquiry but the question the researcher asks and his or her objectives. In my own view, what distinguishes research as progressive or not is the politics and values that infuse the researcher's interpretations of the results. Neither quantitative nor qualitative researchers are immune from such values; neither procedure offers protections against biased interpretations. In short, any research approach can be used for progressive ends or reactionary ones.

Myth #5: Qualitative Psychology Is Just "Psychology Without Numbers"

There are at least three ways in which qualitative investigations (usually) do not "have numbers." First, qualitative workers do not measure or rank research samples on abstract dimensions such as levels of depression or self-esteem or the strength of a particular opinion. Second, they usually do not use statistical inference or probability testing to accept or reject hypotheses. Third, they are usually not seeking to make parametric statements about the incidence or distribution of a particular phenomenon in a defined population. Yet the crucial element of a qualitative stance is not a disavowal of "numbers" per se. The heart of qualitative inquiry is its epistemological stance: its commitment to interrogating subjectivity, intentional action, and experiences embedded in real-life contexts. (Indeed, this commitment does not categorically rule out the use of numerical procedures. Researchers who use Q-sorts and pile-sorting approximate a qualitative stance, even though they subject the resulting data to statistical analyses.) Qualitative inquiry is not so much a different *means* of doing psychology but an approach with different *ends.* It asks different questions and produces a different kind of knowledge. It is to the discussion of these ends that we now turn.

Qualitative Stances in Psychology

The desire to make sense of actual lived experience is the heart of a qualitative stance. William James, writing 100 years ago, urged psychology to incorporate a qualitative stance alongside its "brass instruments" approach:

> Behind the minute anatomists and the physiologists, with their metallic instruments, there have always stood the outdoor naturalists with their eyes and love of concrete nature. . . . In psychology, there is a similar distinction. Some are fascinated by the varieties of mind in living action, others by dissecting out, whether by logical analysis or by brass instruments, whatever elementary processes may be there. (1901/1994, p. 244)

James himself, of course, preferred a qualitative stance. To him, the dissection of elementary mental processes was as boring as studying rocks in a New England farm field.

In *Caste and Class in a Southern Town* (1937), John Dollard examined race relations using an approach that we would now call participation observation. He described his approach this way:

> The basic method used in the study was that of participation in the social life of Southern town. *The primary research instrument would seem to be the observing human intelligence trying to make sense of the experience.* . . . Perhaps it does not compare well with more objective-seeming instruments, such as a previously prepared set of questions but as to this question the reader can judge for himself. *It has the value of offering to perception the actual, natural human contact with all of the real feelings present and unguarded.* (1937, p. 18, emphasis added)

"Varieties of mind in living action"; "actual natural contact with real feelings present"; the research instrument, "an observing human intelligence"; the research task, "trying to make sense of the experience": The vision of psychological knowledge that James and Dollard put forward bears little resemblance to prototypical psychology research in the United States today. On the other hand, the vision matches well with contemporary qualitative approaches. In what follows, I describe some key features of these approaches.

Making the Link Between Individual Lives and Social History

Researchers who assume a qualitative stance situate their investigations in specific historical, social, and cultural contexts. They are not searching for fundamentals of psychic life that exist apart from social context and they do not seek to make universalized claims about psychic life. Instead they set their sights on the ways in which human action and social identities are locally constituted and contingent on their time and place. The work of Abigail Stewart and her colleagues highlights the value of this approach. Two volumes of collected papers (Franz & Stewart, 1984; Romero & Stewart, 1999) have documented the experiences and identities of women situated in varying class, ethnic, and cultural backgrounds. Many of the papers have examined specific historic events or epochs that shaped the meanings, possibilities, and choices available to those they studied (for example, the civil rights movement and the internment of Japanese Americans during World War II).

The assumption that history and circumstance influence psychological processes (and indeed, even the psyche itself) challenges some of the procedural norms of psychology. For example, psychologists have traditionally placed a high value on standardized scales and inventories (for example, measures of self-concept, emotion, and even psychopathology). They freely transport them from locale to locale and administer them to a variety of populations. Many scales have persisted for decades without revision. The reliance (and even insistence) on standardized measures rests on the belief that the aspects of mental life they measure are constituted in the same way across different settings, different epochs, and different social groups.

Asking How, Not Why

Qualitative workers usually ask "How?" not "Why?" Typically, "Why?" questions have been the provenance of psychologists. Psychology has traditionally sought the basic causes of human behavior. In pursuit of ultimate explanations, psychologists have looked for invariant processes lodged inside the individual. For example, some measure underlying motivations, capacities, or attitudes that are assumed to predate the immediate situation. Some seek to establish how universal mental mechanisms (such as information-processing systems) work. Yet others seek to explain human action in terms of proclivities stamped in the brain through genetic selection.

Researchers who assume a qualitative stance set their sights toward a different goal. They ask how human action and meaning are constituted by the ongoing flow of social and cultural life. Stepping outside the controlled context of the laboratory experiment, they seek out a wider and more complex array of human actions than experimenters can be privy to. In addition, they are positioned to observe the fluctuating salience of particular identities and actions. This fluidity is a feature of social life that experiments and self-report scales are not readily able to capture. Qualitative researchers' questions focus on how collective dynamics, institutional arrangements, and shared language practices set in motion, sustain, and interrupt ways of being in the world.

Barrie Thorne's (1993) study of gender in the context of school life is an investigation centered on a "how" question. Her work challenged the claims about male–female differences that occupied a prominent place in professional and popular psychology during the 1980s: for example, that boys played games that took up lots of space, whereas girls confined themselves to small areas; that boys favored large groups, but girls favored intimate dyads; that boys' play was rule-bound, while girls focused on preserving relationships and harmony. Observing children in two schools, Thorne noted that these and other claims about male–female difference and antagonism sometimes held, but sometimes did not. Certain structural features of the school setting and certain forms of social interaction seemed to foster difference, separation, and even antagonism; other features encouraged similarity, cooperation, and shared play.

For Thorne, gender was not a static attribute located "inside" children that produced effects on their behavior. Instead, she analyzed the practices in school settings through which gender (whether difference or sameness, antagonism or cooperation, separation or intermingling) was produced. Her question was a "How?" question: How (i.e., by what set of social and institutional practices) does the flow of daily life at school constitute (and contest) children's gender? Sometimes, these practices were deliberate but often they were unintended. For example, one teacher taught her kindergarten class about using the bathroom by saying, "Babies leave the door open. Big boys and girls close it." Her language usage inadvertently signaled that the stigmatized status of "baby" was without gender, while gender differentiation was the desired grown-up state.

Re-casting People as Intentional and Meaning-Making Agents

Conventional psychological investigations typically pursue a materialist strategy, setting up research designs that bracket research participants' subjective experience. The intent is to observe "pure" mental mechanisms in operation, emptied of any specific local content. This strategy has the goal of discovering information about how the mind works, information that fits with the modernist interest in control. Hugh Lacey (1999) used the analogy of studying an arrow to explore the powers and limits of such a strategy. A materialist investigation of the arrow would focus on its physics and aerodynamics, yielding information about how arrows work. There are questions about arrows that a materialist strategy would not address. It would not tell us about various meanings associated with arrows: what arrows are used for (e.g., hunting food or waging war); the social practices involved in producing, acquiring, and using arrows; or the symbolic meanings of decorations on arrows. These latter questions resemble those that qualitative researchers pursue: questions about people's desires, hopes, fears, and passions. The information that such investigations yield may not further the goal of control. Instead it addresses other goals, such as expanding human agency.

Eva Magnusson's (1998) study of Swedish women workers highlights the active meaning-making of her respondents. For more than 50 years, the Swedish state has developed policies that explicitly promote gender equality in families and at work. Against that backdrop, Magnusson examined how the women in her study drew on various meanings of femininity in discussing their roles at work and in their families. Using successive open-ended interviews, she identified several themes in women's descriptions of their everyday lives.

One theme was the continual necessity to balance the demands of paid work against family commitments in order to keep the household running. Contrary to the ideology of the Swedish state, the responsibility to keep the household running was not shared equally between men and women; rather it fell primarily on women. Another theme was fitting in at work. Many of the women Magnusson interviewed found it difficult to fit in. They tied this difficulty to responsibilities at home that competed with those at work and also to the gender-based organizational structure in the work setting. The women used many different meanings of femininity, using these meanings to accomplish a variety of rhetorical purposes. Consistent across these meanings of femininity, however, was a theme of diminished power, as exemplified in women's diminished freedom of movement, men's entitlement to greater personal time and space, and women's subordinate status.

Language as Key to People's Subjective Worlds

In the view of most qualitative workers, natural language more closely represents the psychological reality of human experience than the formal abstract categories that psychology usually uses (Polkinghorne, 1990). Qualitative investigators thus give priority to ordinary conversation and everyday language. They gather data via focus groups, open-ended interviews, field observations, and other situations in which talk is unconstrained by a research protocol. They approach transcripts, tapes, and texts from multiple angles of vision, searching for patterns of meaning. The *Listening Guide,* an approach devised by Carol Gilligan and her students, is one example of a systematic analytical approach that derives from multiple readings of a transcript or text (see chapter 9, this volume). The *Listening Guide* requires an investigator to "listen" to the respondents at least four separate times, attending to the text in a different way each time. With each listening, the investigator pursues an angle that is tailored to the specific question under investigation.

Diane Kravetz and I (Marecek, 1999; Marecek & Kravetz, 1998) carried out a study of feminist therapists—that is, therapists who espouse a feminist perspective and incorporate that perspective into their work with clients. Our approach involved open-ended interviews—an approach that yielded unruly but rich accounts of their experiences. Although we had not intended to study the antifeminist backlash, backlash quickly became the elephant in the backseat of our study, impossible to ignore. Every therapist spoke about the backlash. Most had confronted antifeminist attitudes that characterized feminists as a fringe group of disturbed and decidedly unpleasant women—angry, man-hating, "ball-busting," abrasive, doctrinaire, lesbian. Diane and I came to ask how this backlash shaped feminist therapists' self-definitions, public and private. How did feminist therapists manage the backlash? What strategies enabled them to reformulate, refute, or otherwise resist the backlash?

Listen to one therapist—a woman who was an experienced feminist therapist and who had a long history of feminist activism that had begun in the 1970s. She struggles, not entirely successfully, to voice the feminist identity that she has cherished, even though she necessarily speaks from within the discursive field of the backlash:

> **Interviewer:** Are there times when you choose to identify yourself as a feminist therapist and times when you don't?
> **Therapist:** Identify myself as a feminist therapist? I don't think I ever do. I mean if someone called up and asked, whatever their intent, I'd say "Yes I am. " But I don't do that. I'm also aware that that might render me less effective. For instance if I said that to someone and it was off-putting to them, they wouldn't come in or they would have a negative attitude. . . . In fact, I'd be surprised if *anyone* kind of goes around the community saying, "Well, I'm a feminist therapist" (said in a high-pitched, singsong voice).
>
> And yet I make no apology about it because it's a healthy framework. But I do think that, um, it has such a political context that in the same way that I wouldn't say, "I vote Democratic, not Republican," I wouldn't say that to anyone calling. I can't imagine that anyone could be an effective healthy therapist without being a feminist therapist. I mean I just don't understand any way that it would be incompatible with being a good therapist.
> **Interviewer:** Have you ever had somebody like, when you were doing therapy with them, all of a sudden understand that you're coming from a feminist perspective?
> **Therapist:** No.
> **Interviewer:** No?
> **Therapist:** I've had people get angry at me, so who knows what they say. . . . I've had people walk out. I don't know what people might have accused me of after leaving. But I don't think I operate in a way that would offend anyone.

This short text contains a profusion of ideas and images of feminism and its relation to therapy, both positive and negative. Although the speaker has long identified herself as a feminist therapist, she now takes care to conceal this from her clients. The text suggests that she might even be tempted to lie if asked directly ("I'd say 'Yes, I am.' But I don't do that"). The speaker parodies a hypothetical therapist who does identify herself as a feminist using a singsong voice that suggests that such a therapist is perhaps naive or out of touch. She defines feminism as "healthy" and even normative for a therapist. ("I don't see how anyone could be an effective healthy therapist without being a feminist therapist.") Yet the analogy she draws between feminism and "vot[ing] Democrat, not Republican" suggests that feminism has no place in therapy. Her choice of words in the closing passage (accuse, offense) have overtones of criminal wrongdoing. Indeed, the list of the negative aspects of her feminist identity gets successively worse (it is off-putting, it drives away business, it makes you ineffective, it is too political, it makes people angry, it is offensive). The list of positive aspects (it is healthy, it is compatible with good therapy) is flaccid and vague in comparison.

Bringing Forward the Researcher's Role in the Research Process

Psychology has long held that, as long as proper technical procedures are followed, the social identity of researchers will not affect their research. For example, in a survey covering 75 years of psychological research, Jill Morawski (1997) observed that few research reports mentioned the investigators' race.

Indeed, more than 90 percent of research reports on race did not indicate the race of the experimenter. Yet, researchers' social identities and value commitments inevitably influence choices they make regarding topics, theoretical frameworks, procedures, and interpretation of the data. Flouting the conventions of the discipline, many qualitative researchers acknowledge the connections between who they are and what and how they study. They acknowledge their active presence at all stages of their research, and they do not attempt to conceal their involvement from the readers of their research reports.

In interviews, focus groups, and fieldwork, qualitative researchers actively engage with their research participants. (Some insist that data gathered in those situations should be regarded as cocreated by interviewer and respondent.) During the analysis phase, qualitative investigators openly draw on their interpretive capacities and judgments. In their writing, many investigators include a description of their actions and voices as participant observers or interviewers as part of the study data. They describe the preoccupations and commitments that led them to the project. Some write their research reports in the first person, a rhetorical strategy that emphasizes the narrative quality of all such reports.

Researchers must acknowledge their subjectivity before they can reflect on how their points of view affect the research process. Such acknowledgments may prompt the researcher and readers to seek alternative interpretations of the data that they might otherwise have missed. An essay by Deborah Belle (1984) illuminates reflexivity and its power as an interpretive tool. Belle reflects on her position as a young, middle-class, White professional carrying out a study of low-income, African American and White single mothers who were roughly her own age. Pondering the similarities and differences between herself and her respondents, Belle arrives at insights about the complex significance of race and socioeconomic class in women's lives. She realizes how inadequate it is to conceive of race and class merely as categories of individual difference. She also gains a critical perspective on some methodological choices that her research team has made. For example, she comes to see that it was shortsighted to assess poverty solely in terms of current household income. Furthermore, she comes to understand the fluctuating significance of social support networks in women's lives. Such networks are not always sources of support; sometimes they drain off a woman's emotional and material resources and act as a brake on her upward mobility.

The Multiplicity of Qualitative Inquiry

The umbrella term *qualitative stance* shelters a diverse array of approaches and ideas. Consider just one potentially contentious issue: language. Although most qualitative researchers give central place to natural language accounts, they take language to mean different things. On the one hand, many, perhaps most, qualitative researchers take their research participants' narratives as realist accounts of reality. Through such accounts, they hope to gain a fine-grained and rich understanding of the lives and experiences of their research participants. On the other hand, postmodern qualitative researchers are skeptical about this representational function of language. In their view, language is metaphoric: It selects, emphasizes, suppresses, and organizes certain features of experience. In that way, language does not offer neutral descriptions of a reality "out there"; it creates what we take to be reality. Following Wittgenstein and others, postmodern qualitative investigators see language as a game one has learned to play. The rules of that game, created by social agreement, shape what we can say and what we can see. In the postmodern vein, an important goal of inquiry is to explore and understand those rules. Language is an object of study in itself, not the medium by which private ideas are communicated to others.

My point is not to call for debate on these issues or to insist on uniformity. Why should qualitative researchers expect to agree? Among conventional psychologists, there is a wide spread of views on many matters, including forms of realism, the value of null hypothesis testing, and the ethics of deception in research. My point is that we should not allow qualitative studies to be hijacked by commentators who conflate qualitative work with postmodernism and then condemn it wholesale as nihilistic or "anti-science." Nor should we allow qualitative work to be demeaned by the false but common assertion that it is new and untried. The history of qualitative research in psychology, as we have seen, stretches back to the very beginnings of the discipline.

Qualitative Psychology: Some New Ideas About Old Dilemmas

All researchers must grapple with issues of objectivity, validity, generality, interpretation, and ethics. This holds equally true for qualitative workers as for quantitative workers. However, qualitative researchers have framed these issues in distinctive ways, unanticipated by but not irrelevant to quantitative research. In what follows, I offer just a few examples.

Objectivity, Subjectivity, and Reflexivity

As previously discussed, for the most part, psychological research proceeds as if it were possible to prevent the social identity of researchers from influencing the research process. Yet feminist psychologists and other critical psychologists have engaged in sustained examination of these issues (cf., Morawski, 1994; Rabinowitz & Martin, 2001). So too have contemporary philosophers of social science called into question the notion of objectivity as knowledge uninfluenced by values and personal commitments (Harding, 1986; Koch, 1981; Lacey, 1999). Decisions about the conduct of research are not solely a matter of dispassionate scientific judgment; they are also shaped by researchers' personal histories and social locations. Furthermore, many philosophers of science see knowledge production as a historical process; they situate research practices, procedures, and outcomes in the social, political, economic, and ideological contexts of their time (Haraway, 1988).

Many qualitative researchers engage in a deliberate process of reflection about how their social location (for example, social class, gender, age, status, ethnicity), value commitments, and personal history have influenced the course and outcome of a research project. In carrying out this reflexive analysis, they may seek feedback and opinions from research participants. This reflexive analysis is an integral part of the study and it is included in the written report. Some have dubbed the recognition of researchers' subjectivity and the analysis of its influence "strong objectivity" (Harding, 1993). The use of this term reflects the view that making this involvement explicit produces a more complete account of the research project (Billig, 1994; Long, 1999).

Generality

Ask many psychologists about qualitative research and the instant response is "You can't generalize from the results. The samples are too small and not representative." But generalization is a problem that bedevils *all* research, even though it may often go unacknowledged. From the 1940s onward, psychological researchers have relied more and more on college student samples, even though such samples are not representative of the population at large with regard to age, social class, ethnicity, marital status, developmental stage, and many other aspects of experience (Sears, 1986). Until a few decades ago, psychological experiments were often conducted with all-male samples. Oddly enough, although these samples were drawn from specific locales (introductory psychology classrooms) and were composed of individuals with particular characteristics, the research participants managed to masquerade as "generic" human beings representative of all. Thus, the results of these studies were cast in universal terms. It is perhaps not surprising that these generalizations have seldom proven to be useful guides to real life.

Qualitative investigators approach generality from a different angle. Most do not try to make statements about enduring or universal causal principles. Nor are most investigations designed to yield parametric information about the population distributions. The primary focus is on a particular case. For some researchers, the goal is to provide local knowledge—that is, to address a specific problem or question. The research is directly intended to benefit the research site (for example, a specific hospital, community, or school). Because it is so richly contextualized, a qualitative project yields more usable information than research that produces generalized but abstract statistical relationships.

Even though qualitative projects are locally focused, they nonetheless contribute to knowledge in more general ways. Glenda Russell's study of the effects of anti-gay politics provides a good example. Russell (2000) studied the responses of gay, lesbian and bisexual people living in Colorado when its voters ratified Amendment 2. Amendment 2 was designed to change the Colorado constitution so that discrimination against nonheterosexuals would be legalized. Russell's primary goal was to assess and document the psychological aftermath of Amendment 2, information that would play an important role in subsequent legal challenges. Yet her study achieves more than that goal. She and her coding team devised a number of innovative theoretical constructs to capture respondents' responses to being (as she puts it) "voted out." These constructs are dense and rich with meanings derived from first-hand reports of the respondents. Furthermore, Russell's analysis traces patterned relationships among the constructs, leading to overarching themes and categories. The Amendment 2 episode can be taken as a paradigm case of antigay political action, with a family resemblance to other such actions. Although other cases will not be identical, some of the themes will be relevant. In Glenda Russell's view, her study can serve as a sensitizing device for future activists and researchers.

Validity

In general terms, validity is an evaluation of the extent to which the research evidence supports or justifies the interpretations and conclusions that are based on it. In the psychology laboratory, a premium is placed on internal validity—that is, on maximizing the likelihood that the effects are attributable to the putative causes. In the service of increasing internal validity, experimenters isolate a few variables and systematically manipulate them, deliberately lifting them out of their context. One consequence is that the laboratory setting bears little resemblance to the real world in which multiple and dynamic factors operate. Thus the quest for internal validity takes precedence over external validity—that is, how well the results generalize to real-world situations. As Campbell and Stanley (1963) put it, internal and external validity "are frequently at odds in that features increasing one may jeopardize the other" (p. 5).

In qualitative investigations, external validity is a strong point. Grounded in real-life contexts, the investigations are attuned to cultural mores, economic arrangements, and structural conditions. Investigators formulate their constructs from the ground up, using respondents' experiences as the starting point. Contextual validity is another strong point of qualitative investigations. Contextual validity involves asking whether all relevant features of the social context have been accounted for in a theoretical model. The broad base of data generated in a qualitative study enables researchers to address contextual validity. For example, many social psychology laboratory experiments have shown that hot temperatures increase the likelihood of aggression. This highly reliable effect has been extrapolated to theories of mob violence and so-called "race riots." From my perspective as a student of ethnopolitical conflict in Sri Lanka, however, temperature dwindles in explanatory significance in comparison to features of social and political life in that country. These include strong ethnopolitical identification; state-sponsored violences and "disappearances"; intractable ethnic, caste, and class injustices; and a long-standing custom of violent engagements surrounding elections (Pieris & Marecek, 1992). In this context, not surprisingly, militant protests, mob violence, and massacres have no discernible seasonal pattern and are not limited to warm climates.

Meaning and Interpretation

All researchers, whether their projects be quantitative or qualitative, face the challenge to find (some would say "create") meaning in their data. For qualitative researchers, this involves sifting out patterned regularities in a data set of transcripts, texts, or notebooks of field observations. The analogous process in a quantitative project occurs when raw data are submitted to statistical analysis. The researcher must decide what meanings to extract from the raw numbers. He or she selects the statistical procedures that will best bring forward those meanings or regularities. Whether numbers or words, data do not speak for themselves; they acquire meaning only within a framework of interpretation created by the researcher. Meaning-making thus demands an "observing human intelligence" (to use Dollard's phrase) no less for quantitative projects than for qualitative ones.

Ethics

Qualitative investigators often face questions of ethics and responsibility that reach beyond the prescriptions of the ethical guidelines of the APA. Those guidelines seem designed with the prototypical psychology study in mind: An encounter that takes place in a clearly demarcated time and place, such as a laboratory session. For qualitative workers, data collection often is not so clearly delimited. In ethnographic studies or participatory action research, for example, field notes may include casual remarks passed in chance encounters, descriptions of unexpected events, or even interchanges between strangers that are accidentally overheard. Should the people whose words or actions are recorded be considered research participants? Is their informed consent required?

The APA ethical guidelines pertain largely to individuals conceived as atomistic, "generic" humans, not as members of communities or social groups. In contrast, qualitative investigators study individuals embedded in specific social organizations or groups, such as neighborhoods, ethnic communities, cultures, or schools. Sometimes these groups cannot be disguised or rendered anonymous. As collective entities, are those groups or organizations entitled to privacy, consent, or protection from harm? Consider the acclaimed ethnography, *Death Without Weeping (*Scheper-Hughes, 1992). Depicting life in an impoverished *favela* in Brazil, it is a searing portrait of a community ethos of predation, exploitation, abandonment, infanticide, and violence. What responsibility does the researcher have for any harm produced by her revelations? Does harm to a community's reputation or harm that might result producing or reaffirming class or ethnic prejudices count? As Lisa Fontes (1998) noted, the question, "How can researchers best understand, interpret, and present findings?" is an ethical question as much as it is a scientific one. And there is no easy answer.

Conclusion

Why is qualitative work enjoying a resurgence of popularity, despite the institutional forces in psychology that persist in stifling it? Despite the conservative traditions that hold sway in American psychology, the discipline has been slowly expanding beyond the study of "generic" humans. Think about the divisions added to the APA in recent decades. They include groups concerned with the study of women; gays, lesbians, and bisexuals; ethnic minorities; families; and men. Not all parts of the discipline are equally ready to move away from a vision of its subject matter as the "human organism" to embrace a psyche constituted by history and culture. But in many quarters and in numerous ways, psychologists are starting to acknowledge personhood and subjectivity.

The face of the profession has altered significantly in the past 25 years. Groups of people who had no place in the discipline have gained entry and risen to positions of leadership: White women; men and women of color; men and women publicly acknowledging themselves as gay, lesbian, and bisexual. The process is by no means complete, but it is under way. I myself was part of the cohort of women (mostly White) in graduate school in the 1970s when federal legislation challenged discriminatory quotas. For many of us in that cohort, there were indelible lessons about strategies of exclusion, the personal effects of being the unwanted Other, and the manifold operations of mundane power. There were also lessons about resistance, solidarity, and making change. Many of us turned our investigative energies toward studying the links between social context and identity and the social dynamics of hierarchy and subordination.

The growth of qualitative psychology has surely been spurred by the rise of interdisciplinary study in universities. Disciplinary boundaries have gotten fuzzy as a variety of hybrid endeavors have sprouted—women's studies, ethnic studies, cultural studies, cognitive science, environmental studies, media and film studies. Moving across disciplinary boundaries and rubbing elbows with colleagues from other backgrounds and programs inevitably fosters reflexivity. In women's studies, for instance, essentialism, ahistoricism, and false universalism—still the norm in psychology—were identified as intellectual traps 20 years ago. Explaining oneself to colleagues from other disciplines, justifying one's ways of producing knowledge, and flirting with other ways of working—all these experiences foster a new consciousness about what one is about.

Qualitative psychologists perch on the fences of the discipline. Some have sought alliances and collaborations with colleagues from the other social sciences. Some have found the richer traditions of psychology outside the United States—traditions more open to both theory and politics—more congenial and more intellectually stimulating. Qualitative psychology cannot budge from its marginal position in American psychology unless the fences come down. Textbooks might make reference to the rich vein of existing qualitative work in psychology, both historic and contemporary. Graduate and undergraduate syllabi might include some qualitative studies. Psychology journals could relax space restrictions so that qualitative studies could be published. Or the APA might support an online journal devoted to qualitative studies in psychology; in the electronic medium, space limitations could be less stringent. The APA publication manual could be revised so that the prescribed style was not coterminus with quantitative methods and experimental studies. Research training could include rigorous courses in qualitative approaches. Teachers and textbook writers might avoid the outdated phrase "the scientific method," which encodes the false ideas that science is unitary and that all scientists share a single method (Hacking, 1996).

Pluralism and openness can help all psychologists do what we do better. With a broader range of accepted investigative options, we can do better at fitting method to question. The point is not that qualitative approaches are categorically better than experimentalism, hypothetico–deductive inquiry, or quantification. However, they enable us to ask and answer certain kinds of questions that those approaches cannot. With only one legitimized way of working in psychology, researchers must recast their questions to fit the method, much like Cinderella's stepsisters trying to cram their oversized feet into a small slipper. Finally, as I argued before, if we make visible the many ways of producing psychological knowledge, all psychologists can develop deeper understandings of what is at stake in choosing any one.

References

Al-Krenawi, A., & Wiesel-Lev, R. (1999). Attitudes toward the perceived psychological impact of female circumcision as practiced among the Bedouin-Arabs of the Negev. *Family Process, 38,* 481–485.

American Psychological Association. (2001). *Publication manual* (5th ed.). Washington, DC: Author.

Bannister, P., Burman, E., Parker, I., Taylor, M, & Tindall, C. (1994). *Qualitative methods in psychology: A research guide.* Buckingham, UK: Open University Press.

Becker, H. S. (1998). *Tricks of the trade: How to think about your research while you're doing it.* Chicago: University of Chicago Press.

Belle, D. (1984). Attempting to comprehend the lives of low-income women. In C. E. Franz & A. J. Stewart (Eds.), *Women creating lives: Identities, resilience, and resistance* (pp. 37–50). Boulder, CO: Westview Press.

Bem, S. L. (1993). Is there a place in psychology for a feminist analysis of social context? *Feminism and Psychology, 3,* 230–234.

Billig, M. (1994). Repopulating the depopulated pages of social psychology. *Theory and Psychology, 4,* 307–335.

Bromley, D. B. (1986). *The case study method in psychology and related disciplines.* Chichester, NY: Wiley.

Brydon-Miller, M., & Tolman, D. L. (1997). Transforming psychology: Interpretive and participatory research methods [Special Issue]. *Journal of Social Issues, 53*(4).

Campbell, D., & Stanley, J. (1963). *Experimental and quasi-experimental designs for research.* Chicago: Rand-McNally.

Cole, M. (1996). *Cultural psychology: A once and future discipline.* Cambridge, MA: Harvard University Press.

Crawford, M., & Kimmel, E. B. (1999). Innovations in feminist research [Special Issue]. *Psychology of Women Quarterly, 23,* 1–458.

Dollard, J. (1937). *Caste and class in a southern town.* Garden City, NY: Doubleday.

Fontes, L. A. (1998). Ethics in family violence research: Cross-cultural issues. *Family Relations, 47,* 53–61.

Franz, C. E., & Stewart, A. J. (Eds.). (1984). *Women creating lives: Identities, resilience, and resistance.* Boulder, CO: Westview Press.

Gavey, N. (in press). To and beyond the discursive constitution of subjectivity. *Feminism and Psychology.*

Hacking, I. (1996). The disunities of the sciences. In P. Galison & D. J. Stump (Eds.), *The disunity of science: Boundaries, contexts, and power* (pp. 37–74). Stanford, CA: Stanford University Press.

Haraway, D. (1988). Situated knowledges: The science question in feminism and the privilege of partial perspective. *Feminist Studies, 14,* 579–599.

Harding, S. (1986). *The science question in feminism.* Ithaca, NY: Cornell University Press.

Harding, S. (1993). Rethinking standpoint epistemology: What is "strong objectivity?" In L. Alcoff & E. Potter (Eds.), *Feminist epistemologies* (pp. 49–82). London: Routledge.

Henwood, K., & Nicholson, P. (1995). Qualitative research [Special issue]. *The Psychologist, 8*(3).

James, W. (1994). *The varieties of religious experience: A study in human nature.* New York: Modern Library. (Original published 1901)

Katzko, M. W. (2002). The rhetoric of psychological research and the problem of unification in psychology. *American Psychologist, 57,* 262–270.

Kidder, L. (1996, Aug.). *Rewriting the rules and reversing the order with qualitative methods.* Paper presented at the International Congress of Psychology, Montreal, Quebec, Canada.

Kleinman, A. (1984). *The illness narratives: Suffering, healing and the human condition.* New York: Basic Books.

Koch, S. (1981). The nature and limits of psychological knowledge: Lessons of a century *qua* science. *American Psychologist, 36,* 257–269.

Lacey, H. (1999). *Is science value free? Values and scientific understanding.* New York: Routledge.

Long, J. (1999). *Telling women's lives: Subject / narrator / reader / text.* New York: New York University Press.

Lott, B. (1981). *Becoming a woman: The socialization of gender.* Springfield, IL: Charles Thomas.

Lykes, M. B. (1997). Activist participatory research among the Maya of Guatemala: Constructing meanings from situated knowledge. *Journal of Social Issues, 53,* 725–746.

Magnusson, E. (1998). *Vardagens könsinnebörder under forhandling-om arbete, familij och produktion av kvinnlighet* (Everyday negotiations of gender, work, family and the production of femininity). Unpublished dissertation, University of Umeă, Umeă, Sweden.

Marecek, J. (1999). Trauma talk in feminist clinical practice. In S. Lamb (Ed.), *New versions of victims: Feminists struggle with the construct* (pp. 158–182). New York: New York University Press.

Marecek, J., & Kravetz, D. (1998). Power and agency in feminist therapy. In C. Heenan & I. B. Seu (Eds.), *Contemporary feminist psychotherapies: Reflections on theory and practice* (pp. 13–29). London: Sage.

Marecek, J., & Ratnayeke, L. (2001). Suicide in rural Sri Lanka: Assessing a prevention program. In O. Grad (Ed.), *Suicide risk and protective factors in the new millennium* (pp. 215–220). Ljubljana, Slovenia: Cankarjev Dom.

Morawski, J. G. (1994). *Practicing feminisms, reconstructing psychology: Notes on a liminal science.* Ann Arbor: University of Michigan Press.

Morawski, J. G. (1997). White experimenters, white blood, and other white conditions: Locating the psychologist's race. In M. Fine, L. Weis, L. C. Powell, & L. M. Wong (Eds.), *Off white: Readings on race, power, and society* (pp. 13–28). New York: Routledge.

Peplau, L. A., & Conrad, E. (1989). Beyond nonsexist research: The perils of feminist methods in psychology. *Psychology of Women Quarterly, 13,* 379–400.

Pieris, S. J. R., & Maracek, J. (1992). *The Welikanda massacre.* Colombo, Sri Lanka: International Centre for Ethnic Studies.

Piran, N. (2001). Re-inhabiting the body from the inside out: Girls transform their school environment. In D. L. Tolman & M. Brydon-Miller (Eds.), *From subjects to subjectivities: A handbook of interpretative and participatory methods* (pp. 218–238). New York: New York University Press.

Polkinghorne, D. (1990). Language and qualitative research. *Theoretical and Philosophical Psychology, 10,* 3–24.

Potter, J. (1996). Discourse analysis and constructionist approaches: Theoretical background. In J. T. E. Richardson (Ed.), *Handbook of qualitative research methods for psychology and the social sciences* (pp. 125–140). Leicester, UK: BPS Books.

Rabinowitz, V. C., & Martin, D. (2001). Choices and consequences: Methodological issues in the study of gender. In R. K. Unger (Ed.), *Handbook of the psychology of women and gender* (pp. 29–52). New York: Wiley.

Richardson, J. T. E. (Ed.). (1996). *Handbook of qualitative research methods for psychology and the social sciences.* Leicester, UK: BPS Books.

Romero, M., & Stewart, A. J. (Eds). (1999). *Women's untold lives: Breaking silence, talking back, voicing complexity.* New York: Routledge.

Russell, G. M. (2000). *Voted out: The psychological consequences of anti-gay politics.* New York: New York University Press.

Scheper-Hughes, N. (1992). *Death without weeping: The violence of everyday life in Brazil.* Berkeley: University of California Press.

Sears, D. O. (1986). College sophomores in the laboratory: Influences of a narrow data base on psychology's view of human nature. *Journal of Personality and Social Psychology, 51,* 515–530.

Stanley, L., & Wise, S. (1983). *Breaking out: Feminist consciousness and feminist research.* London: Routledge and Kegan Paul.

Thorne, B. (1993). *Gender play: Girls and boys in school.* New Brunswick, NJ: Rutgers University Press.

Tolman, D. L., & Brydon-Miller, M. (Eds.). (2001). *From subjects to subjectivities: A handbook of interpretative and participatory methods.* New York: New York University Press.

Weedon, C. (1987). *Feminist practice and poststructural theory.* Oxford: Basil Blackwell.

Weinacker, B., Schmidtke, A., & Kerkhof, A. J. F. M. (2000, Sept.). *The role of anger in persons with a recent suicide attempts.* Paper presented at the Eighth European Symposium on Suicide and Suicidal Behavior, Bled, Slovenia.

Wundt, W. (1921). *Elements of folk psychology.* London: Allen and Unwin.

Part II

Methodologies for Qualitative Researchers in Psychology: The Nuts, the Bolts, and the Finished Product

5

Discourse Analysis and Discursive Psychology

Jonathan Potter

Discourse analysis is the study of how talk and texts are used to perform actions. Discursive psychology is the application of ideas from discourse analysis to issues in psychology. The primary focus of discursive psychology is on the analysis of interaction considered in fine detail; however, its broader ambition is to provide a novel perspective on almost the full range of psychological phenomena. It is not a method as such; rather it is a perspective that includes meta-theoretical, theoretical, and analytical principles.

Using Chomsky's original distinction, if the main traditions of cognitive and social psychology have been overwhelmingly concerned with peoples' underlying competence, discursive psychology is concerned primarily with performance. The competence focus has encouraged psychologists to use experimental manipulations and other procedures in an attempt to access the underlying cognitive entities and procedures. Performance has often been treated as too messy to be analytically tractable. One way of understanding discursive psychology is as an approach that is developing rigorous analytical procedures for studying performance in the form of video- and audio-recorded and transcribed records of interaction. Its focus is on a very wide range of materials ranging from everyday phone calls between family members, relaxed mealtime conversations, to talk and texts in work and institutional settings, to therapy and counseling talk.

Development

Discourse analysis has a publication record in social psychology that goes back nearly two decades. The first analytical article was published in a psychology journal in 1985 (Litton & Potter, 1985), and its first major published statement was the book *Discourse and Social Psychology* (Potter & Wetherell, 1987). This

I would like to thank Alexa Hepburn for making helpful comments on an earlier draft of this chapter.

took a number of the central theoretical topics in social psychology, such as attitudes, categories, and the self and showed the virtue of reworking them in discourse–analytical terms. For example, instead of considering categories in terms of schemata for information processing, they could be studied for their practical and interactional role in conversation (Edwards, 1991). The development of discourse analysis ran in parallel to the emergence of a rhetorical approach to psychology. The first article to use a rhetorical analysis was published in 1985 (Billig, 1985) with the first major theoretical overview appearing in 1987 (now published as Billig, 1996). This highlighted the rhetorical dimension of social psychological notions. For example, attitude expressions can be studied as talk designed for use in settings where there is a possibility of argument and where they are simultaneously justifying a position and implicitly countering alternatives (Billig, 1991). Much of this early work was based on the analysis of tape recordings and transcripts of conversational interviews. It also established the centrality of critical themes as researchers focused on issues of sexism, racism, and ideology (Billig et al., 1988).

The early 1990s saw the blurring together of rhetoric and discourse work and the development of discursive psychology out of discourse analysis. This was partly an attempt to distinguish this particular tradition of work from the range of alternative approaches called discourse analysis in linguistics (Brown & Yule, 1983), sociolinguistics (Sinclair & Coulthard, 1975), poststructuralism (Foucault, 1971), and cognitive psychology (van Dijk & Kintch, 1983). It was also partly an attempt to emphasize that what was being developed was not merely a novel approach to communication or face-to-face interaction but, more ambitiously, a reworking of what psychology is. Edwards and Potter (1992), for example, used analysis of records (including television interviews and newspaper articles) of a set of political disputes to illustrate a novel conception of memory and attribution (see also Edwards & Potter, 1993; for commentaries and responses, see Conway, 1992). Billig (1992) studied conversation about the British Royal Family for the interactional resources they used to undermine arguments for social and political change. Antaki (1994) considered argumentation in terms of its organization in natural settings. More recently, major work in discursive psychology has focused on the way descriptions are made to appear factual (Potter, 1996a) and the way cognitive and psychodynamic notions can be understood in new ways that relate to their role in interaction (Billig, 1999a; Edwards, 1997). I will use the term *discursive psychology* to refer to this tradition of work.

Although early discourse research in psychology tended to be based on a close analysis of conversational interviews, more recent work has focused on records of natural interaction, particularly institutional interaction such as therapy, helpline talk, or case conferences. In part this reflects the influence of successful analytical developments in the related tradition of conversation analysis (Hutchby & Wooffitt, 1998; Sacks, 1992). Conversation analysis has demonstrated that it is possible to do rigorous, cumulative, repeatable qualitative studies of interaction. Although there are a range of differences in emphasis, and potential theoretical tensions, discursive psychology and conversation analysis have important areas of overlap (Edwards, 1995). In this chapter I will be less concerned with these differences and will include conversation analytical work as part of the discussion.

The early work in discourse analysis was influenced by, but distinct from, a number of related developments in social psychology. On the one hand, it picked up, and developed, constructionist themes in the work of Rom Harré, John Shotter, and Kenneth Gergen (Gergen, 1982, 1999; Harré, 1979, 1998; Shotter, 1984, 1993). On the other, it drew on, and modified, ideas from Foucaultian and poststructuralist influenced work that was concerned with the construction of self and mind, and its relation to ideology and the reproduction of oppressive social organizations. Notable research came from Valerie Walkerdine, Wendy Hollway, and others (Henriques, Hollway, Urwin, Venn, & Walkerdine, 1984; Hollway, 1989; Walkerdine, 1988). More recent thinking done under the rubric of discourse analysis by Ian Parker, Erica Burman, and others has also drawn on poststructuralist or Foucaultian ideas (Burman, 1994; Parker, 1992).

Discursive psychology differs from these strands of work in three principal ways. First, discursive psychology has been more concerned with how analysis can be grounded in specific conversational and textual materials than any of the approaches described previously. Second, discursive psychology focuses on talk and texts within specific social practices rather than conceptualizing discourses as abstract objects as in more poststructuralist work (Potter, Wetherell, Gill, & Edwards,1990). Third, discursive psychology conceptualizes construction as a practical process of the manufacture and stabilization of versions of mind, persons, and reality in talk and texts (Potter, 1996a) rather than treating construction as an abstract process. Although there are these areas of difference, discursive psychology still shares much with these traditions, and they are considerably closer to each other than to much of the mainstream North American tradition of psychology.

Discourse Analysis and Theory

One of the difficulties in writing about qualitative methods, and about discourse work in particular, is that the terminology available for describing it—*reliability, validity, sampling, factors, variance, hypothesis testing,* and so on—has evolved over a long period of time to fit the requirements of quantitative research using experiments and surveys. This terminology has become so taken for granted it has become difficult to avoid treating it as obvious and natural. Yet it is bound up with assumptions about the nature of action and interaction that are not appropriate for discourse work. So although this chapter will use a number of these conventional terms, they should be treated with caution.

Another difficulty is the assumption that method can be treated as separate from theory. As philosophers and sociologists of science have shown, this is not the case anywhere in science (e.g., Chalmers, 1992; Knorr Cetina, 1999); and it is certainly not for discourse analysis. To understand the rationale for its methodological procedures it is necessary to understand its basic theoretical principles.

Theoretical Principles of Discourse Analysis

The approach to analysis that has been developed in discourse analysis and discursive psychology is partly a product of its conception of human action. This conception emphasizes the following core features of discourse.

ACTION ORIENTATION. Discourse is the primary medium of human action and interaction. Actions are not merely free-standing but are typically embedded in broader practices. Some are generic (e.g., making invitations); some are specific to settings (e.g., air traffic control management of flight crew). The term action *orientation* is meant to discourage the expectation that analysis will discover a one-to-one relationship between discrete acts and certain verbs.

SITUATION. Discourse is situated in three senses. First, it is organized sequentially, such that the primary environment of what is said is what has just come before, and this sets up (although does not determine) what comes next. Second, it may be situated institutionally, such that institutional identities (news interviewee, say) and tasks (managing neutrality in news interviews) may be relevant (although not determine) what takes place. Third, it can be situated rhetorically, such that descriptions may resist actual or potential attempts to counter them as interested.

CONSTRUCTION. Discourse is construct*ed* and construct*ive*. It is constructed in the sense that it is built from various resources (words, of course, but also categories, commonplace ideas, broader explanatory systems). It is constructive in the sense that versions of the world, of events and actions, and of people's phenomenological worlds are built and stabilized in talk in the course of actions. A person may account for his or her absence at a meeting by constructing a version of the city's traffic problems or of his or her own faulty cognitive processing.

These principles may appear rather abstract. However, they have been developed through analytical practice as well as from broader theorizing. They can be illustrated with an example, which can also show some of the analytical mentality of discourse work and the use it makes of detailed transcript.

The following extract is taken from a call to a child abuse helpline in the United Kingdom. It comes near the start of the call directly after the caller has been asked about her willingness to take part in the research and marks the point where the counselor gets onto the business of the call. (The transcription symbols are explained in Exhibit 5.1.)

Extract One (NSPCC–BC1)

Counselor:	Alright Kath↑ryn .hh so w-what's goin on
Caller:	Well .hh what it <u>i:s</u> is I got
	a really close friend an like
	hh she's been sexually abu:sed an
Counselor:	Mm↓m
Caller:	she's really close to me an I jus
	I wanna tell 'er mum but I can't
	bring myself to do it

Exhibit 5.1. Basic Transcription Symbols

What it <u>i</u>:s	Underscoring represents words or parts of words delivered with added stress or emphasis.
Um::	Colons represent lengthening of the preceding sound; the more colons, the greater the lengthening.
I've-	A hyphen represents the cut-off of the preceding sound, often by a stop.
↑Mm↓hmm	Vertical arrows precede marked pitch movement, over and above normal rhythms of speech. Less marked shifts are dealt with by punctuation marks.
.,?	Punctuation marks show intonation, not grammar; period, comma, and "question mark" indicate downward, "continuative," and upward contours, respectively.
hhh hh .hh P(h)ut	An "h" represents aspiration, sometimes simply hearable breathing, sometimes laughter, etc.; when preceded by a superimposed dot, an (h) marks in-breath; in parenthesis inside a word it represents interpolated laughter.
hhh[hh .hhh] er [I just]	Left brackets represent point of overlap onset; right brackets represent point of overlap resolution.
(certainly) ((slurred voice))	Single parentheses mark problematic or uncertain hearings; double parentheses include additional transcriber's comments.
(0.2) (.)	Numbers in parentheses represent silence in tenths of a second; a dot in parentheses represents a micro-pause, less than a tenth of a second, hearable but too short to easily measure.
°mm hmm°	Degree signs enclose significantly lowered volume.

Counselor: (0.4) tch .hh so:: ↑how did
you find ↑out about ↓that

Action orientation is often the endpoint of analysis rather than the start. Commonly, the analytical goal is to identify the business that is being done in talk, which can be indirect. In this case, for example, the counselor starts with a question and the caller answers. However, this minimal observation does not yet specify what the question is doing. For example, as an opening to the main work of the call the question is asked in such a way that a very wide range of different answers can be offered. This is a valuable practice for a helpline that may receive calls of a highly varied nature. The counselor's question helps to get the interaction going in a way that causes the minimum trouble.

To understand the action orientation of what is going on it is crucial to understand the talk in terms of the way it is situated. First, it is situated in a conversational sequence. For example, the sense of the counselor's question is related to its position at the start of the business. If she had produced it at the end of this sequence, say, it might have appeared challenging, suggesting that the caller is not telling the whole story. Second, there is the more diffuse situation of this being a helpline for reporting abuse. Plainly there is an immediate orientation to this with the caller's answer. For example, she does not build up to talking about troubles through a series of steps, as is common in mundane telephone calls (Jefferson, 1988). Moreover, she does not ask the counselor how *she* is or what is going on with *her*. Rather, she opens her answer with a report of abuse. One has troubles; one helps; they work with distinct and asymmetric institutional identities. Third, there is the rhetorical character of this talk. Again, this is one of the features to be revealed through analysis rather than something immediately apparent. However, we can note that the caller's descriptions may work against alternatives. For example, by describing herself as a "very close friend" of the abuse victim she may be countering the relevant idea that she is a "snitch" or being vindictive.

All of the situated business of talk is done through it being constructed from various discursive resources. Talk is oriented to action through being put together, and delivered, in specific ways. Some of these are obvious and some subtle. For example, the counselor's question depends on the conventional uses of English words such as "what." However, note the detailed construction. We are not seeing words put together as if pasted from a dictionary. Rather than "what is going on" there is a more colloquial, less formal, "what's goin on." This works rhetorically against any expectations of this being a threatening, formal situation such as a job interview or courtroom examination.

This illustrates the way some of the basic theoretical notions of discursive psychology work in practice. It also starts to flesh out the analytical mentality of discourse research. Let us move on to a more explicit discussion of the stages of discourse work.

Questions Discourse Researchers Ask

Discourse researchers typically ask different questions to those common elsewhere in psychology. These questions reflect the understanding of interaction embodied in its theoretical principles. This is a potential source of confusion, as psychological questions often work from a factors-and-outcomes logic that has been developed with notions of experimental manipulation and the multivariate statistics that go with the analysis of results. Discourse work is not designed to answer questions of the kind, "What is the influence of *X* on *Y*" (of health beliefs on diet, of social class on education success, and so on).

Discourse work typically asks questions of the form, "How is *X* done?" How does a speaker use an identity ascription to disqualify a rival's version of events as a product of their stake in what is going on (Antaki & Horowitz, 2000)? How does a schoolteacher present violent or threatening acts toward pupils as inevitable and necessary to maintain classroom control (Hepburn, 2000)? How does a speaker report a "paranormal experience" in a way that attends to the potential for being discounted as mad or deluded (Wooffitt, 1992)? This focus on how-questions leads to a focus on interaction rather than cognition, a focus on concrete settings rather than abstract scenarios, and a focus on processes rather than outcomes.

A number of general themes appear in this work. For example,

1. *Fact and Evaluation:* There has been a focus on questions involving description, factuality, and evaluation. This includes issues of racism and discrimination that come from the critical theme that has been

central in discourse work (Wetherell & Potter, 1992). What procedures do news interviewees use to present their answers as disinterested (Dickerson, 1997)? How are food evaluations organized during family mealtimes (Wiggins & Potter, in press)? How does a speaker (indirectly) display his or her investment in a claim by formulating it in an extreme manner (Edwards, 2000)? This strand of work moves on from rather abstract understandings of construction and constructionism in psychology to consider how construction is done in talk and what is accomplished by it.

2. *Constructions of Psychology:* There has been a focus on the way psychological terms and notions are used in practical settings. How are notions of remembering and forgetting used to manage blame in political hearings (Lynch & Bogen, 1996)? What resources are used to construct and identify "delusional" speech in psychiatric practice (Georgaca, 2000)? How can the psychoanalytical notion of repression be understood in conversational terms (Billig, 1999a)? The challenge is to see how far the basic stuff of psychology can be respecified in terms of practices within particular contexts.
3. *Gender, Psychology, and Feminism:* There has been a major focus on a range of issues related to gender and sexism. This has moved beyond a sociolinguistic concern with gendered speech variations to a consideration of the way particular practices are sustained (Potter & Edwards, 2001). What forms of talk do women have available to understand themselves and their cultural environments when making sense of eating, diet, and body shape (Malson, 1998)? How can the notion of romantic love be reconceptualized in terms of investment in particular stories (Wetherell, 1995)? This is also an area in which important features of the relationship between conversation analysis and discursive psychology are being explored, for example with respect to "saying no" to sex (Kitzinger & Frith, 1999), and considering how gender may be treated as fundamentally relevant to interaction (Stokoe & Smithson, 2001; Wetherell, 1998).
4. *Practices in Work or Institutional Settings:* There has been a focus on interaction as part of the broader organization of activities in a setting such as therapy, medical consultations, classrooms, courtrooms, police or air traffic control rooms, and so on (see Drew & Heritage, 1992a; Engestom & Middleton, 1996; Goodwin, 1997). This is an area in which conversation analysis has made powerful contributions at both analytical and theoretical levels. It is also an area in which important developments in combining analysis of vocal and nonvocal elements of interaction have been made (see Heath, 1997).
5. *Psychologists' Own Work Practices:* There has been a focus on the research practices of psychologists themselves. How are interactional troubles managed in survey interviews (Suchman & Jordan, 1990)? How are questions constructed in market-research focus groups to guide the participants' response style (Puchta & Potter, 1999)? How is interaction in open-ended interviews produced to fit standardized response categories (Antaki, Houtkoop-Steentra, & Rapley, 2000)?

Although it is useful heuristically to split discourse research into particular themes, in practice they overlap with one another.

Preparing for Analysis

Before any analysis can be started the researcher has to collect materials and prepare them for study.

Analytical Materials

Discourse researchers work with a range of different kinds of materials. Although there is considerable disagreement about the virtues of different sorts of material, there has been a general move away from open-ended interviews and focus groups to the consideration of naturalistic materials and texts. All of these materials have one feature—they involve interaction that can be recorded, transcribed, and analyzed. For simplicity, I will concentrate on interviews and naturalistic materials.

For much of the 1980s and early 1990s, open-ended conversational interviews were the principal research materials. The preferred style of interview is a tape-recorded conversation organized around a schedule of topics developed in relationship to the researcher's concerns. Unlike traditional survey interviews, the aim is not to neutrally access information outside the interview but to provide a conversational environment to observe certain practices and to identify the discursive resources drawn on in those practices. For example, in Billig's (1992) study of political ideology he was interested in the way his participants (family groups in the United Kingdom) dealt with issues that raised questions about the legitimacy of British political arrangements. He considered the resources—repertoires of explanation, rhetorical commonplaces—that research participants drew on to sustain that legitimacy against threat. Because of this aim, interviews in discourse work tend to be active and even argumentative.

Interviews in discourse analysis have a range of virtues.

1. *Focus:* Interviews enable the researcher to concentrate on certain predetermined themes. Questions can thus be designed and ordered to provoke participants into using a wide range of their discursive resources.
2. *Standardization:* Interviews provide an opportunity for all participants to address the same set of themes (notwithstanding the contingency of conversation).
3. *Control:* Interviews allow considerable control over sampling. This also eases issues of ethics permissions and recording.

Balanced against this are the following disadvantages.

1. *Psychological Expectations:* Interviews run the risk of flooding the interaction with psychological expectations and categories. Even while the focus is on activities, the research will have to deal with participants' orientation to the interview organization and their speaking position as expert informant or group representative. Such orientations can productively become an analytical focus in their own right (see Widdicombe & Wooffitt, 1995); more commonly there is a tension between the interview as an activity and as a pathway to something else.
3. *Abstraction:* Interviews abstract participants from the settings in which they live their lives and from the stake and interest they typically have in what is going on. They encourage participants to act as theorists rather than actors.
4. *Relative Value:* If you are interested in a particular setting, relationship counseling, for example, and you have the access and the analytical resources to study it, why restrict yourself to people's abstract talk about it?

Naturalistic materials have become central, however, more because of their intrinsic interest than because of the shortcomings in interviews. They are highly varied. They could be audio- or videotapes of flight crew conversation, relationship counseling sessions, social worker assessment interviews, everyday telephone conversation between friends, and so on. They have a range of advantages.

1. *Actuality:* Naturalistic materials document the thing that is being studied directly. If the researcher is concerned with counseling on an abuse helpline, then counseling is studied (not reports of counseling, theorizing about counseling, conventionalized memories of counseling, and so on). There is no extrapolation from something else involved.
2. *Action Orientation:* Such materials make it easier to capture the action-oriented and situated nature of talk. Actions are studied embedded in sequences of interaction. However subtle the analysis, the disruption of such embedding in interviews is likely to lead to analytical difficulties.
3. *Orientation to Settings:* Materials of this kind make it possible to study participants' orientations to settings and institutions. It is hard to see how one could look at the detailed construction of counselors' questions in the abuse helpline (discussed earlier) without using actual recordings from that helpline. Research with naturalistic materials becomes more easily centered on situated practices rather than persons and their abstract cognitive capacities.

Naturalistic materials often present particular problems of access and ethics, of course, and raise issues of reactivity. Nevertheless, perhaps one of the most novel and potentially useful contributions that discourse work can make to psychology is providing a method for collecting, managing, and analyzing naturalistic materials.

Recording and Transcription

One of the major insights of the conversation analyst Harvey Sacks (1992) is the significance of conversational specifics—pauses, intonation, delay, lexical choice, repair, and so on. Rather than seeing such detail as noise blurring the clarity of an underlying signal, Sacks highlighted its key role in interaction. Speakers are enormously attentive to the specifics of interaction. Take the following extract from a phone call.

Extract Two (from Davidson, 1984, p. 105)
A: C'mon down he:re, = it's oka:y,
(0.2 sec)
A: I got lotta stuff, = I got be:er en stuff

Note the way the speaker upgrades the invitation. Why might this be? The likely reason is that the pause of 0.2 of a second is a cue to an impending refusal. Conversational actions such as invitation refusals are typically prefaced by some delay, and research has shown that speakers modify their actions on the basis of such predictions (Drew, in press). This highlights the requirement for research practices that record and represent interaction accurately and in sufficient detail.

Discourse research has been facilitated by the steady improvement of technology in the past two decades. Minidisk recorders are compact and reliable and can capture more than 2 hours of very high quality mono using a flat microphone that is perfectly suited for picking up speech. Videorecorders have likewise become a cheap and compact possibility. Video is more obtrusive and presents certain analytical challenges, but it can provide important information that audio lacks, particularly where the interaction involves important embodied actions.

Digital records make the process of transcribing and managing the materials much simpler and more flexible. Audio and video software allow records to be easily copied, searched, and edited. They also have the capability of disguising voice quality and faces and for eliminating identifying particulars such as names. This is crucial for maintaining anonymity, particularly with sensitive materials.

Various systems for transcribing talk are available. However, discourse researchers have overwhelmingly opted to use the system developed by the conversation analyst Gail Jefferson in the 1960s and 1970s (see Exhibit 5.1). This has the virtues of being quick to learn, being relatively intuitive, and, most important, highlighting features of talk that have been shown to be interactionally important such as intonation and overlap. The simplest way to transcribe is to work with two windows on a computer screen, one running the audio file, the other running the word processor. Audio programs are available that allow a stepwise movement through the file using a physical representation of the wave form that is ideal for timing pauses and noting overlap. (For more detailed discussions of transcription see Hutchby & Wooffitt, 1998, and ten Have, 1999; and for a brief summary of the main transcription symbols and their use see Exhibit 5.1.)

Transcription is demanding and time-consuming. It can take more than 20 hours to produce a decent transcript of an hour of interaction. The time multiplies if the interaction is complex or the recording is poor quality. The compensation is that transcription involves a very careful listening to the material—for this reason it is recommended that researchers do at least some of their own transcription. In addition, this is often when analytical insights are first developed.

Transcription is a crucial element in discourse work. It simplifies the process of analysis and is highly transportable. It is also the prime medium for presenting material in publication, although the Web will increasingly be used to combine audio materials with written articles. Nevertheless, transcripts inevitably have limitations and should be used in combination with the original audio records.

Stages of Analysis

Analysis in discourse research is highly varied and depends to some extent on the nature of the materials that are available and how developed research is on the topic or setting of interest. However, most analysis goes through the following four stages that are overlapping, but broadly distinct.

1. Generating Hypotheses

Discourse research is not hypothesis-based, as is common elsewhere in psychology. Sometimes a researcher comes to some materials with a broad set of concerns or questions. Equally common is an interest in a setting (relationship counseling, say) and how actions are done in that setting. For this reason the first part of discourse research is often the generation of more specific questions or hypotheses or the noticing of intriguing or troubling phenomena.

This stage of the work often starts during transcription, which provides a major opportunity for carefully listening to the material. Discourse researchers often make analytical notes as they transcribe. It is common and productive to continue this open-ended approach to the data in group sessions where a number of researchers listen to a segment of interaction and explore different ways of understanding what is going on.

2. Coding: The Building of a Collection

The main aim of coding is to make the analysis more straightforward by sifting relevant materials from a larger corpus. In traditional terminology it is a form of data reduction; it is a preliminary that facilitates analysis. Typically it involves searching materials for some phenomena of interest and copying the instances to an archive. This is likely to be a set of extracts from sound files and their associated transcripts.

At this stage in the research the coding is inclusive, but coding can continue cyclically throughout the research process as ideas are refined and the understanding of the phenomena changes. Often phenomena that were initially seen as disparate merge together while phenomena that seemed singular become broken into different varieties. Problem or doubtful instances will be included in the coding—they may become most analytically productive when considering deviant cases. This kind of coding is quite different from the sorts of coding practice that take place in content analysis where the goal is typically to develop a set of criteria-based categories, count instances in categories, and perform various statistical analyses of the counts.

3. Doing the Analysis

Analysis does not follow a fixed set of steps. The procedure used is related to the type of materials used and the sorts of questions being asked. This contrasts it to many styles of psychological research where the justification of the research findings depends on following a set of steps in a precise and orderly manner. In discourse research the procedures for justification are partly separate from the procedures for arriving at analytical claims.

Analysis is a craft skill that can be developed through reading discourse research studies and working with sets of materials. It combines elements of hypothetico–deductivism and inductivism. The researcher will typically develop conjectures about activities through a close reading of the materials and then check the adequacy of these hypotheses through working with a corpus of coded materials. For example, imagine one is interested in the design of opening questions in abuse helpline counseling. We have noted in our example earlier an opening question that is open-ended and constructed in a colloquial manner. To establish the relevance of these features for the activity being done, one would do a number of things.

1. *Search for a Pattern:* We would look through our corpus to see how regular this pattern is. If such a pattern is not common, then our speculation will start to look weak. This is a complicated matter. We might find additional fine-grained organizations. For example, the caller in the example is a child (she describes herself as 12 later in the call, and sounds young). The counselor prefaces her question by addressing her by name. It may be that this is more common with child callers and has a specific role in the interaction. These are new questions to follow up.
2. *Consider Next Turns:* Our hypothesis is that the counselor's turn is designed in the way that it is to head off potential problems with what comes next. If next turns typically go smoothly, then this provides support. If we still see trouble arising this would go against the idea. In general, in discourse work the sequential organization of interaction is a powerful resource for understanding what is going on. As conversation analysts have shown, speaker's utterances display an understanding of the earlier utterance. For example, in the first extract the speaker's following turn is hearably an answer. This provides a participant's confirmation of our analytical intuition that the counselor's turn is a form of question.

3. *Focus on Deviant Cases:* These might be ones in which very different question constructions were used; or where surprising next turns appeared. Such cases are rich analytically. For example, they might cast doubt on our general claim and send us back to the drawing board. If no trouble ensues from very specific opening questions, or ones delivered in a very formal speech style, then we will have little evidence for our conjecture about the role of particular question constructions. However, if our unusual cases lead to trouble of various kinds, then the deviant cases will have provided strong support for the conjecture.
4. *Focus on Other Kinds of Material:* Obviously there is an infinite set of alternative materials that we might use for comparison. However, we might consider other telephone helplines, perhaps where calls have a more specific topic (directory inquiries, flight information) or, on the other hand, mundane calls between friends. This will allow us to get a better handle on the specific business being done and how it works in this counseling helpline, drawing on, or differing from, the business taking place in other settings.

It would be wrong to imply that these four analytical tasks happen sequentially or that all of them will be possible or appropriate in any particular case. They are indicative of the sorts of analytical procedures that researchers go through.

4. Validating the Analysis

There is not a clear-cut distinction between validation procedures and analytical procedures in discourse work; indeed some of the analytical themes are also, differently understood, involved in validation. Nevertheless, it is useful to highlight some of the major elements involved in validating claims. Again, not all of them will be relevant in all cases, but individually or together they contribute to establishing the adequacy of particular analyses.

Participants' Orientations

The importance of the turn-by-turn nature of interaction has already been emphasized in the analytical section earlier. Any turn of talk is oriented to what came before, and sets up an environment for what comes next. At its simplest, when someone provides an acceptance it provides evidence that what came before was an invitation. If an analyst claims that some conversational move is an indirect invitation, say, we would want to see evidence that the recipient is orientating (even indirectly) to its nature as an invitation. Close attention to this turn-by-turn display of understanding provides one important check on analytical interpretations (Heritage, 1997). This principle is analytically powerful, although not foolproof, and there have been major disputes on its limits for the analysis of phenomena that involve social categories and power (see Wetherell, Taylor, & Yates, 2001).

Deviant Cases

Deviant cases have already been emphasized. However, it is important to note their significant role in the validation of findings. Deviant cases are often the most analytically and theoretically informative. They can show whether a generalization is robust or breaks down. For example, studies of media interviews show that interviewees rarely treat interviewers as accountable for views expressed in their questions. As Heritage and Greatbatch (1991) have shown, this is the normal (indeed, normat*ive,* pattern). There are occasional deviant cases, however, where a news interviewer is treated as responsible for some view. However, rather than showing that this pattern is not normative, these deviations are the exception that proves the rule. Cases of departure can lead to considerable interactional trouble, which interferes with the interviewee making his or her point (Potter, 1996a).

Coherence

The accumulation of findings from different studies allows new studies to be assessed for their coherence with what comes before. For example, work on the organization of food assessments in mealtime conversations (Wiggins & Potter, in press) builds on, and provides additional confirmation of, earlier work on assessments and compliments (Pomerantz, 1984). Looked at the other way around, a study that clashed with some of the basic findings in discourse work would be treated with more caution—although if its findings seemed more robust it would be more consequential.

Readers' Evaluation

One of the most fundamental features of discourse research is that its claims are accountable to the detail of the empirical materials and that the empirical materials are presented in a form that allows readers to make their own checks and judgments. Discourse articles typically present a range of extracts from the transcript alongside the interpretations that have been made of them. This form of validation contrasts with much traditional experimental and content analytical work, where it is rare for anything close to "raw data" to be included, or for more than one or two illustrative codings to be provided. Sacks's (1992) ideal was to put the reader as far as possible into the same position as the researcher with respect to the materials. Such an ideal is unrealizable, but discourse work is closer than many analytical approaches.

Whether used singly or together, these procedures are not a guarantee of validity. Nevertheless, sociologists of science have shown us that guarantees are hard to find where we are talking about even the hardest of sciences. What these procedures offer is a degree of public quality control. Any study that cannot effectively show participants' own orientations to a phenomenon, that cannot deal with deviant cases, that is out of line with previous research, and that fails to offer convincing interpretations of reproduced extracts is unlikely to be worth serious consideration.

A Research Illustration: Peräkylä on AIDS Counseling

A wide range of different discourse studies could be used to illustrate the research process. Anssi Peräkylä's (1995) investigation of AIDS counseling is worth considering in detail. It is a major and well-regarded integrative study that addresses a related set of questions about interaction. Its topic is a form of counseling that draws on a well-known family therapy approach so it has an additional psychological interest. It draws heavily on the conversation–analytical perspective on institutional talk developed by Drew and Heritage (1992b) and is worth reading in conjunction with Silverman's (1997) complementary study of HIV-positive counseling that focuses more on advice-giving.

Peräkylä researched counseling for HIV-positive hemophilic and mainly gay-identified men and their partners at a major London hospital. The counselors characterized their practices in terms of Milan School family systems theory and, although this is not the start point of Peräkylä's study, he was able to explicate some of the characteristics of such counseling. He concentrated on 32 counseling sessions taken from a wider archive of recordings (450 hours). The wider archive was drawn on to provide additional examples of phenomena of interest but were not otherwise transcribed. The sessions were videotaped and transcribed using the Jeffersonian system. The analytical process was similar to the one described earlier, with an emphasis on identifying patterns and exceptions, and considering the counseling interaction in relationship to other settings.

Part of the study was concerned with identifying the standard normative turn-taking organization of the counseling. Plainly stated, it is that (a) counselors ask questions; (b) clients answer; (c) counselors comment, advise, or ask more questions. When laid out in this manner the organization may not seem much of a discovery. However, the power of the study is showing how this organization is *achieved* in the interaction—that is, how both counselors and clients collaboratively keep it on track, and how it can be used to address painful and delicate topics such as sexual behavior, illness, and death. An understanding of this normative pattern also provides a way for understanding breakdowns and departures.

Peräkylä goes on to examine various practices that are characteristic of family systems theory, such as circular questioning, where the counselor initially questions the client's partner or a family member about the client's feelings, and live open supervision, where a supervisor may offer questions to the counselor that are, in turn, addressed to the client. The study also identifies some of the strategies by which counselors can address dreaded issues in a manageable way.

The general form of Peräkylä's analysis can be illustrated by his treatment of circular questioning. He starts by considering a practice that is extremely common in everyday interaction for eliciting information or actions indirectly.

This practice involves providing a partial experience of some event as a way of fishing for a more authoritative version (Pomerantz, 1980). Note the following example:

Extract Three
A: Yer line's been busy.
B: Yeuh my fu (hh)- .hh my father's wife called me

By reporting her side of the event, A elicits a fuller account from B.

Peräkylä noted that a similar practice appears in AIDS counseling. This involves asking the client's partner to provide his or her own understanding of the client's experience. This generates an interaction where "the clients, in an unacknowledged but most powerful way, elicit one another's descriptions of their inner experiences" (Peräkylä, 1995, p. 110). In the following extract the client is called Edward; his partner and the counselor are also present.

Extract Four (From Peräkylä, 1995, p. 110)
Counselor: What are some of things that you think
E:dward might have to do.=
He says he doesn't know where to go from here
maybe: and awaiting results and things.
(0.6)
What d'you think's worrying him.
(0.4)
Partner: Uh::m hhhhhh
I think it's just fear of the unknow:n.
Client: Mm[:
Counselor: [Oka:y.
Partner: [At- at the present ti:me.
(0.2) Uh:m (.) once: he's (0.5) got a better
understanding of (0.2) what could happen
Counselor: Mm:
Partner: uh:m how .hh this will progre:ss then:
I think (.) things will be a little
more [settled in his=
Counselor: [Mm
Partner: =own mi:nd.
Counselor: Mm:
(.)
Client: Mm[:
Counselor: [E:dward (.) from what you know::
((Sequence continues with Edward responding to a direct question with a long and detailed narrative about his fears.))

Peräkylä emphasized the way that the client's talk about his fears is elicited in part through the counselor asking the partner for his own view of those fears. The point is not that the client is *forced* to reveal his experiences; rather, it is that the earlier revelation of his partner's partial view produces an environment in which such a revelation is *expected* and nonrevelation would be a *delicate* and *accountable* matter. In effect, what Peräkylä documents are the conversational mechanisms that family therapists exploit to do their work and that they characterize in their own literature as using circular questioning to overcome clients' resistance.

Conclusion

Discursive psychology provides a novel account of the relationship between psychology and discourse. Rather than seeing discourse as the product of psychological processes, it considers the ways in which psychology is produced *in talk* as *parts of practices.* Its focus moves from the person to the interaction, and therefore from cognition to discourse. Discourse is conceptualized as (a) oriented to action; (b) situated sequentially, institutionally, and rhetorically; (c) construct*ed* from discursive resources and construct*ive* of events, actions, and minds.

These general principles go along with a reconsideration of the central questions psychologists might usefully ask. In particular, there is a move from causal questions of the form "what is the effect of *X* on *Y*" to practical and interactional questions of the form "how is *X* done?" These questions bring with them new topic areas or reconceptualizations of old ones. The focus on how questions combined with the emphasis on discourse being situated encourages a focus either on records of natural interaction or on interviews treated as interaction in its own right.

The general process of discourse research is quite varied. However, it commonly follows four overlapping but conceptually distinct stages: (a) generating hypotheses; (b) building a collection; (c) doing the analysis; and (d) validating the analysis. Ultimately, however, the quality of the research is derived from the ability to show that claims make sense of the organization of materials in all of their detail rather than following a set of stages.

Discourse analysis and discursive psychology are fast-developing approaches. Although a few years ago there were rather more promissory notes and programmatic statements than actual research examples, there is now a considerable body of published work (for reviews and explication see, e.g., Antaki & Widdicombe, 1998; Edwards, 1997; Wetherell et al., 2001). There is also a range of publications that provide a more detailed account of discourse analytical methods. General overviews of method can be found in Coyle (1995), Gill (1996), Potter and Wetherell (1987), Potter (1996b, 1997), Wood and Kroger (2000), and Wooffitt (1993). Potter and Wetherell (1994) work through the process of analysis with a single example. Billig (1997) and Potter and Wetherell (1995) discussed the analysis of broad themes and interpretative repertoires drawn on in interview talk. Potter (1998) compared grounded theory, ethnography, and discourse analysis in the analysis of clinical materials. Edwards and Potter (2001) discussed discursive psychological analysis of the role of psychological talk in institutions. Wetherell, Taylor, and Yates (2001) introduced and compared a range of different approaches to analyzing discourse. Silverman (2001) considered discourse and conversation analysis in the context of broader issues in qualitative analysis.

I will end by commenting on some of the tensions in current discourse research and some of its future directions. I have already noted a tension between a focus on interview work as against a focus on the use of naturalistic materials. There is also something of a tension between work that starts with a concern with social critique and work that starts with a concern with discovery and understanding. A particularly significant recent tension is around the role of theory in guiding analysis of the categories that are relevant to interaction as opposed to focusing on those categories that are described or oriented to interaction. In a medical interaction, say, are the categories *male doctor* and *women patient* relevant because of a theoretical judgment about the significance of such categories, or should analysis look for evidence of orientations to and displays of gender and medical authority? An illuminating and sometimes heated debate has taken place around this issue (see Billig, 1999b, 1999c; Schegloff, 1997, 1998, 1999a, 1999b; Wetherell, 1998). This debate has raised some important and subtle analytical issues, and encouraged all analysts to consider their practices carefully.

Three themes and directions for the future are worth highlighting. First, there is an increasing interest in the nature of cognition and how it should be understood in interaction. Edwards (1997) has already laid out many of the significant issues. Perhaps the most basic is whether discursive psychology should *supplement* traditional cognitive and social cognitive work in psychology or whether it should provide a respecification of cognition that will *supplant* that work. Chapters in te Molder and Potter (in press) explore various stances on the nature of cognition and its relationship to discourse and interaction.

Second, there is likely to be an increasing focus on institutional talk. There are many institutional settings (classrooms, therapy sessions, drug rehabilitation centers) where psychological issues (learning, insight, change) are both topic and part of the texture of the interaction. In contrast to the psychological project common in much mainstream North American work, which attempts to identify general laws and patterns that will have their effect in any particular situation, this work starts with the specificity of the situation before considering what might be more general.

Third, there is an increasing interest in practical uses of discourse work. How can the detailed study of practices input into training, for example? One possibility is that by explicating practices of counseling, say, counselors will be enabled to make more informed and strategic judgments about what they do. As yet this has been a theme that has been little developed; nevertheless, it is likely to become more prominent as discourse research evolves.

References

Antaki, C. (1994). *Explaining and arguing: The social organization of accounts.* Beverly Hills, CA: Sage.

Antaki, C., & Horowitz, A. (2000). Using identity ascription to disqualify a rival version of events as "interested." *Research on Language and Social Interaction, 33,* 155–177.

Antaki, C., Houtkoop-Steentra, H., & Rapley, M. (2000). "Brilliant. Next Question . . .": High-grade assessment sequences in the completion of interactional units. *Research on Language and Social Interaction, 33,* 235–262.

Antaki, C., & Widdicombe, S. (Eds.). (1998). *Identities in talk.* London: Sage.

Billig, M. (1985). Prejudice, categorization and particularization: From a perceptual to a rhetorical approach. *European Journal of Social Psychology, 15,* 79–103.

Billig, M. (1991). *Ideologies and beliefs.* London: Sage.

Billig, M. (1992). *Talking of the royal family.* London: Routledge.

Billig, M. (1996). *Arguing and thinking: A rhetorical approach to social psychology* (2nd ed.). Cambridge: Cambridge University Press.

Billig, M. (1997) Rhetorical and discursive analysis: How families talk about the royal family. In N. Hayes (Ed.), *Doing qualitative analysis in psychology* (pp. 39–54). Hove, UK: Psychology Press.

Billig, M. (1999a) *Freudian repression: Conversation creating the unconscious.* Cambridge: Cambridge University Press.

Billig, M. (1999b). Whose terms? Whose ordinariness? Rhetoric and ideology in conversation analysis. *Discourse and Society, 10,* 543–558.

Billig, M. (1999c). Conversation analysis and the claims of naivety. *Discourse and Society, 10,* 572–576.

Billig, M., Condor, S., Edwards, D., Gane, M., Middleton, D., et al. (1988). *Ideological dilemmas: A social psychology of everyday thinking.* London: Sage.

Brown, G., & Yule, G. (1983). *Discourse analysis.* Cambridge: Cambridge University Press.

Burman, E. (1994). *Deconstructing developmental psychology.* London: Routledge.

Chalmers, A. (1992). *What is this thing called science?: An assessment of the nature and status of science and its methods* (2nd ed.). Milton Keynes, UK: Open University Press.

Conway, M. (Ed.). (1992). Developments and debates in the study of human memory. *The Psychologist, 5,* 439–461.

Coyle, A. (1995). Discourse analysis. In G. M. Breakwell, S. Hammond, & C. Fife-Schaw (Eds.), *Research methods in psychology* (pp. 243–258). London: Sage.

Davidson, J. (1984). Subsequent versions of invitations, offers, requests, and proposals dealing with potential or actual rejection. In J. M. Atkinson & J. Heritage (Eds.), *Structures of social action: Studies in conversation analysis* (pp. 102–128). Cambridge: Cambridge University Press.

Dickerson, P. (1997). "It's not just me who's saying this . . ." The deployment of cited others in television political discourse. *British Journal of Social Psychology, 36,* 33–48.

Drew, P. (in press). Is confusion a state of mind? In H. te Molder & J. Potter (Eds.), *Talk and cognition: Discourse, cognition and social interaction.* Cambridge: Cambridge University Press.

Drew, P., & Heritage, J. C. (Eds.). (1992a). *Talk at work: Interaction in institutional settings.* Cambridge: University of Cambridge Press.

Drew, P., & Heritage, J. C. (1992b). Analyzing talk at work: An introduction. In P. Drew & J. Heritage (Eds.), *Talk at work: Interaction in institutional settings* (pp. 3–65). Cambridge: Cambridge University Press.

Edwards, D. (1991). Categories are for talking: On the cognitive and discursive bases of categorization. *Theory and Psychology, 1*(4), 515–542.

Edwards, D. (1995). Sacks and psychology. *Theory and Psychology, 5,* 579–596.

Edwards, D. (1997). *Discourse and cognition.* Beverly Hills, CA: Sage.

Edwards, D. (2000). Extreme case formulations: Softeners, investments and doing nonliteral. *Research on Language and Social Interaction, 33,* 347–373.

Edwards, D., & Potter, J. (1992). *Discursive psychology.* London: Sage.

Edwards, D., & Potter, J. (1993). Language and causation: A discursive action model of description and attribution. *Psychological Review, 100,* 23–41.

Edwards, D., & Potter, J. (2001). Discursive psychology. In A. W. McHoul & M. Rapley (Eds.), *How to analyse talk in institutional settings: A casebook of methods* (pp. 12–26). London: Continuum.

Engestrom, Y., & Middleton, D. (Eds.). (1996). *Cognition and communication at work.* New York: Cambridge University Press.

Foucault, M. (1971). Orders of discourse. *Social Science Information, 10,* 7–30.

Georgaca, E. (2000). Reality and discourse: A critical analysis of the category of "delusions." *British Journal of Medical Psychology, 73,* 227–242.

Gergen, K. J. (1982). *Toward transformation in social knowledge.* New York: Springer-Verlag.

Gergen, K. J. (1999). *An invitation to social construction.* London: Sage.

Gill, R. (1996) Discourse analysis: Methodological aspects. In J. E. Richardson (Ed.), *Handbook of qualitative research methods for psychology and the social sciences.* Leicester, UK: British Psychological Society.

Goodwin, C. (1997). The blackness of black: Color categories as situated practice. In L. B. Resnick, R. Säljö, C. Pontecorvo, & B. Burge (Eds.), *Discourse, tools, and reasoning* (pp. 111–140). Berlin: Springer.

Harré, R. (1979). *Social being: A theory for social psychology.* Oxford: Basil Blackwell.

Harré, R. (1998). *The singular self: An introduction to the psychology of personhood.* London: Sage.

Heath, C. (1997). The analysis of activities in face to face interaction using video. In D. Silverman (Ed.), *Qualitative research: Theory, method and practice* (pp. 183–200). London: Sage.

Henriques, J., Hollway, W., Urwin, C., Venn, C., & Walkerdine, V. (1984). *Changing the subject.* London: Methuen.

Hepburn, A. (2000). Power lines: Derrida, discursive psychology and the management of accusations of school bullying. *British Journal of Social Psychology, 39,* 605–628.

Heritage, J. C. (1997). Conversation analysis and institutional talk: Analysing data. In D. Silverman (Ed.), *Qualitative research: Theory, method and practice* (pp. 161–182). London: Sage.

Heritage, J. C., & Greatbatch, D. L. (1991). On the institutional character of institutional talk: The case of news interviews. In D. Boden & D. H. Zimmerman (Eds.), *Talk and social structure: Studies in ethnomethodology and conversation analysis* (pp. 93–137). Oxford: Polity.

Hollway, W. (1989). *Subjectivity and method in psychology: Gender, meaning, and science.* London: Sage.

Hutchby, I., & Wooffitt, R. (1998). *Conversation analysis: Principles, practices and applications.* Cambridge: Polity.

Jefferson, G. (1988). On the sequential organization of troubles-talk in ordinary conversation. *Social Problems, 35,* 418–437.

Kitzinger, C., & Frith, H. (1999). Just say no? The use of conversation analysis in developing a feminist perspective on sexual refusal. *Discourse & Society, 10,* 293–316.

Knorr Cetina, K. (1999). *Epistemic cultures: How the sciences make knowledge.* Cambridge, MA: Harvard University Press.

Levinson, S. C. (1983). *Pragmatics.* Cambridge: Cambridge University Press.

Litton, I., & Potter, J. (1985). Social representations in the ordinary explanation of a "riot." *European Journal of Social Psychology, 15,* 371–388.

Lynch, M., & Bogen, D. (1996). *The spectacle of history: Speech, text, and memory at the Iran-Contra hearings.* Durham, NC: Duke University Press.

Malson, H. (1998). *The thin woman: Feminism, post-structuralism and the social psychology of anorexia nervosa.* London: Routledge.

Parker, I. (1992). *Discourse dynamics: Critical analysis for social and individual psychology.* London: Routledge.

Peräkylä, A. (1995). *AIDS counselling: Institutional interaction and clinical practice.* Cambridge: Cambridge University Press.

Pomerantz, A. M. (1980). Telling my side: "Limited access" as a fishing device. *Sociological Inquiry, 50*(3&4), 186–198.

Pomerantz, A. M. (1984). Agreeing and disagreeing with assessments: Some features of preferred/dispreferred turn shapes. In J. M. Atkinson & J. Heritage (Eds.), *Structures of social action: Studies in conversation analysis* (pp. 57–101). Cambridge: Cambridge University Press.

Potter, J. (1996a). *Representing reality: Discourse, rhetoric and social construction.* London: Sage.

Potter, J. (1996b). Discourse analysis and constructionist approaches: Theoretical background. In J. E. Richardson (Ed.), *Handbook of qualitative research methods for psychology and the social sciences* (pp. 125–160). Leicester, UK: British Psychological Society.

Potter, J. (1997). Discourse analysis as a way of analysing naturally occurring talk. In D. Silverman (Ed.), *Qualitative research: Theory, method and practice* (pp. 146–160). London: Sage.

Potter, J. (1998). Qualitative and discourse analysis. In A. S. Bellack & M. Hersen (Eds.), *Comprehensive clinical psychology* (Vol. 3, pp. 117–144). Oxford: Pergamon Press.

Potter, J., & Edwards, D. (2001). Sociolinguistics, cognitivism and discursive psychology. In N. Coupland, S. Sarangi, & C. Candlin (Eds.), *Sociolinguistics and social theory* (pp. 88–103). London: Longman.

Potter, J., & Wetherell, M. (1987). *Discourse and social psychology: Beyond attitudes and behaviour.* London: Sage.

Potter, J., & Wetherell, M. (1994). Analyzing discourse. In A. Bryman & B. Burgess (Eds.), *Analyzing qualitative data* (pp. 67–56). London: Routledge.

Potter, J., & Wetherell, M. (1995). Discourse analysis. In J. Smith, R. Harré, & L. van Langenhove (Eds.), *Rethinking methods in psychology* (pp. 80–92). London: Sage.

Potter, J., Wetherell, M., Gill, R., & Edwards, D. (1990). Discourse—Noun, verb or social practice? *Philosophical Psychology, 3,* 205–217.

Puchta, C., & Potter, J. (1999). Asking elaborate questions: Focus groups and the management of spontaneity. *Journal of Sociolinguistics, 3,* 314–335.

Sacks, H. (1992). *Lectures on conversation* (Vols. I & II). Edited by G. Jefferson. Oxford: Basil Blackwell.

Schegloff, E. A. (1997). Whose text? Whose context?, *Discourse and Society, 8,* 165–187.

Schegloff, E.A. (1998). Reply to Wetherell. *Discourse & Society, 9,* 413–416.

Schegloff, E. A. (1999a). "Schegloff's texts" as "Billig's data": A critical reply. *Discourse and Society, 10,* 558–572.

Schegloff, E. A. (1999b). Naivete vs. sophistication or discipline vs. self-indulgence: A rejoinder to Billig. *Discourse and Society, 10*(4), 577–582.

Shotter, J. (1984). *Social accountability and selfhood.* Oxford: Basil Blackwell.

Shotter, J. (1993). *Conversational realities: Constructing life through language.* London: Sage.

Silverman, D. (1997). *Discourses of counselling: HIV counselling as social interaction.* Thousand Oaks, CA: Sage.

Silverman, D. (2001). *Interpreting qualitative data: Methods for analysing talk, text and interaction* (2nd ed.). London: Sage.

Sinclair, J. McH., & Coulthard, R. M. (1975). *Towards an analysis of discourse: The English used by teachers and pupils.* London: Oxford University Press.

Stokoe, E. H., & Smithson, J. (2001). Making gender relevant: Conversation analysis and gender categories in interaction. *Discourse & Society, 12,* 217–244.

Suchman, L., & Jordan, B. (1990). Interactional troubles in face-to-face survey interviews. *Journal of the American Statistical Association, 85,* 232–241.

te Molder, H. & Potter, J. (Eds.). (in press). *Talk and cognition: Discourse, cognition and social interaction.* Cambridge: Cambridge University Press.

ten Have, P. (1999). *Doing conversation analysis.* London: Sage.

van Dijk, T. A., & Kintch, W. (1983). *Strategies of discourse comprehension.* London: Academic Press.

Walkerdine, V. (1988). *The mastery of reason: Cognitive development and the production of rationality.* London: Routledge.

Wetherell, M. (1995). Romantic discourse and feminist analysis: Interrogating investment, power and desire. In S. Wilkinson & C. Kitzinger (Eds.), *Feminism and discourse: Psychological perspective.* London: Sage.

Wetherell, M. (1998). Positioning and interpretative repertoires: Conversation analysis and post-structuralism in dialogue. *Discourse and Society, 9,* 387–412.

Wetherell, M., & Potter, J. (1992). *Mapping the language of racism: Discourse and the legitimation of exploitation.* Brighton, UK: Harvester/Wheatsheaf.

Wetherell, M., Taylor, S., & Yates, S. (2001). *Discourse theory and practice: A reader.* London: Sage.

Widdicombe, S., & Wooffitt, R. (1995). *The language of youth subcultures: Social identity in action.* Hemel Hempstead, UK: Harvester/Wheatsheaf.

Wiggins, S., & Potter, J. (in press). Attitudes and evaluative practices: Category vs. item and subjective vs. objective constructions in everyday food assessments. *British Journal of Social Psychology.*

Wood, L. A., & Kroger, R. O. (2000). *Doing discourse analysis: Methods for studying action in talk and text.* London: Sage.

Wooffitt, R. (1992). *Telling tales of the unexpected: The organization of factual discourse.* London: Harvester/Wheatsheaf.

Wooffitt, R. (1993). Analysing accounts. In N. Gilbert (Ed.), *Researching social life* (pp. 287–305). London: Sage.

6

Narrative Psychology and Narrative Analysis

Michael Murray

> It was long ago, and long ago it was; and if I'd been there, I wouldn't be here now; and if I were here, and then was now, I'd be an old storyteller, whose story might have been improved by time, could he remember it. Three good points about stories: if told, they like to be heard; if heard, they like to be taken in; and if taken in, they like to be told. Three enemies of stories: endless talk, the clash of a mill, the ring of an anvil. (Carson, 1999, p. 1)

This quotation is the opening paragraph from a prose work by the Irish writer Ciarán Carson. It provides an introduction to a wondrous book of tales in which Carson intertwines stories told to him by his father with versions of ancient Greek myths and with stories about Dutch painters. It also provides a fitting introduction to this chapter in that it summarizes both the pervasiveness of storytelling in everyday social interaction, the role of plot and memory in narrative, and how in the modern era storytellers have become self-conscious of the telling.

Brian Richardson (2000) began his introduction to a recent special issue of the journal *Style* devoted to the study of narrative with the sentence, "Now, narrative is everywhere" (p. 168). Whereas 20 years ago the study of narrative was confined to literary scholars it has now spread across all the disciplines, from the humanities through the various social sciences and even touching the physical sciences (Nash, 1990). It is perhaps because of the very pervasiveness of stories in everyday life that, until recently, few psychologists have been interested in studying narrative.

Narrative psychology is concerned with the structure, content, and function of the stories that we tell each other and ourselves in social interaction. It accepts that we live in a storied world and that we interpret the actions of others and ourselves through the stories we exchange. Through narrative we not only shape the world and ourselves but they are shaped for us through narrative. In this chapter we review the nature of the narrative turn within psychology, detail how to conduct narrative interviews, and consider some forms of narrative analysis.

Narrative as Theory

Unlike other forms of qualitative research, narrative psychology is not only concerned with methods but also with broader ontological issues. Narrative underlines our very being and our way of acting in the world. We begin by considering some of these theoretical issues before we consider any of the methodological issues.

Narrative Turn in Psychology

The study of narrative accounts has a lengthy history in modern psychology. We can trace it back at least to Wilhelm Wundt (1832–1920), who is often considered the father of experimental psychology but who also developed a parallel approach termed *Volkerpsychologie* that considered the importance of such phenomena as myths in human life (Farr, 1983). Sigmund Freud (1856–1939) was also interested in such broad social stories in his study of mass psychology but more so in the personal stories told by patients in the therapeutic session. It was through his careful analysis of such stories that Freud developed his theory of psychoanalysis.

Throughout the 20th century, despite the domineering approaches of behaviorism and instrumentalism, a steady stream of psychologists turned to the study of more open personal accounts to deepen their understanding of the human condition. For example, during the 1930s, Gordon Allport led a project examining the life histories of refugees from Nazi Germany (Allport, Bruner, & Jandorf, 1941). Subsequently, he prepared a report on the use of personal documents in psychological research (Allport, 1942). In the preface to that report Allport wrote,

> A decade of depression, war and misery has had one benign effect. It has brought out upon the central stage the struggles of the common man, the picture of his daily life, all his homely values. It has brought the documentary film into popularity, the opinion poll . . . autobiographies that give unaccented accounts of ordinary experience. (p. xi)

In the early years of this new millennium, once more the voice of the common man and woman has come to the fore in both popular culture and in the human sciences. Today, one of the most popular of literary genres is the autobiography, not just of the political leader but also of the everyperson. On television one of the most popular formats is not the documentary that gives precedence to the expert voice but the talk show that provides a forum for the ordinary person to tell his or her stories. This enthusiasm to tell and listen to popular life stories could be described as a marker for a society that is losing faith in the more established sacred narratives of religion, preferring more prosaic accounts for advice and guidance (cf. Chandler, 1990). As the novelist Martin Amis wrote in his recent book of memoirs: "We live in the age of mass loquacity. We are all writing it or at any rate talking it: the memoir, the apologia, the c.v., the *cri de coeur*" (Amis, 2000, p. 6).

Narrative Thinking

One of Allport's original research assistants was Jerome Bruner, who has become a leading contemporary advocate of the narrative turn within psychology. Bruner (1986) has argued that there are two ways of knowing—the paradigmatic and the narrative—each distinct and "irreducible to one another" (p. 11). The former is based on the process of classifying and categorizing that is preferred by the natural sciences. It tries to "fulfill the ideal of a formal, mathematical system of description and explanation" (p. 12). The alternative narrative form of knowing is a popular means of making sense of the world by connecting events over time through stories. This narrative mode is the dominant process of thinking within what Bruner termed "folk psychology," mirroring Wundt's earlier term.

One of the central features of this narrative knowing is that it "specializes in the forging of links between the exceptional and the ordinary" (Bruner, 1990, p. 47). It provides a means of integrating the strange and unknown into the realm of everyday life. "The function of the story is to find an intentional state that mitigates or at least makes comprehensible a deviation from a canonical cultural pattern" (Bruner, 1990, pp. 49–50). This argument challenged the dominant atomistic trend within cognitive psychology, and in some forms of qualitative research, that attempted to break human thoughts and language down into the smallest parts. Instead, according to Bruner (1990), "People do not deal with the world event by event or with text sentence by sentence. They frame events and sentences in larger structures" (p. 64). We do not describe our world as a series of bits and pieces but as a series of stories, some more coherent than others.

Other contemporary psychologists (e.g., Gergen & Gergen, 1986; Murray, 1997; Polkinghorne, 1988; Sarbin, 1986) have also argued that narrative is a central human means of making sense of the world. In providing accounts of our everyday lives we speak in narrative form. In addition, we draw on the narrative accounts of others. As Sarbin (1990) stated,

> Simply put, when we are concerned with understanding and communicating about action, we organize our observations according to narrative plots. Whether the target of our interest is random movement or geometric figures, the adventures of a particular person, the history of a social group or the evolution of humankind, our understanding appears to be dependent upon our ability to construct a narrative and to tell a story. (p. 53)

The French philosopher Paul Ricoeur in a series of articles and books has developed a sophisticated thesis for the centrality of narrative in human thought and identity. One of the central planks of Ricoeur's thesis is that we live in a sea of time. Narrative, as it were, provides a map of that sea—it brings order to disorder. A central feature of this narrative process is *emplotment,* whereby we derive "a configuration from a succession" (Ricoeur, 1991a, p. 427). Before we provide this order or shape, Ricoeur argued, there exists a prenarrative structure to our reality that "constitutes a demand for narrative" (1989, p. 74) but also limits the shape we can give to our narrative account.

The narrative interpretation of our reality is central—without it we continue to be awash in a sea of time.

Structure of Narrative

So what precisely does the term *narrative* mean? The very pervasiveness of the term can lead some researchers to suggest that narrative can be any form of text or discourse. However, there are certain distinguishing features. The most distinctive feature is that it provides a coherent causal account of an event that has occurred or that is expected to occur. This definition includes both the causal and temporal dimensions of narrative. The extent of the coherence of the story may vary. Narrative provides a certain shape, structure, or plot to a sequence of events. In any culture there are many such plots that we can draw on to shape our interpretation of events. Some cultures may have a greater range of plot lines than others, and it is even possible that in certain cultures the range is minimal or nonexistent. Because narratives provide shape to our past and projections about our future it would be expected that such cultures would have limited history or plans for the future, but instead their members would live largely in the present.

The plot is what gives the narrative account its structure. As Polkinghorne (1988) argued, it is the narrative plot that can bring coherence to such an expansive sequence of events as those involved in the birth of the universe (e.g., religious stories of creation), as well as allowing us to bring order to the finer details involved in conducting a minor event such as going to the store for groceries. In each case, the narrative brings a sense of order and meaning to the myriad details.

It is the plot that connects the beginning of the story to the end. It weaves different episodes together to make a coherent and meaningful account. It is the plot that gives the story its meaning.

Social Nature of Narratives

The stories that we tell about lives are social constructions. In constructing a narrative account we make use of everyday language. The social nature of language conditions the character of our narrative accounts. "It is together that we remember; and it is within the social medium of language that we articulate our most individual memories in the mode of narrative" (Ricoeur, 1997, p. xliii). In addition, we share stories about our lives with each other. We live within a web of family, community, and other stories. To continue the nautical analogy, we swim in a sea of stories that seeps into our consciousness and into our very identity.

This social nature of narrative is one of its distinguishing features when compared to such other forms of imagination as dreams. Although some researchers suggest that we dream in narrative, this is not clear. According to the early French social psychologist Maurice Halbwachs (1952/1992), one of the particular features of dreams is their lack of structure, their very fluidity.

Dreams could be considered analogous to Ricoeur's prenarrative experience. It is this dimension that provides their mysterious and, sometimes, threatening quality. Dreams exist in a lonely world. They contain disconnected sequences of events that can be strange or "dream-like." They melt away when we awake. When we attempt to recall them it is difficult, whereas when we attempt to recall stories it is more straightforward. Stories exist in a social world. In providing accounts of experience we actively organize them in narrative form so that they can be grasped by the other. In addition, they are partly organized for us by the other person and by the culture in which we live. They are coconstructions (see Mishler, 1997).

The structure of narrative accounts is not fixed but depends on a variety of factors including the narrator, the audience, and the broader social and cultural context (see Murray, 1997a). The character of the relationship between the narrator and the audience is of central importance. The narrative is created in this exchange. As Freud (1937) stated in describing the analyst–analysand exchange:

> The analyst finishes a piece of construction and communicates it to the subject of analysis so that it may work on him; he then constructs a further piece out of the fresh material pouring in on him, deals with it in the same way and proceeds in this alternating fashion until the end. (pp. 260–261).

The story is coconstructed by the two or more parties to the exchange. One of the parties may have more influence than the others such that he or she can shape the narrative. This dominant plot line may or may not accord with the experience of the other. This question regarding the relative contribution of the different participants in shaping a narrative is an ongoing challenge facing the narrative researcher in collecting and analyzing narrative accounts.

We can extend concern with social context to consider broader issues of social power (cf. Murray, 2000). Especially since the work of Foucault (1980), social scientists have broadly accepted that power pervades all social relationships. Societal narratives are not value-neutral but represent various power interests. The adoption of dominant narratives becomes a means of social discipline. People are constantly engaged in a process of negotiating the connection between their personal narratives and these dominant societal narratives. As Morawski (1997) argued,

> Narratives serve as mediations between individual actions and material and social-structural conditions; they reflect the dynamics of ongoing negotiations, interpretations, and construals just as they indicate the constraints operating in these dynamics. (p. 675)

Challenges to Plot Lines

There are events that seem to challenge standard plot lines. These are the events in our lives that do not fit easily into a coherent form. It is this difficulty in creating a narrative about certain personal or societal events that can leave a person or a community adrift, uncertain, and anxious. Narrative therapists such as White and Epston (1990) have suggested that the reason people seek help is because their narrative repertoire does not sufficiently encompass their everyday experiences. The aim of narrative therapy is to help clients expand their repertoire, to construct new and more satisfactory stories. Rather than trying to adjust disconnected cognitive distortions, which is the preferred method of much therapy, narrative therapists prefer to explore the larger plot lines in a person's life story. These plot lines may reflect the dominant societal plot lines that do not accord with personal experience. The aim of the narrative therapist is, together with the client, to challenge these dominant plot lines and to generate alternative stories.

The adequacy of personal and societal plot lines to encapsulate particular social tragedies has been considered by historians such as Lawrence Langer. In his analysis of holocaust testimonies, Langer (1991) found that the accounts of survivors were often disjointed and unfinished—it was not possible to fit the horrors into a standard narrative form. This lack of narrative coherence threatened the survivors' sense of personal interconnectedness. The only way some of them could proceed was by developing a new self built on new stories. However, the foundation for this new self was tenuous and led to ongoing personal and social difficulties (see also Fremont, 1999). Langer argued that it is not just at the personal level but also at the societal level that this challenge to narrative exists. Developing a coherent social narrative for these horrors could contribute to the banalizing of the barbarity of the Holocaust. An agreed social narrative provides a society with an interpretive structure that enables it to grasp, to understand, and possibly to excuse. For Langer and some other Holocaust historians, such a process diminishes the magnitude of the evil and enables Western society to, as it were, move on. Instead, Langer (1998) opts for the alternative literalist discourse that "leads nowhere but back into the pit of destruction." He prefers this discourse because "it has the grace to acknowledge that we learn nothing from the misery it finds there" (p. 22). But as LaCapra (2000) retorts, such an approach also risks "allowing for the apologetic appeal to silence in its aftermath" (p. 104).

Narrative and Identity

The telling of narratives is closely intertwined with the shaping and maintenance of personal identity. We tell stories to ourselves and to others about our lives. In this way our lives are represented in narrative form. McAdams (1985) has been to the fore in promoting a narrative approach to the study of human personality. He argued that:

> An individual's story has the power to tie together past, present and future in his or her life. It is a story that he is able to provide unity and purpose . . . individual identities may be classified in the manner of stories. Identity stability is longitudinal consistency in the life story. Identity transformation—identity crisis, identity change—is story revision. . . . Identity is a life story. (p. 19)

In some ways this characterization of identity can be considered rather individualistic in that it ignores the social context within which the stories are created. It is as if the individual could create any story she or he desires. An alternative approach is to argue that the construction of narrative identity is much more dialogical and occurs within a social context. Further, this social context may be both real and imaginary. As Hermans, Kempen, and van Loon (1992) suggested, "Imaginal dialogues play a central role in our daily lives: They exist alongside actual dialogues with real others and, interwoven with actual interactions, they constitute an essential part of our narrative construction of the world" (p. 28).

Shaping our personal narratives is closely connected with how we shape our social narratives. In discussing the role of narrative in constructing our identities, Ricoeur (1991b) distinguished between *configuration* and *refiguration*. The former is the primary activity by which the narrative brings structure to the world through various forms of emplotment. The latter is the means by which the author defines him- or herself through narrative. There is a constant interchange. We draw on cultural plot lines to create our stories about the world and to define ourselves. In addition, our narrative accounts are not fixed but fluid. This very fluidity is the focus of much contemporary debate about identity (e.g., Gergen, 1991) and about the character of history (White, 1978). It is an issue that influences not only the way we collect but also the way we analyze personal accounts.

Narrative Interviews

Within the research context the primary means of obtaining narrative accounts is through interviews. In the interview situation the participant is often keen to give narrative accounts but is discouraged from doing so by the researcher. As Mishler (1986) has argued,

> Interviewers interrupt respondents' answers and thereby suppress expression of their stories; when they appear, stories go unrecorded because they are viewed as irrelevant to the specific aims of specific questions, and stories that make it through these barriers are discarded at stages of coding and analysis. (p. 106)

Conversely, narrative researchers place the collection of narrative accounts at the center stage of their interviews. They ask for narrative accounts and encourage them wherever possible. One of the particular strengths of the narrative interview is that it gives the research participant much more central control in shaping the agenda. In the standard interview the researcher brings to the interview a series of questions or theories she or he would like to explore. In the narrative interview the researcher asks the participant to identify the major themes.

In this chapter, we will use an example taken from a study of seniors' experience of living with chronic pain to further explore the collection and analysis of narratives. In that study a sample of elderly people who were identified by their physician or public health nurse as suffering from chronic nonmalignant pain were interviewed about the problem. In conducting the interviews a life history approach was adopted. Each of the participants was encouraged to describe his or her life experiences and subsequently his or her experience of living with chronic pain. We will focus particularly on the narrative account of one man who had had his leg amputated and now suffered from chronic phantom pain.

Role of Interviewer

The challenge for the researcher is to encourage the participant to tell his or her story. This brings into play the standard advice on being empathetic and supportive to the participant. For some participants the opportunity of an open agenda is seized and they will proceed to tell extensive stories about their lives with very little encouragement from the interviewer. Conversely, other participants will be reluctant to speak—the very openness of the narrative interview may invite suspicion and anxiety leading to brief answers and long pauses. It is unlikely that one meeting with such a person would be sufficient. Rather, it would be necessary to meet with such an individual on several occasions to allay his or her suspicions. An alternative approach would be to invite such an individual to participate in a group discussion in which he or she could gain confidence through participating in the exchange of stories with colleagues from the community. Another strategy is to suggest that the individual write about his or her experiences or to provide her or him with a tape- or video-recorder to take home on which the individual could detail his or her experiences.

The successful narrative interviewer needs to get to know the research participant. Sometimes, after a brief initial conversation in which the researcher describes him- or herself, the purpose of the interview, and the safeguards on confidentiality, the participants are satisfied and will be prepared to disclose extensive information about their lives. The participants need to feel that their stories are deeply valued. Sometimes this can be difficult. The participants may remain suspicious or feel that their stories are not worthy of research investigation. This resistance can tax the patience of the naive interviewer, who may feel that despite many attempts the participant continues to be excessively restrained.

Fortunately, times are changing. The narrative turn in the social sciences reflects broader changes in society. The public display of personal stories has increased the legitimacy of personal storytelling. Elderly people are especially receptive to the extended narrative interview. It would seem that their very position in the life course provides them with a perspective to look over their lives. Freeman (1997) suggested that later life is the narrative phase *par excellence.* In later life one has gained a certain distance from the life one has lived and it is then possible to size up events and draw connections over time. Because the researcher will often be young, the senior may feel more comfortable about taking control of the interview.

An important issue in the collection of narrative accounts is the issue of reflexivity. This concerns the researchers' own awareness of their role in shaping the narrative. The researcher brings to the interview a range of expectations that may encourage certain narratives and inhibit others. The interviewer needs to be aware of how his or her very presence can shape the interview. An important guide is to refrain from negative comments that might discourage the participants from revealing more about themselves. For some participants the chance to talk in depth about personal experiences can be very emotional. This can be upsetting for the inexperienced researcher. It is advisable that the novice interviewer consult closely with an experienced supervisor. There should be an opportunity for him or her to practice beforehand and to debrief afterward with the supervisor.

Life History Interviews

The aim of the standard narrative interview is to obtain a detailed account of a particular broad area of experience. It is most frequently used in biographical and life history research. In this case the researcher outlines at the outset the purpose of the interview and then encourages the participant to provide a narrative account. For example, the interviewer could start, "I would like you to tell me the story of your life beginning as far back as you wish and recounting as much detail in your life up until the present." During the interview the researcher can interject with such comments as "What happened next?" or "Can you recall anything else?" The main emphasis is on how the participant connects events together.

This life history interview can be extended to different developmental sequences. For example, it can explore the process of "becoming a psychologist" or "leaving home." The main concern is that there is substantial opportunity for the narrator to cast a narrative net over a chronological sequence of events. In his or her narrative account the author can deviate from the sequence, select certain events, and ignore others. The interviews with the seniors in the study of living with chronic pain often began with such general queries as, "Can you just tell me a little about yourself, what you used to do, that sort of thing?" Often such an inquiry was sufficient to obtain a very extended life history. Admittedly, some seniors were more restrained. In this situation, it was sometimes useful to move from the general life history interview to the specific episodic interview.

Episodic Interviews

The episodic interview is more focused than the life-course interview (Flick, 2002). The interviewer has a structured series of topics that she or he introduces. However, unlike the standard interview that is structured on a more abstract level, the episodic interview seeks detailed narrative accounts about the participant's experiences with these topics. The role of the interviewers is to emphasize to the participants that they would like them to expand on their personal experiences. In many ways the episodic interview sets out to deliberately challenge the attitude–scale questionnaire format that has pervaded contemporary society's idea of social research. The aim is not to get the participants to rate their views about the topic on a five-point scale but rather to give extended narrative accounts about their experience with each of the topics.

In the chronic pain study each of the participants was asked to provide an extended account of his or her experience of having pain. That section of the interview provided an episodic narrative that could be analyzed in itself or as part of the larger life history of each participant. Analyzing these pain narratives provided important information on how the participants constructed their experiences of pain. When this was integrated into the broader life narratives it provided an opportunity to explore the broader social and personal context within which the pain narratives were constructed.

Constructing Coherence

In collecting personal narratives we need to be aware that the very interview process may encourage a certain structure for those accounts. In particular, it may encourage a certain narrative coherence. Hollway (1989) has argued, "Participants usually strive for coherence in the narratives they produce (for research as for other purposes). This is one effect on subjectivity of the dominant Western assumption of the unitary rational subject" (p. 43). Similarly, Becker (1997) has asserted that a central belief in Western society is that our lives have a form of linearity. In telling our stories we are expected to convey that linearity. Difficulty in creating a coherent or linear story may be a central challenge inhibiting some participants from providing an extended narrative account.

Squire (2000) in her study of personal accounts of people with HIV questioned the constraints placed on an individual in a narrative life-course interview. She felt that there is a tendency in the contemporary focus on obtaining autobiographical accounts to create a false "seamlessness, homogeneity" (p. 199). In the same way, Eakin (1999) argued that autobiographies emphasize the central role of the author to the neglect of others.

One way to subvert this urge toward coherence and the centrality of the participant is to encourage the telling of a series of autobiographical stories rather than a single autobiography and to deliberately consider the role of different characters (cf. Squire, 2000). Such an approach combines the episodic with the traditional narrative life-course interview and provides for a multivocal narrative.

In the chronic pain study, the participants were encouraged to recount particular pain episodes and the role of different family members rather than giving a single pain account. In this way it was possible to explore how pain was integrated into their everyday lives.

Narrative Analysis

There are a variety of narrative analytical strategies. In other chapters of this book discourse analytical and other strategies are discussed. These can also be applied to the analysis of personal narratives. However, whereas other analytical techniques often start by breaking the narrative down into parts, narrative analysis seeks to consider the account as a whole. In this chapter we will confine ourselves to certain analytical strategies that focus on the narrative structure of personal accounts. The most important feature is the deliberate concern with the narrative structure, not with the particular themes within the narrative. In conducting a comprehensive analysis of personal accounts the researcher will look for particular themes. However, in interpreting these it is important to locate them within the particular narrative framework. It is essential that researchers read the whole interview and familiarize themselves with the various issues. Three broad approaches are considered in this chapter.

Linguistic and Literary Narrative Analyses

The standard linguistic approach to the study of narrative was that developed by Labov (1972). To highlight the narrative structure, this approach breaks the narrative down into clauses that are then categorized into six interconnected components: The *abstract* provides a summary of the narrative; the *orientation* sets the general scene; the *complicating action* contains the central details of the narrative; the *evaluation* can accompany these central details or is confined to the end; and the *coda* or *afterword* can contain a brief or more extensive reflection on the whole narrative. The central component in the narrative is the complicating action. The other components are only introduced in the more sophisticated accounts. In conducting this form of analysis the researcher reduces the transcript down to what is termed the "core narrative" that excludes any material considered extraneous to the story line. There may be a number of such core narratives within any extended interview. The key criterion for including material in the core is that it is a clause with some connection to the main story. Then the clauses are arranged into the six components identified. This approach enables the researcher to grasp not only the action core of the narrative account but also the interpretive orientation the participant adopts and the issues that the participant chooses to emphasize and to ignore.

Extensions of this approach are those narrative analytical techniques that borrow from literary criticism. The *genre* approach attempts to identify the broad type of the narrative. The literary model developed by Frye (1957) can be considered the archetype of this approach. From an extensive review of Western literature Frye argued that there are four main forms: *comedy, romance, tragedy,* and *satire.* More contemporary critics have extended this classification scheme. For example, Plummer (1995) has described the basic plots of the modernist tale as being (a) taking a journey, (b) engaging in a contest, (c) enduring suffering, (d) pursuing consummation, and (e) establishing a home. He suggested that the common elements in these stories are (a) suffering that gives tension to the stories, (b) a crisis or turning point or epiphany, and (c) a transformation. Different plots can jostle with each other in a single narrative and in many narratives certain elements are not apparent. In the example of the senior with chronic phantom pain, the common element was suffering. However, there was no clear evidence of an epiphany that enabled this suffering to be transformed. In many ways, it was this lack of an epiphany that defined the pain experience as suffering. Other researchers (e.g., Frank, 1995) have argued that the epiphany or turning point is the central characteristic of illness stories. It is a narrative means of transforming illness or any personal crisis from something that is threatening into something that is routine or even enhancing.

Gee (1991) has suggested that another literary approach is to consider the poetic structure of narrative accounts. Many contemporary poets are averse to using a narrative plot in verse but Gee has suggested that verse is often implicit in narrative accounts. Using this analytical framework the researcher must be aware of some of the basic poetic strategies used that may implicitly organize the narrative account. The researcher needs to be aware of the rhythm of the narrative that confers stress on certain experiences and also makes connections with more established narratives. For example, does the narrator use a repetitive refrain to emphasize certain experiences or to connect with broader societal narratives? In the chronic pain study considered, the elderly man repeatedly used the phrase "So I . . ." to give his stories momentum and a ballad-like form—for example, "So I went on to Montreal . . . ," "So I went ashore . . . ," and "So two years of that and. . . . " This poetic form of analysis allows the researcher to connect the narrative account to the broader cultural tradition—in this case the popular country and western ballad tradition that highlights the role of suffering in everyday life.

Grounded Narrative Analysis

The inductive approach derived from grounded theory (Glaser & Strauss, 1967) can be applied to narrative analysis. Ruth and Oberg (1996) provided a sustained example of the use of this approach to their analysis of a series of life histories. They approached their analysis in a series of steps:

1. Prepare a summary of each life history.
2. Identify the most "startling" case and a contrast case. In their case they identified two linear stories—one of happiness that they labeled "the sweet life" and one of misery that they labeled "the bitter life."
3. Identify other distinct cases. In their study they identified two discontinuous lives that they labeled "life as a trapping pit" and "life as a hurdle race."
4. Continue reviewing cases and identify remaining types. In their study they identified two gender-specific types, which they labeled "the devoted, silenced life" and "the life as a career."
5. Organize each life history into these story categories and then begin to consider in detail the content of each.

This approach can be useful in providing a descriptive account of the different life histories. Consider the example from the chronic pain study:

> *Summary*: The narrator was a 75-year-old former shopkeeper. He led a varied life in which he worked at a number of different clerical jobs in

> isolated regions. He married and had three children. His family accompanied him on his travels. After a period, he returned to his hometown and bought a small general store that he ran with his wife. In his fifties he developed diabetes and subsequently had one of his legs amputated. He was very frustrated by this impairment. Although during the interview he expressed a stoical attitude to the associated pain, afterwards he wept about how miserable his life was due to the pain.
>
> *Type of story:* The story fell into three main components: life before pain, the advent of pain and how it changed his life, reflections on life with and without pain. This story could be characterized as "a life of struggle." A contrasting story could then be identified that could typify "a life of contentedness."
>
> *Other stories:* The other pain narratives were then reviewed and other contrasting types identified.
>
> *Content of stories*: Each type of story was analysed to identify the particular features and organizing structure. The "life of struggle" was characterized by a) difficult life circumstances, b) limited respect for authority, c) hard work, d) self-sufficiency. (Murray, LeFort, & Ribiero, 2002)

Although this inductive approach provides an excellent descriptive account of narratives, it does not deliberately connect with the theoretical assumptions that guide the analyst. An alternative, more interactive grounded approach is to begin by being explicit about the particular theoretical approach favored and exploring how this provides additional insight into how the narrative is constructed. An example is the work of Hollway and Jefferson (2000), who used psychoanalysis as an interpretive frame for their study of crime narratives. According to their framework the narrative accounts people produce are conditioned by certain unconscious defenses against anxiety. In the chronic pain study, one central anxiety of the senior who had his leg amputated was the fear of being reduced to immobility and the implications of this for his identity. Throughout his life he had been active but now that he was disabled and in constant pain, his whole identity was threatened and he felt unable to act to change it. All his family had been active—for example, "Grandfather stopped working when he was 84, going to sea in his own boat, and mother was 90 and I got an aunt in Montreal who just celebrated her 106th birthday." Now his sense of family and personal identity was being threatened and he felt uncomfortable. This dynamic form of analysis could be pursued to explore other fears that influence the structure of the narrative account. Other theoretical frameworks could also be used depending on their ability to provide insight into how people construct their narrative accounts.

Social Context and Narrative Analysis

Because all narratives are socially constructed it is important that the narrative analyst consider the interpersonal and social context. Mishler (1997) has persistently argued for the necessity of understanding the interpersonal context within which narrative accounts are constructed. As an example he contrasted two doctor–patient interviews. The first he termed "a facilitated story" that was punctuated with periods of silence; when the patient speaks the doctor does not interrupt. Conversely, in "an interrupted story" the doctor deliberately directs the patients to focus on detailing their symptomatology. This process of encouragement through silence and direction through detailed questioning is also at work in the research interview. It is necessary to consider not just what the participant said in the interview but also what the researcher said. In transcribing the accounts it is important to give as much detail as possible of the conversation both in terms of words, paralinguisitics, and silences. The researcher can also return to the interview tapes to clarify issues of emphasis.

In the chronic pain study (Murray et al., 2002) it was important to be aware that the life story was told to a young female interviewer. The senior emphasized throughout that he had always led a vigorous, independent life. His description of his leg amputation was brief and matter-of-fact:

> Dr. Jones tried to save it and everything else. After about six months he decided it would have to come off. There was no way in getting it any better. So it came off about six years ago. But to get back to closing the store, etc. etc.

Throughout the interview he emphasized his vitality, his fortitude and courage in managing the pain. However, when the tape recorder was switched off his tone changed rapidly. The man began to cry and to talk about how the pain had destroyed his life. The narrative of strength that he presented was one that was constructed in a particular interpersonal context and one that he felt he wanted to be recorded. However, it was an identity that was difficult to maintain. This analytical approach can provide the opportunity to explore further the dialogical approach to the construction of narrative identity (Hermans et al., 1992).

The structure of the narrative account is also bounded by the broader social context. As Flick (2002) has emphasized,

> In their concrete shaping, they [narratives] draw upon basic cultural narratives and life histories offered by the culture. The goal of analyzing narrative data is more to disclose these constructive processes and less to reconstruct factual processes. (p. 202)

In interpreting personal narrative accounts we can connect them with the broader social narratives. For example, in her study of the narratives about neurasthenia (nervous exhaustion) of people from the former Soviet republic of Latvia, Skultans (1997) deliberately connected them with the broader social–political context. The participants' narratives of illness were interwoven with a challenge to the dominant political narrative—for example, "I feel that I'm being strangled" (p. 15).

In the chronic pain study (Murray et al., 2002) one of the major issues was the (lack of) connection with broader religious narratives. For some of the seniors these religious narratives pervaded their lives and could provide a coherent explanation of their crisis. However, for the individual previously described, this was not the case. At one point the elderly man said, "I lost all that when I went up North. With the priest, ministers and the holy rollers and all the rest of it there. I lost all faith in their actions." Without this belief in the transformative value of suffering that is a central component of many religions, his pain had no meaning. Instead, he felt lost and confused. This more social analysis enables the researcher to explore the wider social norms that shape our narratives.

These three broad approaches to narrative analysis (cf. Murray, 2000) can each contribute particular insight. The approach used depends on both the narrative and the researcher. There is an ongoing engagement between the researcher and the narrative account to explore which approach provides the best insight. In his commentary on textual analysis Ricoeur (1991a) used the analogy of play. The researcher plays with the interview data and through this engagement explores the value of particular interpretive frames for the analysis. Such advice can be valuable in guiding narrative analysis.

Challenging Narrative Coherence

In this chapter we began by emphasizing that a pervasive feature of narratives is the quest for coherence. However, in the late modern era we are somewhat more skeptical of singular coherence. In the same way, research reports can explore conflicting narrative interpretations. In addition, this awareness of multiple interpretations provides a means of challenging dominant narratives. Narrative research not only explores the social construction of identity and of reality, it also offers a framework for promoting personal and social change.

Although narrative therapy provides a means of challenging inadequate personal narratives, connecting with participant action research provides a strategy to challenge repressive social narratives. Awareness of their role can provide the researcher with the opportunity to question restrictive narratives and to promote more emancipatory ones. This leads away from the traditional value neutrality of the more positivist psychology and enables narrative researchers to adopt a more activist stance. For example, Lykes (1997) has discussed how she engaged Mayan women and children in Guatemala who had suffered sustained political oppression in developing a new story of their lives. Through ongoing group discussion the survivors began to break from their previous silence and to develop a new, shared narrative of strength and resistance.

In her work Lykes (1997) conducted workshop sessions with terror survivors in Guatemala. She wrote,

> In this co-created group space, creativity is a resource for developing the possibility of modifying one's relations, re-establishing previously destroyed social ties, symbolizing one's experiences of the terror that one has lived, recuperating or reconstructing one's story, and searching for one's truth. (p. 730)

As a group the survivors became aware of the distortions in their personal narratives and began to collectively develop a new, more combative narrative. The new stories transformed them from victims into survivors (cf. Greenspan,

1998). This more activist form of research has substantial implications for the researcher as well as for the research participants.

Conclusion

Narrative psychology provides a dynamic approach to understanding human identity and the process of making sense of our ever-changing world. Our personal and social identity is shaped around the stories we tell ourselves and tell each other about our lives. Through detailed analyses of these narratives we can begin to understand our changing identities and our ways of interpreting the world. Narrative psychology provides not only a framework for understanding but also for challenging the nature of ourselves and of our worlds.

References

Allport, G. W. (1942). *The use of personal accounts in psychological research.* New York: Social Science Research Council.

Allport, G. W., Bruner, J., & Jandorf, E. (1941). Personality under social catastrophe: An analysis of 90 German refugee life histories. *Character and Personality, 10,* 1–22.

Amis, M. (2000). *Experience.* London: Jonathan Cape.

Becker, G. (1997). *Disrupted lives: How people create meaning in a chaotic world.* Berkeley: University of California Press.

Bruner, J. (1986). *Actual minds, possible worlds.* Cambridge, MA: Harvard University Press.

Bruner, J. (1990). *Acts of meaning.* Cambridge, MA: Harvard University Press.

Carson, C. (1999). *Fishing for amber: A long story.* London: Granta Books.

Chandler, M. (1990). *A healing art: Regeneration through autobiography.* New York: Garland Press.

Eakin, P. J. (1999). *How our lives become stories: Making selves.* Ithaca, NY: Cornell University Press.

Farr, R. M. (1983). Wilhelm Wundt (1832–1920) and the origins of psychology as an experimental and social science. *British Journal of Social Psychology, 22,* 289–301.

Flick, U. (2002). *An introduction to qualitative research* (2nd ed.). London: Sage.

Foucault, M. (1980). *Power/knowledge: Selected interviews and other writings.* Brighton, UK: Harvester Press.

Frank, A. W. (1995). *The wounded storyteller: Body, illness and ethics.* Chicago: University of Chicago Press.

Freeman, M. (1997). Death, narrative integrity, and the radical challenge of self-understanding: A reading of Tolstoy's *Death of Ivan Ilych. Ageing and Society, 17,* 373–398.

Fremont, H. (1999). *After long silence.* New York: Delta.

Freud, S. (1937). Constructions in analysis. In *Standard edition of the complete psychological works of Sigmund Freud, Vol. 23* (pp. 237–269). London: Hogarth Press.

Frye, N. (1957). *Anatomy of criticism.* Princeton, NJ: Princeton University Press.

Gee, J. P. (1991). A linguistic approach to narrative. *Journal of Narrative and Life History, 1,* 15–39.

Gergen, K. (1991). *The saturated self: Dilemmas of identity in contemporary life.* New York: Basic.

Gergen, K. J., & Gergen, M. M. (1986). Narrative form and the construction of psychological science. In T. Sarbin (Ed.), *Narrative psychology: The storied nature of human conduct* (22–44). New York: Praeger.

Glaser, B. G., & Strauss, A. L. (1967). *The discovery of grounded theory; Strategies for qualitative research.* Mill Valley, CA: Sociology Press.

Greenspan, H. (1998). *Listening to Holocaust survivors: Recounting and life history.* Westport, CT: Praeger.

Halbwachs, M. (1992). *On collective memory* (Ed. and Trans., L. A. Coser). Chicago: University of Chicago Press. (Original published 1952)

Hermans, H. J. M., Kempen, H. J. G., & van Loon, R. J. P. (1992). The dialogical self: Beyond individualism and rationalism. *American Psychologist, 47,* 28.

Hollway, W. (1989). *Subjectivity and method in psychology: Gender, meaning and science.* London: Sage.

Hollway, W., & Jefferson, T. (2000). *Doing qualitative research differently: Free association, narrative and the interview method.* London: Sage.

Labov, W. (1972). The transformation of experience in narrative syntax. In W. Labov (Ed.), *Language in the inner city: Studies in the Black English vernacular.* Philadelphia: University of Pennsylvania Press.

LaCapra, D. (2000). Book review of L. L. Langer's (1998) Preempting the Holocaust. *Holocaust and Genocide Studies, 14,* 102–105.

Langer, L. L. (1991). *Holocaust testimonies: The ruins of memory.* New Haven, CT: Yale University Press.

Langer, L. L. (1998). *Preempting the Holocaust.* New Haven, CT: Yale University Press.

Lykes, M. B. (1997). Activist participatory research among the Maya of Guatemala: Constructing meanings from situated knowledge. *Journal of Social Issues, 53,* 725–746.

McAdams, D. P. (1985). *Power, intimacy and the life story: Personological inquiries and identity.* New York: Dorsey.

Mishler, E. G. (1986). *Research interviewing: Context and narrative.* Cambridge, MA: Harvard University Press.

Mishler, E. G. (1997). Narrative accounts in clinical and research interviews. In B.-L. Gunnarrson, P. Linell, & B. Nordberg (Eds.), *The construction of professional discourse* (pp. 68–81). London: Longman.

Morawski, J. (1997). The science behind feminist research methods. *Journal of Social Issues, 53,* 667–681.

Murray, M. (1997). A narrative approach to health psychology: Background and potential. *Journal of Health Psychology, 2,* 9–20.

Murray, M. (2000). Levels of narrative analysis in health psychology. *Journal of Health Psychology, 5,* 337–348.

Murray, M., LeFort, S., & Ribiero, V. (2002). *Seniors' narrative accounts of chronic pain.* Unpublished data.

Nash, C. (Ed.). (1990). *Narrative in culture: The uses of storytelling in the sciences, philosophy, and literature.* London: Routledge.

Plummer, K. (1995). *Telling sexual stories: Power and change and social worlds.* London: Routledge.

Polkinghorne, D. E. (1988). *Narrative knowing and the human sciences.* Albany: SUNY Press.

Richardson, B. (2000). Recent concepts of narrative and narratives of narrative theory. *Style, 34,* 168–175.

Ricoeur, P. (1989). *Time and narrative (Vol. 3).* (K. Blaney & D. Pellauer, Trans.). Chicago: University of Chicago Press.

Ricoeur, P. (1991a). Life: A story in search of a narrator. In M. J. Valdes (Ed.), *A Ricoeur reader: Reflection and imagination* (pp. 425–437). Toronto: University of Toronto Press.

Ricoeur, P. (1991b). Mimesis and representation. In M. J. Valdes (Ed.), *A Ricoeur reader: Reflection and imagination* (pp. 137–155). Toronto: University of Toronto Press.

Ricoeur, P. (1997). A response by Paul Ricoeur. In M. Joy (Ed.), *Paul Ricoeur and narrative: Context and contestation* (pp. xxxiv–xliv). Calgary, Canada: University of Calgary Press.

Ruth, J.-E., & Oberg, P. (1996). Ways of life; Old age in a life history perspective. In J. E. Birren, G. M. Kenyon, J.-E. Ruth, J. J. F. Schroots, & T. Svensson (Eds.), *Aging and biography: Explorations in adult development* (pp. 167–186). New York: Springer.

Sarbin, T. (1986). The narrative as a root metaphor for psychology. In T. Sarbin (Ed.), *Narrative psychology: The storied nature of human conduct* (3–21). New York: Praeger.

Sarbin, T. (1990). The narrative quality of action. *Theoretical and Philosophical Psychology, 10,* 49–65.

Skultans, V. (1997). A historical disorder: Neurasthenia and the testimony of lives in Latvia. *Anthropology & Medicine, 4,* 7–24.

Squire, C. (2000). Situated selves, the coming-out genre and equivalent citizenship in narratives of HIV. In P. Chamberlayne, J. Bornat, & T. Wengraf (Eds.), *The turn to biographical methods in social science: Comparative issues and examples* (pp. 196–213). London: Routledge.

White, H. (1978). Tropics of discourse: Essays in cultural criticism. Baltimore: Johns Hopkins University Press.

White, M., & Epston, D. (1990). *Narrative means to therapeutic ends.* New York: Norton.

7

Video Methods in Qualitative Research

Donald Ratcliff

An increasing number of qualitative research studies make use of video data in the form of videotape, videodisks, recordable DVDs, and other visual media. Video is useful in a wide variety of contexts for many different purposes. The use of video involves recording and playing back visual and audio components of events, contexts, and interviews, which are the staples of any qualitative study. Because video can transfer this information in a fairly direct manner for later study and analysis, the quality and detail of virtually any research study can potentially be improved by the use of video.

The general area of visual research, of which video is a part, has generated a considerable degree of interest in recent years (Bauer & Gaskell, 2000; Emmison & Smith, 2000; Pink, 2001; Rose, 2000). Although these resources, and others like them, give little focused attention to video methods—at most one chapter—a number of educational psychology studies, that are at least partially qualitative in nature, made use of video data. Examples include a study of latent components in academic counseling (Erickson & Schultz, 1982), rough and tumble play on the playground (Humphreys & Smith, 1987), gender and dominance hierarchies (Charlesworth & Dzur, 1987), and cognitive processes in teaching (Leinhardt, 1989). Psychologists also used video to study counseling sessions, reactions of newborn babies to adult speech (Condon & Sander, 1974), and interpersonal behavior change related to self-observation on video (Shotter, 1983). The wide variety of purposes, advantages, and limitations of video research have been considered in detail elsewhere (Ratcliff, 1996).

Collecting Qualitative Video Data

At the most basic level, qualitative video is created by setting up a camera and recording what happens. However, there are dozens of choices to be made each time video recording occurs. It is important to reflect on the decisions to be made and the likely consequences before recording video data. Although the notion of video being a "mirror with a memory" (Collier & Collier, 1986, p. 7) may overlook the limitations of the camera's perspective both in delimiting what is photographed, when, and from what perspective, perhaps the metaphor can be maintained if it is admitted that the mirror only reflects a part of a phenomenon, and the reflection can be foggy because of the limitations of the medium of video and because of the shortcomings of researchers who aim the cameras and interpret the data.

One area of disagreement among video researchers is whether the camera should be used to reflect a more etic—distanced outsider—view of a social context, or a more emic—insider participant—perspective. Margaret Mead (1995) believed that filmmakers often impose their perspectives on those studied, and thus she advocated that participants be included in the planning and editing of films, reflecting a concern for the emic. Yet Mead also advocated scientific objectivity—the etic view—recommending that the camera remain in one place and "become part of the background scene" (1995, p. 9), a perspective that Erickson (1992) believes is particularly important during the early phases of a study.

Collier and Collier (1986) took the emic a step further by suggesting that participants occasionally run the camera, while MacDougall (1995) advocated short segments of recording, panning, and close-ups to achieve emic "participating cinema." An alternative is to use multiple cameras, although Jackson (1987) reported that his experience in attempting this was a "nightmare." However, Beresin (1993) found that two cameras worked well when one was obvious (on a playground) and the other semihidden (pointed at the playground from a second story window). Another alternative is for a second person to run the camera, relying on cues from the researcher who participates in the activities being filmed (Corsaro, 1985). In my own research, I generally used one camera, although I sometimes had a female assistant do some of the photography to determine if gender influenced the children's behavior (no significant differences were discovered). On one occasion I had my assistant, using a second camera, covertly film children's reactions to the presence of my camera. I found that the reactive influences observed in this manner could just as easily be seen by using a wide angle lens on a single camera.

Another important issue is whether a tripod is a help or a hindrance. Tripods can keep the image from shaking, which results from tiny hand movements that are exaggerated when using a zoom lens (Jackson, 1987). However a large camera on a substantial tripod can be intimidating, as reflected in Andre Bazin's description:

> a sort of god . . . just like a heathen altar . . . [the researcher and camera operator become] high priests . . . who bring victims before the camera, like burnt offerings, and cast them into the flames. And the camera is there, immobile—or almost so—and when it does move it follows the patterns ordained by the high priests, not the victims. (quoted in Segall, 1990, p. 77)

In contrast, Segall (pp. 79–80) used an "affectionate style of shooting" in which extreme close-ups were photographed from her lap, with the camera pointing toward the center of activity. Yet Segall admits that occasionally she panned the room with a wide-angle lens, as might be done with a tripod. I used a tripod for some of my camera work, but often found it to be as much of a hindrance as a help because it was too lightweight to completely smooth the panning. After several weeks of stationary camera placement, I began to carry around the rather large camera and zoom in on events that had emerged as significant in my study. I found this approach was more obtrusive and produced an image that wobbled more than the stationary placement, although I could decrease these difficulties by holding the camera against the wall for stability and keeping a greater distance from filmed activities, which was offset by the use of the telephoto lens.

Reactivity is often a problem in video recordings. I found that children made faces, grinned, used exaggerated movements, made obscene gestures, and even enacted drama for the camera. Although this was most obvious in the early weeks of the study, some reactive effects were noted throughout the duration of the four-month study. However, I found that I could document that reactivity by using a wide-angle lens: More typical activities occurred at the periphery of the screen, then when children entered the area they thought was being pictured they would act in a reactive manner, then return to normal behavior when they thought they were out of the visual field. Similar results were found when a second hidden camera was used to document reactivity. However, reactivity tends to become less likely as the camera becomes a taken-for-granted aspect of the environment and if the camera operator is skilled (LeCompte & Preissle, 1993).

McCarty (1995) argued that early reactive effects to the camera may reflect important personality traits and humor of participants, whereas other researchers advocate the use of one-way mirrors and other blinds to hide the presence of the camera. (Corsaro, 1985; Dowrick, 1991). In contrast, Erickson (1992) found that when trust is developed and participants agree with the reasons for the research, a video camera is no more intrusive than taking field notes.

Sampling decisions in video recording not only involve the question of time but also location and placement of the camera. The degree of zooming the lens might also be considered a sampling issue. Although commercial videos tend to have very brief shots from a wide variety of positions, this may not make for useful research video. Sustained views of an event may permit more detailed analysis later; what may seem boring when being recorded may become invaluable when viewed in slow motion during analysis. For example, some events that may seem repetitive may indeed have minor variations that can only be seen by carefully studying the video. Jackson (1987) recommended that the position of the camera only be changed when there is good reason to do so, although I changed the camera position every hour to study the reactive effects of different placements as well as examine the differences in activities in various areas of the school hallway I studied. I found the highest amount of activity and greatest diversity of activity was in an area near drinking fountains and restrooms of the school, and thus later in the study I did most of my filming near that location.

The position of the camera may make significant differences in the quality of data obtained because of lighting effects that may not be obvious to the naked eye. For example, when recording people standing in front of a window, the light from outdoors can cause the camera lens to close and thus the participants will be underexposed. Many cameras have a "back light" option that may compensate for this to some degree, but even the compensation is a crude general estimate and it may not improve the quality of the view sufficiently.

When recording an interview, there is the additional concern of what position will capture the greatest amount of information. For example, if the camera is pointed toward the participant, the facial reactions of the researcher will probably be excluded, even though this may be an important influence deserving study. Two cameras being combined using a split screen device is a possible solution, although two camera operators may be needed to get details of facial expressions. I tried using a camera that photographed interviews from the side of both the participants and myself, a reasonably good compromise, yet I know that a considerable amount of information was lost in the process.

It is important to log information about the site and the events recorded. Important details to include in this log include the date, time, camera location, participants involved, camera operator, contextual detail, key events, time and length of events, and personal reactions (Jackson, 1987). A related issue that should be considered is whether to set the camera to record the time on the video. I found this to be a useful indexing device, although most cameras at present do not index individual frames, a feature that would be very helpful during analysis. Logging can become so detailed that it can essentially constitute another set of field notes (Erickson & Mohatt, 1982). Logging and field notes constitute an audit trail that can be examined by outsiders or participants to determine strengths and weaknesses in the research process, and thus be a means of establishing validity (Lincoln & Guba, 1985).

These are key issues that need to be considered in the creation of video for qualitative research work. There are also additional issues to consider that are too numerous for inclusion. As part of my research of the school hallway and playground, I tracked hundreds of decisions related to audio and video recording and their effects on the resulting data. Many of these, as well as related comments by other researchers, have been considered in detail elsewhere (Ratcliff, 1996).

Data Analysis and Interpretation

Once video data are created, analysis is required to make the information meaningful. In many qualitative research studies, data collection and analysis is an ongoing, iterative process throughout the study, as analysis provides direction for data collection. This is equally possible when using video data, although the analysis of video may take longer than might the analysis of field notes or audio information alone. This is because video contains an incredible amount of information; one can spend hours describing a 10-minute segment of video if the goal is to include as much detail as possible. For example, an exhaustive account of the colors, textures, shapes, and sizes of contextual detail, in addition to the identification and description of participants' physical characteristics, speech, gestures, gaze, patterns of movement, and other activities (Beresin, 1993) may require several pages of description for even a few seconds of video. Exhaustive video description of a single two-hour video can be a Herculean task (Lancy, 1993). Regardless, it is probably worthwhile to scan a segment of video several times to determine the major structural units that will focus the transcription (Kendon, 1979).

Is Transcription Needed?

In light of the time-consuming nature of complete descriptions, the researcher is confronted with two realistic alternatives: a partial, focused transcription, or no transcription. Focused transcription requires that the researcher either begin broadly and "funnel down" to specifics, or conversely that the transcription be theory-driven. Although the topic of a given study might be thought to delimit the amount of relevant information requiring transcription, it is difficult to predict what additional factors in the video may in some way be related to the topic; discovering these factors and the interrelationships between them may in fact be one of the purposes of using qualitative methods (LeCompte & Preissle, 1993).

An alternative to transcription is to analyze video data directly. One can think of video data as being text, and the methods of analysis used with text can be directly applied to the video data. Qualitative computer programs are capable of video interfacing for the purposes of coding, comparison, and linking video segments to one another, as well as linking video to text, audio, and other visual data. A researcher may also manually code segments of video using either paper or a computer if a time counter is embedded in the video during the recording phase, although this is less functional if the counter does not include seconds or when two screens—one for the computer and one for the video monitor—are required. As qualitative computer programs evolve to greater sophistication, DVD recorders extend memory capacities and provide faster retrieval and computer hardware for interfacing video data improve, entire video data sets may be quickly and seamlessly analyzed with user-friendly programs.

One or Several Sites? One or Several Purposes?

Early qualitative research tended to emphasize a single site to be described and analyzed thoroughly. However, multiple site studies have become more common not only because of the greater potential of determining more continuities and distinctives, but also because of concern for generalizing results. Schaeffer (1995), for example, studied communication between family members in several New York City houses. Initial "mapping" of the environment involved photographing the households to determine the best placement for video cameras. Cameras were connected to monitors in a nearby studio. The researchers noted that family members, particularly the children, became less and less conscious of the cameras over time. Log entries of family activities and participants in events was made for each 3-minute period. Near the end of the study, movie cameras were substituted for the video cameras so that greater clarity could be obtained.

A particularly interesting aspect of this study is that the data were analyzed for several different purposes. In the initial analysis, child-rearing practices of Puerto Ricans were studied by comparing the comments of parents with the actual practices observed in their homes. In a subsequent analysis, patterns of dominance in households were assessed. A third analysis of the data considered behavior associated with food consumption, particularly related control and authority patterns related to household foods. A fourth topic was nonverbal behavior that reflected authority and dominance patterns, as seen in initiating activities, controlling objects, and physically displacing other family members. Another analysis examined the touches between family members, particularly the affection displayed between husbands and wives and between parents and children. An additional topic for analysis was that of cultural norms related to proxemic territoriality and the minute analysis of related body movements.

The question of whether to film one or more sites, and whether one or multiple purposes are considered, are issues that relate to time and personnel available. Often a choice must be made between studying one topic at several locations or one location with several topics. But as the trend toward multiple researchers increases, this may become less of an issue. The ideal, of course, is to let the emerging data inform these decisions. In most cases, the practical scope of the study will be influenced by the nature of the initial purpose and questions that direct the research.

One or More Analysts?

The Schaeffer study (1995) is a good example of multiple analysts being involved in a study. Several of these studies involved ethnography students at Columbia University who learned how to conduct analysis using actual data, while simultaneously producing results that were later published.

The potential for multiple observers viewing the same data, as well as the opportunity to review segments repeatedly, can be a means of establishing reliability of descriptions and constructs (Lancy, 1993), although this possibility has rarely been considered by researchers (Kirk & Miller, 1986). Multiple observers, as well as multiple data sets, also permit triangulation, which is an important means of establishing validity in qualitative research (Mehan, 1979). Because video images are direct and mechanistic reflections of reality (Ball & Smith, 1992), they may be more credible and believable than observation alone because of the assumption that "pictures do not lie." Credibility is the bottom line in establishing a degree of qualitative validity, and multiple analysts increase credibility.

Participants as Analysts? Individuals or Groups of Participants?

Despite the value of the technology of video and computer programs, however, the most important qualitative analytical tools are the human eyes and brain (Jackson, 1987); video can only assist the researcher. Video analysis is a complex task because it involves abstracting and creating new knowledge (Collier

& Collier, 1986). However, the researcher need not accomplish the task alone; analysis can be a cooperative effort of both the researcher and participants, as qualitative inquiry attempts to discover *meanings* of activities and contexts to participants. Participants are educators who teach the researcher their perspectives (Collier & Collier). Participants can view segments of videos, and in the process offer their understandings of what is portrayed. It is also possible to include outsiders, who bring with them different experiences and thus a wider variety of interpretations. Teams of participants, researchers, and outsiders can interact with one another as they observe video, producing a higher level of analysis than one person in isolation (Collier & Collier). However, fine-grained examination of video by multiple analysts can be costly (Lancy, 1993), time-consuming (Collier & Collier), and be undermined either by conformity influences or by friction between group members.

In my own research with children, I showed school hallway videos to small groups of three to six upper elementary-level children and asked them to describe events and the meanings of the events portrayed. These self-selected groups—formed by using snowball sampling (LeCompte & Preissle, 1993)—readily talked about events as they watched, but comments tended to center on identifying the children in the video rather than describing meanings of events. After the video ended, however, they were able to go into greater detail about what was observed, as one child's comments often prompted reactions and detail from other youngsters in the group. However, it was not until the second or third half-hour interview with additional videos that I heard children begin to unfold some of the *meanings* of events in the videos and their own corollary experiences. Near the end of the study when I interviewed children individually, I found they provided more details about personal meanings of events. Perhaps this was a function of having previously interviewed them in group settings, but my impression from reading the literature as well as other interviews I have conducted is that children—if comfortable with the interviewer—are more likely to discuss meanings at a deeper level in the one-to-one context, but it is at the expense of greater detail in the descriptions of events provided by children in groups of peers.

Separate or Simultaneous Analysis?

There is disagreement on whether the audio track and the video information should be analyzed separately or simultaneously. Collier and Collier (1986) emphasized the unity of the analysis and thus argued that both forms of data should be analyzed at the same time. In contrast, Mehan (1982) analyzed the audio track for three components of classroom communication—initiation, reply, and evaluation—then analyzed the video for visual cues in classroom communication, such as children raising their hands. Similarly Erickson and Schultz (1982) examined kinesic and other nonverbal components of communication using video data, then used "voice print analysis" to analyze the audio track. My own experience suggests that there may be value in separate analysis when followed up by simultaneous observation and listening, but I suspect that the specific topic of a given research study may determine the best approach. This may be an issue that may require some trial and error, particularly in the early phases of analysis.

Constant Comparison and Analytic Induction

Although it is possible to use preexisting categories of behavior and impose them on video data, qualitative research historically has emphasized the emergence and description of categories inherent to the research context. Indeed, this is considered one of the key values of qualitative research; the intention to set aside assumptions about what is important in a given setting, and to be open and experience the fluid wholeness of the video record (Collier & Collier, 1986).

Constant comparison, sometimes termed "grounded theory," is a qualitative analysis procedure that involves coding data, developing categories from codes, which are then further abstracted into "axial categories," and finally the "core category" to which all other categories are related. Chapter 8 of this volume describes constant comparison in detail, and video adaptation of this method is detailed elsewhere (Ratcliff, 1996).

In my research of children in a school hallway, I used the initial phases of constant comparison to generate categories. Although I could have used video data to determine axial categories, early observations without the camera highlighted three social formations of children: phalanxes (children walking side-by-side), clusters (stationary groups of children, usually in the form of a circle or semicircle), and school lines. Later in the research, detailed components of these three axial categories were examined in detail by sampling the video data. The videos became an "elicitation" approach (Collier & Collier, 1986), as children responded to videos during these interviews. Although in a sense the idea of "social formations," which encompasses all three kinds of groupings, could be considered a core category, I did not want to prematurely foreclose the data from other kinds of analysis for additional constructs and understandings. At one point, my own children helped me sort categories and subcategories of hallway activities; I felt they might reflect children's perspectives, similar to those I studied, because of their age.

Znaniecki (1934) formalized a procedure of data analysis that can also be adapted to video data analysis. Curiously, this method is often included as an *aspect* of qualitative analysis, whereas at other times it is treated as a separate *method* of qualitative analysis. Stranger yet, the originator of the method only used it in analyzing *quantitative* data. "Analytic induction" involves the development of a hypothesis from observing specific events and, as additional examples of those events are examined, the hypothesis is tested and compared with alternative explanations. The hypothesis is then reformulated, and again tested with more examples observed at the research site. By regularly revising the hypothesis, it eventually fits all of the observed examples, and it approaches the status of a "law" of behavior.

Later advocates of Znaniecki's approach avoided the designation "law" and emphasized the search for exceptions as central to the hypothesis reformulation process (e.g., Robinson, 1951). The goal of the testing and reformulation of the hypothesis is an explanation that is comprehensive, and thus is isomorphic to the data. Znaniecki's work, and later development of the analytic induction approach to qualitative data analysis, is explored in detail elsewhere (Ratcliff, 1994), as is the adaptation of this approach to qualitative video research (Mehan, 1979, 1982, Ratcliff, 1996).

Microanalysis

An approach somewhat similar to constitutive ethnography is Erickson's (1992) "microanalysis," which is probably the most commonly used method of qualitative analysis specific to video data. Microanalysis emphasizes the *how* of human interaction rather than the *what.* Erickson has argued that this method should only be used when other methods fail to produce needed details. Like Mehan, Erickson links his procedure with analytic induction, emphasizing that an event or behavior is described, measured, or tracked in detail by repeated examination of sequences. By noting key contrasts between recurring events, as well as commonalties and distinctives of unique or rare events, the researcher determines how well conclusions generalize within the immediate context and then across different contexts.

The initial analysis begins while collecting video data, as the choice of what people or events to record is itself an analytical decision. However, the majority of the analysis takes place subsequent to recording (Erickson, 1992). Erickson outlined five steps in the analysis of video data.

During the first stage of analysis, the researcher examines an entire sequence without pausing or using slow motion. Field notes are written while watching the video, emphasizing the whole of the event, much as would be done in a standard field setting.

The second stage involves the identification of major boundaries between events by locating major shifts in activity and then playing and replaying the video recording—both forward and in reverse—to discover the precise frames that begin and end the event. Three phases to the event are thus highlighted: the beginning, the focus of the activity, and the conclusion that leads to the next event. Predictable changes in body language and use of space often accompany these three phases, according to Erickson.

The organization of each of the three phases in several selected tape segments makes up the third stage of the analysis. Linkages between segments of activities are located, elaborating the skeletal structure of the second stage. The researcher seeks to determine how each participant in the interaction contributes to the event, concentrating on mutual influences rather than events in isolation.

Stage four involves the transcription of statements and nonverbal communication of individual participants, guided by the analytical purposes of the research. During this phase the cultural influences on interaction become most salient.

In stage five, segments analyzed in earlier stages are compared with the remainder of the video data to determine their degree of representativeness. Other segments may be microanalyzed for comparison, and typical and nontypical events may be counted. The researcher examines the entire video record for exceptions.

Erickson illustrated the use of microanalysis in a research study comparing the interaction styles of a Native American teacher and an Anglo American teacher teaching Odawan students in Canada (Erickson & Mohatt, 1982). The styles of teaching and classroom management of the two teachers were compared to examine patterns of participation by the teacher and children. Analytical charts were created for each tape, listing events and their durations, functioning as an index for quickly locating specific events for analysis. The product included quantitative analysis in addition to qualitative description. Erickson and Mohatt found that the Odawan teacher spent more time waiting for children to finish their activities and used small groups more often than the Anglo teacher, whereas the Anglo teacher provided more time for children to play. The Anglo teacher also differentiated work time and free time to a greater degree than the Odawan teacher, and the Odawan teacher attended to the children's readiness for changing activities to a greater extent than did the Anglo teacher. Activities in the Odawan teacher's classroom were initiated slowly and smoothly but ended quickly in comparison with the Anglo teacher. The Odawan teacher made fewer movements around the room and generally interacted at a smaller distance with students, only calling out to groups rather than individuals from across the room. The Anglo teacher used more directives and stated them more quickly. The researchers concluded that the Odawan teacher's pedagogy was more congruent with the cultural principles of social organization of the tribe than was the Anglo teacher's instruction. Over the year, video analysis revealed that the Anglo teacher increasingly adapted to the local cultural norms in her teaching.

Other researchers have found microanalysis to be a very useful analytical tool for qualitative video research. Beresin (1993), for example, studied the socialization of third, fourth, and fifth grade children on a playground, emphasizing the microtransitions that framed the school day, which she considered rites of passage that marked changes in activities. She microanalyzed children's eye movements, patterns of movement, speech, gestures, and other activities, and documented components of children's folklore, such as rhymes, jokes, and other games. Beresin found that misbehavior was most likely to occur at the end of a recess period, as aggression was associated with the pressure of the limited amount of time remaining and the forced proximity of lining up to return to the school building. Later she used video segments while interviewing children, and near the end of the study made a video presentation to school teachers and the principal.

Corsaro (1985) studied preschool children using a variation of microanalysis. He outlined the emergence of peer culture in the nursery school setting by studying interactive episodes between children using a one-way mirror. Corsaro repeatedly played segments of the video, sometimes frame by frame, to discover what activities initiated and maintained interactions. His form of microanalysis revealed that friendship was established by excluding *other* children from group activities. A sense of "we-ness" between preschoolers developed from challenging adults and avoiding adult detection of shared activities. Corsaro (1982) noted that some units of behavior were more clearly boundaried than others; some events had definite beginning and ending points, whereas other interactions occurred within a continuous stream of events, as beginnings and endings were more ambiguous in the video data. When such ambiguities exist, Corsaro recommended that a unit of interaction be generated by blending various theoretical assumptions with data.

Collier and Collier (1986) suggested that microanalysis can be an optional component in a broader process of video data analysis. The more encompassing process includes (a) watching an entire video in its totality, an "immersion" that can last for weeks; (b) inventorying the video by categories or codings of activities, spaces, or other components; (c) focusing the analysis on newly discovered ideas and the original questions for the research, using microanalysis of details if needed; and (d) making conclusions by organizing the details within a contextual description. The Colliers emphasized that video can reveal the internal dynamics of activities, as similar segments of video can be viewed side by side, using slow motion—to find details—and fast scanning to find broader patterns of events. Both reverse and forward viewing can be helpful, they concluded.

Research Case Example: Hallway Rituals

Throughout this chapter I have described my own research with children in a school hallway (Ratcliff, 1995). After successfully completing this study, I continued to use the 116 hours of video data for secondary analysis related to the ritualistic behavior of children.

The research question was open-ended: "What, if any, activities in the hallway fit ritual theory?" Before the research study, I had studied Van Gennep's (1960, pp. 15–24) idea of "territorial passage" in which a person throughout most of history who wished to pass from one country to another had to cross a neutral area between national boundaries. This neutral area is a place of "wavering between two worlds." Customarily there are rituals that are performed as the person moves across the boundaries and the neutral region, the equivalent of modern day travelers going through customs. I found that the school hallway is also a place of "wavering between two worlds" that separates the *school culture* of the classroom—that emphasizes work and submission to adult authority—from the *child culture* of the playground, where child autonomy is more predominant. The hallway is sometimes predominantly school culture, as when teachers insisted on silence and moving in lines, yet at other times it was more like child culture, with exuberant play and talking.

Several years after the original study was completed, I began to examine some of the more elaborate rituals, recorded on video, when the hallway was a mixture of the two cultures. The guiding paradigm was that of postpositivist qualitative research (Seale, 1999). I did not know exactly what to anticipate, although I knew rituals—especially elaborate rituals—were the focus. Participants were not selected; anyone who was in the hallway had been videotaped. The site was originally chosen on the basis of a high degree of activity and movement, to maximize the variety and frequency of behavior, so that as many relationships and events as possible would be produced (Ratcliff, 1995). As noted earlier, the camera was positioned in a location that had the highest level of activity of the hallway—near the restrooms and drinking fountains.

The data analysis procedure chosen was microanalysis. This procedure was selected in part to demonstrate the method for this chapter, but also because it permits a wide variety of activities to be analyzed simultaneously for many possible relationships and understandings. Because only one microanalytical segment will be considered, these results are preliminary.

A video made about five weeks into my research was selected, because it was recorded after students had come to ignore the camera most of the time yet before I began recording video that specifically targeted the main topic of the study, social formations. The tape also reflected one of the more dynamic time periods of the school day, the mid-morning; afternoons were less dynamic, with a relatively constant flow of children in the hallway. Seven minutes after the tape begins a boy—probably in fourth grade—does a brief dance routine, a prime example of a spontaneous dance ritual.

For the first stage of microanalysis, I carefully examined the first 12 minutes of the video, writing field notes on the entire segment. I noted several activities that were ritualistic, such as children rubbing the walls and a boy rocking backing forth in an exaggerated manner as he walked. The video began in the midst of a transition; many children were changing classrooms, then the number of children in the hallway decreased markedly for several minutes and that part of the hallway was even empty at times. Finally, the hallway again seemed to explode with children coming out and going into several different doorways at the same time.

The second stage of microanalysis involved the assignment of event boundaries. By using the play, scan, slow motion, pause, and reverse functions several times, I was able to locate the beginning of the relatively inactive portion of time between the two transitions. The inactive segment began at 3:23—3 minutes and 23 seconds from the beginning of the tape, when the last of a large group of sixth graders walked past the camera and the end of the hallway was empty. The end of the inactive segment was at 9:47 when a teacher emerged from her classroom, followed by her entire class, which was quickly joined by several other classes entering the hallway at one time. During most of the approximately 6 minutes of this segment of video, there were no more than two or three children in the hallway at one time.

The third stage involved the examination of the segments (Erickson terms them "strips of activity") that make up the boundaried time period. Because I had noticed a rather elaborate ritual by one child in the latter half of this 6-minute period, I decided to concentrate on that segment. Seven specific strips of activity were found between 6:45 and 9:48, several that were fragmented by the individuals moving out of the sight of the camera, then returning. Strip 1a was a teacher walking from her room past the camera (6:45–7:06) and strip 1b when the teacher returned to her room (9:28–9:48). Strip 2a portrayed an African American boy who left the classroom and walked past the camera (7:10–7:26) and strip 2b when he returned after visiting the restroom/drinking fountain area (8:59–9:48). Strip 2b involved the elaborate ritual of interest. Strip 3 (7:29–7:42) pictured four boys walking by the camera who then began to run to their classroom doorways. Strip 4 (7:34–7:45) portrayed two girls who walked by the camera, one began to run, but she resumed walking when the other girl did not run. Three other strips of children's activity were also observed.

Several of these seven strips overlapped, indicating multiple trajectories and activities. Perhaps most striking was the amount of running or fast walking that is observed. Teachers were in the hallway for a few seconds at a time, but not continuously. The multiple strips constituted a hallway in transition from the silence and emptiness of the early morning, to the chaotic and overwhelming impact of several classes in the hallway at one time. The boys running (strip 3), the one girl who begins to run (strip 4), and the rapid movement of a girl in strip 5 were quite different from the leisurely stroll of a sixth grader in strip 6. One could anticipate the impending change of classes would affect all of the children photographed except the sixth grader, which was confirmed. Thus the majority of the strips of behavior suggest a time of "wavering between the two worlds," wavering between complete inactivity and bewildering class change.

The fourth stage in microanalysis examined in detail the event selected as central to the analysis, in this case the entry of the dancing child. At 7:10 the African American boy, probably a fourth grader, walked around the corner from a classroom entryway, toward the camera next to the left wall. At first he walked straight, then at 7:13 he moved into a hunched position, leaned down as if to avoid detection, and rubbed the wall intermittently as he walked. At 7:19, he resumed standing up straight and slowed down as he approached the camera. At 7:23 he moved to the middle of the hallway to get past the camera, apparently on his way to the drinking fountain or rest room, and disappeared from the screen at 7:26. At 8:59 he returned, walked around the camera, looked back into the camera, and again rubbed the wall with his hand at 9:01, then rubbed the entire side of his body against the wall at 9:02, as he continued to walk. He then began to make a first turn with his hands out like a dancer, completed the first spin midway across the hallway at 9:04. He then moved his arms up to a vertical position and raised one leg as he moved to the opposite side of the hall for a second complete 360 degree turn at 9:05. At 9:06 his arms came down, he raised his head to face the ceiling as he turned to make a third circle. As he completed the third circular movement, and lowered his head, he took one step backward, then walked forward raising his face to the ceiling at 9:07. At 9:08 he extended his right arm out to the side, as he continued walking forward. His left arm was raised some, then lowered and the right arm was raised to the ceiling in a graceful manner, followed by lowering both arms at 9:09. At 9:10 his arms resumed a more typical position, he entered the doorway of the classroom at 9:12, only to reemerge slightly as he swung around a support pole one time at 9:13, then he reentered the doorway to the classroom at 9:14, completing the elaborate ritual.

Stage five involved a comparison of the event in stage four with other similar events. The dancing boy was an example of numerous dances, of almost endless variety, observed in the hallway. Dancing could involve walking backwards or sideways, walking heel to toe, skipping, jumping, hopping, strutting with arms and body moving in rhythm with steps, and walking with books balanced on the head.[1] Dancing is a key activity of the hallway, at least when teachers are not present or nonresponsive, probably one of many expressions of children's resistance to adult-imposed rules, or alternatively expressing a desire for recognition as a dancer or musician. These conjectures relate closely to the theoretical bases of child culture and the sense of transcendence implicit in ritualistic behaviors, themes I have developed elsewhere (Ratcliff, 2000, 2001). Other aspects of stage five are addressed to some extent in creating the taxonomy of rituals in the next section of this chapter, but to use microanalysis completely, the analysis I just described would be repeated dozens, preferably hundreds of times with as many segments of video, preferably involving multiple analysts who compare their findings and work together to explore and refine emerging hypotheses and conclusions.

Extending the Analysis Into a Taxonomy of Rituals

In addition to my own secondary analysis, students at the University of Georgia and Toccoa Falls College conducted secondary qualitative analysis of my video data. Students[2] were given the option of analyzing videos or an alternative assignment for the class. The students who chose to do analysis signed a confidentiality pledge, in keeping with the original provisions of my school hallway research. They were then asked to apply a rather elastic variation of Erickson's microanalysis and analytic induction to analyze videotapes that I selected in a fairly random manner from the video corpus.

The products of this first level of analysis were then subjected to my own taxonomic analysis, which my students corrected and elaborated. Videotapes, each approximately two hours in length, were viewed by students who sought examples of ritualistic behavior by children. I described several such ritualistic activities, such as wall rubbing, jumping and hitting door frames, and dancing around poles that supported the roof of the school building. I showed my students a sample video, portraying such activities. I specifically defined a ritual as unnecessary activity that was either repeated or likely to be repeated. Each ritual observed on the tapes was to be described, with emphasis on the beginning and ending of each ritual.

After several weeks, the students met with me and listed the activities they found on their videotapes. Although most students clearly understood the concept of ritual, there was some confusion about the presence, beginnings, and endings of rituals. Using the research tapes, we located several examples and as a group attempted to identify when rituals occurred, as well as their duration. To determine if these could be consistently applied to data, I used a rough measure of interrater reliability for the length of rituals. Estimated lengths of many rituals were very inconsistent, suggesting that the definitions

[1]These variations were described by my students who viewed similar situations on several other videotapes, as described in the next section of this chapter.

[2]I wish to thank Dena Darr, Kristen Hoober, Bill Matko, Jessica Nisewonder, Jennifer Parks, Jared Ritter, and Chrissy Tackett for their significant input to my analysis.

Exhibit 7.1. Taxonomy of Hallway Rituals

I. Drinking rituals
   A. Entering to drink
      1. Like a bird (flapping arms)
      2. With hands clasped
      3. From the side of the drinking fountain, as wall is touched
   B. Drinking from the side (to monitor approaching students)
   C. Taking multiple drinks by leaving momentarily and then returning

II. Tactile rituals
   A. Wall
      1. Purposeful rubbing
      2. Touching the wall
      3. Leaning against the wall
   B. Pole (located at classroom entryways, presumably to support the building roof)
      1. Touching the pole
      2. Swinging around the pole
   C. Hit and run (touching a person with the presumed expectation of a chase)
   D. Holding hands (with another student, usually girls and usually same sex)

III. Walking/dancing rituals
   A. Jumping and touching a doorframe
   B. Shooting hoops (same as A except with hand movements used in basketball)
   C. Dancing with another child
   D. Dance walk
      1. With broadened shoulders and strutting
      2. With spasm-like movements
      3. With books on child's head
      4. While hopping on one foot
   E. Jogging, skipping, or jumping as child leaves classroom

IV. Athletic/fighting rituals
   A. Pretending to fire a gun
   B. Boxing/fake punches
   C. Pretending to fight with swords
   D. Wrestling or rough-and-tumble play

needed refinement. My students and I redefined the beginnings and endings of several such rituals and eventually gained a degree of consistency in estimates of length. A few rituals continued to produce inconsistent estimates, and thus were discarded. The remaining rituals were then made into a taxonomy (see Exhibit 7.1).

Conclusion

Video can be central to a research study by providing important data to be analyzed in detail. Video can also be used as a supplement to qualitatative research by providing visual content to which participants respond, or an audit trail for external examination. In some research studies participants can even produce video data by operating the camera. Without question, video data can be an important component to virtually any qualitative research project.

References

Ball, M. S., & Smith, G. W. H. (1992). *Analyzing visual data.* Newbury Park, CA: Sage.

Bauer, M. W., & Gaskell, G. (2000). *Qualitative researching with text, image and sound.* Thousand Oaks, CA: Sage.

Beresin, A. R. (1993). *The play of peer cultures in a city school yard.* Doctoral dissertation, University of Pennsylvania, Philadelphia. (University Microfilms No. 9331755)

Berger, M. M. (1970). *Techniques in psychiatric training and treatment.* New York: Brunner/Mazel.

Charlesworth, W. R., & Dzur, C. (1987). Gender comparison of preschoolers' behavior and resource utilization in group problem solving. *Child Development, 58,* 191–200.

Collier, J. C., & Collier, M. (1986). *Visual anthropology: Photography as a research method.* Albuquerque: University of New Mexico Press.

Condon, W. S., & Sander, L. W. (1974). Synchrony demonstrated between movements of the neonate and adult speech. *Child Development, 45,* 456–462.

Corsaro, W. (1982). Something old and something new: The importance of prior ethnography in the collection and analysis of audiovisual data. *Sociological Methods and Research, 11,* 145–166.

Corsaro, W. (1985). *Friendship and peer culture in the early years.* Norwood, NJ: Ablex.

Dowrick, P. W. (1991). *Practical guide to using video in the behavioral sciences.* New York: Wiley.

Emmison, M., & Smith, P. (2000). *Researching the visual.* Thousand Oaks, CA: Sage.

Erickson, F. (1992). The interface between ethnography and microanalysis. In M. D. LeCompte, W. L. Millroy, & J. Preissle (Eds.), *The handbook of qualitative research in education* (pp. 201–225). San Diego, CA: Academic Press.

Erickson, F., & Mohatt, G. (1982). Cultural organization of participant structures in two classrooms of Indian students. In G. Spindler (Ed.), *Doing the ethnography of schooling* (pp. 132–174). New York: Holt, Rinehart, and Winston.

Erickson, F., & Schultz, J. (1982). *The counselor as gatekeeper: Social interaction in interviews.* New York: Academic Press.

Humphries, A. P., & Smith, P. K. (1987). Rough and tumble play, friendship, and dominance in school children: Evidence for continuity and change with age. *Child Development, 58,* 201–212.

Kendon, A. (1979). Some theoretical and methodological aspects of the use of film in the study of social interaction. In G. P. Ginsburg (Ed.), *Emerging strategies in social psychological research* (pp. 67–87). New York: John Wiley and Sons.

Kirk, J., & Miller, M. L. (1986). *Reliability and validity in qualitative research.* Beverly Hills, CA: Sage.

Jackson, B. (1987). *Fieldwork.* Urbana: University of Illinois Press.

Lancy, D. F. (1993). *Qualitative research in education.* New York: Longman.

LeCompte, M. D., & Preissle, J. (1993). *Ethnography and qualitative design in educational research* (2nd ed.). San Diego, CA: Academic Press.

Leinhardt, G. (1989). Math lessons: A contrast of novice and expert competence. *Journal of Research in Mathematics Education, 20,* 52–75.

Lincoln, Y. S., & Guba, E. G. (1985). *Naturalistic inquiry.* Newbury Park, CA: Sage.

MacDougall, D. (1995). Beyond observational cinema. In P. Hockings (Ed.), *Principles of visual anthropology* (2nd ed., pp. 115–132). New York: Mouton de Gruyter.

McCarty, M. (1995). McCarty's law and how to break it. In P. Hockings (Ed.), *Principles of visual anthropology* (2nd ed., pp. 69–75). New York: Mouton de Gruyter.

Mead, M. (1995). Visual anthropology in a discipline of words. In P. Hockings (Ed.), *Principles of visual anthropology* (2nd ed., pp. 3–10). New York: Mouton de Gruyter.

Mehan, H. (1979). *Learning lessons: Social organization in the classroom.* Cambridge, MA: Harvard University Press.

Mehan, H. (1982). The structure of classroom events and their consequences for student performance. In P. Gilmore & A. A. Glatthorn (Eds.), *Children in and out of school* (pp. 59–84). Washington, DC: Center for Applied Linguistics.

Pink, S. (2001). *Doing visual ethnography.* Thousand Oaks, CA: Sage.

Ratcliff, D. (1994). *Analytic induction as a qualitative research method of analysis.* Unpublished manuscript, University of Georgia. Retrieved Sept. 4, 2002, from http://don.ratcliff.net/qual/analytic.html

Ratcliff, D. (1995). *An elementary school hallway: Social formations and meanings outside the classroom.* Doctoral dissertation, University of Georgia. (University Microfilms No. 9531229)

Ratcliff, D. (1996). *Video and audio media in qualitative research.* Retrieved Sept. 4, 2002, from http://don.ratcliff.net/video

Ratcliff, D. (2000). Peer culture and school culture theory. *Christian Education Journal, 4,* 57–76.

Ratcliff, D. E. (2001, Jan.). *Rituals in a school hallway: Evidence of a latent spirituality of children.* Paper presented at the Annual Conference on Interdisciplinary Qualitative Research, Athens, GA.

Robinson, W. S. (1951). The logical structure of analytic induction. *American Sociological Review, 16,* 812–818.

Rose, G. (2000). *Visual methodologies.* Thousand Oaks, CA: Sage.

Schaeffer, J. H. (1995). Videotape: New techniques of observation and analysis in anthropology. In P. Hockings (Ed.), *Principles of visual anthropology* (2nd ed., pp. 255–284). New York: Mouton de Gruyter.

Seale, C. (1999). *The quality of qualitative research.* London: Sage.

Segall, R. G. (1990). *Learning constellations: A multimedia ethnographic research environment using video technology for exploring children's thinking.* Unpublished dissertation. Cambridge, MA: MIT Media Laboratory.

Shotter, J. (1983). On viewing videotape records of oneself and others: A hermeneutical analysis. In P. W. Dowrick & S. J. Biggs (Eds.), *Using video* (pp. 199–210). London: John Wiley & Sons.

Van Gennep, A. (1960). *The rites of passage.* Chicago: University of Chicago Press.

Young, C. (1995). Observational cinema. In P. Hockings (Ed.), *Principles of visual anthropology* (2nd ed., pp. 79–113). New York: Mouton de Gruyter.

Znaniecki, F. (1934). *The method of sociology.* New York: Farrar and Rinehart.

8

Grounded Theory in Psychological Research

Karen Henwood and Nick Pidgeon

Generating theory that is grounded in semistructured interviews, fieldwork observations, case-study notes, or other forms of textual documentation is one important principle of much qualitative social science today. It is often specifically associated with the methodological approach adopted by the American sociologists Barney Glaser and Anselm Strauss during their investigation of the institutional care of the terminally ill (1965), which they subsequently termed *grounded theory* (1967). Grounded theory studies are often prompted by quite general research interests at the outset. These might include identifying actors' views or perspectives on a topic or investigating processes or phenomena of interest within their local contexts and settings, and from there arriving at insights and explanatory schemes that are relevant to ("grounded in") real-world problems, a previously unresearched topic area, or both.

Since the late-1980s psychologists have been interested in using the principles and practices of grounded theory (see Henwood & Pidgeon, 1992; Rennie, Phillips, & Quartaro, 1988). In this chapter we argue that its usefulness for psychologists is both as a node around which there are discussions of a wide range of contemporary methodological issues (e.g., epistemology, design, interpretive practice, and validity) and as a resource for framing studies and analytical strategies that deal in principled and practical ways with the exigencies of conducting systematic but creative qualitative research that has clear relevance to substantive problem domains. In so doing we also hope to avoid presenting grounded theory as a unitary method (for some it is *the* method of thematic qualitative inquiry), instead preferring to reflect contemporary developments in thinking about the place of the approach within qualitative inquiry in general.

We wish to thank Marcus Sangster, Huw Davies, Paul Finch (of the Forestry Commission), Sarah Pearce, Ffion M. Roberts, Sue Hunter, and all of the individuals who contributed to both the North Wales Community Focus Groups and the Stakeholder Panel. Our colleague Barry Turner, who died unexpectedly in 1995, shared with us many of his insightful thoughts on the use of grounded theory method. Mildred Blaxter has been a valued commentator and discussant. The opinions expressed here are, however, solely ours.

We will also argue that grounded theory's apparent philosophical foundation in a process of "pure" induction (of theory from data) hides an epistemological dilemma. Resolving this requires constructivist readings of the approach that more closely reflect the actual processes of grounded theory analysis. If it is perplexing to find complex, multiple, and divergent ways of presenting the philosophical positions associated with grounded theory, this is no less than should be expected in circumstances where qualitative researchers, and indeed social scientists in general, are having to juggle with many epistemological tensions. Denzin and Lincoln (2000, p. 2) described these tensions as existing within a "complex historical field" where modernism and postmodernism represent two "crosscutting historical moments" that overlap and simultaneously "operate in the present."

The chapter references exemplar studies, which we believe provide particularly good written accounts of various grounded theory projects and principles (drawn primarily from psychology but also related disciplines where appropriate). The main illustrative study we use is based on an extensive corpus of discussion data from focus groups we have ourselves conducted with members of the public in Wales—a devolved region of the United Kingdom—about the symbolic importance and value they attach to the woodlands, forests, and trees within their environment (Henwood & Pidgeon, 2001). The study is unusual in that it deals more explicitly than many other accounts of grounded theory with the thorny but essential issue of how interpretive, qualitative research necessarily involves developing an understanding of the topic in question that is embedded in particular kinds of psychological and, in this case, sociopolitical/cultural theory. In addition to showing how this embeddedness influences the design and course of research we also demonstrate how our research deploys some of the principles and practices of grounded theory.

Background to the Approach

In their book *The Discovery of Grounded Theory,* Glaser and Strauss (1967) observed that, at the time of publication, sociological research placed excessive reliance on the quantitative testing of hypotheses derived from a small number of grand (totalizing) theories, typically through numerical survey and other statistical approaches. They argued that this ultimately led to empirically impoverished abstract theory, in the sense of having restricted relevance to any particular "substantive" problem domain. Closing this "embarrassing gap between theory and empirical research" (Glaser & Strauss, 1967, p. vii), therefore, required a radical change of philosophy. Specifically, what was needed, they argued, was an approach aimed at generating more insightful accounts, contextual explanations, or middle-range theories that would as a consequence "work" (hold clear relevance to problems and phenomena identified in the course of study, in context or in situ) and also be relevant to those being studied. In historical terms, as noted by Cathy Charmaz (2000):

> Grounded theory served at the forefront of "the qualitative revolution" . . . at a critical point in social science history . . . defended qualitative research

> and countered the dominant view that quantitative studies provide the only form of systematic social scientific inquiry. (p. 509)

Glaser and Strauss (1967) also made the basic observation that a new methodology was needed to realize this alternative goal of generating innovative theory that is well-grounded in qualitative data. Accordingly, they took the step of formalizing a range of principles, methods, and tactics (which we outline in greater detail later) to promote creativity in conceptualizing in parallel with rigorous analysis of "ill-structured" qualitative data.

It is debatable to what extent the procedures and methods of grounded theory are distinctive to the approach, or alternatively should be conceptualized as one part of a core, generic set of techniques for conducting theory-building from qualitative data. What has made grounded theory particularly attractive to researchers from a range of disciplines subsequently is its claim to describe a *formal set of methods or procedures* for guiding or gaining credibility for qualitative interpretive inquiry more generally. Many who are new to qualitative research, and especially analysis, find the provision of such explicit techniques both reassuring and genuinely useful. Equally, there is considerable work still to be done in relating grounded theory to other researchers' ways of depicting qualitative study design, data gathering, and analysis. In our view the qualitative researcher should not, therefore, approach grounded theory today in a naive or simplistic way. As with any other systematic approach to research, principled choices, both of epistemology and methodology (see Henwood & Pidgeon, 1994; Madill, Jordan, & Shirley, 2000) have to be made at various stages in the grounded theory research process—choices that will subsequently guide the conduct of study, its analysis, and outcomes.

As a philosophy of inquiry, there are a number of historical antecedents to grounded theory. In psychology these can be first traced to the ideas of Dilthey (1894/1977), who in arguments with the early experimentalists, such as Ebbinghause, maintained that the human sciences would be mistaken to exclusively pursue causal explanation at the expense of establishing understanding (*Verstehen* or meaning). This idea subsequently became significant in interpretive phenomenology (Schutz, 1962), as well as in the ideographic school of 1950s and 1960s psychology.

Grounded theory also has an especially long-standing association with the pragmatic and symbolic interactionist philosophical traditions (see, e.g., Blumer, 1969; Mead, 1934) that have served to frame several generations of researchers' theorizing, questions, and inquiries within some areas of social psychology and microsociology. The American interactionist tradition also holds an important historical place in the development of generic qualitative research practice to the present day. It provided an early and coherent case for (and practical examples of) studies that took for granted the importance of the actor's point of view and that sought to explore the activities and interactions involved in the interpretive and symbolic production of meaningful social and cultural worlds, often through detailed in situ case studies. Accordingly, the philosophical, theoretical, and methodological mix of ideas that often guide grounded theorists' interpretive practice can be seen in their stated aim of initially focusing on problems and issues that have to do with people's substantive activities, interactions, sense-making, and locatedness within particular settings, before moving on to elucidate more general or formally theorized understandings of such problems, including the wider significance of their socially situated experiences and the conditions and consequences of their activities and ways of living.

The basic philosophy of grounded theory inquiry may appear to represent a considerable conceptual break from that conventionally taught within experimental and survey design courses. It opens out a range of new and exciting challenges and opportunities for psychological research—particularly where existing theory is inappropriate, too abstracted, or absent entirely—without also losing sight of necessary rigor in analytical practice (Henwood & Pidgeon, 1992). Reflecting its symbolic interactionist roots, at the interface of sociology and social psychology, it is no surprise to find those working in the applied or practitioner areas of psychology to be the first to take up this challenge. Good exemplar studies can now be found particularly within health psychology (Houston & Venkatesh, 1996; Sque & Payne, 1996), psychotherapy and clinical psychology (Bolger, 1999; Borrill & Iljon-Foreman, 1996), and also in social (Annesley & Coyle, 1998; Henwood, 1993; Marsliglio, Hutchinson, & Cohan, 2000), feminist (Currie, 1988; Willott & Griffin 1999), organizational (Crook & Kumar, 1998), and environmental psychology (Tuler & Thomas, 1999).

The Dilemma of Qualitative Method

The perspective adopted in the original 1967 account of grounded theory hides an epistemological tension, which Martyn Hammersley (1989) labeled the *dilemma of qualitative method.* Put simply this arises from a simultaneous commitment on the one hand to scientific process and realism (by claiming to directly reflect the "data"—for example, participants' own accounts and viewpoints), and on the other a form of constructivism (inherent to the approach of symbolic interactionism) that involves the researcher in the *creative and interpretive* process of generating new understandings and theory. Philosophically speaking, theory cannot simply emerge from or reflect data, because interpretation and analysis is always conducted within some preexisting conceptual framework brought to the task by the analyst.[1] This then raises the thorny question of what grounds grounded theory (Henwood & Pidgeon, 1992, 1995a, 1995b).

For some analytical purposes it might be simplest to just ignore this dilemma. However, the risk is that the approach might then be followed as if it were a prescriptive method—a standardized procedure for guaranteeing "true" representations of the psycho–social world. Our own preferred response has been to argue for a constructivist revision of grounded theory (Henwood &

[1]Alvesson and Sköldberg (2000) also argue that grounded theorists cannot simply assume that the raw "data" of analysis are themselves unproblematic or uncontested. In a related discussion, Rennie (2000) suggests that grounded theory involves a "double hermeneutic" in that both its processes (theory generation) and "objects" of inquiry (the psychosocial world) invevitably involve preinterpretation.

Pidgeon, 1994, 1995a; Pidgeon & Henwood, in press; see also Charmaz, 1990, 2000; Costain Schou & Hewison, 1996). This framing captures more nearly the essential characteristic of its combination of systematic rigor in analysis with the essentially creative and dynamic character of the interpretive research process. A constructivist revision also alerts the researcher to the fact that data should *guide* but certainly should not *limit* theorizing (Layder, 1993). For this reason we have used the term *generation of theory,* rather than discovery, as more accurately describing both the epistemological and practical realities of the approach (Henwood & Pidgeon, 1992). Similarly, Martin Bulmer (1979) has commented that, rather than theory being discovered or emerging from a purely inductive process, grounded theory always involves a constant two-way dialectical process or "flip-flop" between data and the researcher's conceptualizations. Such a position is also in keeping with an additional principle of grounded theory—that of *emergent design* that we discuss in greater detail later.

From a constructivist perspective, the logic of interpretive practice requires that researchers remain aware that knowing always involves seeing or hearing from within particular individual, institutional, and other socioculturally embedded perspectives and locations. It also means taking into account other complexities associated with the multiple, fragmented, and shifting character of discursively patterned or "ordered" frameworks of meaning (Denzin, 1997; Gubrium & Holstein, 2000; Schwandt, 2000). Otherwise one will simply lack awareness of the preconditions that inevitably structure understanding and that would remain tacit or hidden under the guise of emergent ideas and theory. To be able to "discover" or "generate" questions, meaning, insights, and theory researchers must be able to retain their disciplinary knowledges and use their theoretical sensitivities (Bulmer, 1979). Theoretical sensitivities are qualitative researchers' way of approaching the analysis of data: Rather than being held as true until found to be false, such sensitivities are viewed as tools that can be vision-creating or vision-blinkering, depending on a complex mix of individual, structural, and cultural conditions. Paradoxically, theoretical sensitivities tell us where to look at the same time as, potentially, keeping us from seeing (Vaughan, 1992, p. 195). We illustrate the ways in which theoretical sensitivities are central to grounded theory interpretive practice—and the very real practical consequences that follow—in our example study later in the chapter.

Methodology

It is impossible in a chapter such as this to encapsulate what is now a considerable body of methodological literature, as well as the many examples of published grounded theory studies available. This literature now includes all the various aspects of Glaser and Strauss's original (1967) work, how it has been followed up and developed in different ways by the individual authors and coworkers (Glaser, 1978, 1992; Strauss, 1987), and, as discussed earlier, different renditions by researchers influenced by more recent postmodernist and constructivist thinking within the social sciences. In large measure, however, the term grounded theory indicates, to us at least, an *intertwining* of research process and outcomes—where the *process* involves the detailed, systematic but flexible interrogation of (a range of) initially unstructured data selected for its close relationship to the problem under investigation and the analytical *outcomes* (often with the powers of formal explanatory theory) combine a demonstrable relevance and "fit" to the substantive problem, phenomenon, or situation under investigation. Accordingly, although grounded theory indicates a property of a conceptual system (strictly an outcome), the term has become associated with the methodological strategies advocated by Glaser and Strauss (a set of processes) within their original template for grounded theory research (Glaser & Strauss, 1967; see also Pidgeon & Henwood, 1997; Strauss & Corbin, 1998; Turner, 1981). The phases of grounded theory analysis reflecting the order of their expected first occurrence within a single project, are as follows:

1. Open-coding to capture the detail, variation, and complexity of the basic qualitative material (sometimes also referred to as substantive coding);

2a. Constantly comparing data instances, cases, and categories for conceptual similarities and differences (the method of constant comparison);

2b. Sampling new data and cases on theoretical grounds as analysis progresses (theoretical sampling to extend the emergent theory by checking out emerging ideas, extending richness and scope, and in particular to add qualitative variety to the core data included within the analysis;

2c. Writing theoretical memoranda to explore emerging concepts and links to existing theory;

3a. Engaging in more focused coding (including focused, axial, and theoretical coding) of selected core categories;

3b. Continuing to code, make comparisons, and sample theoretically until the point at which no new relevant insights are being reached (theoretical saturation); and

4. Additional tactics to move analysis from descriptive to more theoretical levels: for example, grouping or reclassifying sets of basic categories; writing definitions of core categories; building conceptual models and data displays; linking to the existing literature; writing extended memos and more formal theory.

This list presents discrete stages. In overall terms the analyst typically works from an initial topic or research question(s), to data gathering, through initial treatment of unstructured materials (using the varied analytical operations listed), possibly more data gathering and analysis, and on to a set of theoretical categories, interpretations, models, and written accounts of theory. As we demonstrate later, this flow is accompanied by a gradual development of the conceptual focus away from local descriptions inherent to the data toward more ordered and analytical (i.e., theoretical) concepts and categories.

However, in detail the core processes of generating grounded theory exhibit both linear and iterative qualities, reflecting both the ongoing flip-flop between data and conceptualization described earlier and the fact that research design with grounded theory is emergent rather than inexorably fixed in advance. Strauss and Corbin emphasize that

> because our approach to theory building is one of *emergence* . . . the design, like the concepts, must be allowed to emerge during the research process. As concepts and relationships emerge from data through qualitative analysis, the researcher can use that information to decide where and how to go about gathering additional data that will further the evolution of the theory. (1998, p. 33)

As a result, the researcher will cycle from later back to earlier operations where this is necessary to promote theory development, fit, and conceptual integration. Hence, the research question itself, which Turner (1981) pointed out may only be tacitly understood at the outset of inquiry, is often sharpened and refined—sometimes changed entirely—by the process of data analysis (see, e.g., Michie, McDonald, & Marteau, 1996). In a similar way, a recategorization of initial codes can follow the development of the emerging theoretical analysis or a realization by the analyst that initial terms and concepts used do not in fact fit the data in the ways originally assumed.

In our view, presenting the linearity and nonlinearity in the process of grounded theory design invites a nondidactic view of the principle of flexibility, emergence, and iterativeness in relation also to a defined origin to inquiry and to qualitative research design. Our own experience of teaching grounded theory is that new researchers enthusiastically glean from the classic writings on the topic that they should approach their initial fieldwork and data analysis without any previous theoretical preconceptions or reference to earlier literature. Glaser and Strauss recognize that it is logically impossible to approach inquiry as a true *tabula rasa.* But it would be equally fair to say that many writings in the tradition of grounded theory are less than helpful on the issues surrounding study origin and (at least initial) research design. We would accordingly recommend Marshall and Rossman (1999) as an aid to designing any grounded theory study. They help to elucidate a number of initial design choices that grounded theorists often leave unresolved or unstated in their written accounts. For example, although grounded theorists emphasize theoretical sampling, in practice the very first data to be collected are often sampled on other grounds—as when interviews with key informants or a particularly rich case, thought likely in advance to maximize the chance of obtaining both good quality data and pointers to additional relevant samples are used (see also Cutliffe, 2000).

One aspect of design decision making seems particularly problematic. This is the tension between keeping to a general statement of initial substantive interests and problems and of formulating more specific research questions (including the use of the theoretical literature to sharpen initial focus). We should note at this point that, following the initial writing of *Discovery,* Glaser and Strauss have explicated rather different positions on a number of critical issues, including this one. Glaser (1992) has argued strongly for an initially generalist position to any study: One approaches a problem area because it is interesting, but without strong preconceptions. He thereby continues the theme of many qualitative researchers' refusal to subordinate open-ended, exploratory research activities to any form of theory verification by stating that "the problem emerges and questions regarding the problem emerge" (Glaser, 1992, p. 25). Strauss and Corbin (1998), on the other hand, argue for enhancing the early focus of grounded theory studies by making explicit the questions guiding a researchers' choice of topic or interest in investigating a particular setting, and then using these to direct attention to the specific phenomena that are to be subjected to intensive data gathering and analytical scrutiny. This latter suggestion is more in line with recent and widely read resource books on interpretive qualitative methods (Flick, 1998; Marshall & Rossman, 1999; Mason, 1996; Miles & Huberman, 1994), all of which caution against the dangers of too loose, as well as overly restrictive, initial research designs. Novice researchers, in particular, are deemed to be at risk of being unable to focus their studies sufficiently if they do not make explicit what interests them about their chosen topic area and state these interests as research questions fairly early on in their investigations.

Embedding projects in background and disciplinary knowledges to formulate workable and maximally useful research questions early on also brings the role of the theoretical literature into question. The principle that people new to grounded theory often read into descriptions of the approach—of completely setting aside the literature at the start of the project to maintain sensitivity to relevance in the data—may sometimes need to be displaced by a more discriminating strategy of using the literature early on in specific ways. Cutliffe (2000) emphasized the importance, when investigating relationships between concepts (in his case between hope and bereavement counseling) of using the theoretical literature before entering the study to promote clarity in thinking about concepts as it "helps the researcher to reach conceptual density, enhance the richness of concept development, and subsequently the process of theory development" (2000, p. 1481).

The special counsel that remains within grounded theory is to avoid being wedded to particular theoretical positions and key studies in the literature in ways that overly direct ways of looking and stymies the interactive process of engagement with the empirical world being studied. *Theoretical agnosticism* is a better watchword than theoretical ignorance to sum up the ways of using the theoretical literature—as well as initial research questions—at the early stages of the flow of work in grounded theory.

Grounded theorists typically treat any relevant medium or combination of media as data;[2] whether archival documents, official records and reports

[2]If the principal objective is theory building, this could even include quantitative data, as in some forms of exploratory statistical analysis (cf. Tukey, 1977). Glaser himself brought his background in statistics to the writing of *Discovery*, and one chapter of the monograph is devoted solely to the use of quantitative survey data for the inductive generation of theory. Although this chapter has subsequently puzzled many qualitative researchers who read the book, and as a result has received very little attention, it too represents a considerable break with mainstream (in this case statistical) research practice. In particular, by arguing that the conventional canons for statistical verification (e.g. strictures guarding against type I error in statistical inference: that is of rejecting the "null" hypothesis where no "true" difference actually exists) might be temporarily

(Turner, 1978), letters (Banks, Louie, & Einerson, 2000), fieldwork observations (Wright, 1997), focus group data (Green, 1997; Henwood & Pidgeon, 2001), or interview notes and transcripts (Kimle & Damhorst, 1997; Sarlio-Lahteenkorva, 2000). Some studies combine multiple sources of data (e.g., Crook & Kumar, 1998; Karp & Tanarugsachock, 2000; Friedlander, Heatherington, & Marrs, 2000). Selection of precisely what form of data to collect will depend primarily on the aims of the study.[3] To outline just one example, Turner (1978; Turner & Pidgeon, 1997) used reports from government accident inquiries to generate a theory of the human and organizational preconditions to major industrial accidents and disasters, precisely because these provided a rich, and the best, store of information on such administrative "failures of foresight."

In the early stages of generating grounded theory the researcher must adopt a stance of maximum flexibility in generating new categories from the data. This is a creative process, which taxes fully the interpretive skills of the researcher, who is nevertheless disciplined by the requirement that codes and categories generated should *fit* (provide a recognizable description of) the data. Success in generating theory, which is well-grounded, depends on maintaining a balance throughout between full use of the researcher's own imagination and theoretical sensitivities against this basic requirement of fit. Turner (1981) suggested starting open coding with the first paragraph or segment of the material and asking, "What categories, concepts, or labels do I need to account for what is of importance to me in this paragraph?" (p. 232). This initial label then serves as the first indicator for the concept (or category) described by the card header. Open coding continues by checking whether further potentially significant aspects of the paragraph suggest different concepts (almost certainly they will), and continues systematically with subsequent paragraphs or segments in the data.

The aim of open coding is to generate an indexing system through which any particular segment of raw text can be quickly identified, accessed, compared to other segments, and interrogated during subsequent analytical operations. In the terminology of information technology this amounts to a code and retrieve paradigm. It is accordingly no surprise to find many computer-aided qualitative data analysis software (CAQDAS) packages, founded on such a paradigm, and some explicitly reference grounded theory as their source of analytical logic (see Kelle, 1997; Weitzman, 2000). Such software is invaluable where a project involves large and complex data sets, which the analyst needs to organize, sift, and sort for complex comparisons and emergent relationships. In our experience CAQDAS programs greatly simplify the mechanics of open coding, although this may be outweighed by the effort to properly set up a database in ways that fully exploit a particular program's capabilities. Even more important it is still the researcher who must provide the *interpretative* work that generates

---

set aside where "discovery" of new theory or patterns from exploratory analysis of complex quantitative data sets is the principal objective.

[3]Grounded theory is sometimes inappropriately portrayed as being solely associated with the collection and analysis of interview data. By contrast, interviews are typically the main material of analysis in phenomenological studies that aim to explore participants' life worlds through their own expressed understandings of this (see Baker, Wuest, & Stern, 1992).

the label and who decides which segments of data to compare. Accordingly, our general recommendation is that such software should be used by the beginning grounded theorist only with care.

The exercise of coding to explore similarities and differences is basic to implementing the analytical method of constant comparison, on which the generation of grounded theory is founded. This involves continually sifting and comparing elements (basic data instances, emergent concepts, cases, or theoretical propositions) throughout the lifetime of the project. By making such comparisons the researcher is sensitized to similarities (e.g., at more general levels of abstraction) and nuances of difference as a part of the cognitive exploration of the full range and complexity of the data. In short, similarities and differences are central to promoting dense conceptual development. Taken together the commitments of constant comparison and theoretical sampling define the analytical dynamic of the grounded theory process, which involves the researcher, as we have suggested, in a highly interactive and iterative process.

As the number of coded concepts increases, some indexed to many facets of the data and some indexed to few, the analysis increasingly involves other core activities designed to both raise the conceptual level and construct an orderly theoretical account. Pidgeon, Turner, and Blockley (1991) liken the early phases of grounded theory (open coding and initial memoing) to stepping deeper into a maze, a confusing place that may generate considerable uncertainty and anxiety. During the later phases of analysis suitable routes out of this maze have to be found. Perhaps the most critical stage of the whole analysis (and paths to escape the maze) is prompted at the point of theoretical saturation, where the researcher also often focuses on an important core category or group of categories.

Research Case Example

Our illustrative case is drawn from a policy study we carried out to investigate the symbolic importance and value that community members attach to their environment. The study (Henwood & Pidgeon, 1998, 2001) was sponsored by the Forestry Commission, which has national responsibility for planning, and in some commercial cases managing, tree and forest cover across the United Kingdom. Traditionally, the "value" of forestry had been assessed purely in economic terms, either via actual timber prices or—where more intangible community benefits such as access to recreation were concerned—using quantitative "contingent valuation" attitude surveys of users (e.g., Mitchell & Carson, 1989). The sponsors realized that such quantitative approaches were failing to reflect fully the reasons why people desire to have woods and trees in their local environment. Our study attempted to move forward efforts that have been made fairly recently in academic and policy research to understand the more tacit and intangible personal and cultural meanings and values that inform such environmental perceptions and evaluations (e.g., Burgess, 1995; Burgess, Harrison, & Limb, 1988; Tuler & Thomas, 1999). We reasoned that our chosen method had to be sensitive to—and build its account from—the local and cultural layers of meaning that are expressed in lay discourse about woods, forests, and trees.

At the outset we were personally aware that trees and forests featured prominently in the ancient Celtic tales, myths, and legends of Wales (e.g., the Mabinogion stories; see Gantz, 1976). Also, some studies had suggested that views about environmental and other recent changes in Wales (such as housing, work, transport, lifestyle, community, etc.) might symbolically represent contested concerns about the impact of social and economic transformation on people's lives, identities, and culture (Cloke, Goodwin, & Milbourne, 1997). However, no equivalent study of perceptions of trees, forests, and woodlands had been conducted previously in Wales.

The Fieldwork Context

The data for the study were collected early in 1998 in Bangor, a small city in rural North Wales. Wales as a whole is culturally distinctive from the rest of the United Kingdom in that there are many living signs and symbols of Welsh heritage (flags, festivals, literature). In North Wales, where nationalist commitments are strongest, a large percentage of the population speak Welsh as their first language. As we were constrained to a very short time scale for delivery of initial findings (three months) we had agreed with the sponsors to limit fieldwork to Bangor, an area of outstanding natural beauty (mountains, coastline, beaches) that attracts many visitors for outdoor recreational activities. Economically this part of rural Wales has suffered over the past 30 years as traditional industries have declined and very recently because of the effects of poor agricultural prices and the Bovine spongiform encephalopathy (BSE; "mad cow") crisis in farming. Reversing the numerical decline in the rural population in the immediate post-war period there is now a significant inward movement of people over the Wales/England border for reasons such as environmental preference and other lifestyle improvements (e.g., flexible work, relatively inexpensive housing, "country living").

The Sample and Methods of Data Collection

The data were collected from five community focus groups. As we wished to reflect a broad spectrum of beliefs and values across the local voting age community the overall sample comprised a wide spread of ages (17 through to 65+). All of the participants had to have lived in the area for at least five years. Although this had *not* been an explicit sampling criterion about half of our participants had been born in North Wales and half had moved there from outside (typically the North West of England).

Focus groups are a technique increasingly used in research to explore talk about a topic, or set of topics, in depth with participants (see, e.g., Barbour & Kitzinger, 1998). The aim is to encourage, by means of the interactional dynamics operating in the group, free discussion of *shared meanings* (including contestation and debate) of a kind not ordinarily attainable in a one-to-one interview study. The ground covered in the focus groups included, "How did participants think about the forests, woods, and trees that were of personal significance to them?" "What difference did it make when this topic is placed in its relevant community and cultural context (i.e. within Wales)?" "What specific meanings attached to forests, woods, and trees in discussions of their cultural role and significance?"

All group sessions were audio-recorded. Tapes were first listened to thoroughly by the authors both independently and jointly. They were then transcribed by us at a level of inclusiveness dictated by the developing analysis. Although with tape-recorded interview or focus group studies one would often work from full transcripts, our preferred strategy was to initially work directly from the tapes before transcribing those parts that were central to the analysis. This was in part for pragmatic reasons—the short time scale for the study—and partly because doing one's own transcription is a way for researchers to start early on the path of thinking analytically about the data and its properties.

Interpretive Analysis

The accounts given by participants about the importance of woods, forests, and trees were paid detailed attention—not as repositories of facts from which can be read off transcendental realities or "truths" but as rich, detailed, and complex tapestries into the wefts and warps of which are woven personally held and more widespread cultural values and meanings. Our task as analysts was to generate compelling, credible, trustworthy ways of investigating and then theorizing about (at least some of) the threads in these tapestries, and, finally, to present comparably rich, detailed, and meaningful ways of addressing our research questions. We report on three facets of our investigations: the initial work of open coding; use of constant comparison of initial codes to sift, sort, and develop higher order descriptive and conceptual themes; and, finally, theoretical integration that, in our case, involved making explicit our previously tacit theoretical sensitivities.

INITIAL WORK OF OPEN CODING. Two extended sections from two different focus groups (A and B), shown as they appeared in our original transcription notes, are given in the left-hand columns of Exhibits 8.1 and 8.2. Direct quotes are shown in double quotation marks, and the précis used where a long section of talk encapsulated a single issue are indicated by square [ ] brackets. Also shown in square brackets are researcher comments on such things as how interactions between group members suggested particular ways of interpreting remarks, in ways not made explicit by the verbatim text. For example, in focus group B (Exhibit 8.2), after 12.7 minutes, the second author (NP) comments that "sounds dead cool" was made in an ironic, mocking tone.

Following Turner's (1981) approach to open coding, described previously, the codes initially generated are shown in capitals on the right-hand side of the boxes. We recorded these literally as handwritten "jottings in the margin" of the transcripts. For example, with group A we have coded the following: implicitly valuing *trees as part of everyday life;* feelings of *local community ownership* and the *threat* posed to this by cutting down trees; and *age of trees*

Exhibit 8.1. Initial Open Codings: Focus Group A

Data transcript	Interpretation
VERBATIM REMARKS shown in " "	CODES
Researcher comments/precis shown in [ ]	Memos shown in { }
Numbers 14.6, 15.1 etc. give location (minutes) on tape	
F2 [incomer] people do come for the trees the beeches →	AMENITY FOR VISITORS
14.6 F1 [local] "I think people living [born?] here it's → an everyday part of their lives watching the trees as they change the leaves change and just having them around because I live on Cae Llepar the other side of the valley and if you look out across Bangor you don't really notice it when you are on the ground but looking across it there are an awful lot of trees across the whole city"	TREES AS PART OF EVERYDAY LIFE {Memo by KH - though aesthetic value mentioned it is qualified; it may have a taken for grantedness for local people}
15.1 M3 [born Bangor, responding mentions view of → Anglesey from Bangor mountain and how its all green behind] "like you say you don't notice it unless you actually are somewhere like that and you think hang on here it's really beautiful what's going on"	{Memo by NP - 'insider's view of the environment'}
15.6 F1 "people sort of associate themselves with the → area and with the trees that are in it so if people threaten to chop down trees whatever they feel threatened because it is their area and their locality and the trees stand for that because there is a lot of things about the Newbury bypass [a prominent environmental protest against road building in England] and all that sort of thing the trees being chopped down and partly because of the natural beauty of the environment and rare shrubs or whatever but partly just because people associate it with their area and they don't like the government coming and chopping everything down without asking people first"	STABILITY (COMMUNITY, LOCALITY, LOCAL OWNERSHIP, THREAT) {Memo by KH - 'chopping trees is a threat to us'}
16.2 M4 "trees are so old when they are full grown → that they can be 100s of years old and almost like symbols of longevity not eternity but things → lasting longer than I'll last" F1 "yes stability" M4 [agrees] "stability yes"	STABILITY AGE/LONGEVITY

Exhibit 8.2. Initial Open Codings: Focus Group B

Data transcript	Interpretation
7.2 "probably as important or more important than even Wales is to people who live in cities as it acts as a contrast to their own life of concrete and clay" [as somebody who has lived in a city] "one of the things I come to the country for is to live in that sort of environment for a time everything the perceptions the greenery the mountains whether they are true of freshness purity clean environment" [NP asks view of those born here]	→ NATURE AS CLEANLINESS (AS OPPOSED TO DIRTY CITIES)
8.6 [all born here] M1 "its like stability really you keep seeing the same thing" M2 "but that's not because its Welsh but because it's where you live but Wales is like the final frontier isn't it" [laughter] M1 "its like stability you don't notice it but you would notice it when it goes" M3 "but that's nothing Welsh"	STABILITY → {Memo by NP - reluctance here about expressing Welsh Nationalism - looks like 'don't impose a nationalist discourse upon us'}
9.0–11.3 [somebody (English) raises question of whether removal of a part of a city would be the same. Complex discussion of whether removing trees is the same or different - one speaker thinks differently as it's not just physical objects but also removing communities (cites Splott by Cardiff docklands) whereas removing a tree is nothing particularly if it is caused by act of God]	→ FORESTS AND COMMUNITY
11.2 "I was very lucky in that where I grew up I lived all of my childhood within easy reach of trees and forests and I'm not sure I can explain why but I'm very grateful that I did and I think it would be a great shame if even more areas of woodland and forest were decimated because children growing up in the future would lack the experience"	→ COMMUNITY → FUTURE GENERATIONS → STABILITY
12.7 M1 "would it be pompous to say that one of the parts of the human condition is that we have a natural affinity with nature and possibly a non-natural affinity with man-made artifacts like cities and towns so the loss of trees forestation vegetation is much more fundamental than say the loss of buildings or whatever" M2 [Welsh participant - ironic/mocking?] "sounds dead cool" [laughter] M3 "there have been trees around for many years" M4 "symbolic of country living isn't it the tree" M1 "it's more fundamental than that we all lived in the country one time and urban living is a relatively new thing"	→ NATURAL/ARTIFICIAL {Memo by NP - is nature more fundamental than man-made artifacts?} → TREES SYMBOLIZE NATURE {Memo by NP - M1 and M4 both ex-city dwellers and incomers. My feeling was the NW participants - e.g. M2 - were far more skeptical of this stereotype of 'things country'}

contributing to a sense of community and (a recurring concept) *stability*. In group B we have comparisons between *clean* rural and dirty urban environments; references to the value to *future generations* of the sense of (recurring once more) "*stability*" or "community" that can be contributed when children grow up with accessible woodland areas nearby; and contrasting *natural and artificial landscapes* to make a judgment about people's sense of fundamental well-being ("the human condition").

At the same time as coding, it is often necessary to comment on aspects of the data being coded, which in turn can often prompt writing a memo. Our short pointers to memos are again written in the margins, within curly { } brackets. For example, the debate shown in group B, an all male group comprising half locally born and half incomers, was only one of a series of contestations within this group over "Welsh" and "English" versions of issues. A suitable heading for an extended memo to the note shown to the right of the text at 12.7 minutes might be skepticism about views of the goodness of natural living—perhaps a case of differences between insider and outsider viewpoints? This, and a number of other instances of note–memo writing, flagged for us some troubling and potentially productive issues that we had not considered explicitly in the original study design. Why the apparent reluctance on the part of our participants who self-identified as Welsh (either personally, culturally, or nationally) to link their own environmental views to Welsh nationalism? How should we as researchers find a satisfactory way of interpreting such remarks? What are the pros and cons of using specific labels (insiders/outsiders, incomers/long-term residents) to reference possible cultural categories and differences?

Unlike categories (which have to fit the data), the contents of memos are not constrained in any way and can include hunches and insights; comments on new samples to be checked out later; and explanations of modifications to or grouping of categories. Perhaps most important, memos serve both as a means of further stimulating theoretical sensitivity and creativity, generating links to the literature, and as a vehicle for making public the researcher's emerging theoretical reflections. Another especially useful function of memoranda is in creating records of research decision making: for example, the reasons for believing that a concept has reached theoretical saturation, or the grounds for seeking additional theoretical samples of data (see later).

Constant Comparison to Develop Higher Order Descriptive and Conceptual Themes. Flexible and open-ended coding itself often promotes the development of fruitful lines of analysis (e.g., our interpretations of participants' ambivalence about linking their views of the environment to national identity and cultural difference, as mentioned earlier). Usually, however, additional data handling and analytical devices are used to *systematically* build up and sort through the "maze" of initial codes, notes, and memoranda, which in turn gives credibility and support to researchers' developing propositions, interpretative accounts, or theoretical schemes.

In the current case, having completed open-coding, we used constant comparison to contrast a set of "higher order" themes encapasulating the main codes that recurred across the different groups in a range of similar and different ways. These are shown in the left-hand column of a data analysis matrix

(Table 8.1). The middle column gives illustrative quotations, and the right-hand column shows how each theme subsequently contributed to the conclusions drawn from the analysis.

Initially these themes served merely as data description devices, as labels indicating that there was a weight of participants' comments and personal and cultural meanings bearing on each theme. Subsequently, the segments of text coded within each higher order theme were worked through and compared with one another in more detail (an additional use of the principle and technique of constant comparison as a mean of focused-coding core or important concepts). At this point the themes moved from being merely higher order labels to theoretically meaningful resources that could be mined to provide complex and useful ways of unpacking and addressing the central research question: What is important to people personally and culturally about woods, forests, and trees?

The two text boxes contain a number of extracts coded with the label "stability" (group A 15.6 and 16.2; group B 8.6 and 11.2) in association with labels such as age, locality, community. The group A codes and extracts convey, in an extremely direct way, a composite statement of a commonly articulated theme: the high value placed on woods and trees because of their longevity and everyday presence to people. The association was especially strong when trees were part of people's places of birth or the local communities in which they grew up. Often woods and trees were valued for contributing to a sense of local community belonging, place, and, in some cases, a wider cultural identity.

Other within- and across-group comparisons then resulted in a more detailed, in-depth, and complexly textured account of the stability issue, and introduced more varied personal and cultural aspects of meaning. Equating trees with a sense of community and the comforts of home, for example, did not, for some, express wholesale resistance to cultural and landscape change (contrary to the view that such a sentiment might be asserting essential virtues of county life or living a rural idyll). Rather, harvesting, developing—and even commercially exploiting—the natural landscape was itself viewed as a vehicle for sustaining community life and cultural identity (see verbatim comment by Morris, group D, in Table 8.1; also Cloke et al., 1997).

The issue of who counts as members of local communities, and the claiming and unclaiming of links between the woods and valleys of the Welsh landscape and Welsh community, national or cultural identity, became a major faultline in discussions of the theme of stability and familiarity. Placing sole emphasis on the specular or aesthetic qualities of the landscape potentially signified a speaker's position as an outsider, because self-defined insiders viewed the landscape as inspiring feelings of both pain and pleasure when invoking a sense of belonging and home. These different meanings associated with expressions of landscape appreciation are illustrated in the group B discussion of the impacts on local people and communities of rural and urban environmental change. The remark at the beginning (7.2), by a participant who self-identifies as English and a previous city dweller, values the freshness and greenery of the landscape from which he gains lifestyle and health benefits. But this contrasts with the views of long-term local residents who remark on the importance of

Table 8.1. Data Analysis Matrix: Lists Four Overarching Themes, Illustrative Text Extracts, and Summarizes Ways in Which Each Theme Contributed to the Conclusions Drawn From the Study

Higher order theme	Illustrative data extract	Contribution to study conclusions
Symbolisation of nature	"trees and forests are so . . . large for want of a better word, they are very symbolic of nature as a whole" (Keith, Group B)	A pervasive, intangible quality of woods and trees is their symbolization of the wholeness, goodness, or value of nature; this is one way of providing additional benefits to people in ways that derive from but also transcend their physical presence
Threat of urbanization	"if you continually knock just one small forest down sooner or later it's going to be no forests. It's going to be just one concrete block. It's going to be nothing" (Aled, Group D) "conifers are the McDonalds of trees" (Mike, Group A)	Valuing trees is a way of communicating desire for life sustaining over life-threatening forms of landscape use and development; however, there are times when trees appear on the life-threatening side of the equation (global environmental protests that take no account of local concerns; regimented commercial conifer plantations)
Stability/ familiarity	"it's like stability really you keep seeing the same thing all the time it's like comfort" (Llewelyn, Group B) "if we got cracking and got our own mills and processing plants here it would provide work for um Welsh people . . which would be clean and provide a good environmental point for the nation as a whole" (Morris, Group D)	Through their sustained contribution to the everyday life of people trees, can signify comfort, home, and a sense of community, place, or cultural identity; equating trees with this sentiment need not express resistance to cultural and landscape change as harvesting the natural landscape can be a vehicle for sustaining community and cultural identity
Protection of wildlife/ biodiversity	"trees belong to the earth they belong to the animals . . . a lot of humans treat them in a way they shouldn't..they are supposed to be there just for a home and for food (for the animals)" (Sarah, Group C) "we must accept that a great deal of what we think is beautiful and natural has in fact been produced by man (sic) for his own use. . .you see these lovely little woods and they have been planted as pheasant covers" (Graham, Group A)	Valuing woods and trees as wildlife habitats often simultaneously expresses older style conservationist beliefs and more recent environmental discourses; a dislike of human domination of nature is often featured, but this dislike is countered by fears of the chaotic potential of nature and a more modern (sometimes entepreneurial) tolerance of a blurring of the boundaries between nature, human intervention, and culture

"stability," of "seeing the same thing daily," and joke about Wales "as like the final frontier" (8.6).

As with many approaches to qualitative research, the success of our study depended on combining clear lines of analysis with a sufficiently complex interrogation of data to study the broad topic in question. Constantly comparing codes with codes (to generate a set of main themes) and then codes with data and data with data (to develop an account of those themes' wefts, warps, and weaves) enabled us to move creatively and systematically between complexity and simplicity: to show that we had not just looked at but rather examined our topic and our data. By using principles now depicted in guidelines for ensuring analytical trustworthiness and quality (see, e.g., Elliot, Fisher, & Rennie, 1999; Yardley, 2000), we were able to achieve credibility and support for our finally presented, interpretive account and write-up.

Using Theoretical Sensitivities to Arrive at Theoretical Integration and Closure. One of the most perplexing features of generating grounded theory is how researchers move from early and intermediate stages to theoretical integration and closure, for any individual study. Although helpful on matters of ensuring trustworthiness and credibility, in truth neither systematic coding nor grouping of themes, nor using constant comparison to develop layers of analysis will, in themselves, enable this to happen. In our case, bringing the analysis to fruition involved making explicit the initially implicit theoretical sensitivities at work. The main theoretical resources that informed the project as a whole are illustrated in Figure 8.1.

It was at the point where we began to move from using themes as descriptive categories to theoretically meaningful resources when input from such multiple sources on the process of analysis most noticeably began to happen. Overall, we took seriously the approach of qualitative researcher as "bricoleur" (Denzin & Lincoln, 2000), conjoined with the tapestry metaphor that is concordant with cultural theories of mosaics, webs, or discourses of meaning. We had access to many sensitivities via our academic positions, activities, and backgrounds, and set these alongside the other knowledges that the design of the study had made central: participants' local knowledges and various specialized or expert domains, especially in forestry planning and management and Welsh life and culture, for which we had convened a stakeholder panel of forestry experts and other interested parties before the focus groups. We also began to adopt an additional, complementary strategy of interrogating each new instance of a thematic category for different interpretive viewpoints. For example, when participants offered remarks about the value of woods and trees to wildlife and biodiversity, were they in fact making straightforward comments about the need for conservation, or were they addressing the rights and wrongs of people's domination of nature (as in different environmental world views; see Pidgeon & Beattie, 1998)?

The analytical practice of seeking out different interpretive viewpoints was supported by our knowledge of various interpretive approaches to the analysis of cultural worlds, practices, and meanings (Clifford & Marcus, 1986; Denzin, 1997; Geertz, 1973). These efforts were oriented toward building up

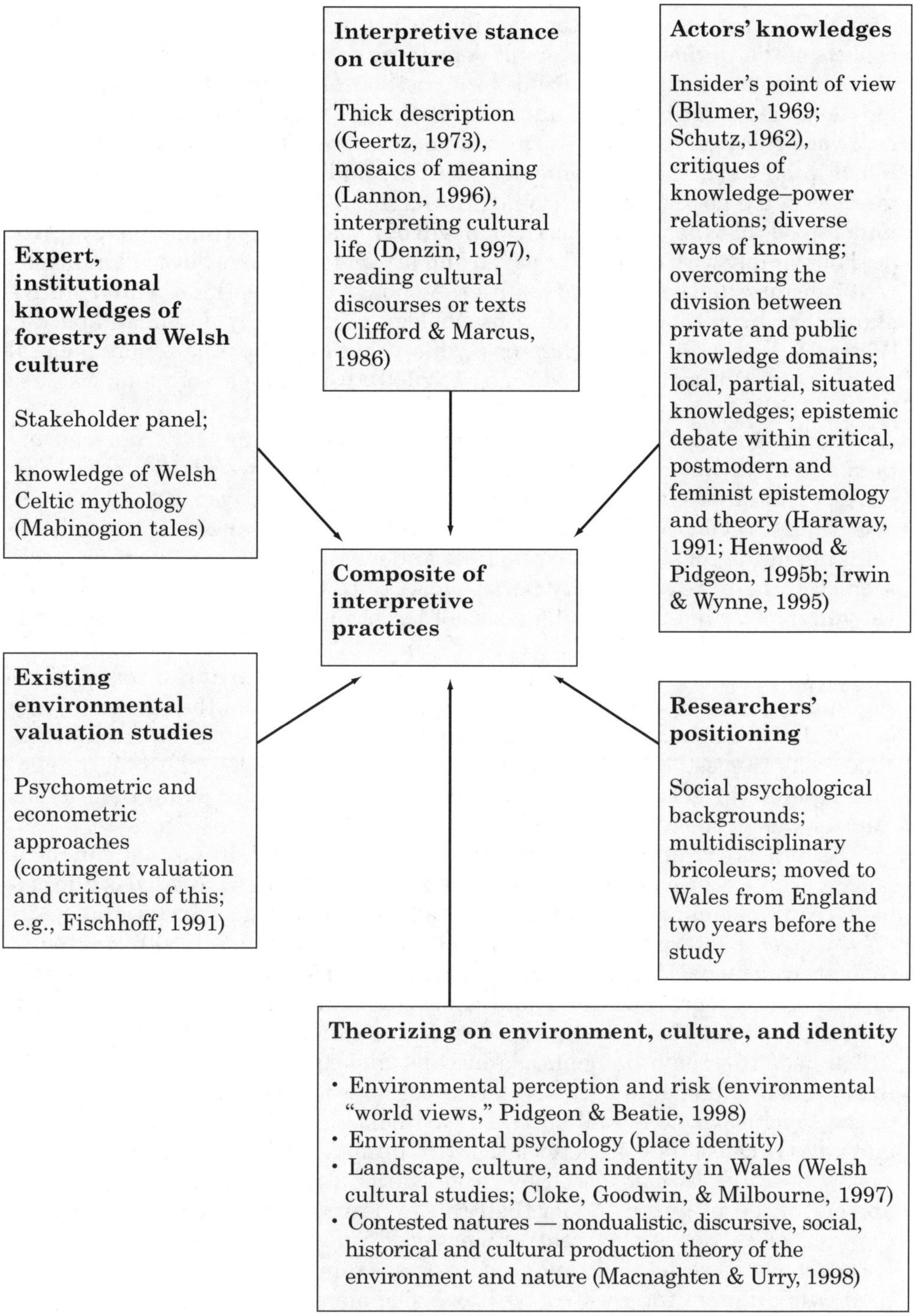

Figure 8.1. Theoretical sensitivities: Data as guides that do not limit theorizing.

a richly layered account of the different ways in which it is possible to "see" aspects of the worlds people inhabit depending on the cultural contexts, orders of meaning, and situational frames—a position also supported by arguments for more democratic, social, and pluralistic epistemologies (Haraway, 1991; Henwood & Pidgeon, 1995b; Irwin & Wynne, 1995). Theorizing about the relationship between the environment, identity, and culture has taken up such ideas within a postmodernist frame (Macnaghten & Urry, 1998). From this we understood that the work of participants in our focus groups might have been to deal not simply with complexly woven and layered meanings but with multiple, contradictory, and fragmented realities. Although the latter kind of interpretive stance has been taken up within psychology primarily by discourse analysis (Potter & Wetherell, 1987; chapter 5, this volume) rather than more general interpretive cultural theory (cf. Squire, 2000), we were ourselves able to use this to further our analytical efforts.

Because we did not construe participants' accounts as truly representing public opinion but as insights into people's symbolic worlds, we were also sensitive to other ways to read for interpreted meaning (see, e.g., chapter 9, this volume). Our analysis attended to the role of dualistic or contrastive thinking in the construction of practices and meanings. Hence, "valuing trees" seemed to be a way for study participants to communicate a desire for life-sustaining over life-threatening forms of landscape use and development (our theme headed "threat of urbanization") through repeated use of interrelated bipolar contrasts: clean versus dirty, urban versus rural, artificial versus natural, and so forth. Woods, forests, and trees routinely fell on the life-sustaining side of these contrasts (clean, rural, natural) and, when they did not, comments reflexively suggested that they were in some sense exceptional, ironic, or running against the grain (e.g., regimented, commercial conifer plantations as the "McDonalds of trees").

As indicated (although of course not fully articulated) by our data analysis matrix (Table 8.1), when members of the groups were asked to discuss intangible forestry meanings and values this enabled them also to express (fragments of) a range of interpreted opinions and meanings that were both related to their own personal, biographical, and local cultural positions *and* responsive to wider contemporary concerns and issues (including development, modernization, and globalization; governance, decision making, and legitimacy; communities and identity; environmental, landscape, and cultural change). Out of these interpreted opinions and values it was possible for us to identify a range of policy conclusions (see Table 8.1). In particular, people value woods, forests, and trees because they are associated with human–environment relationships that oppose the threats posed by urbanization; as leitmotifs for community and cultural continuity; and for their role in nature and biodiversity conservation and protection. Other central messages from the research, however, followed from a more detailed, nuanced, textual examination within each of these themes of different interpretive positions, fragments, and contested meanings. Ultimately our research came to articulate concerns for more fundamental beliefs, fears, and desires about the relationship between people, culture, and nature, and the question of identity within contemporary Welsh rural society.

Further Developing the Study: Using Theoretical Sampling

How far we had moved from substantive theorizing about a very particular kind of interactional and cultural setting to develop insights that have merit at a more formal theoretical level was an issue that remained outstanding for us at the end of the analysis of the North Wales focus group data. Our initial purposive sample had allowed us to take into account criteria that had seemed necessary to introduce diversity of members of the public and communities in the North Wales area (and, fortuitously, length of residency in Wales). However, if we were to be able to arrive at supportable answers to the question about the research in terms of Wales as a whole, it seemed that we would need to use theoretical sampling to develop the project further (during the period 1999–2001).

We came to view three aspects of the initial sample as possibly marking limits to the scope of our analysis and, accordingly, as suggesting lines for developing additional theorizing: the markedly rural character of the North Wales area; differences in type and amount of woodland and tree cover across Wales; and the highly diverse social geography of Wales (e.g., the southeast is more strongly socialist in terms of values, more urbanized, and historically industrialized). We therefore decided (in 1999) to extend the study by sampling theoretically from four other geographical locations, giving additional consideration also to different perspectives to be derived from locally born and incomer participants. Accordingly, the additional fieldwork was devised with residency as an explicit sampling criterion, by convening not only mixed but also homogeneous long-term and incomer resident groups in each new area visited. In these ways, outstanding issues arising from the original fieldwork could be addressed, such as the different ways issues of cultural identity play out depending on the social geography of the local area. Our final analysis of the data from this extended project is currently ongoing.

Conclusion

We would not wish to present the combination of methods we used in our particular study to shift from codes encapsulating the descriptive detail of local accounts, to drawing on them in more theoretically informed and integrated ways, as a standard form for researchers using grounded theory. In part this is because no such standard form exists, in our view. Indeed, as a postscript to this chapter, we can briefly note that the two originators of the grounded theory approach have themselves gone on to suggest competing pathways. Strauss (with Corbin, 1998) has developed a process of axial coding (relating properties, dimensions, or axes of main codes together) to specify a spatially or temporarily organized theoretical model—particularly in terms of antecedents, intervening causes/conditions, and consequences of a selected core category. In essence, Strauss and Corbin recommend the exhaustive coding of the intersecting properties of core conceptual categories along important dimensions or axes in ways that link socio–structural causes with local contexts and consequences (e.g., Crook & Kumar, 1998; Konecki, 1997), as well as to elaborate hypotheses within the emergent theory.

Glaser (1992), on the other hand, has reemphasized reliance on using constant comparison alone to generate and integrate focused and theoretical codes *from* initial substantive (open) codes and to then select from explanatory families (or model types) as appropriate to achieve theoretical integration. For Glaser (1992), the attempts by Strauss and Corbin (1998) to formalize grounded theory procedures and methods (although undoubtedly useful for some beginning researchers) has led them down the path of verification and away from discovery, on the way displacing use of the method of constant comparison and forcing data into preconceptions (particularly of cause and consequence) rather than enabling researchers to hear what is relevant and meaningful in their data. Glaser described their approach as "full conceptual description" rather than grounded theory (for detailed comment, see Kendall, 1999). It is not our purpose to enter into this ongoing debate about what constitutes the "true" legacy of grounded theory. Our view is that to survive, grounded theory ideas and practices must retain an openness to current thinking so that they retain their relevance within changing climates and conditions (see also Rennie, 2000). Accordingly, we stress again our belief that there is no set way of achieving the most difficult task of all in grounded theory research: getting out of the maze of detailed and complex codings, deciding on the limits to making constant comparisons, and reaching theoretical closure or integration. This is both the challenge and excitement that using grounded theory brings.

References

Alvesson, M., & Sköldberg, K. (2000). *Reflexive methodology: New vistas for qualitative research.* London: Sage.

Annesley, P., & Coyle, A. (1998). Dykes and psychs: Lesbian women's experiences of clinical psychology services. *Changes, 16*(4), 247–258.

Baker, C., Wuest, J., & Stern, P. N. (1992). Method slurring: The grounded theory/phenomenology example. *Journal of Advanced Nursing, 17,* 1355–1360.

Banks, S., Louie, E., & Einerson, M. (2000). Constructing personal identities in holiday letters. *Journal of Personal and Social Relationships, 17*(3), 299–327.

Barbour, R. S., & Kitzinger, J. (Eds.). (1998). *Developing focus group research: Politics, theory and practice.* London: Sage.

Blumer, H. (1969). *Symbolic interactionism.* Englewood Cliffs, NJ: Prentice-Hall.

Bolger, E. A. (1999). Grounded theory analysis of emotional pain. *Psychotherapy Research, 9*(3), 342–362.

Borrill, J., & Iljon-Foreman, E. (1996). Understanding cognitive change: A qualitative study of the impact of cognitive-behavioural therapy on fear of flying. *Clinical Psychology and Psychotherapy, 3*(1), 62–74.

Bulmer, M. (1979). Concepts in the analysis of qualitative data. In M. Bulmer (Ed.), *Sociological research methods* (pp. 241–262). London: Macmillan.

Burgess, J. (1995). *Growing in confidence: Understanding people's perceptions of urban fringe woodlands.* London: Countryside Commission.

Burgess, J., Harrison, C. M., & Limb, M. (1988). People, parks and the urban green: A study of popular meanings and values for open spaces in the city. *Urban Studies, 25,* 455–473.

Charmaz, C. (1990). Discovering chronic illness: Using grounded theory. *Social Science and Medicine, 30,* 1161–1172.

Charmaz, K. (2000). Grounded theory: Objectivist and subjectivist methods. In N. Denzin & Y. Lincoln (Eds.), *Handbook of qualitative research* (2nd ed., pp. 509–535). Thousand Oaks, CA: Sage.

Clifford, J., & Marcus, G. E. (Eds.). (1986). *Writing culture.* Berkeley: University of California Press.

Cloke, P., Goodwin, M., & Milbourne, P. (1997). *Rural Wales: Community and marginalisation.* Cardiff: University of Wales Press.

Costain Schou, K., & Hewison, J. (1996). Health psychology and discourse: Personal accounts as social texts in grounded theory. *Journal of Health Psychology, 3*(3), 297–311.

Crook, C. W., & Kumar, R. L. (1998). Electronic data interchange: A multi-industry investigation using grounded theory. *Information and Management, 34,* 75–89.

Currie, D. (1988). Re-thinking what we do and how we do it: A study of reproductive decisions. *Canadian Review of Sociology and Anthropology, 25,* 231–253.

Cutliffe, J. R. (2000). Methodological issues in grounded theory. *Journal of Advanced Nursing, 31*(6), 1476–1484.

Denzin, N. (1997). *Interpretive ethnography.* Thousand Oaks, CA: Sage.

Denzin, N., & Lincoln, Y. (2000). The discipline and practice of qualitative research. In N. Denzin & Y. Lincoln (Eds.), *Handbook of qualitative research* (2nd ed., pp. 1–28), Thousand Oaks, CA: Sage.

Dilthey, W. (1977). *Descriptive psychology and historical understanding* (Trans. R. M. Zaner and K. L. Heiges). The Hague: Martinus Nijhoff. (Original published 1894)

Elliott, R., Fischer, C. T., & Rennie, D. L. (1999). Evolving guidelines for publication of qualitative research in psychology and related fields. *British Journal of Clinical Psychology, 38,* 215–229.

Fischhoff, B. (1991). Value elicitation: Is there anything in there? *American Psychologist, 46,* 835–847.

Flick, U. (1998). *An introduction to qualitative research.* London: Sage.

Friedlander, M. L., Heatherington, L., & Marrs, A. L. (2000). Responding to blame in family therapy: A constructivist/narrative perspective. *American Journal of Family Therapy, 28,* 133–146.

Gantz, J. (1976). *The Mabinogion.* Harmondsworth, UK: Penguin.

Geertz, C. (1973) *The interpretation of cultures: Selected essays.* New York: Basic Books.

Glaser, B. (1978). *Theoretical sensitivity: Advances in the methodology of grounded theory.* Mill Valley, CA: Sociology Press.

Glaser, B. (1992). *Emergence versus forcing: Basics of grounded theory analysis.* Mill Valley, CA: Sociology Press.

Glaser, B., & Strauss, A. (1965). *Awareness of dying.* Chicago: Aldine.

Glaser, B., & Strauss, A. (1967). *The discovery of grounded theory.* New York: Aldine.

Green, J. (1997). Risk and construction of social identity: Children's talk about accidents. *Sociology of Health and Illness, 19*(4), 457–479.

Gubrium, J., & Holstein, J. A. (2000). Analysing interpretive practice. In N. Denzin & Y. Lincoln (Eds.), *Handbook of qualitative research* (2nd ed., pp. 487–508). Thousand Oaks, CA: Sage.

Hammersley, M. (1989). *The dilemma of qualitative method: Herbert Blumer and the Chicago tradition.* London: Routledge.

Haraway, D. (1991). *Simians, cyborgs and women: The reinvention of nature.* New York: Routledge.

Henwood, K. L. (1993). Women and later life: The discursive construction of identities within family relationships. *Journal of Ageing Studies, 7,* 303–319.

Henwood, K. L., & Pidgeon, N. (1992). Qualitative research and psychological theorizing. *British Journal of Psychology, 83,* 97–111.

Henwood, K. L., & Pidgeon, N. F. (1994). Beyond the qualitative paradigm: A framework for introducing diversity in qualitative psychology. *Journal of Community and Applied Social Psychology, 4*(4), 225–238.

Henwood, K. L., & Pidgeon, N. (1995a). Grounded theory and psychological research. *Psychologist, 8*(3), 115–118.

Henwood, K. L., & Pidgeon, N. F. (1995b). Remaking the link: Qualitative research and feminist standpoint theory. *Feminism and Psychology, 5*(1), 7–30.

Henwood, K. L., & Pidgeon, N. F. (1998). *The place of forestry in modern Welsh life and culture. Report to the U.K. Forestry Commission.* Edinburgh, Scotland: U.K. Forestry Commission.

Henwood, K. L., & Pidgeon, N. F. (2001). Talk about woods and trees: Threat of urbanisation, stability and biodiversity. *Journal of Environmental Psychology, 21,* 125–147.

Houston, H. R., & Venkatesh, A. (1996). The health care consumption patterns of Asian immigrants: Grounded theory implications for consumer aculturation theory. *Advances in Consumer Research, 23,* 418–423.

Irwin, A., & Wynne, B. (1995). *Misunderstanding science? The public reconstruction of science and technology.* Cambridge: Cambridge University Press

Karp, D. A., & Tanarugsachock, V. (2000). Mental illness, caregiving and emotion management. *Qualitative Health Research, 10*(1), 6–25.

Kelle, U. (1997). Theory building in qualitative research and computer programs for the management of textual data. *Sociological Research Online, 2*(2).

Kendall, J. (1999). Axial coding and the grounded theory controversy. *Western Journal of Nursing Research, 21*(6), 743–757.

Kimle, P. A., & Damhorst, M. L. (1997). A grounded theory model of the ideal business image for women. *Symbolic Interaction, 20*(1), 45–71.

Konecki, K. (1997). Time in the recruiting search process by headhunting companies. In A. Strauss & J. Corbin (Eds.), *Grounded theory in practice* (pp. 131–145). London: Sage.

Lannon, J. (1996). Mosaics of meaning: Anthropology and marketing. In R. Paton (Ed.), *New management reader* (pp. 24–40). London: Routledge.

Layder, D. (1993). *New strategies in social research.* Cambridge: Polity Press.

Macnaghten, P., & Urry, J. (1998). *Contested natures.* London: Sage.

Madill, A., Jordon, A., & Shirley, C. (2000). Objectivity and reliability in qualitative analysis: Realist, contextualist and radical constructivist epistemologies. *British Journal of Psychology, 91,* 1–20.

Marshall, C., & Rossman, G. B. (1999). *Designing qualitative research* (2nd ed.) London: Sage.

Marsiglio, W., Hutchinson, S., & Cohan, M. (2000). Envisioning fatherhood: A social psychological perspective on young men without kids. *Family Relations, 49*(2), 133–142.

Mason, J. (1996). *Qualitative researching.* London: Sage.

Mead, G. H. (1934). *Mind, self and society.* Chicago: University of Chicago Press.

Michie, S., McDonald, V., & Marteau, T. (1996). Understanding responses to predictive genetic testing: A grounded theory approach. *Psychology and Health, 11,* 455–470.

Miles, M. B., & Huberman, A. M. (1994). *Qualitative data analysis* (2nd ed.) Beverly Hills, CA: Sage.

Mitchell, L. A., & Carson, R. T. (1989). *Using surveys to value goods: The contingent valuation method.* Washington, DC: Resources for the Future.

Pidgeon, N. F., & Beattie, J. (1998). The psychology of risk and uncertainty. In P. Calow (Ed.), *Handbook of environmental risk assessment and management* (pp. 289–318). Oxford: Blackwell Science.

Pidgeon, N. F., & Henwood, K. L. (1997). Using grounded theory in psychological research. In N. Hayes (Ed.), *Doing qualitative analysis in psychology* (pp. 245–273). Hove, UK: Psychology Press.

Pidgeon, N. F., & Henwood, K. L. (in press). Grounded Theory. In A. Bryman & M. Hardy (Eds.), *Handbook of Data Analysis.* London: Sage.

Pidgeon, N. F., Turner, B. A., & Blockley, D. I. (1991). The use of grounded theory for conceptual analysis in knowledge elicitation. *International Journal of Man–Machine Studies, 35,* 151–173.

Potter, J., & Wetherell, M. (1987). *Discourse and social psychology.* London: Sage.

Rennie, D. (2000). Grounded theory methodology as methodological hermeneutics: Reconciling realism and relativism. *Theory and Psychology* 10(4), 481–502.

Rennie, D. L., Phillips, J. R., & Quartaro, G. K. (1988). Grounded theory: A promising approach to conceptualisation in psychology. *Canadian Psychologist, 29*(2), 139–150.

Sarlio-Lahteenkorva, S. (2000). The battle is not over after weight loss: Stories of successful weight loss maintenance. *Health, 4*(1), 73–88.

Schutz, A. (1962). *Collected papers: The problem of social reality.* The Hague: Martinus Nijhoff.

Schwandt, T. (2000). Three epistemological stances for qualitative inquiry: Interpretivism, hermeneutics and social constructionism. In N. Denzin & Y. Lincoln (Eds.), *Handbook of qualitative research* (2nd ed., 189–214). Thousand Oaks, CA: Sage.

Sque, M., & Payne, S. (1996). Dissonant loss: The experiences of donor relatives. *Social Science and Medicine, 43*(9), 1359–1370.

Squire, C. (Ed.). (2000). *Culture in psychology.* London: Routledge.

Strauss, A. (1987). *Qualitative analysis for social scientists.* Cambridge: Cambridge University Press.

Strauss, A., & Corbin, J. (1998). *Basics of qualitative research* (2nd ed.). London: Sage.

Tukey, J. W. (1977). *Exploratory data analysis.* Reading, MA: Addison-Wesley.

Tuler, S., & Thomas, W. (1999). Voices from the forest: What participants expect of a public participation process. *Science and Natural Resources, 12*(5), 437–451.

Turner, B. A. (1978). *Man-made disasters.* London: Wykham Press.

Turner, B. A. (1981). Some practical aspects of qualitative data analysis: One way of organizing the cognitive processes associated with the generation of grounded theory. *Quality and Quantity, 15,* 225–247.

Turner, B. A., & Pidgeon, N. F. (1997). *Man-made disasters* (2nd ed.). Oxford: Butterworth-Heinemann.

Vaughan, D. (1992). Theory elaboration. In C. C. Ragin & H. C. Becker (Eds.), *What is a Case?* (pp. 173–202). New York: Cambridge University Press.

Weitzman, E. (2000). Software and qualitative research. In N. Denzin & Y. Lincoln (Eds.). *Handbook of qualitative research* (2nd ed., pp. 803–820). Thousand Oaks, CA: Sage.

Willott, S., & Griffin, C. (1999). Building your own lifeboat: Working class male offenders talk about economic crime. *British Journal of Social Psychology, 38*(4), 445–461.

Wright, K. B. (1997). Shared ideology in alcoholics anonymous: A grounded theory approach. *Journal of Health Communication, 2*(2), 83–100.

Yardley, L. (2000). Dilemmas in qualitative health research. *Psychology and Health, 15,* 215–228.

9

On the *Listening Guide:* A Voice-Centered Relational Method

Carol Gilligan, Renée Spencer, M. Katherine Weinberg, and Tatiana Bertsch

The *Listening Guide* is a method of psychological analysis that draws on voice, resonance, and relationship as ports of entry into the human psyche. It is designed to open a way to discovery when discovery hinges on coming to know the inner world of another person. Because every person has a voice or a way of speaking or communicating that renders the silent and invisible inner world audible or visible to another, the method is universal in application. The collectivity of different voices that compose the voice of any given person—its range, its harmonies and dissonances, its distinctive tonality, key signatures, pitches, and rhythm—is always embodied, in culture, and in relationship with oneself and with others. Thus each person's voice is distinct—a footprint of the psyche, bearing the marks of the body, of that person's history, of culture in the form of language, and the myriad ways in which human society and history shape the voice and thus leave their imprints on the human soul (Gilligan, 1993). The *Listening Guide* method comprises a series of steps, which together are intended to offer a way of tuning into the polyphonic voice of another person.

As voice depends on resonance or relationship in that speaking relies on, and is affected by, being heard, this method is intended to offer "a pathway into relationship rather than a fixed framework for interpretation" (Brown & Gilligan, 1992, p. 22) and shares a set of assumptions about the human world with what are now being called relational psychologies (e.g., Aron, 1996; Gilligan, 1982; Miller, 1976; Tronick, 1989). These assumptions include the premise that human development occurs in relationship with others and, as such, our sense of self is inextricable from our relationships with others and with the cultures within which we live (Spencer, 2000). In addition, this method draws from psychoanalytical theories that have long-emphasized the layered nature of the psyche, which is expressed in a multiplicity of voices (e.g., Fairbairn, 1944; Mitchell, 1988; Winnicott, 1960). The *Listening Guide* method provides a way of systematically attending to the many voices embedded in a person's expressed experience.

The origins of the *Listening Guide* method lie in the analyses conducted in Gilligan's (1982) work on identity and moral development. The effort to render this method systematic began in 1984, and was undertaken in collaboration with graduate students—diverse in gender, race, sexual orientation, and age—over a period of about 10 years.[1] The *Listening Guide* was developed in part as a response to the uneasiness and growing dissatisfaction with the nature of the coding schemes typically being used at that time to analyze qualitative data. These techniques did not allow for multiple codings of the same text, thereby reducing the complexity of inner psychic processes to placement in single static categories. At that time, many social scientists were becoming more interested in developing methods for studying and interpreting narratives as a way of understanding meaning-making processes (e.g., Bruner, 1986; Geertz, 1983; Josselson, 1987; Mischler, 1979; Polkinghorne, 1988). This interest in, and attention to, narratives was a part of a growing awareness that the emphasis on quantitative methods in psychology was limiting what we could learn about human experience to what could be captured numerically, and many researchers were working to develop and define systematic methods for examining qualitative data in more complex ways.

The *Listening Guide* method picks up on the clinical method developed by Freud and Breuer (Breuer & Freud, 1895/1986) in *Studies on Hysteria* and that of Piaget (1929/1979) in *The Child's Conception of the World.* These works emphasize the importance of following the lead of the person being interviewed and discovering in this way the associative logic of the psyche and the constructions of the mind. The *Listening Guide* method was also inspired by literary theory, including new criticism and reader response theory, as well as by the language of music: voice, resonance, counterpoint, and fugue. It joins feminist researchers, cultural psychologists, and psychological anthropologists in their concerns about the ways in which a person's voice can be overridden by the researcher and their cautions about voicing over the truth of another (e.g., Borland, 1991; Fine & Macpherson, 1992; Scheper-Hughes, 1994).

The *Listening Guide* method has been used by many researchers interested in the psyche and in relationship, and it has been brought to bear in analyzing a range of phenomena within psychology, including girls' sexual desire (Tolman, 1994), adolescent girls' and boys' friendships (Way, 1998), girls' and women's experiences with anger (Brown, 1998; Jack, 1999), women's experiences of motherhood and postnatal depression (Mauthner, 2000), and heterosexual couples' attempts to share housework and childcare (Doucet, 1995). It has also proved useful in analyzing and interpreting U.S. Supreme Court decisions as well as a variety of literary and historical texts, including novels and diaries.

In this chapter we detail the steps involved in the *Listening Guide* method and focus specifically on the use of the guide to analyze and interpret qualitative interview data. In doing so, we demonstrate how we have been thinking about and using the *Listening Guide* method most recently, drawing on the insights of those who first developed this series of steps, the work of other researchers

[1]These conversations involved many people over the years, including as central participants Dianne Argyris, Jane Attanucci, Betty Bardige, Lyn Mikel Brown, Elizabeth Debold, Andrea Doucet, Carol Gilligan, Dana Jack, Kay Johnston, Natasha Mauthner, Barb Miller, Dick Osborne, Pamela Pleasants, Annie Rogers, Amy Sullivan, Mark Tappan, Jill Taylor, Deborah Tolman, Janie Ward, Grant Wiggins, and David Wilcox.

who have since applied the method in a wide range of projects, our own recent research, and our experiences in teaching the guide.

The *Listening Guide*

The *Listening Guide* method comprises a series of sequential listenings, each designed to bring the researcher into relationship with a person's distinct and multilayered voice by tuning in or listening to distinct aspects of a person's expression of her or his experience within a particular relational context. Each step requires the active presence of the researcher and an acute desire to engage with the unique subjectivity of each research participant. The voice of the researcher is explicitly brought into the process, making it clear who is listening and who is speaking in this analysis (Brown & Gilligan, 1991).

This approach to listening is centered on a set of basic questions about voice: Who is speaking and to whom, telling what stories about relationship, in what societal and cultural frameworks (Brown & Gilligan, 1992, p. 21)? With these larger framing questions in mind, we read the texts (in this case the interview transcripts) through multiple times, with each listening tuning into a particular aspect. Each of these steps is called a "listening" rather than a "reading," because the process of listening requires the active participation on the part of both the teller and the listener. In addition, each listening is not a simple analysis of the text but rather is intended to guide the listener in tuning into the story being told on multiple levels and to experience, note, and draw from his or her resonances to the narrative. In this sense, as Tolman (2001) has noted, the *Listening Guide* "is distinctly different from traditional methods of coding, in that one listens to, rather than categorizes or quantifies, the text of the interview" (p. 132).

Although the first two listenings are more prescribed, the later listenings are shaped by the particular question the researcher brings to the interview. No single step, or listening, is intended to stand alone, just as no single representation of a person's experience can be said to stand for that person. The listenings of each step are rendered visual through underlining the text, using different colored pencils for each listening. Each listening is also documented through notes and interpretive summaries the researcher writes during the implementation of each step. The marked interview transcript, notes, and summaries help the researcher to stay close to the text and keep track of "a trail of evidence" (Brown, Tappan, Gilligan, Miller, & Argyris, 1989), the base for later interpretations.

The need for a series of listenings arises from the assumption that the psyche, like voice, is contrapuntal (not monotonic) so that simultaneous voices are co-occurring. These voices may be in tension with one another, with the self, with the voices of others with whom the person is in relationship, and the culture or context within which the person lives. Voices are fluid and we register the continuous changes in our own and others' voices. As one young boy in the work by Chu and Gilligan noted, his mother had "a happy voice," but he also heard "a little worried voice." Each listening amplifies another aspect of a person's voice in a manner akin to listening to and following the oboe through a piece of music and then listening again, this time following the clarinet (Gilligan, Brown, & Rogers, 1990).

We describe and illustrate each step of the *Listening Guide* method by focusing on a small section of an interview conducted by Katherine Weinberg for her research with mothers who have a history of depression (e.g., Tronick & Weinberg, 1997). Weinberg extended this study in response to her observation that her quantitative work with these mothers did not fully capture the power and richness of their stories. The *Listening Guide* offered Weinberg a way of hearing what each mother was saying and of understanding the mother's experiences with depression, the ways she was coping with this illness while also coping with the demands of motherhood, and the meaning of these experiences for her. In her use of the *Listening Guide* for research with depressed women, Weinberg was guided by the work of Jack (1991) and Mauthner (1993, 1998).

The interviewee, Vanessa,[2] was 39 years old at the time of the interview. The focus of the interview was on Vanessa's history of depression and her life as a new mother. She had volunteered for Weinberg's study of the effects of depression and anxiety on maternal and infant functioning. Weinberg conducted, audiotaped, and transcribed this interview. In her verbatim transcription she maintained a respect for the spoken language by including pauses, inflections, false starts, unfinished sentences, and overlapping speech.

Step 1: Listening for the Plot

The first listening comprises two parts: (a) listening for the plot and (b) the listener's response to the interview. First, we read through the text and listen for the plot by attending to what is happening or what stories are being told, in the manner characteristic of many forms of qualitative analyses (e.g., Reissman, 1993; Strauss & Corbin, 1998; Werber, 1990). We also attend to the landscape, or the multiple contexts, within which these stories are embedded (Brown & Gilligan, 1992). We begin by first getting a sense of where we are, or what the territory is by identifying the stories that are being told, what is happening, when, where, with whom, and why. Repeated images and metaphors and dominant themes are noted as are contradictions and absences, or what is not expressed. The larger social context within which these stories are experienced is identified, as is the social and cultural contexts within which the researcher and research participant come together.

In this plot listening, we also attend to our own responses to the narrative, explicitly bringing our own subjectivities into the process of interpretation from the start by identifying, exploring, and making explicit our own thoughts and feelings about, and associations with, the narrative being analyzed. Because many have pointed out that a researcher is not and can never be a "neutral" or "objective" observer (e.g., Keller, 1985; Morawski, 2001), we consciously and actively focus on and document our own response to what is being expressed and to the person speaking. Following basic principles of reflexivity (Mauthner

[2]Vanessa is a pseudonym.

& Doucet, 1998), we note our own social location in relation to the participant, the nature of our relationship with this person, and our emotional responses. As we go through the interview text, we notice and reflect on where we find ourselves feeling a connection with this person and where we do not, how this particular person and this interview touches us (or does not touch us), what thoughts and feelings emerge as we begin to listen and why we think we are responding in this way, and how our responses might affect our understanding of this person and the stories being told. We work to identify our own responses to this particular interview, like a clinician who identifies her countertransference, or responses to her client, in the hope that she will be better able to not confuse her own experiences with those of her client, or to not allow her own responses to the material the client brings to interfere with her ability to listen to and connect with her client.

As multiple listenings are at the heart of this method, a *Listening Guide* analysis is enhanced by work within interpretive communities (e.g., Taylor, Gilligan, & Sullivan, 1995) that provide multiple listeners. Here the goal is not necessarily agreement, but rather the exploration of the different connections, resonances and interpretations that each listener naturally brings to the analytical process. In the excerpt that follows, we listen to Vanessa's description of the effect that her own mother's depression had on her.

> And then I think you know everything kind of went underground for me and I stopped talking to people. . . . Hmmm. I think when there is a mental illness in the house and it's and there . . . can be . . . and some of it can be out of control that hmmm a lot of families tend to isolate and that I think is what my family did and hmmm besides I didn't have anything to talk about. What was I going to say? My mother is a raging maniac? Or or she's she's a rock and I can't talk to her. It's not something you share with people at school. Hmmm and hmmm I think it made me chase my dad for for some kind of attention and of course that made him run faster. Hmmm. And so hmmm. . . . and you know at that point I think that's when I stopped sleeping. And I kept worrying that one of them was going to drop dead you know. And I think that hmmm some of that was behind the not sleeping.

In listening for the plot, we hear Vanessa, a 39-year-old White woman, talking about herself when she was about 10 or 11 years old. Her mother was quite depressed and Vanessa took over many of the responsibilities her mother could no longer handle, including the care of her younger siblings, two of whom were born during this time period. She portrays herself as isolated, not just from people outside the family but also from both of her parents. She attributes her isolation from people at school to not having "anything to talk about" because what was most salient for her was the fact that her mother was a "raging maniac" and that was "not something you share with people." She also states that she stopped sleeping and worried that one of her parents was "going to drop dead." Although Vanessa's family had financial resources because her father was a practicing physician, the psychological resources seem scarce.

Typically all of the people involved in the analysis of this interview would write a listener's response. Here we offer the responses of two of us for the sake of example.

Renée's response:

> I found myself filled with images of and associations with being surrounded by depression and the isolation that comes with feeling like you cannot tell anyone about it. I noticed I was tuning into the severity of her mother's depression and was both awe-struck by Vanessa's capacity to function (she continued going to school) and to take care of her younger siblings when her own needs were not being met and deeply saddened by the heavy burden she had to bear at such a young age. I also found myself a bit troubled by Vanessa seemingly taking responsibility for father's distancing as she indicates that her efforts to connect with him "made him run faster." Rather than her father's response being the natural response ("of course"), I thought there were many other ways her father could have responded to her suffering and requests for attention.

Carol's response:

> When Vanessa says she went "underground," I find myself wondering where she went and also where she is now. I think of the times I went underground and did not feel I could speak about what I was seeing. Vanessa's description of her mother's depression is so vivid ("raging maniac," "a rock"), that I found it hard to keep track of the 10-year-old girl. Listening to this interview, I know I will be listening for her.

Step 2: I Poems

The second listening focuses in on the voice of the "I" who is speaking by following the use of this first-person pronoun and constructing what Elizabeth Debold (1990) has called "I poems." The purpose of this step is twofold. First, it is intended to press the researcher to listen to the participant's first-person voice—to pick up its distinctive cadences and rhythms—and second, to hear how this person speaks about him- or herself. This step is a crucial component of a relational method in that tuning into another person's voice and listening to what this person knows of her- or himself before talking about him or her is a way of coming into relationship that works against distancing ourselves from that person in an objectifying way (Brown & Gilligan, 1992).

Two rules govern the construction of an I poem: (a) underline or select every first-person "I" within the passage you have chosen along with the verb and any seemingly important accompanying words and (b) maintain the sequence in which these phrases appear in the text.[3] Then pull out the underlined "I" phrases, keeping them in the order they appear in the text, and place each phrase on a separate line, like lines in a poem. These guidelines are intended to foster a process of following the free-fall of association. Often the I poem itself will seem to fall readily into stanzas—reflecting a shift in meaning or

[3]We are using the same passage throughout this chapter to demonstrate how multiple readings of the same text (the heart of this method) yield different information. When working with an entire interview, the plot listening gathers information from the whole text, whereas the I poems may be constructed selectively from certain passages.

change in voice, the ending of a cadence or the start of a new breath. Sometimes the I poem captures something not stated directly but central to the meaning of what is being said. Other times it does not. In either case, the I poem picks up on an associative stream of consciousness carried by a first-person voice, cutting across or running through a narrative rather than being contained by the structure of full sentences. Cutting the text close and focusing in on just the I pronoun, the associated verb and few other words moves this aspect of subjectivity to the foreground, providing the listener with the opportunity to attend just to the sounds, rhythms, and shifts in this person's usages of "I" in his or her narratives.

Constructing an "I poem" from the passage selected from Vanessa's interview would involve first underlining the I statements, as indicated in the text that follows.

> And then I think you know everything kind of went underground for me and I stopped talking to people. . . . Hmmm. I think when there is a mental illness in the house and it's and there . . . can be. . . . and some of it can be out of control that hmmm a lot of families tend to isolate and that I think is what my family did and hmmm besides I didn't have anything to talk about. What was I going to say? My mother is a raging maniac? Or or she's she's a rock and I can't talk to her. It's not something you share with people at school. Hmmm and hmmm I think it made me chase my dad for for some kind of attention and of course that made him run faster. Hmmm. And so hmmm. . . . and you know at that point I think that's when I stopped sleeping. And I kept worrying that one of them was going to drop dead you know. And I think that hmmm some of that was behind the not sleeping.

These phrases are then lined up, like lines in a poem:

I think
I stopped talking
I think
I think
I didn't have anything to talk about

What was I going to say?
I can't talk
I think
I think
I stopped sleeping
I kept worrying
I think

Although in the full text Vanessa's isolation is apparent, by listening to this "I poem" we can hear how her description of this time is dominated by her own inner thoughts, not speaking about what was going on to anyone else, not sleeping, and worrying. Compiling several I poems from this interview highlights how much Vanessa thinks, as "I think" is repeated like a refrain.

This way of expressing herself is in contrast to her description in another section of the interview of how taking an antidepressant affected her life.

> Well, I think that hmmm. . . . well actually I quit a job that I had been in for a very long time that I had started the program. I was very good but it was taking so much out of me that I was exhausted all of the time and one of the first things I did when I started to feel better was quit this job and shock myself. Like I walked into my boss's office and handed him my resignation and said "I'm leaving in a month. I'm going. I, I . . This is the end of this. I can't do this anymore.

I think
I quit
I had been
I had started
I was very good
I was exhausted

I did
I started to feel better
I walked
I'm leaving
I'm going
I
I
I can't do this anymore

In this passage, the I poem highlights how much more physical and emotional activity Vanessa became engaged in while taking antidepressants. Her reflections on this time are filled with a wider range of action on her part—walking, leaving, quitting, and going. These two I poems allow us to hear in Vanessa's own words her sense of going from feeling "very small" and "very hidden" when she was depressed to experiencing herself as "getting bigger and bigger and bigger" when she started taking the medication. Selecting several different passages throughout the interview to focus on in this step and examining them in relation to one another can facilitate hearing potential variations in the first-person voice that may include a range of themes, harmonies, dissonances, and shifts.

Step 3: Listening for Contrapuntal Voices

The next step, listening for contrapuntal voices, brings the analysis back into relationship with the research question. It offers a way of hearing and developing an understanding of several different layers of a person's expressed experience as it bears on the questioned posed. The logic behind this step is drawn from the musical form counterpoint, which consists of "the combination of two or more melodic lines" (Piston, 1947, p. 13). Each melodic line has its own rhythm and "melodic curve" (the shape and movement of a melody within a range of low and high notes). These melodic lines of music are played simultaneously and move in some form of relationship with each other. This third step in the *Listening Guide* method offers a way to listen for the counterpoint in the text we are analyzing, or the multiple facets of the story being told. The first two steps—establishing the plot or the story lines and the psychic landscape and bringing in the first-person expressions of the speaker—build up to, and provide a context for, the contrapuntal listenings. It is in this third step that we begin to identify, specify, and sort out the different strands in the interview that may speak to our research question. This process entails reading through the interview two or more times, each time tuning into one aspect of the story being told, or one voice within the person's expression of her or his experience. The researcher's questions shape this listening, which may be based on the theoretical framework guiding the research, or the questions raised by the previous listenings, or both.

To begin, we specify the voices we will listen for and determine what the markers of a particular contrapuntal voice are or, more simply, how we will know this voice when we hear it. The text is then read through, listening for just one voice at a time, and the appearance or evidence of this voice is underlined in a color chosen to mark it. Reading through the text a separate time for each contrapuntal voice allows for the possibility that one statement may contain multiple meanings, and therefore may be underlined multiple times, and also allows the researcher to begin to see and hear the relationship between the person's first-person voice and the contrapuntal voices. The contrapuntal voices do not have to be in opposition to one another; they may be opposing or complementary in some way. Listening for at least two contrapuntal voices takes into account that a person expresses his or her experience in a multiplicity of voices or ways. It is important to note that it also allows for the possibility that some of these voices may be in harmony with one another, in opposition to one another, or even contradictory.

Examples of contrapuntal voice analyses range widely, depending on the nature of the particular study. Building on *In a Different Voice* (Gilligan, 1982), the voices of a separate and connected self, and of justice and care, have been distinguished and followed (see Gilligan & Attanucci, 1988; Johnston, 1988; Langdale, 1983; Lyons, 1988, 1989). In the work of the Harvard Project (e.g., Brown & Gilligan, 1992; Taylor et al., 1995), the analysis of girls' development from childhood into adolescence was shaped by the counterpoint in girls' interview texts between a voice of resistance or resilience (a strong, clear, confident voice) and a voice of distress or capitulation. Rather than characterizing these girls' voices as either resistant or capitulating, the counterpoint between both of these voices was followed both within a given interview and in the interviews conducted over time (Gilligan et al., 1990). Dana Jack (1991), in her study of depressed women, followed the counterpoint between an "I" who spoke clearly and directly (I feel, I know, I want, I believe) and what she called the "over-eye," the part of the self that observed, judged, shamed the self—the voice of the depression (I should, I have to). Through her contrapuntal analysis of the relationship between these two voices, Jack observed how the voice of the over-eye came in to silence the I, and how the resistance or resilience of the I, as it was repeatedly overruled by the over-eye, contributed to the exhaustion of depression (the extraordinary effort it took to silence the self). This analysis led her to conceptualize depression as a silencing of the self.

Returning to the excerpt from the interview with Vanessa, in light of our question about motherhood and depression, we noticed in the I poems two possible contrapuntal voices; a voice of knowing and a voice of silence. In the first contrapuntal voice listening we decided to underline the places in this passage in which Vanessa, speaking about herself as a child, described her knowledge of herself and her response to her mother's depression. Here, we show these phrases in italics below.

> And then I think you know, *everything kind of went underground for me,* and I stopped talking to people. Hmmm. I think when *there is a mental illness in the house,* and it's, and there can be . . . and *some of it can be out of control,* that hmmm, *a lot of families tend to isolate.* And *that I think is what my family did.* And hmmm, besides, I didn't have anything to talk about. What was I going to say? *"My mother is a raging maniac?"* Or, or "She's, *she's a rock and I can't talk to her." It's not something you share with people at school.* Hmmm, hmmm, I think for, *it made me chase my Dad for some kind of attention,* and of course *that made him run faster.* Hmmm. And so, hmmm ? and you know at that point, I think that's when *I stopped sleeping.* And *I kept worrying that one of them was going to drop dead,* you know. And *I think that hmmm, some of that was behind the not sleeping.*

Pulling out just what we have underlined in this listening, we hear how much Vanessa knew about what was going on for her, and her family, at that time:

> everything kind of went underground for me I stopped talking to people there is a mental illness in the house some of it can be out of control . . . a lot of families tend to isolate that, I think, is what my family did my mother is a raging maniac . . . she's a rock and I can't talk to her it's not something you share with people at school it made me chase my Dad for some kind of attention that made him run faster . . . I stopped sleeping I kept worrying that one of them was going to drop dead I think that hmmm, some of that was behind the not sleeping.

This listening goes to the heart of Weinberg's question about how much this mother knows about her experience with her own depressed mother. Vanessa recalls being aware of the severity of the situation with her mother ("my mother is a raging maniac") and what her own response to her mother's depression was. She began having difficulty sleeping and worried that one of her parents was going to die. Although she did try to reach out to her father, it unfortunately seemed to have contributed to her father pulling even further away ("that made him run faster"). This listening also highlights Vanessa's conflicts or uncertainties about knowing. Her repeated phrases, "you know," suggest that she wonders what others know about what she knows, and her hesitations, the "hmmms" that interrupt the flow, similarly could possibly be interpreted as a manifestation of her conflicts around speaking.

The second contrapuntal voice we listened for was a voice of not speaking. We underlined the passages in which Vanessa talked about her sense that she could not speak about what was happening to her family during this time. These passages are noted in bold text.

> And then I think you know, *everything kind of went underground for me,* and ***I stopped talking to people*** . . . Hmmm. I think when *there is a mental illness in the house,* and it's, and there can be and *some of it can be out of control,* that hmmm, *a lot of families tend to isolate.* And *that I think is what my family did.* And hmmm, besides, **I didn't have anything to talk about. What was I going to say?** *"My mother is a raging maniac?"* Or, or "She's, *she's a rock and I can't talk to her."* ***It's not something you share with people at school.*** Hmmm, hmmm, I think for, *it made me chase my Dad for some kind of attention,* and of course *that made him run faster.* Hmmm. And so, hmmm and you know at that point, I think that's when *I stopped sleeping.* And *I kept worrying that one of them was going to drop dead,* you know. And *I think that hmmm, some of that was behind the not sleeping.*

In this listening, we hear how Vanessa became isolated by virtue of her sense that she could not talk to anyone about what was happening to her, leaving her with little to say and perhaps little around which to connect with her peers—"it's not something you share with people at school."

In the counterpoint between these two voices, we hear evidence of Vanessa's own depression and also of her resistance, her strategy of going underground. Rather than having to choose which voice best characterizes what Vanessa is expressing, we listen for the relationship between these voices as her depression might also carry some aspects of her strategies for resistance. Together, these voices convey that Vanessa went underground because of what she knew. Here she conveys that she was aware of how out of control her mother's depression was but she had the sense that saying something about it was not possible for her.

Together, these contrapuntal voice listenings raise questions about what Vanessa knows in the present that she perhaps feels she cannot talk about and whether this possible silence may be contributing to her depression. We also return to Weinberg's inquiry, which began with her observation that in our search for understanding how maternal depression affects the mother–infant relationship, the women's own experiences with depression needed to be incorporated. These observations suggest the shape of the next step, composing an analytical summary based on the series of listenings we have conducted.

Once the contrapuntal voice listenings have been completed, with each voice underlined in a different color, the transcript provides a visual way of examining how these voices move in relation to one another and to the Is. In musical counterpoint, the two or more lines of music may each develop a distinct theme, at times moving in consonance with one another and at other times in dissonance. Here too, the contrapuntal voices within one person's narrative are in some type of relationship with one another, and this relationship becomes the focus of our interest. A range of questions could be asked at this point. Does one contrapuntal voice move with particular I poems more than others, and if so how do these voices move in relationship with one another? Does one or more of the voices move completely separate from the Is? What are the relationships among the contrapuntal voices? Do some of them seem to take turns? Do they seem to be opposing one another? How do they move in and out of relationship with one another? Although we only listened for two contrapuntal voices in this example, we could have decided to listen for more, depending on the questions guiding our analysis.

The development of these listenings for contrapuntal voices is an iterative process. The researcher begins with an idea about a possible voice, creates an initial definition or description of this voice, listens for it, and then assesses whether the definition of this voice makes sense and whether it is illuminating some meaningful aspect of the text. The researcher may then fine-tune this particular contrapuntal voice and try to listen for it again. In addition, once two or more contrapuntal voices have been identified, the researcher may reflect on whether something that felt important in the other listenings is getting left out, whether something needs to be added to an already defined voice, or whether a new voice needs to be listened to. In studies that involve several interviews, the contrapuntal voices may evolve out of the analyses of many different interviews through a process of going back and revisiting this step, this time reading for voices that have been redefined or newly defined through the analysis of other interviews.

Step 4: Composing an Analysis

In the final step of the *Listening Guide* method, having gone through the text a minimum of four times (plot, I poem, and listening for two or more contrapuntal voices), leaving a trail of underlinings, notes, and summaries each time, the researcher now pulls together what has been learned about this person in relation to the research question. In essence, an interpretation of the interview or text is developed that pulls together and synthesizes what has been learned through this entire process and an essay or analysis is composed. Returning to the research question that initiated this inquiry, several questions can be considered. What have you learned about this question through this process and how have you come to know this? What is the evidence on which you are basing your interpretations? Sometimes in this step it may become apparent that the research question itself needs to be modified, or perhaps even transformed, in response to this series of listenings.

Through our analysis of Vanessa's description of her experiences as a child living with her mother who was severely depressed, we hear a tension between how much Vanessa knew about what was happening in her family and how she also felt that there was no one with whom she could talk about how out of control some things had gotten. She held on to her own knowledge by taking it with her as she went underground psychologically. We wonder whether this tension between knowing and silence highlighted in the passage is still alive for Vanessa today, though we cannot answer this question based on the evidence in this passage.

In this chapter we focused on one small passage within one interview to provide an example of how each of the steps of the *Listening Guide* can be operationalized. A full analysis of this interview would involve working with the entire transcript. Although listening for one voice at a time in the earlier steps can illuminate different aspects of a person's experience as expressed in an interview, these separate listenings must be brought back into relationship with one another to not reduce or lose the complexity of a person's expressed experience. In a study that includes multiple interviews, these *Listening Guide* analyses may be examined in relationship to one another, illuminating similarities in the themes that may begin to emerge across several interviews and also marking distinct differences between them.

Conclusion

The *Listening Guide* method is a way of analyzing qualitative interviews that is best used when one's question requires listening to particular aspects of a person's expression of her or his own complex and multilayered individual experiences and the relational and cultural contexts within which they occur. It is a particularly useful tool for discovery research; to uncover new questions to pursue through focusing in on and learning from individual experiences. It is a relational method in the sense that it intentionally brings the researcher into relationship with the participant through making our responses, experiences, and interpretive lenses explicit in the process, and by listening to each participant's first-person voice before moving in to listen for answers to our own research questions. It is also relational in that the specific way the method is operationalized changes in response to, and via the process of, analysis. Through each of these steps we actively bring ourselves and our research question into relationship with the person's spoken experience to direct the analytical process, creating an opening for that person to shift our way of listening, the questions that we ask, and the ways in which we ask them.

This method requires the active engagement of the researcher throughout the analysis because it is intended to be a guide, or a set of steps that provide a basic frame, rather than a set of prescriptive rules to be followed. The researcher must make decisions with regard to how precisely to implement each step of this method in a particular research project. We have demonstrated the particular way that we have been implementing the *Listening Guide* method. As with any analytical tool, others have necessarily developed different ways of conducting the four basic steps to fit the specific needs of their various studies and sets of research questions.

Finally, although a *Listening Guide* analysis may serve as a primary method of analysis, it has also been used in conjunction with other qualitative methods of analysis such as narrative summaries (Way, 2001) and conceptually clustered matrices (Brown, 2001), as well as with a statistical analysis of thematic codes derived from interview texts (Tolman & Szalacha, 1999). These methods each offer a different pathway into and through qualitative interviews. The *Listening Guide* method offers a way of illuminating the complex and multilayered nature of the expression of human experience and the interplay between self and relationship, psyche and culture.

References

Aron, L. (1996). *A meeting of the minds: Mutuality in psychoanalysis.* Hillsdale, NJ: Atlantic.

Borland, K. (1991). "That's not what I said": Interpretive conflict in oral narrative research. In S. B. Gluck & D. Patai (Eds.), *Women's words: The feminist practice of oral history* (pp. 63–75). London: Routledge.

Breuer, J., & Freud, S. (1986). *Studies on hysteria* (James Strachey, Trans.). New York: Basic Books. (Original published 1985)

Brown, L. M. (1998). *Raising their voices: The politics of girls' anger.* Cambridge, MA: Harvard University Press.

Brown, L. M. (2001). White working-class girls, femininities, and the paradox of resistance. In D. L. Tolman & M. Brydon-Miller (Eds.), *From subjects to subjectivites: A handbook of interpretive and participatory methods* (pp. 95–110). New York: New York University Press.

Brown, L. M., & Gilligan, C. (1991). Listening for voice in narratives of relationship. In M. Tappan & M. Packer (Eds.), *Narrative and storytelling: Implications for understanding moral development. New directions for child development* (Vol. 54, pp. 43–62). San Francisco: Jossey-Bass.

Brown, L. M., & Gilligan, C. (1992). *Meeting at the crossroads: Women's psychology and girls' development.* Cambridge, MA: Harvard University Press.

Brown, L. M., Tappan, M., Gilligan, C., Miller, B., & Argyris, D. E. (1989). Reading for self and moral voice: A method for interpreting narratives of real-life moral conflict and choice. In M. Packer & R. Addison (Eds.), *Entering the circle* (pp. 141–164). Albany: State University of New York Press.

Bruner, J. (1986). *Actual minds, possible worlds.* Cambridge, MA: Harvard University Press.

Debold, E. (1990, April). *Learning in the first person: A passion to know.* Paper presented at the Laurel–Harvard conference on the psychology of women and the development of girls, Cleveland, OH.

Doucet, A. (1995). *Gender equality, gender differences, and care: Towards understanding gendered labour in British dual earner households.* Unpublished doctoral dissertation, University of Cambridge, Cambridge.

Fairbairn, W. R. D. (1944). Endopsychic structure considered in terms of object relationships. *International Journal of Psychoanalysis, 25,* 70–93.

Fine, M., & Macpherson, P. (1992). Over dinner: Feminism and adolescent female bodies. In H. Radtke & H. Stam (Eds.), *Power gender: Social relations theory in practice* (pp. 219–246). Newbury Park, CA: Sage.

Geertz, C. (1983). *Local knowledge: Further essays in interpretive anthropology.* New York: Basic Books.

Gilligan, C. (1982). *In a different voice: Psychological theory and women's development.* Cambridge, MA: Harvard University Press.

Gilligan, C. (1993). Letter to readers, 1993, *In a different voice: Psychological theory and women's development* (pp. ix–xxvii). Cambridge, MA: Harvard University Press.

Gilligan, C., & Attanucci, J. (1988). Two moral orientations: Gender differences and similarities. *Merrill-Palmer Quarterly, 43*(3), 223–237.

Gilligan, C., Brown, L. M., & Rogers, A. (1990). Psyche embedded: A place for body, relationships and culture in personality theory. In A. I. Rabin, R. A. Zucker, R. Emmons, & S. Frank (Eds.), *Studying persons and lives* (pp. 86–147). New York: Springer.

Jack, D. C. (1991). *Silencing the self: Women and depression.* Cambridge, MA: Harvard University Press.

Jack, D. C. (1999). *Behind the mask: Destruction and creativity in women's aggression.* Cambridge, MA: Harvard University Press.

Johnston, D. K. (1988). Adolescents' solutions to dilemmas in fables: Two moral orientations—Two problem solving strategies. In C. Gilligan, J. V. Ward, & J. M. Taylor (Eds.), *Mapping the moral domain: A contribution of women's thinking to psychological theory and education* (pp. 49–71). Cambridge, MA: Center for the Study of Gender, Education, and Human Development, Harvard University Graduate School of Education.

Josselson, R. (1987). *Finding herself: Pathways to identity development in women.* San Francisco: Jossey-Bass.

Keller, E. F. (1985). *Reflections on gender and science.* New Haven, CT: Yale University Press.

Langdale, C. H. (1983). *Moral orientations and moral development: The analysis of care and justice reasoning across different dilemmas in females and males from childhood through adulthood.* Unpublished doctoral dissertation, Harvard University Graduate School of Education, Cambridge, MA.

Lyons, N. P. (1988). Two perspectives: On self, relationships, and morality. In C. Gilligan, J. V. Ward, & J. M. Taylor (Eds.), *Mapping the moral domain: A contribution of women's thinking to psychological theory and education* (pp. 21–45). Cambridge, MA: Center for the Study of Gender, Education, and Human Development, Harvard University Graduate School of Education.

Lyons, N. P. (1989). Listening to voices we have not heard: Emma Willard girls' ideas about self, relationships, and morality. In C. Gilligan, N. P. Lyons, & T. J. Hammer (Eds.), *Making connections: The relational worlds of adolescent girls at Emma Willard School* (pp. 30–72). Cambridge, MA: Harvard University Press.

Mauthner, N. (1993). Towards a feminist understanding of "postnatal depression". *Feminism & Psychology, 3*(3), 350–355.

Mauthner, N. (1998). "It's a woman's cry for help": A relational perspective on postnatal depression. *Feminism & Psychology, 8*(3), 325–355.

Mauthner, N. (2000). *The darkest days of my life: Stories of postdepression.* Cambridge, MA: Harvard University Press.

Mauthner, N., & Doucet, A. (1998). Reflections on a voice-centered relational method. In J. Ribbens & R. Edwards (Eds.), *Feminist dilemmas in qualitative research: Public knowledge and private lives* (pp. 119–146). Newbury Park, CA: Sage.

Miller, J. B. (1976). *Toward a new psychology of women.* Boston: Beacon Press.

Mischler, E. G. (1979). Meaning in context: Is there any other kind? *Harvard Educational Review, 49*(1), 1–19.

Mitchell, S. A. (1988). *Relational concepts in psychoanalysis: An integration.* New York: Basic Books.

Morawski, J. (2001). Feminist research methods: Bringing culture to science. In D. L. Tolman & M. Brydon-Miller (Eds.), *From subjects to subjectivities: A handbook of interpretive and participatory methods* (pp. 57–75). New York: New York University Press.

Piaget, J. (1979). *The child's conception of the world.* Totowa, NJ: Littlefield Adams. (Original published 1929)

Piston, W. (1947). *Counterpoint.* New York: W. W. Norton.

Polkinghorne, D. (1988). *Narrative knowing and the human sciences.* Albany: State University of New York Press.

Reissman, C. K. (1993). *Narrative analysis.* Newbury Park, CA: Sage.

Scheper-Hughes, N. (1994). The violence of everyday life: In search of a critical and politically engaged psychological anthropology. In M. Suárez-Orozco, G. Spindler, & L. Spindler (Eds.), *The making of psychological anthropology II* (pp. 135–157). Fort Worth, TX: Harcourt Brace.

Spencer, R. (2000). *A comparison of relational psychologies. Project Report No. 5.* Wellesley, MA: Stone Center Working Paper Series.

Strauss, A., & Corbin, J. (1998). *Basics of qualitative research: Techniques and procedures for developing grounded theory* (2nd ed.). Thousand Oaks, CA: Sage.

Taylor, J. M., Gilligan, C., & Sullivan, A. (1995). *Between voice and silence: Women and girls, race and relationship.* Cambridge, MA: Harvard University Press.

Tolman, D. L. (1994). Doing desire: Adolescent girls' struggles for/with sexuality. *Gender and Society, 8*(3), 324–342.

Tolman, D. L. (2001). Echoes of sexual objectification: Listening for one girl's erotic voice. In D. L. Tolman & M. Brydon-Miller (Eds.), *From subjects to subjectivities: A handbook of interpretive and participatory methods* (pp. 130–144). New York: New York University Press.

Tolman, D. L., & Brydon-Miller, M. (Eds.). (2001). *From subjects to subjectivities: A handbook of interpretive and participatory methods.* New York: New York University Press.

Tolman, D. L., & Szalacha, L. (1999). Dimensions of desire: Bridging qualitative and quantitative methods in a study of female adolescent sexuality. *Psychology of Women Quarterly, 23*(1), 7–93.

Tronick, E. Z. (1989). Emotions and emotional communication in infants. *American Psychologist, 44*(2), 112–119.

Tronick, E. Z., & Weinberg, M. K. (1997). Depressed mothers and infants: Failure to form dyadic states of consciousness. In L. Murray & P. J. Cooper (Eds.), *Postpartum depression and child development* (pp. 54–81). New York: Guilford Press.

Way, N. (1998). *Everyday courage: The lives and stories of urban teenagers.* New York: New York University Press.

Way, N. (2001). Using feminist research methods to explore boys' relationships. In D. L. Tolman & M. Brydon-Miller (Eds.), *From subjects to subjectivities: A handbook of interpretive and participatory methods* (pp. 111–129). New York: New York University Press.

Werber, R. P. (1990). *Basic content analysis.* Newbury Park, CA: Sage.

Winnicott, D. W. (1960). Ego distortion in terms of true and false self, *The maturational processes and the facilitating environment* (pp. 140–152). London: Hogarth.

10

Participatory Action Research: From Within and Beyond Prison Bars

Michelle Fine, María Elena Torre, Kathy Boudin, Iris Bowen, Judith Clark, Donna Hylton, Migdalia Martinez, Missy, Rosemarie A. Roberts, Pamela Smart, and Debora Upegui

Participatory action research represents a stance within qualitative research methods—an epistemology that assumes knowledge is rooted in social relations and most powerful when produced collaboratively through action. With a long and global history, participatory action research (PAR) has typically been practiced within community-based social action projects with a commitment to understanding, documenting, or evaluating the impact that social programs, social problems, or social movements bear on individuals and communities. PAR draws on multiple methods, some quantitative and some qualitative, but at its core it articulates a recognition that knowledge is produced in collaboration and in action.

With this essay, we aim to accomplish four ends. First, we provide a cursory history of PAR, beginning with Kurt Lewin (1951) and traveling too briskly through the feminist and postcolonial writings of critical theorists. Second, we introduce readers to a PAR project we have undertaken in a women's prison in New York, documenting the impact of college on women in prison, the prison environment, and on the women's postrelease outcomes. Third, we present a glimpse at our findings and offer up an instance of analysis, demonstrating closely how we analyzed thematically and discursively data about "transformation" as a research collective of inmate and university-based researchers. Fourth, we articulate a set of reflections on our work as a PAR collective, the dilemmas of writing openly under surveillance.

The authors would like to thank the Leslie Glass Foundation, the Open Society Institute, and the Spencer Foundation for funding the research; Superintendent Elaine Lord, Paul Korotkin, and E. Michele Staley for their feedback; and Shura Saul for her design inspiration.

The roles and responsibilities of outside scholars in relation to inside scholars have long been a question for theorists and researchers of social injustice. Many have agitated for a form of participation but few have articulated the nature of the work-together (see Chataway, 1997, for an exception; also McIntyre, 1997). This chapter invites readers into a prison-based PAR project, in which a team of university-based researchers and inmate researchers collaborated to document and theorize the impact of college within and beyond the prison environment. Like many before us, we sought to organize all aspects of the intervention and the research through democratic participation. Like those, our practice did not always live up to the design. We do not see insiders or outsiders as the "true" bearers of truth or knowledge, but more like Brinton Lykes (2001), Linda Tuhiwai Smith (1999), and Ignacio Martín-Baró (1994) we recognize in our souls the relative freedom and therefore responsibility of outside researchers to speak critically and constructively with insiders about the possibilities and limits of participatory research within the walls of prison.

A Too Brief History of Participatory Action Research

Kurt Lewin has long been the name attached to the "genesis" of action research in the United States. From the 1940s onward, with vision, critique, and intellectual courage, Lewin dared to assert participant knowledge as foundational to validity; democratic and participatory research as foundational to social change. Working very much within a psychological paradigm for a greater social good, Lewin carved a space for "the development of reflective thought, discussion, decision and action by ordinary people participating in collective research on 'private troubles' (Mills, 1959) which they have in common" (quoted in Adelman, 1997). Lewin challenged the artificial borders separating theory, research, and action, insisting: "No action without research; no research without action" (quoted in Adelman, 1997). At the core of Lewin's project was, like John Dewey, a refusal to separate thought from action; an insistence on the integration of science and practice; a recognition that social processes could be understood only when they were changed (see Cherry & Borshuk, 1998).

Frances Cherry and Catherine Borshuk place in historic context the power of Lewin's work while he was director at the Commission for Community Interrelations (CCI) of the American Jewish Committee. According to Cherry (personal communication, 2000), "Perhaps closest to contemporary participatory action research would be the category of research conducted by CCI: a community self-survey of civil rights in which the importance of members of the community conducting the research was stressed as essential . . . Lewinian thinking [recognized] that science and social problem-solving should be intimately connected, and that action research was inevitably participatory."

The community self-survey of civil rights, initiated under Lewin's leadership, exemplifies the kind of democratic progressive community projects CCI advocated, "attempting to move beyond academic expertise and to place the tools of research in the hands of concerned citizens" (Cherry & Borshuk, 1998, p. 129). Lewin's vision of democratic social research was compromised significantly over time by the increasing conservatism of U.S. psychology, McCarthyism, and scientism and converted into a set of techniques and axioms rather than a radical challenge to science as practiced.

Central and South American theorists and practitioners, including Orlando Fals-Borda (1979), Paulo Freire (1982), and Ignacio Martín-Baró (1994) have structured a set of commitments to PAR that move Lewin well beyond the borders of psychology, into an explicit analysis of the relation of science to social inequality, community life, and radical social change. As Martín-Baró explained,

> If our objective is to serve the liberation needs of the people [of Latin America]. . . . [We must] involve ourselves in a new praxis, an act of transforming reality that will let us know not only about what is but also about what is not, and by which we may try to orient ourselves toward what ought to be" (1994, pp. 27–29). Like Martín-Baró, Fals-Borda and colleagues sought a set of practices that would reveal "facts" as processes, "causality" as circular or "spiral in nature," and "multiple determinations" rather than "immediate antecedents" (Fals-Borda, 1979). For Fals-Borda, like Lewin, a dynamic or dialectical confrontation between common sense and systematic observations, followed by intensive reflection and action, engaged at the provocative borders between insiders and outsiders, were the recursive steps of PAR.
>
> Deeply critical of the relation of science to social inequity, and equally hopeful about science for radical social change, Fals-Borda recognized "the possibility for the masses of workers themselves to create and possess scientific knowledge; that social research and political action can be synthesized and mutually influential so as to increase the level of efficiency of action as well as the understanding of reality" (1979, p. 40). Across history and current texts, these PAR scholars have worked to articulate specific principles of PAR. At root, participatory research recognizes what Antonio Gramsci (1971) described from a prison cell in Italy, the intellectual and political power of "organic intellectuals" from whom counter-hegemonic notions derive, whose lives are deeply grounded in class struggles. Herein lies the fundamental challenge to what Habermas called "scientism" or what John Gaventa called "official knowledge" as the sole legitimate claim to truth (Gaventa, 1993; Habermas, 1971; Hall, 1993; Kemmis & McTaggart, 2000; McIntyre, 2000). With similar commitments, Hans Toch (1967) authored a powerful article that spoke about PAR in prison, about the knowledge of "convicts" and the humility of outside researchers, an article well ahead of its time. We owe much, in this chapter and in our work, to the wisdom and foresight of Hans Toch.

Relationships, Responsibilities, and Action at the Heart of Participatory Research

> In the participatory research propounded here, the silenced are not just incidental to the curiosity of the researcher but are the masters of inquiry into the underlying causes of the events in their world. In this context research becomes a means of moving them beyond silence into a quest to proclaim the world (Gaventa, 1993).

In the past five years, with both feminist and explicitly critical turns, the writings on the stance of participatory researchers have broken important new ground. Our work has been enormously influenced by five such turns. To begin, there has been a sharp recognition of participation *with,* not only *for,* community. Psychologist Brinton Lykes marked this move in her language, reflecting her stance on a project in which she

> agreed to *accompany* a friend to her community of origin in the Highlands of Guatemala. . . . [Recognizing myself] as a "situated other" within a *praxis of solidarity* [which] informs my ongoing efforts to develop alternative methods for "standing under" these realities and participating with local actors in responding to problems in daily living. (2001, p. 1)

Second, we are inspired by participatory action researchers, who drawing from critical race and legal theories have recognized the intellectual power and searing social commentary developed at the bottom of social hierarchies (Ladson-Billings, 2000). Mari Matsuda (1995), a critical legal scholar writing for an "outsider's jurisprudence," wrote, "When notions of right and wrong, justice and injustice, are explained not from an abstract position from the position of groups who have suffered through history, moral relativism recedes . . . [toward] a new epistemological source for critical scholars looking to the bottom"(p. 6).

Third, from the growing literature on research for and by indigenous peoples, some participatory researchers, ourselves among them, draw from the writings of Maori theorist and researcher Linda Tuhiwai Smith (1999), who recognizes not only the knowledge accumulated in indigenous communities but also that indigenous values, beliefs, and behaviors must be incorporated into the praxis of participatory research. From Tuhiwai Smith we take profound insights about respect for local custom and practices, not as an obstacle to research but as a site for possible learning and shared engagement and long-term social change.

Fourth, we have been inspired and moved by the writings of critical psychologist Kum Kum Bhavnani (1994), who has authored an essay in which she struggles aloud with questions of objectivity—that is, feminist objectivity in her self-consciously political research. Holding herself responsible to satisfy high standards for quality work, Bhavnani writes about three criteria for "feminist objectivity": inscription, micropolitics, and difference. Inscription entails holding herself accountable to produce stories about young women and men that counter—and do not reinforce—dominant, stereotypic scripts. Micropolitics demands that she explicitly analyze, in her empirical texts, her relation to and with the "subjects" of her research. And "difference" reminds her that she must theorize not only the strong trends that sweep across her data, but interrogate, as well and with equal rigor, the subtle and significant "differences" within.

And fifth, Glenda Russell and Janis Bohan (1999) argue that it is crucial to theorize and strategize how PAR "gives back" to communities generous enough to open themselves up for intellectual scrutiny. Russell and Bohan are two of the very few scholars who deliberate on the questions of audience, product, and what is left behind. For these activist scholars, creating a legacy of inquiry, a process of change, and material resources to enable transform are crucial to the PAR project.

These five turns—toward working "with," recognizing local knowledge, respecting local practices, stretching toward a grounded "feminist objectivity," and giving back—emerge for us as guiding refinements in the practice of PAR (see also Brydon-Miller, 1997; Olesen, 1999).

A Note on Limits and Responsibility

Although many scholars have begun to write on the power of PAR, a number of feminist and critical race theorists have wandered into the other side of the conversation, daring to reveal what Venezuelan community psychologist Esther Weisenfeld (1999, p. 2) has called the "unfulfilled promises of PAR." We are indebted to these writers, because it is in their firm belief about the power of participation that they feel compelled to write honestly with caution. Thus, Patricia Maguire (2001) reflected on her training of participatory researchers in the new South Africa, and reported a low level but pervasive resistance to the dialogic, nonauthoritarian nature of the work, such that participants were as eager to contribute fully as they were to be taught or led in traditional relations of authority, disappointment emerging when they were not. Anne Bettencourt, George Dillman, and Neil Wollman (1996) wrote on participatory research as a form of grassroots organizing, and noted with concern that once a compelling project is stirred up, participatory researchers have an obligation to find, build, and then pass the torch on to an interior leadership structure to move the action forward and to resist taking up that role themselves. Cynthia Chataway (2001) offered a very careful analysis of her work with a Native American community, respectfully recognizing that although equal and public participation may be the goal of outside researchers, those who work and dwell in communities that are oppressed and highly surveyed may, indeed, be grateful for the research and yet prefer privacy as a form of public responsibility. John Stanfield II (1998) noted that participatory research has become a "partial solution" to the historic oppression of people of color in social sciences but, he continued, "rarely do researchers share career rewards with 'subjects' of color, such as coauthorships and access to authoritative credentializing processes" (p. 336).

In a useful move, Brinton Lykes, who has worked, read, and thought carefully about the delicate praxis of participatory methods in Guatemala, Ireland, South Africa, and the United States, offers a crucial and generous set of reflections on working criteria for evaluating participatory methods, including:

> the method's compatibility and/or complementarity with other existing resources in local communities with a majority population living in extreme poverty, thereby enhancing sustainability of the project . . . [and] the method's capacity to facilitate an action/reflection dialectic when new ways of thinking and/or alternative cultural practices emerge within and among local participants and their communities in response to the PAR process. (2001, pp. 195–196)

We hear all of these cautions as wisdom. We are privileged to be working within a maximum-security prison with a supportive superintendent and correctional staff and prison-based researchers and respondents, and we understand the stakes for these inmates, should they broach some forms of honesty or critical action, could be devastating. We have learned, as Tuhiwai Smith would warn us, that what appears to be "paranoia" may just be local wisdom; and not to confuse "finding your voice" and "speaking out" with courage. Thus we have learned that "equal" participation and responsibility does not mean the "same." Instead, it means endless ongoing conversations, among us, with every decision always revisited, about who can take risks, who dares to speak, who must remain quiet, and what topics need never see the light of day. As Linda Martín Alcoff (1995) has written, we are painfully aware that we always need to "analyze the probable or actual effects of [our] words on the [many, contradictory] discursive and material contexts [both within and beyond the prison]" (p. 111).

The Context for the Project

The 1980s and 1990s in the United States were decades of substantial public and political outcry about crime and about criminals. During these years, stiffer penalties were enforced for crimes, prisons were built at unprecedented rates, parole was tougher to achieve, "three strikes and you're out" bills passed, and college was no longer publicly funded for women and men in prison. Indeed, with the signing of the Violent Crime Control and Law Enforcement Act, President Bill Clinton stopped the flow of all federal dollars (in the form of Pell grants) that had enabled women and men in prison to attend college. It was then up to the states to finalize the closing of most prison-based college programs around the nation. At Bedford Hills Correctional Facility, a vibrant college program had been coordinated by Mercy College for more than 15 years. In 1995, this program, like more than 340 others nationwide, was closed. This decision provoked a sea of disappointment, despair, and outrage from the women at Bedford Hills, who had been actively engaged in higher education and in GED/ABE (adult basic education) preparation. Within months, a group of inmates met with the superintendent and, later, an active community volunteer, Thea Jackson, and soon they, with Marymount Manhattan College president Regina Peruggi, resurrected the college—now a private, voluntary consortium of colleges and universities dedicated to inmate education.

The design of the college was conceptualized through pillars of strong, ongoing participation by the prison administration, staff, the inmates, faculty, and volunteers. Students, in particular, are expected to "give back" in any number of ways. They teach, mentor, pay the equivalent of a month's wages for tuition, contribute to the prison community, and demonstrate high levels of community engagement once they are released (see Fine et al., 2001). Structurally, the design of the college program called for the college administrators at Bedford to meet regularly with the prison administration, the inmate committee, and a representative of the board to create and sustain a "safe" context for serious conversation–reflection, revision, and re-imagining of the college program. It was felt to be important to design the program with core participation from every constituency because many, including the long-termers who witnessed the loss of the college, did not want the younger women to ever take the program for granted, assume its permanence, forget its fragility, or view it as an entitlement. Little did we know that the forms of participation within the college would emerge, powerfully, as one of the central positive outcomes of the college program. That is, women who have, for the most part, spent the better (or worst) part of their lives under the thumbs of poverty, racism, sexism, and violence could, in college, "hear my own voice" or "see my own signature" or "make my own decisions"—re-imagine themselves as agents who make choices, take responsibility, create change for themselves and others (e.g., family, children, and younger women at Bedford) and design a future not overdetermined by the past.

At its heart, this college program has not been simply about the taking of courses, but instead about deep immersion in an intellectual and ethical community of scholars. The physical space of the learning center—equipped with nonnetworked computers (use of the Internet is banned in prisons), contributed books, magazines, newspapers, flags from colleges and universities in the consortium—holds what Seymour Sarason (1974) called the "sense of community," a place where, the women will attest, "if I need help I can find it—even if that means someone to kick me in the ass to get back to work and finish my papers." This intellectual community also spills out onto the "yard," where you can overhear study groups on Michel Foucault, qualitative research, Alice Walker; or in the cell block where the ticking of typewriter keys can be heard late into the night; or a "young inmate may knock softly on [my] wall, at midnight, asking how to spell or punctuate. . . . " For the women at Bedford Hills, 80% of whom carry scars of childhood sexual abuse, biographies of miseducation, tough family and community backgrounds, long lists of social and personal betrayals, growing back the capacity to join a community, engage with a community, give back, and trust are remarkable social and psychological accomplishments.

Thus, when the first author was asked to conduct the empirical documentation of the impact of college on the women, the prison environment and the world outside the prison, it seemed all too obvious that a participatory design behind bars would be nearly impossible—albeit essential.

Research Design

In 1997, the Leslie Glass Foundation offered to fund the documentation of the impact of college on the prison community. Fine, professor of psychology at the Graduate Center of the City University of New York, agreed to become the principal investigator of the project, and hired a team of graduate students to help conduct the study: Melissa Rivera,[1] Rosemarie A. Roberts, María Elena Torre, and Debora Upegui. It was determined, early in the design phase, that

[1]Melissa Rivera relocated to California early in the project and is no longer active in the research.

the project would be maximally informed, useful, and productive if there were a set of inmate researchers on the team as well (see Toch, 1967). We consulted with the superintendent, who agreed with the design, after the New York State Department of Correctional Services (NYSDOCS) provided official approval. The following inmate researchers joined the team: Kathy Boudin, Iris Bowen,[2] Judith Clark, Aisha Elliot,[3] Donna Hylton, Migdalia Martinez,[4] Missy, and Pamela Smart. Over time, NYSDOCS, through the efforts of E. Michele Staley, grew to be a crucial member of our research team, computing the postrelease reincarceration rates for women who enrolled in, graduated from, or did not participate in the college program.

Study Design

The design of the research called for both qualitative and quantitative methods (see Table 10.1). The research questions required that a quantitative analysis be undertaken to assess the extent to which college, in fact, reduced recidivism and disciplinary incidents; and a qualitative analysis to determine the psychosocial effects of college on the women, the prison environment, their children, and the women's lives postrelease.

A Glimpse of the Findings

Using very different methods, we were able to research intensively a number of questions about the impact of college on women in, and released from, prison. Integrating both quantitative and qualitative methods allowed us to more deeply probe questions that needed further explanation.

To What Extent Does Involvement in College Affect Women's Reincarceration Rates?

In the fall of 1999, the research team approached the New York State of Correctional Services, requesting that a longitudinal analysis of reincarceration rates be conducted on those women from Bedford Hills Correctional Facility who had attended the Mercy College Program and had subsequently been released. Staley, program research specialist, conducted the analyses for the project and provided data on return-to-custody rates for all participants at any

---

[2] Iris Bowen was transferred to another correctional facility mid-way through the research. Though her relocation, far from family, friends, and support networks, has put incredible strains on her, she remains a vital member of the research committee.

[3] Aisha Elliot, a starting member of the research committee, stopped participating early in the project because of personal commitments.

[4] Migdalia Martinez was granted clemency in December 2000 and released, after serving 11 years, 3 months, on January 31, 2001. She remains a member of the research team.

Table 10.1. Research Questions, Methods, Sample, and Outcomes

Research Questions	Method	Sample[a]	Outcomes
1. What is the impact of the college experience on *inmate students*?	1. Archival analysis of college since inception 2. One-on-one interviews conducted by inmate-researchers 3. Focus groups: with inmates, faculty, children, and college presidents	 N = 65 10 focus groups: N = 43 (inmates) N = 20 (faculty) N = 9 (children) N = 7 (presidents)	• Academic achievement • Personal transformation • Expression of responsibility for crime and for future decisions • Reflection on choices made in the past and decisions to be made in the future • Civic engagement and participation in prison and outside
2. What is the impact of the college experience on the *prison environment*?	4. In-depth interviews with former inmates 5. Interviews with correction officers and administrators	N = 20 N = 5	• Changes in prison disciplinary environment • Prison climate • Correction officers views of and experiences with prison • Attitudes of women not in the college program about college • Faculty's views of college program
3. What are the *postrelease effects* of college on the women and on their reincarceration rates?	6. Surveys of faculty 7. Student narratives 8. Statistical analysis of former inmates who attended college while in prison	N = 20 N = 18 N = 454 total students (N = 274 released)	• Reincarceration rates • Economic well-being • Health • Civic participation • Persistence in pursuing higher education • Relations with family and friends

Continued

Table 10.1. *Continued*

Key Methodological Decisions			
1. Create a research committee consisting of outside researchers and inmates with administrative advisors.	3. Racial/ethnic mix in research committee leadership and focus group facilitators and cofacilitators.	5. Inmate researchers choose between anonymity and authorship.	8. Conduct focus groups, facilitated by inside and outside researchers, with subsamples to: (a) pursue themes that emerged from individual interviews and (b) maximize opportunities for dissenting opinions.
	4. Conduct focus group within prison with teen group children of inmate, rather than conduct interviews in teen homes.	6. Participants choose a name by which they are known in the report.	9. Individual interviews rather than focus groups for correction officers.
2. Teach inmates how to be researchers in a semester-long research methods college course.		7. Sample. Include inmates who left college in sample and those in precollege program.	10. Interpretation session. Data analysis by inside and outside researchers.
			11. Writing final report in a single voice.

[a]*Some women participated in more than one data source.*

time since release, and then return to custody rates for all participants within 36 months of release.[5]

Using the standard NYSDOCS measure of 36 months, out of the 274 women tracked longitudinally, 21 college participants returned to custody. Thus, women who participated in college while in prison had a 7.7% return-to-custody rate. In contrast, an analysis tracking all female offenders released between 1985 and 1995 revealed a 29.9% return-to-custody rate within 36 months. Women without college are almost four times more likely to be returned to custody than comparable women who participated in college while in prison. Women with no college are twice as likely to be rearrested for a "new term commitment" (a new crime) than women with some college. In addition, women with no college are 18 times more likely to violate parole than women with some college. In other words, *college in prison reduces the amount of postrelease crime and even more significantly heightens responsible compliance with parole expectations.*

To What Extent Does Engagement in College, and Completion of a Degree, Affect Women's Psychological Sense of Themselves, Past, Present, and Future?

We review, now, how we analyzed the qualitative individual and focus group interviews for evidence of "transformation." We were struck, in examining all of the data, with the extent to which women spoke of college as a source of personal change, transformation, and new selves. Theorizing transformation, however, proved to be a multilayered task. The process of analysis moved us through four readings of "transformation."

Initially all of us read all of the transcripts and heard a *discourse of split selves:* As the research team first read through the transcripts, we all noted recurring talk of "old" and "new" selves; the "before-college me" and "after-college me." Women in prison and those recently released repeatedly credited college with facilitating a personal change from their old ways to their new (read "better") way of life. With an intentional and sharp separation of old and new, the women drew clear distinctions between the "me before" and the "me now:"

> I'm not the same person that went to prison. If you knew me before, you would never know it's the same person. [I made] a complete turn around.

---

[5] Staley relied on the following methodology:

[NYSDOCS] matched the file [of college students from the Mercy College registrar's office] with our department's release file that included releases between 1985 and 1999, using DIN (Departmental Identification Numbers assigned to each inmate). . . . [I]ncluded in the analysis were only the inmates that were released from NYSDOCS' custody subsequent to their participation in the college program. Of the 454 cases provided, 274 college participants have been released from NYSDOCS since their college participation. This is the sample that was used in the follow-up analysis to determine how many of these participants returned to NYSDOCS' custody. With respect to the return-to-custody analysis, I used the same survival analysis methodology that is used to prepare our department's standard return-to-custody report, *1995 Releases: Three Year Post Release Follow Up.* (Personal correspondence, Staley, Aug. 22, 2000)

> And I'm proud of that, 'cause I like me now . . . college made me face me and like me now. (Ellie)

> When I first came to Bedford Hills, I was a chronic disciplinary problem, getting tickets [issued for disciplinary infractions] back to back. I had a very poor attitude as well, I was rude and obnoxious for no reason, I did not care about anything or anyone. . . . Then I became motivated to participate in a number of programs, one of which was college. I started to care about getting in trouble and became conscious of the attitude I had that influenced my negative behaviors. . . . College is a form of rehabilitation, one of the best. (Denise)

Within this discourse of split selves, there was a particularly relentless attempt by the women to derogate their past selves. This, then, produced the occasion for our second reading through the transcripts. Heeding the advice of Celia Kitzinger (2000), we wanted to avoid the tendency to rush too quickly through material that seemed obvious or superficial, even idiomatic. The research team reread and discussed the transcript sections on transformation generating and pressed for deeper interpretations with each pass.

As the earlier excerpts illustrate, we were interested to hear how harshly many of the women described their "former selves": angry, antisocial, drug abuser, disrespectful both to self and others, having little to offer the world. These characterizations were typically followed by descriptions of "complete" and "total" personal changes: productive, working, motivated, knowledgeable, worthy of pride. This trashing of women's past lives was read initially by Graduate Center researchers as a language of internalized self-blame and self-hatred.

> Cause we were some wild kids when we were younger. We were angry. We didn't understand the system. This was our first time ever being in trouble. So all we wanted to do was fight. We didn't interact with anybody, we weren't social. So now [we're] like totally different. We look forward to coming to college. . . . And it's like I changed, just totally changed. And my sister came [to college] a couple of months afterwards and changed, but we did it together. (Erica, describing herself and her sister early in their incarceration)

The inmate researchers, on the other hand, heard in the same transcripts a familiar language of redemption that echoed the kind of talk heard in counseling, 12-step programs, support groups, church, and even in discussions about upcoming parole board meetings. An old "bad," "unworthy," "negative" self is vilified and then redeemed as a new "positive," "productive," "good" self.

> When I first came here I had a chip on my shoulder that I wanted somebody to knock off. . . . I stayed in trouble. I was disrespectful. I had no self-respect, no respect for others. And it took a while for me to change gradually through the years, and . . . when I started going to college that was like the key point for me of rehabilitation, of changing myself. And nobody did it for me, I did it for myself. . . . And I went and I did it and I accomplished things that I didn't think I could accomplish. (Roz)

Together as researchers, we worried that this language, used by the women about themselves, sounded so much like the language used by those in some policy circles attacking women in poverty, women of color, and indeed women in prison. Thus across the transcripts we analyzed for overlapping discourses of redemption as well as social ideologies that place blame for social problems squarely and exclusively within individuals (usually racialized), with no history and no context.

As we theorized the relationship between the discourses of redemption and derogation of poor women, inmate researchers reminded the research team of a simple fact that, though obvious, Graduate Center researchers had looked beyond: Crimes had been committed by most of the women with whom we spoke. The discourse of redemption, it was suggested, serves as a powerful coping strategy for women desperate to understand themselves as separate from the often destructive behavior that led them to prison. By staying within a story of two separate selves, women can assert judgment over their past actions without having to face the pain of integrating complicated histories—past selves now despised, past behavior now regretted—into their present selves. The task of analysis then became to look back across the data for connective tissue between past and present selves, for instances where women reflect critically on their lives.

> But then just to sit down and read it all and discover that you don't even like half of this stuff here about you. But this is you. You know, you from you. And it was like, oooh! . . . so I [re-]wrote it and I read it and I re-read it and I re-wrote it and I sort of like condensed it [from 20 pages] into like about six pages. . . . it was like really deep because it was no escaping then. (Rhonda, on documenting her past for her clemency petition)

Through reconceptualizing past, present, and future selves as connected, we began to understand that personal change, or transformation, was not a simple declaration of starting anew with a "clean slate." The women were trying to describe personal change or transformation as a process in which a woman recognizes her past, present, and future selves in relation to each other and within social context, both in and outside the prison. And most were articulating the role that college played in helping them draw these lines of connections.

Using this line of analysis, we resisted thinking of lives and selves as existing outside of social context, without community, without history. In addition, we began to understand that women bring pieces of "old" selves into "new" selves, and that these pieces of the past selves inform and cocreate, within a social historical context, a present ever-changing self. And that college is one of those sites in which women can, in a community, acquire a language and the skills of reflection, through which these lines of connection can be drawn. Thus we undertook our third reading of the transcripts, seeking this connective tissue. For Sondra, a student, this means recognizing her multiplicity and negotiating which pieces of herself are useful in moving her life in the direction she chooses:

> It's still in my character, but I don't let it come out. It doesn't prove anything. Before, I didn't care. Now I see I can achieve, do anything I put my mind to. I have matured. . . . I can set examples now. (Sondra, addressing past behavior that led to disciplinary problems)

> I know the decision to continue my education will help me in the long run, yet my aspiration is to somehow help the young women who are coming into prison in record breaking numbers. My past allows me to speak from experience, and the academic knowledge I have obtained allows me to move forward productively, hopefully enabling me to help these younger women recognize and reach their potentials. (Crystal)

In Crystal's comment, we can see that recognizing these connections in oneself can lead to an understanding of self in community and responsibility across generations. Crystal sees her past in the younger women's presents and her present in their futures. This recognition led our research team to a fourth stage of analysis, in which we sought evidence of transformation talk located within a discourse of community and social responsibility.

Finally, after many readings and much discussion, we came to see that *a discourse of responsibility* was operating to link old and new selves, and that the women viewed college as the intellectual and personal site in which they could develop such a discourse in community while in prison. As fundamental, the women recognized that in the absence of programs like college, they would not have been able to move into reviewing their pasts, reseeing their crimes, narrating a sense of responsibility for past and future.

> I can think and talk about my victim now. It's not just "the bitch cut me and I cut her back." Even that idea comes out differently now, "the girl cut me and I chose to strike back." Those words weren't in me before, but now, just having the words to articulate things, puts them into perspective differently. (Tanisha)

> My involvement with college . . . has opened my eyes to all of the things that were wrong in my life. Now I have a sense of priority, a sense of accountability and I have made a legitimate premise for myself on which to build . . . my needs are still important, but not at someone else's expense. (Vanessa)

As these women testify, our quantitative and qualitative data confirm what other researchers and prisoners have found: Core elements of higher education, such as self-reflection and critical inquiry, spur the production of critical subjectivities, transformed and connected selves, and in turn transformed communities (Conway, 1998; Faith, 1993; Germanotta, 1995; Rivera, 1995). These interior transformations in self bear significant consequence for the women and for their incarceration rates. Said another way, individuals move from being passive objects to active subjects—critical thinkers who actively participate in their lives and social surroundings; who take responsibility for past and future actions; who direct their lives, networks, and social actions in the world. Moving across readings of the transformation narratives, we came to see the social psychological links between college, transformation, and social responsibility. We turn now to our transformation as researchers on a participatory research team.

We Created Among Us: A Team of Women Scholars

A world may come into being in the course of a continuing dialogue.
Maxine Greene (1995, p. 196)

We met often as a team, sometimes once a month, sometimes more and sometimes less. Encumbered by limitations on privacy, freedom, contact, and time, we are as profoundly moved by our shared capacity and desire to climb over the walls that separate and carve a small delicate space of trust, reciprocity, and the ability to argue respectfully about what is important to study, to speak, and to hold quietly among ourselves.

In this space for critical inquiry, we walked across barbed wires outside the windows and inside the room, through our racialized and classed histories, between biographies filled with too much violence and too little hope and biographies lined with too much privilege and too little critique. We engaged in what Paulo Freire (1982) would call "dialogue," a "relation of 'empathy' between two 'poles' who are engaged in a joint search" (p. 45). Freire deployed dialogue in an effort to provoke critical consciousness or *conscientizacao,* which "always submits . . . causality to analysis; what is true today may not be so tomorrow" (p. 44). Freire sought to create educational spaces, in our case both a community of learners and a community of researchers, in which "facts" were submitted to analysis, "causes" reconsidered, and, indeed, "responsibility" reconceived in critical biographic, political, and historical context. The task, then, was not merely to educate us all to "what is," but to provoke analysis of "what has been" and release, as Greene would invite, our imagination for "what could be."

As one of the inmate researchers, Missy, explained, "I look at this research project as a way of giving back, motivating and hopefully helping the program and the participants, and even the researchers—I want them to hopefully have a different outlook on what education means in prisons. I'm hoping that we reach a younger generation. To pass on our stories. . . ."

And Yet: Between Us Inside and Out

This space of radical openness is a margin—a profound edge. Locating oneself there is difficult yet necessary. It is not a "safe" place. One is always at risk. One needs a community.
bell hooks (1984, p. 149)

We are, at once, a team of semifictional coherence, and, on the ground, a group of women living very different lives, defined in part by biographies of class, race, and ethnic differences. Half of us go home at night; half of us live in the prison. Many of us bring personal histories of violence against women to our work, and all of us worry about violence against, and sometimes by, women. Some of us have long-standing experience in social movements for social justice; others barely survived on the outside. Some of us are White, Jewish, Latina, Caribbean African American, some mixed. Most of us are from the mainland of this country, a few born outside the borders of the United States. The most obvious divide among us is that between free and imprisoned, but the other tattoos and scars on our souls weave through our work, worries, writings, and our many communities. Usually these differences enrich us. Sometimes they distinguish us. At moments they separate us. We understand ourselves to carry knowledge and consciousness that are, at once, determined by where we come from and shaped by who we choose to be (Harding, 1983; Hartsock, 1983; Jaggar, 1983; Smith, 1987).

Pamela Smart, inmate researcher, wrote,

> Most research on prisons is conducted by outside investigators. However, there is an incredible source of skills right inside these walls. Inmate researchers can establish a comfort zone with interviewees that many outside researchers cannot. Because a lot of people in prison are less trusting of outsiders, they may not be entirely forthcoming with their responses. However, inmate researchers, by the nature of their statuses as inmates, are often viewed by participants as more trustworthy. Just because I am in prison does not negate the fact that I am also a competent researcher. Using prisoners as researchers is a valuable experience that is beneficial to both the participants in the study and the readers of the results.

Questions of Design: How Participation Shifted Our Questions, Methods, Analyses, and Writings

We offer next a series of key methodological, ethical, and theoretical decisions we, as a team, made within the prison project and try to articulate what difference the participatory design made with respect to the questions we asked, the methods we used, the sample we selected, the procedures we undertook, the analyses we generated, and the writings we produced.

Creating the Conditions for Collaboration: The Undergraduate and Graduate Seminars. With the wisdom of C. Wright Mills (1959) and Franz Fanon (1967) and buoyed by the commitments of participatory researchers before us, we began our work with an understanding that full participation of all researchers requires common and complementary skills, understandings, trust, and respect. Artificial collaboration would have been easy to accomplish. Simply having women in prison around the table would have been an exercise in what Nancy Fraser (1990) recognizes as the bourgeois version of a public sphere: inviting political unequals to the table and calling that democracy. A number of the women from inside the prison were already published (Boudin, 1993; Clark, 1995), but most were not. Thus, from the start, we committed to working through questions of power, trust, and skill by offering a set of courses on research methods within the prison facility, an undergraduate course and a graduate-level seminar. In the undergraduate course, students were assigned a final project in which they would have to generate a specific question of personal interest under the larger umbrella question, "How does college impact the women in the facility, the prison environment and the women/children postrelease?" Once questions were formed and reformed, each inmate interviewed at least five other women about her question, analyzed, interpreted, and wrote up her results.

What was profound about this experience—a simple exercise in building a cadre of inmate researchers—was that the women came to see their personal experiences as fundamentally social and political. And they acquired research experience.

In the graduate seminar, the same kinds of social scaffolding occurred. Personal problems of "having a crazy neighbor who screams all night" unraveled crucial analyses of the politics of mental health and prisons. An off-hand remark about the proliferation of gangs in women's prisons sparked a rich theoretical discussion of the power of college and other programs to create intellectual and political spaces for personal and community engagement.

Thus, a crucial feature of participatory work is the building of a community of researchers—this means shared skills, respect, trust, and common language. This does not mean, however, consensus.

CREATING SPACE FOR DISSENT AND INSIDER KNOWLEDGE. As indigeneous researchers (Smith, 1999) and participatory action researchers have long recognized, insiders carry knowledge, critique, and a line of vision that is not automatically accessible to outsiders (Park, Brydon-Miller, Hall, & Jackson, 1993; QSE, 2000). There were three ways in which insider knowledge profoundly moved this project. First, prison staff and administrators, as well as inmates, simply know things that outsiders do not—formal and informal procedures, lines of authority, practices and their consequences, for instance. Second, insiders understand the profound connections between discrete features of a community that outsiders might erroneously see as separate and divisible. Understanding life at the intersections, as Kimberle Crenshaw (1995) has so beautifully articulated, is critical to the sustenance of an organization and can be perversely misunderstood by researchers who work to extract "variables" from the tightly woven fabrics of organizational life. Third, these insiders understand the power and politics of privilege, privacy, surveillance, and vulnerability.

PRIVACY, VULNERABILITY, AND SURVEILLANCE. Women living in prison have little privacy. Layering a participatory research project atop of this absence of privacy seemed problematic to the Graduate Center researchers. In this facility—one recognized nationally as respectful, participatory, high on commitments to women's growth and low on troubles—even here, given the concerns of security, women's diaries and books have been searched during our time in the facility; notes taken away; poetry destroyed. Questions of where to store the data, and still provide access to the inmates for analysis and interpretation, continue to plague us as outsiders. Indeed, at one point one of the inmate researchers asked the appropriate question about exploitation, "So we just collect the data with you, and then you get to analyze and interpret it?"

It was clear that although all the inside interviews were coconducted by an inmate and a Graduate Center researcher, that the Graduate Center researchers would interview the corrections officers. Some inmates we interviewed wanted to change their names for the final report and others demanded that their original names be kept intact, pointing out that in too many instances they have been erased from the outside world. At many moments in our work, we would need a document, a report, or materials from offices around the prison. When an inmate would ask for such information, there might be nervous caution about giving her requested documents, and yet when one of the Graduate Center researchers would ask, she would more often be told, "Take it—return it whenever you finish." These incidents constantly reminded us of the realities of being in a prison and about our denial about prison.

SELF-CENSORSHIP: AN INSIDER'S DILEMMA. An inmate doing research is also a person trying to survive and to get out of prison. This dual reality is always present in the mind of the inmate researcher. As researchers and writers of the research, we are always looking for truths, or the closest that we perceive to be "true." As prisoners we are always saying, "Is it safe to say this?" "What kind of harmful consequences might flow from this either for ourselves personally or the program or individuals about whom we are writing?" Self-censoring is as much a part of being an inmate researcher as "truth seeking."

We worry that writing something negative about the prison or a program may lead to negative consequences, removing those of us who are inmate researchers from a program, from one living unit to another, far from friends or increasing pressure around any of the life details of living in prison. As inmate researchers, we worry that defining negative truths may create tension between ourselves and the women with whom we live and work. Our relationships with our peers are a basis for survival. We live in a closed community in which everything is tied together. There is no exit.

All researchers have to make decisions about what to put in or take out of the research. These decisions relate to protecting individuals, protecting communities, or protecting groups or programs within a particular community. In this sense, insider researchers in a prison are not alone in making choices—many of these issues have been raised by Tuhiwai Smith (1999) on indigeneous researchers, feminists of color including Aida Hurtado (1996), hooks (1984), Beth Richie (1996), all working on questions of gender and sexuality subordination within racialized communities. However, operating among these choices of inmate researchers is a tendency for self-censorship that is almost survival instinct. Self-censoring comes from the instinct of self-protection in a context that is one of total control over one's day-to-day living conditions, day-to-day work, and personal freedom.

ISSUES OF POWER AMONG THE PAR TEAM. One of the values of qualitative research is to challenge the traditional power relations between those who do the research and the object of the research through a participatory process. But the realities and dynamics of prison, as the social context of this project, also affects the quality of work and the participation of the prisoner researchers in stated and unstated ways. As prisoners, we are always bounded by roles and rules of a closed institution. Some argue that we are in prison to be punished; others argue that we are in prison to be corrected. But in any case, we are essentially objects that must be controlled. On the other hand, we are striving to take responsibility for our lives, to become active, responsible *subjects.* This conflict of roles and expectations plays itself out in our roles as researchers in this project.

As the research evolved over time, some of us felt more constraints. Inmate researchers each had some area of involvement, but we had less knowledge of the whole. What was our role and how did it differ from the "outsiders"? Toch (1967) argued that prisoners can be useful as translators/"bridgers" in the interviewing and analysis of the data. But what was their relationship to the larger project, its conclusions and results?

At points some inmate researchers felt cut off from the project. An inmate researcher explained these feelings as a series of plaguing questions: "Was it just my imagination? Should I raise this in a meeting? Would I be seen as an interloper, a troublemaker? Am I stepping over the bounds? Whose bounds? Who has the power?" Some of these power issues can be addressed by creating a process among all the researchers. But another dimension has to do with the great divide between inside and out; the very physical and practical nature of our being cut off and limited as prisoners. As *inmate* researchers, we cannot meet among ourselves without permission and oversight. We cannot tape-record interviews. At the end of the day, Graduate Center researchers leave and we stay.

As we moved toward the data analysis stage of the research project, and each of us took on some writing, a few of us began to articulate some of these questions and concerns. The research team talked about how to overcome some of the restraints imposed by time and place. Transcripts of focus group interviews were brought in, so that the insider researchers could read through them. This provoked a conversation about how to increase researcher access to the data without compromising the confidentiality and privacy of the participants. When two of the outside researchers raised that they were presenting some of our work at a conference outside, we discussed how to include the insiders' perspectives and spirits. These discussions went beyond seeking practical solutions, as we became aware of the dimensionality of time and space, shaping the contours of our collective efforts. Over time our work as a team, particularly in the process of analysis and writing, we became a research team in which the distinctions between insiders and outsiders faded as other dimensions of our experiences emerged—women, mothers, graduate students, Spanish-speaking, comfortable with writing, spiritually focused, and so on. Our team had a life and a spirit, which grew inside our walls; now all of us together had to figure out how to transcend the walls to communicate what we had learned together.

As our work moved toward analysis of the data, our roles got fuzzier. Often the inmate researchers were the ones to caution against romanticizing inmates or using a highly politicized phrase like "the prison industrial complex," fearing that we would alienate our audience. We are not just "insiders," which denotes place. Most of us feel acutely responsible for the crimes that brought us here and for the impact of our actions on others. We truly do feel for the public's anger about crime and feel responsible to address the legitimacy of that anger in our work. But it is hard for us to climb out of our own sense of responsibility, to feel entitled to claim a critical voice. Our work with outside researchers, who brought their sense of freedom to level clear critiques of social policy—so long as it was grounded in the data—stretched our capacities to think the unimaginable, to be socially responsible and critical.

Emotions at the Table. The consequences of our work are many. We research and write to document the impact of college on women in prison; to support the continuing of a college program that is, as one inmate researcher described, on "sandy footing"; to encourage other prisons and universities to consider similar collaborations and to illustrate the power of education in prison. On a personal level, we write to secure a program of which some of us are students, some are staff, and some are board members. These intimate relationships bring both a passion and fever to the work, as the future of the program moves between solid and unstable ground. The emotions that flow around this tenuous nature of the program have an impact on our research effort as they demand time and space from us, often in our meetings together. In a research meeting it is common for us to flip-flop between hope and despair, possibility and fear as we face the realities of our relationships to the college program, the research, and to each other. These emotions and our commitments to reflexivity in our work at times leave us numb—the result of too many feelings. Sometimes in a research meeting we pause as a research member details the difficulty of registering new students eager to start the program with one or two courses, as she silently fears the program may close before these students graduate. Other times we deliberately stay clear of conversations that are too painful, keeping on task as a way to feel control when there is little available. We wrestle with how to communicate these emotions in our writings, how to honor their influence without getting derailed. The context and physical environment of our research is harsh, noisy, and without privacy, by design. We sit, after all, in a maximum-security prison where half of us are prisoners and all of us are human.

Lost Bodies. One of the challenges of participatory work is the coordination of bodies around the research table. People bring outside commitments, unexpected illness, and even unexplained absences because of hectic lives. At the prison we have the added challenge of working within the rules, regulations, and limitations set by the facility and the state. Inmate members of our research team have been randomly called out of our meetings by officers and at times have not been given notice about changes in meeting times. As inmates, Bedford Hills researchers have little control over being called to the doctor, the visiting room, or even to a cherished trailer visit with family. One inmate researcher was transferred, mid-project, to a facility near the Canadian border, almost 500 miles away, and another inmate researcher has had to focus her energies instead on issues related to her case.

This movement of bodies in and out of our meetings has meant that, at points, the research has taken longer. At other moments, the process of updating each other has served to keep our articulations of the research clearer and more focused. In addition, the extra time we have been afforded through this process has strengthened our sense of being a true research "team" as our relationships have grown over time. Each struggle we have individually and collectively undergone has helped us to better understand each other's ideas and theoretical perspectives. Overall, when we sit around the research table we pay attention to who is missing, and in this sense the bodies are never truly "lost." Rather, what results is a discussion and writing that is infused with the bodies, minds, thoughts, and spirits of the women, coresearchers, who have come and gone. And though our hearts often ache, our collective work, without question, is richer for it.

AUDIENCE. Throughout this project, we constantly reminded each other, whether subtly or overtly, that we must consider our audience. The inmate researchers, in particular, were extremely cognizant of the public sentiment regarding crime and regarding prisoners in general. We anticipated a hostile, angry audience bred in times where popular "tough on crime" attitudes prevailed. Probably because of our awareness regarding the animosity toward prisoners, at times some of the inmate researchers became our own worst enemies, as their fear fueled a desire for self-censorship. Playing the roles of devil's advocates inmate researchers forecast the concerns and arguments of those we imagined would challenge our findings.

Anticipating reaction outside of the prison was often overshadowed by the stark reality that both the inmate and graduate center researchers also had to consider the prison administration's reaction. As the data collected were discussed and analyzed, strong opinions formed. Some of us wanted to include those opinions as part of our interpretation of the findings. However, the inmate researchers often reminded the group that, although they might not actually suffer a typical prison "punishment" (e.g., cell confinement, loss of privileges, etc.), vocalizing strong opposition to some facility policies might result in angering the very people who hold power over them. As a result, some voices have remained silent. The realization of our limitations has made some of us both disappointed and angry. It is interesting to note, however, that these moments have seemed to weigh as heavily on the outside researchers as on the inside researchers. Perhaps the concern of the graduate center researchers results from the fact that the suppression of any one voice in the symphony of PAR alters the final composition of the research.

QUESTIONS OF GENERALIZABILITY. There were many moments in this work, particularly in writing up the final report (Fine et al., 2001), and even in writing this chapter, that we sought to understand what is particular to the Bedford Hills experience of college in prison, but as important, which findings and dynamics are generalizable to other contexts. That is often a question asked of qualitative material—if the analysis is so rich, context-dependent, and particularized, have we learned anything that can be taken to other contexts?

We believe, with respect to both the substance of college in prison and the praxis of participatory work, there is much to be generalized. In this project, as in all other projects with which we are connected, we begin with a commitment to theorize the relations of the part to the whole so that we can ask here and in universities, high schools, community-based organizations, and prisons around the nation, "How does education transform young adult lives, biographies and sense of possibility—in prison or out? How does achievement, earning a diploma, and graduation further affect sense of self and responsibility to community? How do mothers returning to college affect children's academic well-being? How does college afford social critique and personal responsibility?" Certainly there are specific features of this prison, with this college at this moment in time, that shape the experience and consequences; but there are also significant dynamics that carry across time and space that may look very different in rural Minnesota, in a men's prison, or a community college on a Native reservation. But some of the deep complex relations of education, voice, and community appear to resonate across very divergent contexts.

Turning to participatory research, we discover that here, too, many of the issues that have plagued—and defined—our work together are knotty for any group of insiders working within an organization. Writing *as an insider* on domestic violence in Native communities, racism within gay men's organizations, sexism in a Black church, exploitation of domestic labor in suburban White communities, domestic violence within the lesbian community—for each of these topics, we have met researchers and practitioners who have self-censored, worried that the material was "too hot" and would be "badly used" against the community, that the researcher would be shunned, the research attacked, the story silenced even more. In most instances, the researchers ultimately figured out ways to talk about the material so that the right questions of theory, politics, and practice could be opened up. So we place the concerns of women inmate researchers writing from within prison inside a broad, ethical community of scholars working on critical issues within the local webs of organizational and community life.

HOW DO WE EVER WALK AWAY? As we enter the final stages of the research, many of us have been filled with the mixed emotions of pride, hope, and sadness. There is a shared sense of pride in the success of our collective efforts and the potential for our work; hope that this potential will be fulfilled; and sadness that to end this project will end our ability to meet regularly and therefore lose our personal relationships and intellectual intimacy. Again the reality of working across razor wire and steel bars reminds us of the limitations of our social positions.

How do we continue what is no longer allowed? An inmate researcher, perhaps in an attempt to move beyond her own feelings of loss, describes the oncoming transition as "arriving at dessert," recognizing that once the project is over we can finally indulge in all the digressions and tangential conversations that were put aside because of the time constraints of our rigorous research agenda. However, the levity of this light-hearted comment lasts only a moment as we remember that just as we will no longer be able to meet regularly, the prison does not allow outsiders to bring in food.

What's to Be Gained From Participatory Action Research?

We spent much time, as a research collective, discussing what is to be gained from PAR. There are, of course, the instrumental gains—insiders know more, know better, and know more details of how an organization, community, and indeed a prison operates. Outsiders, in contrast, have the freshness to ask the deliberately naive questions (Kvale, 1996) and have the relative freedom to speak a kind of truth to power that may provoke new lines of analysis. We dance between detachment and engagement. Yet, on reflection, rarely did we operate as two separate and coherent constituencies. Instead we grew to be, over time, a group of women with very distinct and sometimes overlapping commitments, questions, worries, and theoretical and political concerns.

In prison, as in any institution under external surveillance, insiders know details of daily life, understand the laser-like penetration of external scrutiny, and are more likely to refuse to simply romanticize—or pathologize—that which happens within. Indeed, in our collaborations it has been the inmate researchers who recognized that our design needed to include dissenting voices, narratives of critique, perspectives from dropouts. It is entirely possible that if outsiders, alone, collected the qualitative material we would have gathered material that would have been essentially a sugar-coated greeting card of praise for the program, collecting discourses of redemption, transformation, and positive affect, unchallenged and underscrutinized. "Research performances" of the good student would likely have gone unchallenged. In contrast, inmate researchers are able and willing to say in an interview, "Are you kidding, *you* have changed? You just got a ticket. . . . " or identify a correction officer known to be ambivalent about or hostile to the college, or arrange an interview with a recently arrived young woman member of a gang not yet ready for college. To the question, "Don't the inmates *bias* the research design in favor of positive results?" we respond that the inmates, far more than the outsider researchers, knew where to gather more problematic material, how to press for complex—not just sugar-coated—responses, and consistently refused to romanticize inmates as powerless or as victims.

Inmate researchers understand intimately and thereby theorize profoundly the complex interconnections that constitute prison life, both as inmates and as researchers within the facility. Although Graduate Center researchers assumed college to be a "variable" connected to, but relatively insulated from, other aspects of prison life, the inmates understood the connections that had to be recognized. Thus, for example, we learned that because of a recent shift in disciplinary policy in the facility, women can no longer bring pens out to the yard. Anyone seeking or offering tutoring or homework assistance on the yard must be denied—or helped with a crayon. With metal detectors and sometimes pat-frisking required for women to enter the yard, the numbers who do go to the yard have diminished. Tutoring, study groups, homework assistance in the yard dwindles. A seemingly remote policy has a profound impact on the college community. Outsiders would never have guessed.

PAR may indeed bend toward a kind of "strong objectivity," as Sandra Harding (1983) might say, because we pool our many partial truths toward understanding the power of college in prison. But PAR also provides an interior legacy and power—within the prison—of respect for insider knowledge and recognition of inmate authority. This research project refuses to speak *for* but stretches to speak *with*. Inmate "subjects" are not exploited or edited by outsiders, but rather have become part of a hybrid team of women have worked together with deeply contradictory material to produce an analysis of rigor, policy, and respect.

So, to the question, "What's to be gained from PAR?" we answer that all research is collaborative and participatory, even though typically, respondents are given code names and rarely acknowledged as coauthors. More researchers must acknowledge the coconstruction of knowledge, and that material gathered from, with, and on any community—including a prison—constitutes a participatory process.

We believe that we have simply—and with enormous effort—recognized the profound influence of collaboration that is constitutive of research. Insiders *and* outsiders know much, and know much deeply. Between us there is a powerful coconstruction of critical knowledge about the effects of college on prison life. We consider participatory work simply an acknowledgment of the strength of our intellectual and action-based collaboration.

References

Adelman, C. (1997). Action research and the problem of participation. In R. McTaggart (Ed.), *Participatory action research: International contexts and consequences* (pp. 79–106). Albany: State University of New York Press.

Alcoff, L. M. (1995). The problem of speaking for others. In J. Roof & R. Wiegman (Eds.), *Who can speak?: Authority and critical identity* (pp. 97–119). Urbana: University of Illinois Press.

Bettencourt, B. A., Dillman, G., & Wollman, N. (1996). The intragroup dynamics of maintaining a successful grassroots organization: A case study. *Journal of Social Issues, 52,* 207–220.

Bhavnani, K. K. (1994). Tracing the contours: Feminist research and objectivity. In H. Afshar & M. Maynard (Eds.), *The dynamics of "race" and gender: Some feminist interventions* (pp. 26–40). London: Taylor & Francis.

Boudin, K. (1993). Participatory literacy education behind bars: AIDS opens the door. *Harvard Educational Review, 63,* 207–232.

Brydon-Miller, M. (1997). Participatory action research: Psychology and social change. *Journal of Social Issues, 53*(4), 657–666.

Chataway, C. J. (1997). An examination of the constraints on mutual inquiry in a participatory action research project. *Journal of Social Issues, 53,* 747–765.

Chataway, C. J. (2001). Negotiating the observer–observed relationship: Participatory action research. In D. L. Tolman & M. Brydon-Miller (Eds.), *From subjects to subjectivities: A handbook of interpretive and participatory methods* (pp. 239–255). New York: New York University Press.

Cherry, F., & Borshuk, C. (1998). Social action research and the commission on community interrelations. *Journal of Social Issues, 54,* 119–142.

Clark, J. (1995). The impact of the prison environment on mothers. *The Prison Journal, 75(3)*, 306–329.

Conway, K. (1998). *The impact of attending college while incarcerated on women's self-esteem.* Unpublished manuscript, Bedford Hills, New York.

Crenshaw, K. (1995). Mapping the margins: Intersectionality, identity politics, and violence against women of colour. In K. Crenshaw, N. Gotanda, G. Peller, & K. Thomas (Eds.), *Critical race theory: The key writings that formed the movement* (pp. 357–383). New York: New Press.

Faith, K. (1993). *Unruly women: The politics of confinement and resistance.* Vancouver: Press Gang.

Fals-Borda, O. (1979). Investigating the reality in order to transform it: The Colombian experience. *Dialectical Anthropology, 4,* 33–55.

Fanon, F. (1967). *Black skin, white masks.* New York: Grove Press.

Fine, M., Torre, M. E., Boudin, K., Bowen, I., Clark, J., et al. (2001). *Changing minds: The impact of college in a maximum security prison.* New York: Graduate School and University Center, City University of New York.

Fraser, N. (1990). Rethinking the public sphere: A contribution to the critique of actually existing democracy. *Social Text, 25/26,* 56–80.

Freire, P. (1982). Creating alternative research methods. Learning to do it by doing it. In B. Hall, A. Gillette, & R. Tandon (Eds.), *Creating knowledge: A monopoly* (pp. 29–37). New Delhi: Society for Participatory Research in Asia.

Gaventa, J. (1993). The powerful, the powerless, and the experts: Knowledge struggles in an information age. In P. Park, M. Brydon-Miller, B. Hall, & T. Jackson (Eds.), *Voices of change: Participatory research in the US and Canada* (pp. 21–40). Westport, CT: Bergin and Garvey.

Germanotta, D. (1995). Prison education: A contextual analysis. In H. S. Davidson (Ed.), *Schooling in a "total institution": Critical perspectives on prison education* (pp. 103–121). Westport, CT: Bergin & Garvey.

Gramsci, A. (1971). *Selections from prison notebooks.* New York: International.

Greene, M. (1995). *Releasing the imagination: Essays on education, the arts, and social change.* San Francisco: Jossey-Bass.

Habermas, J. (1971). *Knowledge and human interests.* Boston: Beacon Press.

Hall, B. (1993). Introduction. In P. Park, M. Brydon-Miller, B. Hall, & T. Jackson (Eds.), *Voices of change: Participatory action research in the United States and Canada* (pp. xiii–xxii). Westport, CT: Bergin & Garvey.

Harding, S. (1983). *Discovering reality: Feminist perspectives on epistemology, metaphysics, methodology, and philosophy of science.* Dordrecht, Holland: D. Reidel.

Hartstock, N. C. M. (1983). *Money, sex, and power: Toward a feminist historical materialism.* New York: Longman.

hooks, b. (1984). *Feminist theory from margin to center.* Boston: South End Press.

Hurtado, A. (1996). *The color of privilege: Three blasphemies on race and feminism.* Ann Arbor: University of Michigan Press.

Jaggar, A. M. (1983). *Feminist politics and human nature.* Totowa, NJ: Rowman & Allenheld.

Kemmis, S., & McTaggart, R. (2000). Participatory action research. In N. K. Denzin & Y. S. Lincoln (Eds.), *Handbook of qualitative research* (2nd ed., pp. 567–605). Thousand Oaks, CA: Sage.

Kitzinger, C. (2000). How to resist an idiom. *Research on Language and Social Interaction, 33*(2), 121–154.

Kvale, S. (1996). *InterViews: An introduction to qualitative research interviewing.* Thousand Oaks, CA: Sage.

Ladson-Billings, G. (2000). Racialized discourses and ethnic epistemologies. In N. K. Denzin & Y. S. Lincoln (Eds.), *Handbook of qualitative research* (2nd ed., pp. 257–277). Thousand Oaks, CA: Sage.

Lewin, K. (1951). *Field theory in social science: Selected theoretical papers.* New York: Harper.

Lykes, M. B. (2001). Activist participatory research and the arts with rural Maya women: Interculturality and situated meaning making. In D. L. Tolman & M. Brydon-Miller (Eds.), *From subjects to subjectivities: A handbook of interpretive and participatory methods* (pp. 183–199). New York: New York University Press.

Maguire, P. (2001). The congruency thing: Transforming psychological research and pedagogy. In D. L. Tolman & M. Brydon-Miller (Eds.), *From subjects to subjectivities: A handbook of interpretive and participatory methods* (pp. 276–289). New York: New York University Press.

Martín-Baró, I. (1994). *Writings for a liberation psychology.* Cambridge, MA: Harvard University Press.

Matsuda, M. (1995). Looking to the bottom: Critical legal studies and reparations. In K. Crenshaw, N. Gotanda, G. Peller, & K. Thomas (Eds.), *Critical race theory: The key writings that formed the movement* (pp. 63–79). New York: New Press.

Mauer, M. (1995). *Young Black Americans in the criminal justice system: Five years later.* Washington, DC: Sentencing Project.

McIntyre, A. (1997). *Making meaning of Whiteness: Exploring racial identity with White teachers.* Albany: State University of New York Press.

McIntyre, A. (2000). *Inner-city kids: Adolescents confront life and violence in an urban community.* New York: New York University Press.

Mills, C. W. (1959). *The sociological imagination.* London: Oxford University Press.

Olesen, V. L. (1998). Feminisms and qualitative research at and into the millennium. In N. K. Denzin & Y. S. Lincoln (Eds.), *Handbook of qualitative research* (2nd ed., pp. 215–255). Thousand Oaks, CA: Sage.

Park, P., Brydon-Miller, M., Hall, B., & Jackson, T. (1993). *Voices of change: Participatory research in the United States and Canada.* Westport, CT: Bergin and Garvey.

Qualitative Studies in Education (QSE). (2000). Through our eyes and in our words—The voices of indigenous scholars. *International Journal of Qualitative Studies in Education, 13*(4).

Richie, B. (1996). *Compelled to crime: The gender entrapment of battered black women.* New York: Routledge.

Rivera, J. A. (1995). A nontraditional approach to social and criminal justice. In H. S. Davidson (Ed.), *Schooling in a "total institution": Critical perspectives on prison education* (pp. 159–171). Westport, CT: Bergin & Garvey.

Russell, G. M., & Bohan, J. S. (1999). Hearing voices: The uses of research and the politics of change. *Psychology of Women Quarterly, 23,* 403–418.

Sarason, S. B. (1974). *The psychological sense of community: Prospects for a community psychology.* San Francisco: Jossey-Bass.

Smith, D. (1987). *The everyday world as problematic: A feminist sociology.* Boston: Northeastern University Press.

Smith, L. T. (1999). *Decolonizing methodologies: Research and indigenous peoples.* London: Zed Books.

Stanfield, J. H. (1998). Ethnic modeling in qualitative research. In N. K. Denzin & Y. S. Lincoln (Eds.), *Handbook of qualitative research* (pp. 175–188). Thousand Oaks, CA: Sage.

Toch, H. (1967). The convict as researcher. *Trans-Action* (Sept.), 72–75.

Weisenfeld, E. (1999). *The researcher's place in qualitative inquiries: Un-fulfilled promises?* Paper presented at the 27th Interamerican Congress of Psychology, Caracas, Venezuela.

11

Balancing the Whole: Portraiture as Methodology

Jessica Hoffmann Davis

Portraiture in art is a process of representation through which the artist recreates the subject of the image, interpreting nuances of physicality and personality through artistic elements such as line, color, and composition. This artistic process results in a tangible imprint of the artist's understanding of and relationship with the subject of the portrait. Similarly, the research portrait, a written narrative, is imprinted with the researcher's understanding of and relationship with the individual or site that is represented in the text. Like the artist, the research portraitist works to balance elements of context, thematic structure, relationship, and voice into an aesthetic whole that is so carefully constructed that every part seems an essential ingredient in the clarity of cohesive interpretation (Lawrence-Lightfoot & Davis, 1997).

As a qualitative research methodology, portraiture is distinguished in part by this preoccupation with artistic coherence. The quest for coherence, for balancing a whole, plays a constant role in the researcher's efforts to construct a narrative that authentically portrays the central story of the subject or site. Portraiture is based on a belief in narratives or stories as primary and valid structures through which personal and professional identities are framed, sustained, and shared (see, e.g., Bruner, 1996). The narrative in portraiture is respected as an essential vehicle for meaning making in the life of the individual or group (Bateson, 1989; Lawrence-Lightfoot, 1994) and in the work of the attendant researcher. Narratives taken from literature are frequently used as foils for individual experience and as fodder for the interpretive process (see, e.g., Gilligan, 1982). In portraiture, however, the interpretive product (the research portrait) itself embodies artistic and literary elements. Simultaneously holding to empirical rigor and to artistic mandates, portraiture participates in a tradition of forging bridges across social science and art (Lawrence-Lightfoot & Davis, 1997).

Portraiture may be regarded as embracing ethnographic objectives and techniques even as it rewrites both the form and function of traditional case

Material from Davis et al. 1993 quoted by permission of Harvard University, Graduate School of Education.

studies. Like exemplary case studies, successful portraits provide detailed and responsible accounts of individuals or groups. Unlike case studies that focus, for example, on analyses of strengths and weaknesses, portraiture embraces the notion of a "good" whole—one that necessarily incorporates challenge and error even as it functions effectively. Finally, like other recent research traditions, such as grounded theory (Haig, 1995; Kinach, 1995), portraiture relies on inductive rather than deductive analysis, the generation rather than testing of theories, and a humanistic determination to speak through relevant voices, rather than academic codes, thereby reaching a broader audience.

Introduction

The artist stands before her subject confident that, after various conversations back and forth, a relationship of trust has been forged. The person whose portrait is being painted relaxes on the chaise. The artist's eye moves from sole of bright blue shoe, to rounded hip, to resting elbow, to melancholy eyes. What major forms emerge for the artist as central to the figure she is interpreting on canvas? How will she organize these emergent central forms into a cohesive whole that will make sense to a viewer and seem an apt portrayal to the subject of the work? Imprinted with the unique style of the artist, the final portrait does not contain every detail of what the artist sees; but in its organization of central shapes against a backdrop that illuminates the whole, the artist somehow captures the essence of the subject. Rising from her chaise to take in the final work, the subject nods with a look of both surprise and interest, "Yes," she says, "I can see that that is me."

Far from the artist's studio, on the third floor of Longfellow Hall at the Harvard Graduate School of Education, I sit with a small team of researchers. Together, we are making aesthetic decisions about the context, content, and structure of the research portraits that we are constructing. One of the researchers shares her progress in organizing her understanding of the site she has been studying, a community art center in the Fruit Belt section of Buffalo, New York. After weeks of careful review of contextual documents, field notes, and interview data, things are coming together. From the language of the center, as documented in 200 pages of transcriptions, she has identified three major themes that emerge and seem to authentically organize her interpretation of the nature of arts learning that is provided at the site. Resonant constituent language has rendered as titles for these themes: "the model of the professional artist, realistic accessibility, and constant survivor" (Davis, Soep, Remba, Maira, & Putnoi, 1993).

The artist critiques and revises his selection and portrayal of form through a lens that is tempered both by his understanding of the particular subject and his broader knowledge of art and art history. Similarly, this researcher has tested the selected themes across dimensions deemed relevant through extensive study of the broader scene of community arts education. She has created a backdrop as if on the canvas of her portrait, made out of data she has selected from observation, interview, and close study of written materials. And this backdrop illuminates her portrayal as surely as the negative space on the artist's canvas makes its positive counterpart more vivid. Attending as the artist does to aesthetic details such as metaphor, vivid description, and cohesive composition, this research portraitist has created a balanced whole that is grounded in rigorous research but accessible to readers including and transcending the academy. When the directors of the community art center read what they call the "story" of their center, they let us know, "Yes, we can see that that is us."

In the pages that follow, I hope to shed light on the inner workings of a research methodology that I view as inherently interdisciplinary, integrating rigorous standards of qualitative research with the aesthetic qualities of works of art. In unpacking the elements of this apparently seamless process of interpretive description, I focus on the rigorous dialectic that persists between process (the triangulation of data through observation, interview, and material review) and product (the carefully constructed narrative portrayal). The variety of portraiture that I describe draws on the work of Sara Lawrence-Lightfoot (1983, 1994) and on my own adaptation of her individualistic approach into a collective endeavor suitable for use by a group of researchers (Davis et al., 1993, 1996; Pruyne et al., 1998). Lawrence-Lightfoot and I have outlined in some detail foundations and guidelines for the use of portraiture (Lawrence-Lightfoot & Davis, 1997). But in the limited space of this chapter, I hope to provide a vivid if condensed account of the methodology in action, implemented by a group of researchers working together to create research portraits that resonate with authenticity to readers across disciplines and circumstance.[1]

This unfolding of the process in action is organized around the component parts of the portraiture process: context, group voice, relationship, emergent themes, and aesthetic whole. I hope throughout my discussion to be able to make convincing links between the methods of research portraitists and the process of working artists. Perhaps the distance between the artist's studio and the research office is shorter than we think and perhaps there is much to learn from a look in both directions.

Context

Education, like art, does not happen in a vacuum. The physical neighborhood in which schools or art centers work, like the size and diversity of the community that is served, are all important elements that contribute from the outside to the inside of the walls of the site. Artists know well that a change in the shade or scene selected for the background of the portrait can transform the effect of the image. Similarly, research portraitists choose well what to include in an introduction to a portrait to set the stage for what will follow. The palette from which the researcher constructs an introduction is made up of selected

[1]Examples are based on the author's past work in Project Co-Arts and current work in the Arts in Education Program Portraiture Project. She is grateful for support for these initiatives from the Bauman, Cummings, Ford, Dodge, Julian, and Warhol Foundations and from the National Arts Learning Foundation.

pieces of information reviewed carefully with an eye to an understanding of the environment in which the site functions.

When I wrote the portrait of the Artists Collective in Hartford, with the help of my research team, I immersed myself in newspaper articles, census reports, annual reports of the center, and other data that would let me know about the North End of Hartford and the Collective's then-home on Clark Street. Leaving out extraneous details, I tried to provide threads that would help clarify the details I would share as I wove my interpretation of the education provided. For example, the following excerpt from the introduction to the portrait sets the stage for both the Afro-centric art center and the community it serves:

> Judging from the bustle of working people, a visitor might be surprised to learn how hard hit financially Hartford has been in recent years or the high percentage of Hartford's residents who are actually unemployed. Judging from the predominance of white pedestrians downtown, a visitor might also be surprised to know that almost three quarters of Hartford's population is either African-American or Latino—many living at or below the poverty line. The white executives who crowd the street by day leave the city for the suburbs at night, and the African-American and Latino residents maintain their respective places in the North and South Ends of Hartford. The rooftops of the small two and three-decker homes of the largely African-American community of the North End are visible from the upper floors of the downtown buildings. It is difficult to convince a cab driver to take a fare there; but the North End is an easy walk from downtown. (Davis et al., 1993, p. 14)

The process of creating a research portrait of a site begins a long time before the site is visited. Studying relevant written materials provides a context for the researcher's encounter with a site and provides a respectful familiarity with the place that will positively affect the relationship with constituents. This preparation also provides a cachet of data from which to draw not only for the context that is provided at the start of the portrait (what fellow researchers and I have entitled the "outside in") but also on the contextual threads that will be woven throughout. Contextual elements ranging from the neighborhood in which the site is located to the details of a room in which a moment of teaching and learning is described shed different and important hues on the individuals, and action, and the increasing clarity of the portrayal.

In the following contextual description, the reader moves from outside to inside the center and experiences the setting of the Artists Collective as a series of selected details that reflect priorities of the education and community promoted at the site:

> From outside to in, the change in atmosphere is as dramatic as the change experienced crossing "the line" into the North End. Opening the double doors into the main floor's hallway, eyes are drawn upwards to the colorful banners hung from the ceiling in rows of three. Neatly hung posters line the hallways. Some announce performances by noted black artists, others advocate a drug free America: "Drugs don't care about you; connect with

> people who do." On the tops of skirted tables lie well ordered stacks of free brochures: "Cocaine/crack, The Big Lie"; "Thinking about Drugs? Think about this." There are brochures that announce local arts events, tours of West Africa, and programs to help you, "if someone close, has a problem with alcohol or other drugs." An order form for a new publication announces, "Finally, a guide for the unique issues facing black parents: Different and Wonderful, Raising Black Children in a Race-Conscious Society." (Davis et al., 1993, p. 3)

Against this level of carefully described internal physical context, the interactions of constituents is illuminated and made sensible both from a visual and pedagogical perspective. We see the colorful banners and posters that densely line the walls and we understand that a large emphasis is being placed at this site on building community and keeping children away from drugs.

Throughout the text, references to contextual details gathered from numerous relevant sources (field notes, documents collected before and throughout a site visit, information gleaned in interview settings) ground both the observations and interpretation of the portraitist. In setting the stage for a dance class in which well-known New York choreographer Aca Lee Thompson is working with young dancers, I include as background physical detail that provides context for the scene. The selection of this detail highlights the contributions that persist in which world-class artists link up with a tiny but powerful center for arts learning:

> Overhead against the classroom wall above a wall-wide mirror is a mural painted by the late renowned artist Keith Haring. Outlined in black on a white ground, the dancing figures are characteristic of Haring's familiar style: a cross between Aztec/Egyptian/primitive and modern/media/cartoon. Haring was visiting Hartford's Wadsworth Athenaeum one day and Ms. McLean says, "It was such a nice day; he came on a Saturday. He left this with us." Haring's mural art adorns city and subway walls in New York City and a wall in this classroom in Hartford, Connecticut. The juxtaposition of world class art and minimally renovated classrooms exemplifies the achievement of the Oasis on Clark Street. An independent arts space expert contracted in 1986 observed, "This is a very successful organization in a very makeshift facility." (Davis et al., 1993, p. 23)

As in a painted portrait in which favorite objects of the subject may be included, contextual details help the reader see and understand the action and structure at the portrayed site. The various kinds of contextual elements that inform a research portrait fall into the categories of (a) physical context, clarifying detail that sets the stage like the skyscrapers and sidewalks of Hartford or the Herring mural described earlier; (b) personal context as detail that clarifies an understanding of individuals and interactions from details of appearance to life stories that inform the portrait; and (c) historical context, data that places the here and now portrait within the continuum of the individual site's journey from past to future. Examples of personal and historical context can be found in the following excerpts, describing the founders and directors of the Artists Collective:

> Dollie McLean is a petite woman of African/Caribbean origin whose former life as a dancer and actress is imprinted on her straight posture and graceful gait. Her hair, edged with blonde highlights, is pulled straight back off her face and tightly drawn above her head into an upright ponytail wrapped in fabric. Her high style appearance would seem to reflect her New York City roots.
>
> Jackie McLean also strikes an urbane New York image. He is dressed for an interview in an elegant dark suit with a floral print tie in purples and greens. His gold watch, bracelet, and rings echo "show biz," "big city," "New York." A light-complexioned African-American, Jackie McLean sports a goatee and his feathery brown hair is laced with threads of gray. Mr. McLean describes his wife's shopping days on New York's Orchard Street: " . . . and Dollie's shopping was always more looking and thinking about something a long time. She is very frugal. She runs the Artists Collective the same way which is why we never had a deficit." (Funding cuts in the last year have resulted in the Collective's first deficit.) (Davis et al., 1993, p. 17)

Providing personal context as visual description seems always the hardest challenge for research portraitists. What sort of physical detail is appropriate to include? How much should be left out of the scene? When personal contextual information is included superficially, it reads as if it were an intrusion rather than an integral part of the portrait. To just tell the reader that the individual speaking has red hair informs very little. Personal and historical contextual details, like all the elements the portraitist is balancing, are carefully chosen to inform, clarify, and enrich (rather than decorate) the written account and the reader's consequent understanding.

In the example just given, selected details in description of the McLeans enable the reader to visualize these two individuals. Moreover, they help to contextualize them against the backdrop of the story of their New York roots, a thread that informs the narrative throughout. The McLeans's connections with New York enable them to bring top-notch professional artists into the Collective. But the New York connection also emerges as a dissonant thread in the tension that persists on the part of community members who mistrust individuals coming from New York to help adolescents in Hartford's North End. Later in the portrait we hear that

> Jackie McLean recognizes the tension within the community and voices their sentiment: "Who do they think they are coming in here to help us? We coulda' done it!" He says, "When I get them all together, I say, 'Why didn't you do it? You didn't do it, so stop talking about it. We did it.' " (Davis et al., 1993, p. 48)

Similarly, when we first meet the McLeans, physically and personally, we encounter relevant contextual historical data introduced even in the small detail of Dollie's frugality. Dollie's shopping encounters become important historical context, useful to include in the portrait, because they set the stage for her careful financial management of the center.

Issues of what to include or leave out persist throughout the writing of the portrait and the data collecting that informs that process. Just as our portrait painter is leaving out extraneous visual information and focusing on highlighting particular elements in her painting, the research portraitist is "testing" information and its relevance to the understanding and portrayal of a cohesive interpretation of the subject or site. A description of personal sacrifice adds important perspective to an understanding of the founder's motivation.

> The move from New York City to Hartford in 1970 was not an easy one for Dollie McLean. It came at a time when her children had reached the age where she could spend a little more time paying attention to what she wanted to do. Although she had given up dance, she had continued to attend weekly dance classes to keep in shape and, as a propitious head start for the acting career to which she had long aspired, she was accepted as an actress in New York's Negro Ensemble Company.
>
> But Jackie McLean's two and then three day weekly trips to Hartford to teach a few music courses at the University of Hartford's Hartt School of Music were growing as they would into a full time position as professor, founder, and chair of the African-American Music Department Jazz Degree Program in 1973. "By 1969," Mr. McLean tells the story, "it looked like most of my work was going to be not in New York City but here in Hartford. I began to talk to Dollie very carefully about moving. . . . "(Davis et al., 1993, p. 17)

Group Voice

No matter how realistic in detail (suggesting objective or photographic representation) an artist's portrait may be, the individualism of the artist is indelibly imprinted on the work. We see in the work of the famous portraitist John Singer Sargent, for example, a stylistic tone that suggests a level of comfort with Boston's elite. The trappings and furnishings of the rich from jewelry to china to ornate costumes are not accentuated in his work—they present almost as expected givens in the settings portrayed. We are not surprised to learn that Sargent sat at table with members of the society he portrayed, devoted patrons such as the wealthy Boston icon Isabella Stewart Gardner. Beyond the ease in presentation we may sense behind the brush strokes, in the brush stokes themselves, there is a distinctive style. Those familiar with paintings will be able to note without the benefit of a label, "That's by Sargent of course." Similarly, in a research portrait, the voice of the researcher is imprinted on the rapport with the research participant, the language used in portrayal, and even on the particular details that are chosen to be included in a work.

For example, if I were to visit and portray the community art center Plaza de la Raza in Los Angeles, many elements of the scene would be unfamiliar to me. Dias de los Muertos (Day of the Dead) might, for me, be especially intriguing. But when our Mexican portrait researcher visited the center and wrote about the holiday as if it were a given, she had to be reminded that a reader like me might not know about it as she did. This researcher was bilingual and was able therefore to achieve a more nuanced understanding of many of the aspects of the center's effectiveness. We decided that because her voice was bilingual, the researcher should share that perspective with the reader.

An example of this literally bilingual approach to portraitist voice can be found in this brief but representative moment from her portrait:

> Speaking in Spanish, the migajón (bread dough sculpture) instructor, Ofelia Sánchez, tells the story of a 73 year old woman who came from Argentina to the United States to live with her daughter, but her daughter always left her at home alone. The older woman constantly said that she wanted to die, *"¡Ay, Dios mío! ¿Porqué no me recoges? Yo ya no más no sirvo para nada."* (Oh, My God! Why don't you bring me to you? I am no longer of any use). According to Sánchez, after joining the migajón class, this woman said that her daughter's absences no longer bothered her. Indeed, she wanted her daughter to leave so that she could have more time to make flowers, *"¡Ay Diosito! ¡No te vayas a creer que te dije que me llevaras, si tengo que hacer muchas flores todavía!"* (Oh My God!, disregard what I said to you earlier about bringing me to you. I still have many flowers to make!). (Remba in Davis et al., 1996, p. 147)

Different individuals bring different backgrounds and understandings that have an impact on what they see, hear, and make sense of in any setting. An experienced artist visiting a community art center would ask different questions of a print maker than a researcher who had never seen a printing press. On a very basic level, voice is what makes individual researchers see what they see and include or leave out what they choose to in a portrait. Voice necessarily affects observation, understanding, and reportage. Beyond individual perspectives, however, both individuals and groups of researchers working collectively on a set of portraits need a set of foundations and constraints with which responsibly to focus their ultimately indelible individual voices. How is that achieved?

The study to which I refer throughout these pages (Davis, 1994; Davis et al., 1993, 1996) had as its research question "What does educational effectiveness look like in community art centers in economically disadvantaged communities?" A frequent misconception about portraiture is that it is not driven by a research question; that it is instead some kind of comprehensive interpretation of a subject or site. All research begins with a question and the best research begins with a question to which we don't know the answer (Curtis, personal communication, 1989). Like any research initiative, portraiture is grounded in one or more questions, and the data gathering, from selection of relevant written materials for study to the establishment of an interview protocol, is informed by that question.

Researchers (individuals or groups) embarking on a portrait need to do some sort of preliminary study such as a literature review as a preparatory step. Project Co-Arts, for example, began with a full-scale national study exploring what counted as "educational effectiveness" in the field of community art centers. The preliminary study included a review of articles from and on the field, reviews of descriptive materials from more than 300 centers, in-depth telephone interviews with educational directors at more than 100 centers, and on-site visits to 32 centers (Davis, 1994). This research into the general scene provided a context for our selection of particular portraiture sites and a tenor of expertise for our collective researcher voice. Knowledge of the broader field links the individual example and context to the more universal scene and context. That knowledge informs the researcher's voice and, through that voice, the ways in which the narrative will be framed.

When a research team sets forth, as we did, to do one or a series of portraits, it will very consciously work to establish some version of what I have called "group voice" (Davis et al., 1993, 1996; Lawrence-Lightfoot & Davis, 1997). Group voice is simply the agreed on parameters that lend harmony and coherence to the individual voices of team researchers as they meet various sites in their portraiture research. Group voice does not replace individual voice, even when a research team decides to remove the "I" or "we" from the portrayal—to write the portraits in the third-person. Individual voice will always guide vision, understanding, and choice as described earlier. But group voice provides shared constraints that ground the individual forays and ensures that they will all provide links between portrayal of individual sites and a broader vision of the field.

In creating a group voice, researchers may begin by identifying what we call "relevant dimensions" with which to guide their study. My view of relevant dimensions is similar to what Lawrence-Lightfoot has called the "preoccupations" of the researcher as "her disciplinary background, her theoretical perspectives, her intellectual interests, and her understanding of the relevant literature" (Lawrence-Lightfoot & Davis, 1997, p. 93). Relevant dimensions are the salient areas of study identified by preliminary research and consequent researcher expertise. The dimensions not only frame the portrait, they connect the subject or site of the portrait to the broader field of which it is a representative.

Accordingly, our large-scale preliminary study of a few hundred community art centers (as described earlier) helped us to identify four relevant dimensions within and across which educational effectiveness (as determined by the field) in these settings seemed to occur. Those relevant dimensions were

1. Community: The community that the center serves;
2. Teaching and learning: The overall educational philosophy;
3. Administration: The organizational structure of the center; and
4. Journey: The overall history of the center from its origins to its vision of itself in the future.

These dimensions would guide our research in various important ways. From the start we would be sure, when collecting written materials from a portrait site, that we had data that informed our understanding of these areas of preoccupation. Appropriate materials might include, for each dimension, (a) letters from or articles about the community (community); (b) teacher journals or written descriptions of curricula (teaching and learning); (c) documents that had to do with funding or leadership (administration); and (d) documents such as annual reports over a series of years that included the history of the site or five-year plans that contained visions for the future (journey).

Similarly, our interview protocol was guided by these dimensions. For example, to inform the dimension of community, a question we would ask was, "Can you tell me about the community you serve?" For teaching and learning:

"Can you tell me what counts as success in your classroom?" For administration: "Who is in charge here? What can you tell me about the leadership of the place?" For journey: "Can you tell me about the history of the place and where you see it going in the next five years?" And for all constituents: "What would you tell someone on the other side of the country who wanted to start a place like this? What makes this place so special?"

Individual researchers can formalize their grounded preoccupations as relevant dimensions with which to achieve a similar focusing of their portraiture work. For example, a student writing a portrait on a community school of music was particularly interested in self-image as an artist and its impact on adolescent development. In her preliminary review of pertinent psychological and sociological research, she identified four relevant dimensions that were associated with self-image as an artist. She incorporated these dimensions into her individual portraiture voice as mentorship: master/apprentice relationships; family: familial support; flow: commitment to optimal experience; and performance: affecting the formation of identity (see Powell, 1995).

For individual researchers, the determination and application of relevant dimensions lends a certain integrity to individual voice. For a research team, relevant dimensions provide a common frame—a group voice that is grounded in broader research—a unified disposition to the individual perspectives represented and valued on a research team. Of importance, relevant dimensions are brought into the site by the portraitist—informing the voice through which the narrative will be told. While focusing data collection, relevant dimensions provide an instrument through which themes may emerge from the site and a sounding board against which the resonance of emergent themes may be tested, as described in a later section.

A group of researchers working together on individual portraits benefit from regular team meetings at which developing ideas can be shared, individual questions addressed, and group voice continuously refined and agreed on. Although it is always most practical to have one writer or senior writer for each portrait, subsets of the research team can work together as we did in the Co-Arts work, visiting sites in pairs, expanding the reach of the portrait writer both in data collection and affirmation of observations (Davis et al., 1993, 1996). Typically, a pair of researchers on site will meet at the end of each day to share notes and consider such process issues as to what extent relevant dimensions have been thoroughly explored, what themes may be emerging to be "listened for" the next day, and how the relationship with the site is developing. On one project (Pruyne et al., 1998), six researchers collected data separately, met regularly around these issues, and wrote different sections of one shared portrait. In current work, individual researchers are data collecting and working on their own. But in all these settings, the team's work is linked by group voice and grounded by group meetings that serve as sounding boards for developing ideas and an arena in which concerns and directions are reviewed.

One important protocol determined at such meetings concerns attitudes and personal presentation for group members entering a site and forging a relationship. "Never be late." "Be a listener and learner." "Dress for each visit as an honored and honoring guest." Such "nuts and bolts" decisions about entering a site, as micro as they may seem, help set the stage for generative relationships and a team standard across all site visits by the research team.

Relationship

Artist and subject reflect on the work together. As the model expresses her pleasure and interest in the portrayal that she is reviewing, she is measured with her language. Understanding the time and intensity the artist has put into the work, she is grateful to see that she recognizes herself in the portrayal and can celebrate what she had not anticipated. "I look sad in this image. Is that what you saw?" "I believe what you have painted is an expression of me." The artist has been measured in her portrayal of the sadness she sees, careful to link it to the comfort of the chaise—careful not to turn the image into a treatise on sadness rather than a portrayal of the individual subject she has come to know well from days of looking, painting, and relationship building. "This image is about you," the artist shares, "but it is my vision of you, so it is part yours and part mine." Through this sharing—the model's hours of sitting, the artist's concentration on the figure before her—a relationship of trust has been forged. "You may look and see because I know that you will not betray me in your expression of your vision."

"Do no harm" is the researcher's mandate. In the telling of a story, a story that through the telling is no longer just that of the site or subject, the researcher holds to that mandate. In entering the site, the researcher has initiated a respectful relationship simply by studying carefully contextual materials about the site. "There's that picture of Jackie McLean," I comment as I enter the halls of the Artists Collective. "I read about it in an article about the center and am excited to see it for myself." Constituents realize that the researcher is earnest in his or her interest and has spent some time preparing for the visit. In the tone of questions, in the attention given to listening and observing carefully, to the expectation of goodness rather than a search for the problem, the researcher is building a positive relationship. This relationship will scaffold the time spent in on-site observation and discourse and demonstrate throughout the visit that there is mutual respect and a level of trust that will not be violated. Beyond that, relationship guides what will or will not be included in a portrait as the researcher determines protectively what information illuminates and what intrudes.

In our group portraits, this relationship is prioritized from first contact made with the site to last. In initial contact, we demonstrate our preparation for a visit we care about—through informed and respectful interaction—and in the final portrait, we demonstrate our dedication to doing no harm—through carefully monitored portrayal. Indeed, before a portrait is read by anyone beyond the research team and the constituents at the site, a final draft is shared with research participants so that they can review it in detail. They let us know what, if any, erroneous information we may have included and where, if any place, we may have inadvertently offended.

It is interesting to note that at this juncture in the work, my repeated experience has been that we can never accurately anticipate what we have included that might offend and what will cause no distress. Invariably in the portraits we have produced in various projects, we have been surprised by what aspects of the text caused disagreement. One participant reports, "The researchers say my smock was batik. I hate batik clothes and would never wear them. That smock was handpainted by me and my granddaughter." A change is respectfully inserted. When asked whether the financial distress of the site is treated with a level hand, the surprising response, "Actually it felt to me as if you 'sugar-coated' our pain. It was much worse than you describe" (Davis et al., 1996).

The construction of an authentic interpretation—one that is affirmed by the site as well as by the researchers—results from a redefinition of the boundaries that traditionally separate insider from outsider knowledge. A trusting relationship between research participant and researcher allows for the co-constructing of a story that belongs to and honors them both. Furthermore, that relationship extends beyond the limits of the portrait. It is not uncommon for constituents at a site to stay in touch with a portraitist, to call long after the research portrait is completed to share some news that is assumed of interest to the researcher.

At a gathering at the White House in 1996, Hilary Rodham Clinton was honoring the work of community arts educators and the publication of the President's Committee Report on programs like the Artists Collective that serve youth who have been placed at risk (Weitz, 1996). As Dollie McLean and I wound up the marble stairwell to the reception area, I was taking the scene in—the elegance, the gorgeous portraits, the famous guests. Dollie took my arm and leaned in close, "Let me tell you about the new meals project we're starting at the Collective. We want to focus on manners and the art of listening at the table. . . . " It had been three years since the portrait had been completed.

Relationship is developed and cultivated in every element of the portraiture process, but in the interaction that is essential to interview, its significance is clear. For example, in training for such back and forth, the group of researchers role-plays the technique of writing down key words that are spoken by the interviewee. These brief notations help guide additional questions and confirm, in the researcher's repetition of these words, a listening and attentive attitude. Empowering research techniques (Mishler, 1991) scaffold the exchange and assure the respondent that the researcher really cares about the answers and the integrity of the story being told.

In our portraiture initiative, after Lawrence-Lightfoot (1983), we set out to study goodness. This expectation of goodness, as opposed to a deficit model based on the identification of problems, sets a tone for relationship that is positive and trusting. Sites like those we studied in the Project Co-Arts/Safe Havens study (1993) are accustomed to having evaluators come and assess their practice. It takes time to assure these constituents that evaluation is not our mandate. In recognizing goodness, challenges are assumed as part of the process not identified as signs of a problem, and a positive perspective is promised and maintained. This approach, coupled with the displayed appreciation of a supplicant learner gratefully welcomed to a site, set the stage for a relationship marked by trust. As with all features of portraiture, that relationship informs the data-collecting process as well as the creation of the final narrative.

Emergent Themes

The artist has decided which forms will be highlighted in her portrayal: the chaise, the resting elbow, and the melancholy eyes of her subject. The chaise is clearly an organizing force, representing comfort both literally and metaphorically—its rounded edges and restful contours echoing the shape and tone of its occupant. The resting elbow, punctuating the subject's contact with and reliance on the chaise—and the melancholy eyes, taking restful comfort a step further to the edge of sorrow. Rounded drooping lines embody these resonant themes: comfort, contact, and sadness. These themes resonate throughout the lines and textures in the image and also offer coherence to the portrait's portrayal.

Back at the research table, the research team is considering the coherence that is offered by the three major themes that have emerged at the Artists Collective in Hartford: family, safe haven, and the process of becoming somebody (Davis et al., 1993). Having demonstrated the resonance of the language of these themes throughout the repeated refrains heard in interview, voiced in daily rituals, or used in descriptive written materials, we now "walk" the theme of "safe haven" through the relevant dimensions that scaffolds the portrait team's work.

In terms of teaching and learning, I point out, the center is a safe haven from the low academic expectations that its African American students face in schools. In terms of the community, it is a safe haven as a place full of celebration of art replete with positive African American role models in a community in which negative stereotypes abound. In terms of its administration, it is a safe haven for the artist educators who have joined together as founders, board members, and faculty to build a program offering alternatives to urban youth. At the collective, their lives as artists are valued and space is designated for the pursuit of their talents in various artistic domains. And in terms of the journey of the center, it echoes the journey of its founder Jackie McLean, who found a safe haven in music from the drug addiction he was fighting decades ago in New York. Following the inspiration of that journey, the founding and future of the center will be dedicated to providing such a safe haven for its constituents.

Although these examples represent only a portion of resonance within and across the dimensions—there are many more that unfold in the narrative—and they serve to illustrate the ways in which the emergent themes, like the dimensions, are both distinct and porous. Illustrating the theme of safe haven as perceived by community members and expressed in educational context by director Dollie McLean, an excerpt from a section of the portrait makes the point:

> A staff member says of the Collective: " . . . people call this an oasis and it is because [here] people are not overwhelmed by a culture that feels alien to them. . . . " One parent explains: "They don't observe black history and holidays in school—just segments of that; we reinforce that at home that you are capable, that you are no more or less than anybody else. But that ain't happening at school." At the Collective, Ms. McLean says they "lay" the art "on top of culture and heritage." She believes, "the origin of many of the problems we have with our youth is the fact that they've been taught . . . whether it's from the school system, television, whatever—that they come from nothing; they're nobody; they're thieves, they're pimps, all of the worst things. . . . "
>
> The achievements celebrated on the Collective walls proclaim a different reality and Dollie McLean finds the students "behave quite differently" at the Collective. She remembers at one of their first open houses (Open House At The Artists Collective ="OHATAC"): "A teacher came [and saw] the young man that we had at the door taking donations, or taking names. The teacher pulled me aside and said, 'Dollie, do you know who that boy is that you have sitting at the desk?' I said, 'Yes, that's Marvin and he's one of our star students.' Marvin was just wonderful with us, but obviously all his school childhood—it was that thing, he was labeled as a bad kid. So I just think a lot has to do with what kids accomplish, you know their own sense of self-worth." (Davis et al., 1993, p. 21)

There is something about works of art that makes the representations they contain not just depiction but valid expression of human experience. It is the way in which the portrayal of the subject on the chaise in the artist's portrait focuses on one woman's sadness, but speaks of sadness writ large. There is a similar quality about the interpretation that a research portrait provides that tells the reader not just about the Artists Collective as an individual site but more generally about other sites of this nature in urban centers around the country. The emergent themes organize the account of experience and make it comprehensible to the constituents at the site who know it first-hand as well as to the readers of the portrait who reinterpret the experience through their reading.

Ultimately a series of portraits on the same subject (e.g., community art centers) can be analyzed through a comparison of emergent themes with an eye to a clearer vision of a field. In reflecting on emergent themes across community art centers, we consider whether there are, for example, informative links between the themes identified for the Molly Olga Center in Buffalo *(the model of the professional artist, realistic accessibility,* and *constant survivor)* and those of the Artists Collective in Hartford *(family, safe haven,* and *the process of becoming somebody;* Davis et al., 1993). What principles of effectiveness can be derived from the resonance of themes across sites? In a final reflective chapter in the Safe Havens collection, I address this question and derive from such considerations a set of overarching descriptive criteria (see Davis et al., 1993, pp. 184–186). These activities demonstrate the way in which emergent themes organize what we discover internally (within the site) and offer structures that can be useful to external consideration (from the perspective of the field). In this way, portraiture functions as inductive reasoning and generates theory that can inform broader understanding.

Summarizing the process, in end-of-day on-site reflection and in consultation with coresearchers, portraitists record their developing ideas and evidence for emergent themes and consider, as I have described, their aptness. Reflecting in this way at regular junctures throughout the site visit allows the portraitist to maintain an ongoing rapport with both the process (the collection of data) and the product (the portrait), both of which, as the interpretation comes together, are organized around emergent themes.

After the site visit, in the ongoing analysis of data, emergent themes are implemented in a new way, as structures for coding and triangulating data from a number of sources. But even in this stage of the data analysis, the portraitist, like the artist reflecting on process, is ready to change. A researcher working on a recent portrait of the Boston Arts Academy wrote a first draft of a section of the portrait around the theme of "passion and satisfaction"—an expression he heard frequently in his time at the school. But in reading the draft, it was clear that constituent language throughout the data sorted under the title of this theme repeatedly addressed the issue of, in constituent language, "meeting challenge." Indeed, reviewing his transcription data with an eye to relevant dimensions, it was "meeting challenge" that seemed more apt for the naming of this theme and for the structuring of his portrait.

From data collection (triangulated around material review, site observation, and in-depth interview) to the final stages of writing the portrait, then, the emergent themes taken together structure the researcher's interpretation as an aesthetic whole. The presentation of emergent themes and the interrelationships among them illuminates the structure of both the site and the portrait—the parts of the interpretation and their necessity to a view of the whole.

Aesthetic Whole

The artist looks at her painting and at her subject. At first the gaze is from subject to portrait and portrait to subject in almost rapid and rhythmic motion. But after a while attention is focused on the canvas. Does everything fit? Does this look right? When the artist decides a work is done—when it is complete and "right"—may be the most important decision of the ongoing process. In reaching this decision, the visual artist plays the role of producer and perceiver all at once, considering the work as fulfilling her artistic objectives and trying hard to view it from the eyes of the other who will be making sense of the image. Does this make sense? Do the parts fit together into a sensible whole? When the image has reached this level of coherency, the artist will say, "Yes. That's right." At least for now.

In considering as a final methodological element, the most comprehensive feature of the research methodology of portraiture—the aesthetic whole—we realize that it has been a beacon in the process from its inception. From selection of materials to review, from scenarios observed, and interviews staged, the end in view, the mounting of a coherent interpretation, has been the ballast for both developing process and product. The portraitist, like the artist, is constructing and communicating her understanding for the reconstruction and reinterpretation of the reader. This communicative expression of understanding relies on the creation of a balanced composition, a unified whole.

As psychologist of the arts Rudolf Arnheim put it, "In a balanced composition, all factors of shape, direction, location, etc. are mutually determined by each other in such a way that no change seems possible, and the whole assumes the character of 'necessity' in all its parts" (Arnheim, 1966, p. 76). He continues, "Under conditions of imbalance the artistic statement becomes incomprehensible" (1974, p. 20). Accordingly, the researcher needs to assemble the respective parts of the interpretation and to justify the inclusion of each separate entity in terms of its relation (even as a dissonant refrain) to the congealing whole. Without unity, without the parts fitting together into an intelligible articulation, there is no communication, no understanding to be shared or found.

At every juncture, the researcher is balancing three areas of judgment: aesthetic and empirical concerns, the separate parts of the overarching interpretation, and the various features of the methodology through which the interpretation has been attained. Three broad concerns—questions of "how to"—underscore the numerous queries that have been raised and fuel the portraitist's process of composing the narrative: (a) how to fit together what is included; (b) how to decide what to exclude; and (c) how to know when the whole is unified.

In addressing these issues, and giving shape to our group voice, our research group was supported in the final writing stage by an agreed on schema for the creation of the overarching aesthetic whole of final team portraits. Project Co-Arts' pattern or skeletal framework was called a "generic outline" (generic in that it could serve all of the separate portraits). It delineated a plan of action in which each portrait began, as we have discussed, with an opening section that introduced the site in terms of its context or setting as well as the emergent themes that would structure the aesthetic whole of the portrait.

Thereafter, the generic outline calls for individual sections, one for each emergent theme, in which evidence of the resonance (and dissonance) of the theme is included with regard to each of our identified relevant dimensions. Presenting each theme section as a more linear construction than portraitists could or would want to achieve (for example, many more than three sources of evidence and dissonance would appear in a given theme section), the generic outline specified the following broad brushed pattern:

THEME I (e.g., safe havens)

a. Relevant Dimension 1 (Teaching and Learning)
   - i. evidence (e.g., the story of the student not doing well in school who finds success at the center)
   - ii. evidence (another resonant example/story/refrain)
   - iii. evidence (another resonant example/story/refrain)
   - iv. dissonance (e.g. the parent who resents the cost of education at the center)

b. Relevant Dimension 2 (Community)
   - i. evidence (e.g. the story of the center as a source of celebration of African-American history)

ii. evidence (another resonant example/story/refrain)
iii. evidence (another resonant example/story/refrain)
iv. dissonance (e.g. the mother who is not allowed on the basis of her gender to present her daughter in the Rites of Passage ceremony)

c. Ibid. for dimensions 3 (Administration) & 4 (Journey)

For each subsequent theme (3 and 4), the same approximate girders were suggested. Giving shape to the process of testing emergent themes by virtue of their resonance across dimensions (as described earlier), the generic outline helps to scaffold the researcher's final process of creating an aesthetic whole. Finally, our outline called for a conclusion, a brief retrospective holistic view that might be accomplished explicitly through the portraitist's reflection or implicitly through a story that seemed both emblematic and integrative. With the Artists' Collective portrait, I used a concert at the Children's Museum in Boston as a synthesizing final event.

Researchers use the generic outline specifically to ensure that they include stories that exemplify the resonance of themes across dimensions and that they balance their examples of evidence thoughtfully throughout the text. But the outline offers the same sort of structural tool as sorting data according to dimension and later by theme. Just as it is important in the writing not to line evidence up sorted by dimension for each theme, it is important to vary literary elements in the text. Context leads the way in balancing observations of classroom pedagogy with physical details of site and individuals and various direct quotations from constituents. Applying expressive language, rich metaphor, and vivid descriptions, the research portraitist, like a Spiderwoman, is weaving elements into a vibrant multifaceted whole.

The subject or site itself, then, as it is perceived and understood by the portraitist, is the governing force in the construction of the aesthetic whole. Patterns or substructures, like the generic outline, are there to be adapted in response to the portraitist's interpretation of the overall gestalt. Portraitists' ongoing considerations of the structural requirements of the final portrait ensure that a view of the whole is guiding the development of each unfolding part. The weaving together of the parts of the whole exemplifies the ongoing portraiture dialectic between process and product. It is out of this continuous weaving that the aesthetic whole is created.

Unity is expressed in the methodology of portraiture as surely as in the research portrait. Just as the close attention to each separate part of the portrait is obscured from the reader through the invisibility of seams, so too is the methodology of portraiture, that I have unpacked here part by part, in the end, a seamless endeavor. Enriched throughout by carefully constructed context, expressed through theoretically grounded group and indefatigable individual voice, informed by cautiously guarded relationships, and organized into scrupulously selected themes, the research portrait is the result of a subtle synthesis of rigorous procedures that unite in an expressive aesthetic whole. Just as the portrait (product) is perceived as one unified whole, so too is the methodology of portraiture (process) performed from start to finish as a unified endeavor.

At the children's museum:

> Jackie McLean has arrived. He is smiling and clapping and speaking back to the musicians. The sparsity of the crowd has been overwhelmed by the intensity and electricity of the audience's experience. We are yelling and clapping; we are entirely engaged. Dollie McLean, dressed in white, looks worried. One of the children is ill; she needs to get him back to Hartford. As the performance comes to an end, the announcer says there will be a second performance in just a few minutes. The thought that the performance will begin again is almost unbelievable. The intensity and accuracy of this work seems impossible to duplicate without even a rest. But in the dressing room, the energy is uplifting. Even an onlooker can experience what the Collective mother describes as "the self-esteem and the good feeling you get after a good performance—that natural high that will encourage you to do a lot of things. . . . " The audience has experienced the "high" Cheryl Smith noted in the prison audiences: "they are high not for one day but they are high for a year until we return. . . . " It seems possible.
>
> All the Collective family members are there to celebrate the children's success, to gather and share in Jackie's that evening. . . . It seems as if all the training has been rehearsal for a moment like this. And Dollie McLean agrees, "Yes, you get to see the finished product . . ." She adds with a smile, "but it is never finished" (Davis et al., 1993, p. 51)

References

Arnheim, R. (1966). *Toward a psychology of art.* Berkeley: University of California Press.

Arnheim, R. (1974). *Art and visual perception: A psychology of the creative eye.* Berkeley: University of California Press.

Bateson, M. C. (1989). *Composing a Life.* Boston: Atlantic Monthly Press.

Bruner, J. (1996). *The culture of education.* Cambridge, MA: Harvard University Press.

Davis, J. (1994). *The Co-Arts assessment handbook.* Cambridge, MA: President and Fellows of Harvard College

Davis, J. (1996). *The wheel in motion: The Co-Arts plan from theory to application and the final toolbox of assessment tools.* Cambridge, MA: President and Fellows of Harvard College.

Davis, J., Eppel, M., Galazzi, M. Gonzalez-Pose, P., Maira, S., et al. (1996). *Another safe haven: Portraits of Boulevard Arts Center, then and now.* Cambridge, MA: Presidents and Fellows of Harvard College.

Davis, J., Soep, L., Remba, N., Maira, S., & Putnoi, D. (1993). *Safe havens: Portraits of educational effectiveness in community art centers that focus on education in economically disadvantaged communities.* Cambridge, MA: President and Fellows of Harvard College.

Gilligan, C. (1982). *In a different voice.* Cambridge, MA: Harvard University Press.

Haig, B. (1995). Grounded theory as scientific method. In A. Neihan (Ed.), *Philosophy of Education Society yearbook.* Illinois: University of Urbana at Champaign Press.

Kinach, B. (1995). Grounded theory as scientific method: Haig-inspired reflections on educational research methodology. In A. Neihan (Ed.), *Philosophy of Education Society yearbook.* Illinois: University of Urbana at Champaign Press.

Lawrence Lightfoot, S. (1983). *The good high school.* New York: Basic Books.

Lawrence Lightfoot, S. (1994). *I've known rivers.* Reading, MA: Addison Wesley.

Lawrence-Lightfoot, S., & Davis, J. H. (1997). *The art and science of portraiture.* San Francisco: Jossey-Bass.

Mishler, E. G. (1991). *Research interviewing: Context and narrative.* Cambridge, MA: Harvard University Press.

Powell, K. (1995). *Musicianship at the Community Center of Boston: Nurturing artistic identity in adolescents.* Unpublished manuscript, Harvard University, Cambridge, MA.

Pruyne, E., Anisko, E., Hamovit, L., Kennedy, S., Lehmann, A., et al. (Eds.). (1998). *The Walnut Hill School, Natick, MA: The educated artist, gift of responsibility, and welcome as I am.* Natick, MA: National Arts Learning Foundation.

Weitz, J. (1996). *President's committee on the arts and the humanities coming up taller: Arts and humanities programs for children and youth at risk.* Washington, DC: President's Committee on the Arts and the Humanities.

12

Ethnographic Methods: Applications From Developmental Cultural Psychology

Peggy J. Miller, Julie A. Hengst, and Su-hua Wang

Ethnographic modes of inquiry have had a long and distinguished history in the social sciences, especially in anthropology and sociology. Like all interpretive methods, ethnographic approaches are oriented to the study of meaning, but, in the case of ethnographic methods, meaning is understood to be structured by culture—that is, by collectively shared and transmitted symbols, understandings, and ways of being. The word *ethnography* dates from the emergence of anthropology as a discipline in the late-19th century. Anthropologists coined the term to describe monograph-length descriptions of people who were *ethnoi* or "other" (Erickson, 1986). Intrigued by distant cultures, many of which were European colonies, they traveled to far-off outposts to see them first-hand. Ethnographic methods evolved out of these cross-cultural encounters. The goal was to understand a particular culture on its own terms, to represent the meaning of actions and institutions from "the native's point of view" (Malinowski, 1922). In his ground-breaking study of the Trobriand Islanders, Malinowski combined long-term *participant-observation* with in-depth *interviewing,* the two hallmarks of modern ethnography (Erickson, 1986). Ethnographic methods remain the privileged mode of inquiry in cultural anthropology and have become increasingly important in the fields of education and communication.

In psychology, where the prevailing orientation has been positivist, proposals for a "second" or "cultural" psychology were part of the intellectual landscape from its inception as a discipline (Cahan & White, 1992; Jahoda, 1989). Wilhelm Wundt wrote extensively on cultural psychology and was "captivated by the ethnographic material he pursued so tirelessly" (Jahoda, 1993, p. 181). Despite this early history, modern psychology has excluded ethnographic approaches from its methodological repertoire. Even community psychology, with its commitments to contextual understandings and to collaborative models of research, has marginalized ethnographic methods (Stewart, 2000).

However, the recent renewal of interest in cultural psychology makes it timely to consider the nature of ethnographic methods, given the affinity of ethnography for problems in cultural psychology. Although psychologists from many corners of the discipline have contributed to recreating a cultural psychology (e.g., Bruner, 1990; Cohen, Nisbett, Bowdle, & Schwarz, 1996; Gergen, 1985; Markus & Kitayama, 1991), scholars of child development have played a particularly important role, and some have written extensively about ethnographic methods. In addition, there are several traditions of interdisciplinary study of child development in which ethnographic methods have been privileged. For these reasons, this chapter will draw heavily on developmental questions to illustrate the assumptions and aims of ethnographic methods.

But before we turn to specific instantiations, it is necessary to provide additional background about the nature of ethnographic methods. First, it is important to stress that ethnographic modes of inquiry do not constitute a single, unified perspective or set of methods. Rather, here, as in qualitative inquiry in general, diversity reigns. This is amply illustrated in Denzin and Lincoln's (1994) *Handbook of Qualitative Research.* Denzin and Lincoln's introduction to their volume provides an excellent survey of the diversity of interpretive paradigms. They see this diversity as anchored in positivism, on the one extreme, and postmodernism, on the other. The naive realist position—there is a reality out there that can be studied objectively and understood—is countered by the postmodern, poststructuralist position of radical doubt. Articulating the latter position, Denzin (1996) wrote, "There can never be a final, accurate representation of what was meant or said, only different textual representations of different experiences" (p. 132).

Between these two extremes are the middle-ground positions of postpositivism and constructivism. According to Denzin and Lincoln (1994), postpositivism rests on the assumption that reality can never be fully apprehended, only approximated. Postpositivists use multiple methods to capture as much of reality as possible; emphasize the discovery and verification of theories; and apply traditional evaluative criteria, such as validity. Denzin and Lincoln (1994) defined constructivism as involving "a relativist ontology (there are multiple realities), a subjectivist epistemology (knower and subject create understandings), and a naturalistic (in the natural world) set of methodological procedures" (p. 13). Evaluative criteria include trustworthiness, credibility, and confirmability.

Some Examples of Problems for Study

Denzin and Lincoln emphasized that these various positions are realized within particular disciplinary traditions that inflect them in distinctive ways and that each researcher enters the research process from the vantage point of his or her particular interpretive community, with its unique history of research practices. The interpretive community to which we belong is an interdisciplinary community that has tried to bring together culture and children into a culture-sensitive understanding of child development. For the most part, this community has drawn on the middle-ground positions of postpositivism and constructivism (e.g., Gaskins, 1994; Goncu, 1999; Grau & Walsh, 1998; Jessor, Colby, & Shweder, 1996; Rizzo, Corsaro, & Bates, 1992; Shweder et al., 1998).

Consider, for example, Gaskins, Miller, and Corsaro's (1992) framing of a set of papers pertaining to children's socialization, one of the fundamental problems in developmental cultural psychology. Gaskins et al. advocated an interpretive approach that views reality as socially constructed; recognizes that the complex relationship between the researcher and the participants is part of the research question; and defines knowledge as understanding that makes sense to the actors themselves in terms of collectively shared interpretive frameworks, a criterion that privileges the actor's point of view. This approach makes sense given the kinds of problems that this community of scholars has identified as central to their interests, problems that rest on the premise that all children grow up to be cultural beings. This characteristic is unique to our species and is perhaps the most important reason why human beings experience a prolonged period of immaturity (Bruner, 1972). The process of human development is thus inextricably bound to the process of enculturation, of orienting oneself within systems of meaning.

But, as Gaskins et al. (1992) pointed out, no child orients him- or herself within culture in general. Rather, each child navigates a specific culture, with a specific set of beliefs, practices, and interpretive frameworks. The process of becoming a participant in a culture is therefore enabling and limiting at the same time. Socialization, the universal process of becoming a participant in a culture, cannot be understood except by studying enculturation, the process of meaning creation in particular cultures (Mead, 1963).

Thus, the fundamental developmental question from this perspective is how do children come to invest cultural resources with meaning? Born into a world of already existing traditions and semiotic systems, children use their growing interpretive abilities to participate in cultural practices. This process is constructive and it is necessarily individual and collective. It is individual in that each child creates personal meaning out of the particular, necessarily limited set of resources to which he or she is exposed. It is collective in that these resources were created by previous generations and are made available to the child by other people. By participating with caregivers and peers in day-by-day encounters with cultural resources, children shape their own developmental experiences while at the same time contributing to the production of social order (Cook-Gumperz & Corsaro, 1986).

No one has probed a child's meaning-making process more profoundly than Jean Briggs in her book, *Inuit Morality Play* (1998). Offspring of *Never in Anger* (J. Briggs, 1970), a classic of psychological anthropology, and informed by three decades of work with the Inuit, this study focuses on a single three-year-old child, Chubby Maata, as she engages a distinctive kind of emotional drama that is common to many Inuit families. J. Briggs sees culture as a " 'bag of ingredients' actively used by individuals in creating and maintaining their social-cognitive worlds" (p. 14). This view allows her to realize that she cannot provide a full interpretation of the meanings that Chubby Maata is making because every fragment of data "explodes with potential meanings" (p. 20). But it is not only the witnessing ethnographer but the child herself who has to live with this ambiguity. Chubby Maata is making educated guesses, based on her past and present apprehension of the patterns in her own and other people's words and actions. The ethnographer's task is to follow the child. She is making educated guesses about Chubby Maata's educated guesses. The resulting ethnography is "a cloth full of holes, the very sort of cloth that Chubby Maata herself was weaving" (p. 20).

The metaphor of a cloth full of holes is compatible with Howard Becker's (1996) understanding of a key interpretive challenge. Operating out of the Chicago school of sociology, Becker focuses not on geographically distant cultures but on poor urban neighborhoods, medical schools, the art world, and other contexts that are nearer at hand. He says that people—he is speaking of adults, not children—are "not sure what things *do* mean: they make vague and woolly interpretations of events and people" (p. 60). The implication for ethnographers is that we should respect people's confusion and indecision and not represent their meanings as more coherent or stable than they are.

The general problem of how children make meaning out of cultural resources implies several questions: What exactly is happening here? That is, what kinds of activities are these children and their companions engaging in? What are the folk theories—informal, local belief systems about children, child-rearing, and development—that inform and rationalize their activities? What are the larger contexts and activities in which these activities are embedded? To some social scientists, these will seem like uninteresting questions, inviting "mere" description. But as Becker (1996) stressed, it is all too easy to think we know what people are up to. He cautioned, "Don't make up what you could find out" (p. 59).

Play provides an excellent example of how these general questions have been applied in a specific research arena. In the past decade, play has inspired several substantial ethnographic studies in different parts of the world. Scholars have asked questions about the types of play that occur under everyday conditions (e.g., pretend play, exploratory play, teasing), about the folk theories that parents hold about the nature of children, of development, and of play itself (e.g., play develops naturally to children vs. play must be taught), and about the larger contexts and activities in which play is embedded (e.g., do children contribute to the family's livelihood, and if so, how and from what age, and how much time does this leave for play? Gaskins, 1996; Goldman, 1998; Goncu, 1999; Lancy, 1996; Taylor & Carlson, 2000).

These studies have produced findings that challenge fundamental assumptions about the nature of play (Miller, 2001). They show that play is constituted differently within and across cultures: communities vary in the types of play; the time, space, and personnel available for play; whether play is valued by adults; what role, if any, play is seen to have in children's development; and the kinds of imaginative resources that are drawn on for play. These findings challenge developmentalists to revise our assumption that pretend play belongs to a single ontological category. When viewed from the perspective of this or that local meaning system, pretend play emerges as a blessed spiritual encounter, demon possession, deceit, or self-indulgent idleness.

Ethnographic Methods: An Overview

Ethnographic research involves taking up a rigorous program of scientific inquiry marked by repeated and varied observations and data collection; detailed recordings of, and reactions to, such observations; a skeptical stance by the researcher that forces as many questions from the continuous interpretation of the data as it provides answers; and the presentation of ongoing interpretations to the larger scientific community. Despite the diversity, common issues and practices cut across ethnographic research, whether conducted in the originating discipline of anthropology for the purposes of documenting whole cultures or conducted by researchers addressing a diversity of questions across multiple disciplines. In this section we first address characteristics common to ethnographic methods, then briefly outline four key phases in ethnographic research. For more detailed discussions of how to conduct ethnographic research see Agar (1980), Erickson (1986), Hymes (1982), and Wolcott (1995).

Characteristics of Ethnographic Inquiry

One important characteristic of ethnographic methods is the *sustained and engaged nature* of data collection. "Classic" ethnographic studies within anthropology focus on cultures "foreign" to the researcher and, as a consequence, fieldwork necessarily includes time for the researcher to become familiar with, and learn to navigate within, unfamiliar physical, social, and communicative environments (e.g., Basso, 1996; C. L. Briggs, 1986; J. Briggs, 1970; Schieffelin, 1990). As ethnographic methods have been taken up by researchers in other disciplines, such as education and psychology, and applied to problems closer to "home," the researcher often enters a research site where he or she has already spent time and is acquainted with "local" linguistic, social, or institutional histories and practices (e.g., Baym, 2000; Denzin, 1993; Giorgio, 1999; Heath, 1983; Prior, 1998; Wolf & Heath, 1992). In such cases, time "in the field" may be shorter as the researcher is able to draw more heavily on personal experiences and communicative practices in customizing data collection. In either case, to penetrate participants' meaning systems, ethnographers must familiarize themselves with the participants' community—the physical and institutional settings in which they live, the daily routines that they and their companions follow, the beliefs that guide their actions, and the linguistic and other semiotic systems that mediate all of these contexts and activities.

Through such sustained community contact, researchers necessarily become deeply engaged in the lives, practices, celebrations, and problems of their participants. In remote and isolated sites, the very survival of the researcher may depend on the strengths of the relationships the researcher has been able to forge and the goodwill of the community members under study (e.g., J. Briggs, 1970; Gottlieb & Graham, 1993). Even when life and limb are not at stake, the research itself is shaped and strengthened by the willingness of individuals to participate in the researcher's project. Much has been written about the complexities of researcher–participant relationships in the interpretive process (see Behar, 1993; Scheper-Hughes, 1992; Wolcott, 1995; Wolf, 1992). In fact, Engstrom (1996) argued that one way to measure the validity and generalizability of research findings is to look for successful collaborations between the researchers and the participants. In ethnographic work, researchers often find that because of their relationships with participants and their developing emic understandings, they are in a unique position to help speak across cultures on behalf of the group being studied (e.g., Basso, 1996; Philips, 1983) and to help identify avenues of change that support community goals (e.g., Engstrom, 1996). These opportunities for personal, social, and political intervention make ethnographic research an attractive choice for action research traditions in education (e.g., Cochran-Smith & Lytle, 1993) and community psychology (e.g., Stewart, 2000).

Ethnographic methods also carry with them *an implicit multicultural perspective,* a perspective that is often made explicit within particular research programs (e.g., Miller, Fung, & Mintz, 1996; Rogoff, Mistry, Goncu, & Mosier, 1993). In attempting to apprehend local meanings, ethnographers try not to mistake their own deeply taken-for-granted, culturally saturated understandings for those of the study participants—a challenge that is never fully met. To anticipate an example that will come later in the chapter, if the goal is to appreciate the interpretive frameworks of parents from a particular American community, and the ethnographer is Taiwanese, then the process of bringing these parents' (American) frameworks into focus will also expose the ethnographer's own (Taiwanese) frameworks. Thus, even when ethnographers study a single cultural case, they aim for double vision at least. In fact, American parents and Taiwanese ethnographers belong to multiple communities and are likely to live and breathe meanings that flow within and across multiple cultures. This does not mean that cultural boundaries have no reality, but it does make a mockery of the idea that cultural boundaries can be neatly drawn in this increasingly globalized world.

Another characteristic of ethnographic inquiry is that data collection and analyses are *both microscopic and holistic* (Gaskins et al., 1992). Focusing on the details of particular participants and practices, ethnographic methods capture unanticipated nuances and variations of human interaction. However, Geertz (1973) argued that detailed description of behavior alone, what he calls "thin description," is not sufficient to recoup meaning. Instead, ethnographers engage in what Geertz (1973) termed "thick description." To ensure that their understandings are culturally valid, ethnographers ground their interpretations of cultural events in an accumulation of specific details from the events of everyday life and from the participants' reflections on those events. It is in this way that ethnographers approach broad interpretations "from the direction of exceedingly extended acquaintances with extremely small matters" (Geertz, 1973, p. 21). By way of illustrating the distinction between "thin" and "thick" description, Geertz (1973) borrowed Ryle's example of two boys who are "rapidly contracting the eyelids of their right eyes" (p. 6). Are they blinking, winking, parodying a wink, faking a wink, practicing a wink? It is impossible to say without understanding the multiple embedded contexts in which these actions took place and the socially established communicative code that renders them intelligible. Thus, it is necessary not only to examine actions microscopically but also to contextualize them in a more holistic sense to successfully describe an event as it was understood by the actors themselves.

Finally, ethnographic inquiry is a *dynamic process* marked by generative and self-corrective methodologies (Gaskins et al., 1992). Successful researchers need to be flexible from the beginning, prepared to revise or discard initial research questions and adjust data collection procedures as they position themselves physically and socially in the research site. J. Briggs (1970), for example, set out to study shamans among the Inuit, only to discover that shamans no longer existed in the community she had entered. When Miller, Sandel, Liang, and Fung (2001) formulated their research questions about the role of personal storytelling in Longwood, hell-raising stories were not on their list; the parents in this community brought such stories to their attention. In addition, researchers must be open to learning locally appropriate ways to ask questions and hold interviews (C. L. Briggs, 1986); they must develop effective ways to present their research project and their role as researcher to the participants, a problem that is especially complex when the participants are children (Corsaro, 1985, 1988); and they must learn to situate themselves physically and socially in ways that allow them to observe the phenomena of interest (Ochs, 1988). Often, such negotiations include a willingness on the part of the researcher to accept the interactions that are offered and to look for new ways to augment data collection (Prior, 1998).

The generative and self-correcting nature of ethnographic inquiry is also evident during data analysis and writing. The interpretive process, guided by the notion of cultural validity, is theory-generating. The goal is to provide a deeper understanding of the multiple perspectives that are operating in all human interactions. Therefore, categories used in analysis are not predetermined but are developed through a continual process of iterative division, classification, and evaluation (Bloom, 1974; Strauss, 1987). The researcher begins with a tentative descriptive framework—what Pike (1967) called an etic classification—often gleaned from other data sets or theoretical positions, and proceeds to test that framework through successive passes through the data. The outcome of this self-corrective process of constant comparison is an emic classification (Pike, 1967) that captures the patterns in the participants' meanings. In addition, deepening interpretations of the data emerge when researchers revisit earlier work. For example, accounts written early in a research program are necessarily expanded in later accounts as researchers combine existing data with new data. (This process will be described more in the latter half of this chapter.) In other cases, researchers apply their evolving perspectives to a reinterpretation of earlier work. When Wolf (1992) reexamined her 30-year-old field notes concerning the case of a young Taiwanese mother who suddenly began behaving in a decidedly aberrant manner, she was dissatisfied with her earlier account. In an effort to better display the multiple perspectives of participants and researcher, she ended up producing three separate accounts of the same incident. (See J. Briggs, 1998, for an excellent example in the same vein.)

Phases of Ethnographic Research

Despite the flexibility inherent in ethnographic research practices, the research process generally unfolds in a series of phases.

Developing Questions and Gaining Access. The ethnographer begins the research process by formulating a problem for study, drawing on previous scholarship, and learning as much as possible about the particular community or institution in which the study will be conducted. Any previous ethnographic work and other formal or informal sources of information about the same community are invaluable in allowing the researcher to hone the initial research questions, anticipate field conditions, and design an approach that will best address the research questions. It is in this phase that the researcher makes initial decisions about what in psychology is referred to as subject sampling. Ethnographers, however, are less concerned about random sampling than they are about specifying the social positioning of the participants who agree to work with them, thereby delimiting their interpretations. The researcher must make preliminary contacts to obtain initial institutional permission to conduct research and work to establish relationships with possible participants. In the classic case, the ethnographer enters the research site as an outsider, and the task of gaining access to particular groups or institutions may take a great deal of patience and interpersonal skill. In our own work, which spans several working-class and middle-class communities in the United States and Taiwan, we have found that doors open much more rapidly if the ethnographer has a trusted associate in the community.

The importance of the process of negotiating access to a research site cannot be overstated. The physical and social positioning the researcher is able to establish and maintain within the community of study critically shapes the entire research enterprise. Nor is this a task that applies only to the initial phase of fieldwork. Ethnographer–participant relationships must be renegotiated throughout the course of study, and this requires ongoing documentation and reflection. In other words, this relationship becomes an object of study in its own right, adding to the broader research questions. The epistemological assumptions outlined earlier for constructivist ethnographies imply that the knowledge that is gained through ethnographic inquiry will be conditioned by the ethnographer's positioning in the local scene and by the nature of the relationships that he or she is able to create with participants. For example, a female ethnographer will have access to certain kinds of contexts and informants, a male ethnographer to others. An ethnographer who has connections to cultural elites will have access to different perspectives than an ethnographer who has connections to the poor. Each ethnographer will come to an understanding that is inevitably partial. The rigor of this approach lies partly in delineating that partiality, which itself contains clues as to how local meanings are constructed.

Collecting and Managing Data. Ethnographic research is known for producing copious amounts of data. Learning to direct data collection and organize data for ongoing interpretation are daunting tasks for novice ethnographers. The bulk of the data collection occurs during fieldwork as the researcher carefully compiles detailed records of research-related activities and his or her initial reactions and interpretations (Wolcott, 1995). Such documentation takes many forms, including field notes, interviews, indirect observations, and artifacts.

Field notes (Emerson, Fretz, & Shaw, 1995) are written descriptions and reflections about the participant–observation. Most researchers make notes in their logs as frequently as possible, jotting down short notes "on the fly" and more detailed notes later. Field notes may contain physical descriptions of the site (augmented by photographs, maps, sketches, etc.), descriptions of daily routines of the participants (augmented by work schedules, seasonal activities, etc.), and detailed descriptions of observed interactions and participant interviews. To facilitate such detailed record keeping, researchers routinely make use of any technologies appropriate to the site (e.g., audiorecording, videorecording, etc.).

Interviews may be conducted with individuals or groups, and the general organization of the interview is usually planned in advance. However, specific interview techniques depend on the nature of the community and research questions (see C. L. Briggs, 1986; Mishler, 1986), as will be illustrated in the final section of this chapter. Whenever possible, interviews are audiorecorded and transcribed for analysis. In addition to more formal interviews, ethnographers find opportunities to insert their questions into casual conversation.

The researcher may also collect indirect observations by working with participant–collaborators, especially in cases where the phenomenon of interest occurs infrequently or only with limited audiences. In such cases, research assistants are taught to take notes or make recordings, ask questions, and make specific observations to address the research questions.

Finally, collecting artifacts about the community, the participants, the physical setting, the institution, and the practices may also be a critical form of data collection. Which artifacts are appropriate to collect will depend on the goals of the research project but may include maps, newspapers, legal documents, popular texts, diaries, letters, tools, and so forth. In addition, the researcher will need to make notes about the circumstances and reasons for obtaining each artifact.

INTERPRETING AND ANALYZING DATA. Data analysis begins early in the research process and continues throughout what is often a long program of ethnographic inquiry, with new research projects building on previous ones. In fact, effective fieldwork requires the direction such ongoing interpretation provides (e.g., who to interview next, what questions to ask, what activities to observe, etc.). Fitting with ethnography's general goal of developing understandings consistent with the meaning-making practices of the community being studied, the interpretive process is primarily inductive in nature, and coding systems and categories evolve from a continual comparison of the growing data set (see Strauss, 1987; Wolcott, 1994). Novice ethnographers who are familiar with preset coding systems applied intact to complete data sets often find the evolving and inductive coding practices of ethnographic work difficult to manage.

The specific nature of the coding systems and types of analyses vary widely, depending on the goals of the specific research project and the disciplinary training and theoretical inclinations of the specific researchers. Early analysis is often focused on developing categories that account for the diversity and breadth of the data being collected. As the analysis progresses, categories are filled in with more depth, and interconnections within and across categories are analyzed. Particular examples may be extracted for in-depth analysis, as we illustrate in the next section of this chapter.

The credibility of the findings is in part a result of a well-documented and systematic analysis of the data. Although not focused on reliability in a traditional sense, ethnographic researchers are very concerned about presenting "accurate" or "valid" representations of the phenomena in question from the participants' perspective—that is, getting the "story" right. One way trustworthiness of interpretations is achieved is through comparing and integrating data from different sources, a process often referred to as triangulation (Denzin, 1978; Marshall & Rossman, 1995; Rizzo et al., 1992). In addition, researchers will discuss their interpretations with participant–collaborators, seeking both contesting and supportive responses, which will allow them to thicken their analysis or reinterpret their data.

Though uncommon, it is possible for ethnographic studies to blend quantitative coding systems with qualitative coding strategies (Gaskins, 1994; Rizzo et al., 1992). For example, qualitative analysis of interview data can be used to illuminate the meaning of survey data obtained via conventional quantitative methods. As well, emic descriptions derived from fieldwork can be used to construct interview protocols or questionnaires that yield quantifiable results. However, it is important to dispel the myth that qualitative analyses are valuable only insofar as they can be converted into quantitative analyses (Hymes, 1982).

WRITING. One way of stating a guiding principle for ethnographic writing is "write early, write often." This process begins with the researcher's log and field notes and continues through the construction of published accounts. However, it is in the culmination of writing up and disseminating ethnographic accounts that the fieldwork of specific research projects is connected with broader programs of scientific inquiry. Like all research projects, "Fieldwork is validated only through the requisite reporting that results from it" (Wolcott, 1995, p. 66). Written accounts of ethnographic work take many forms, but typically the ongoing analyses of the data obtained during an ethnographic research project yield multiple publications.

In recent decades, the textual practices of ethnographers, as well as the appropriateness of various types of ethnographic accounts, have been at the center of intense debates (see Behar & Gordon, 1995; Clifford & Marcus, 1986; Geertz, 1988; Richardson, 1997; Van Maanan, 1988; Wolf, 1992). As ethnographers have grappled with poststructuralist views of culture, issues of representation have become a critical consideration. These issues include how to represent "others" or let "others" represent themselves; how to represent the researcher's roles, limitations, and biases within the research site; how to appropriately blend multiple, often contesting, perspectives; and how to respect the diversity and complexity of cultural practices. This has led to a diversification in published research accounts as ethnographers have experimented with issues of representation in ethnographic writing (see Behar, 1993; Seremetakis, 1991).

The Nonnarration of Children's Transgressions: An Interpretive Puzzle

In this section we address an interpretive puzzle from our own work by way of illustrating how ethnographers proceed in analyzing and interpreting data. The puzzle arose from a program of ethnographic research that is comparative in design, involving middle-class Taiwanese families in Taipei, Taiwan, and middle-class European American families in Longwood (a pseudonym), a neighborhood in Chicago (Fung, 1999; Miller, Hengst, Alexander, & Sperry, 2000; Miller, Wiley, Fung, & Liang, 1997; Miller et al., 2001).

How the Puzzle Arose

To set the stage for this puzzle, it is necessary to present some background about earlier phases of this research. The initial goal of the project was to investigate how personal storytelling is used to socialize young children within the family context. Do these families engage in personal storytelling—telling oral stories about one's past experiences—in ways that involve young children? If so, how is personal storytelling defined and practiced with young children? We were particularly interested in the modes of participation and interpretive strategies that families used in narrating young children's past experiences. Note that all of these questions are versions of the "What exactly is happening here?" question.

Through participant–observation and video recording of ordinary family interaction, we discovered that stories involving the focal child (2 years, 6 months, of age) as protagonist occurred at remarkably similar rates (about four per hour on average) in the Taipei and Longwood families. In addition, in both cases, stories were conarrated with young children, and stories were told about the child in the child's presence.

These similarities coexisted with a striking difference in the content and manner of narration. The Taipei mothers were much more likely than their Longwood counterparts to treat children's past transgressions as a didactic resource, as opportunities to teach young children the difference between right and wrong. Transgressions were talked of openly in front of siblings, researchers, and guests; explicitly, often in strong language; and at length. Rarely was the language mitigated, although subtle nonverbal cues were used to signal humor. The ethnographer was treated as a judging witness to the child's misdeeds. By contrast, the Longwood families operated with a distinct self-favorability bias in narrating young children's experiences. They rarely told stories about the child's past transgressions. When they did so, they managed to portray the child in a positive light despite his or her misdeed, casting the researcher as an appreciative audience to the child's exploits.

Defining the Puzzle

The puzzle, then, is this: How can we make sense of the Longwood practice of not narrating children's transgressions? (The complementary puzzle from the

Taipei data is: How can we make sense of the narrative practice of foregrounding children's past transgressions? See Fung, 1999; Miller et al., 1996; for discussions of this puzzle.) From a Taiwanese perspective, this is baffling. This looks irresponsible. What are these Americans up to when they downplay or mitigate young children's transgressions or strike them entirely from the narrative record?

Notice that this puzzle has been defined, in part, by the Taiwanese comparison, which casts the American practices in relief. Although many ethnographic studies focus on a single cultural case, there is usually an implicit comparative perspective that informs what the ethnographer is able to identify as interesting problems. The inclination to emphasize children's strengths is so common among middle-class Americans that it is next to invisible. We might have overlooked this puzzle were it not for the contrast with the Taiwanese findings. In other words, having a comparative vantage point on one's own cultural ways is often crucial in rendering the familiar strange (Erickson, 1986; Ochs & Schieffelin, 1984).

Notice too that this puzzle arose out of careful documentation of a pattern that occurred in everyday family interaction, a pattern that emerged in response to our initial questions. In observation after observation we witnessed and participated in a baseline of personal storytelling activity in which children's transgressions were rarely narrated. It is important to emphasize that to document that baseline we followed a complex set of analytical coding steps that, for lack of space, can only be briefly mentioned: We devised a descriptive code for defining personal storytelling in the two cultural cases, applied the code to the video-recorded observations for each family, transcribed the full set of personal storytelling events that were identified for each family, and devised and applied additional codes for describing the content and manner of narration (see Miller et al., 1997). Some ethnographers might have described the resulting baseline pattern as "routine," without attaching any numbers; our preference was to count the stories that occurred and to calculate the proportion that involved child transgressions. In both cases, whether or not numbers are attached, there is a recognition that specific examples of interaction are interpretable only against a documented baseline of ordinary activity.

Microanalysis of a Strategically Chosen Example

Ethnographers often use the interpretive strategy of lifting out an example for microlevel analysis as a way of deepening their understanding of the phenomenon in question. This strategy illustrates the "microscopic and holistic" feature of ethnographic research that we discussed earlier in which an event is described in minute detail as a way of illuminating the meaning of some larger pattern. In the following analysis we illustrate this strategy, borrowing from an analysis presented more fully in Miller et al. (1996). Although ethnographers often choose "typical" examples to work with, Miller et al. chose a story that was exceptional within the baseline distribution. They focused on a rare instance in which a Longwood family not only told a story about the focal child's transgression but structured the story so as to establish the child's transgression as the point of the story, thereby mimicking the Taiwanese practice. This exceptional story was important analytically because it allowed us to disentangle two possible interpretations. Perhaps Longwood families narrated child transgressions in the same didactic manner as their Taipei counterparts but did so far less frequently. Or perhaps they narrated child transgressions in a qualitatively different manner on those rare occasions when they narrated them at all.

The story in question actually involved two transgressions. As narrated by the mother—in collaboration with Mollie (2 years, 6 months), the researcher, and Mollie's older sister—Mollie first wrote on the wall and then tried to evade responsibility for her misdeed by falsely accusing her sister.

> **Mother:** [To child] Did you tell Judy [the researcher] what you wrote on the dining room wall with?
> **Child:** Ah . . . key.
> **Researcher:** [To child] You wrote on the dining room wall?
> **Mother:** With a key, not even a pencil.
> **Researcher:** [To mother] You must have loved that.
> **Mother:** A key, the front end of that key.
> **Sister:** And behind a living room chair.
> **Mother:** I was sort of napping in there and I saw this and I thought it was a pencil. And I woke up and said [whispering], "Mol, you didn't write on Mommy's wall with a pencil, did you?" Oh, she was so relieved, she said, "No! Me no use pencil, me use key!" and I was like, "OH GOD! Not a key!" And she said, "No, no, ME no use key, Mom. Kara [her sister] use key," and then I was even more upset.
> **Sister:** I didn't even see her do it!
> **Mother:** But it's so funny. You look at her and she's like, "I didn't use pencil."
> **Researcher:** So, I'm in the clear.
> **Mother:** Oh, yeah.
> **Sister:** I didn't even see her do it. I was at school.

In this excerpt, Mollie's mother prompts her to confess her wrongdoing to the researcher. Mollie complies, and the researcher invites additional response. Several turns ensue in which the mother emphasizes that Mollie used a key to write on the wall, the researcher aligns herself with the mother through an ironic expression ("You must have loved that!"), and Mollie's older sister—whom Mollie falsely blamed—contributes further information about the incident, emphasizing that she was not even there when the incident happened. Having established Mollie's wrongdoing by eliciting supporting accounts from the parties involved, the mother then explains more fully to the researcher what happened. That is, she tells a story about Mollie, referring to her in the third-person, in which she situates the wall-writing incident within the events that preceded and followed it. She explains that she was napping when the misdeed occurred. Her dawning realization that Mollie wrote on the wall while she napped is recreated through the mounting suspense of parallel, but increasingly damaging, admissions by the child. The mother represents Mollie as trying to mitigate her responsibility for wrongdoing, first by explaining that she used a key and not a pencil and second by falsely accusing her sister. The humor lies in the fact that the child's inept and increasingly transparent attempts to explain away her misdeeds have exactly the opposite effect. Her mother's subsequent comment, "But it's so funny," explicitly frames the narration as nonserious. Note also that although the mother says that she was "even more upset" by the child's lie than by the misdeed that occasioned it, there is no further mention of the more serious transgression. Also, the interaction that preceded the story about the child, including the elicited confession from Mollie, includes no mention of her false accusation.

Miller et al. (1996) compared this story with a Taiwanese story that is strikingly similar in content and structure: Angu, like Mollie, wrote on the wall and then tried to shift blame to someone else. Although it is beyond the scope of this chapter to present the parallel microanalysis of Angu's story, it is important to summarize some of the key differences in how Angu's misdeeds were narrated: Angu's caregiver developed the story at far greater length; foregrounded the more serious transgression of falsely accusing another person; shamed the child for her misdeeds; and framed the story as serious. What, then, do these twin microanalyses tell us? Even in the rare instance in which an American family constructed a story around the child's transgression, creating a story that resembled a Taiwanese story in content and structure, close analysis revealed that it conveyed a qualitatively different interpretation of the child and of her experience. Instead of creating an opportunity for moral education and remediation, Mollie's mother developed the amusing dimensions of the incident. She created a charming and naive mischief maker, not a transgressor.

The Puzzle Partially Unraveled

To summarize, we made several analytical moves in attempting to understand this interpretive puzzle. First, we established, through participant–observation and transcription of video-recorded home observations, that personal storytelling occurred routinely in Longwood and Taipei families. Second, we documented a contrasting pattern in the content and structure of personal storytelling such that Longwood families, compared with Taipei families, were far less likely to narrate young children's transgressions. In other words, the initial analytical moves involved documenting an observed pattern in ordinary family interaction, drawing on comparative observations to aid in the identification of that pattern. The third analytical move involved microanalysis of a particular story that was strategically chosen because of its outlier status in the baseline distribution of storytelling. This microanalysis deepened our understanding of the meaning of the baseline pattern by zeroing in on a violation of that baseline. Although the story, in this exceptional instance, was "about" Mollie's misdeeds, it was also "about" how funny those misdeeds were. This series of analyses, thus, supports the following rendering of Longwood parents' perspective on young children's misdeeds: best to leave them un-narrated; if one happens to slip through, background it, mitigate it, laugh about it, or in some way undercut its importance. These analyses suggest that young children's wrongdoing has a qualitatively different meaning for Longwood parents, compared with Taipei parents. Apparently, young children's wrongdoing is a somewhat delicate matter for Longwood parents.

Although this series of analyses allowed us to deepen our understanding of the nonnarration of children's transgressions, it is important to emphasize that no analysis is the final analysis. In the constructivist ethnographic approach that we advocate, each analysis leads seamlessly to a more pointed set of questions; thus, the boundary between one research report and the next is somewhat arbitrary. In the case at hand, our interpretations were based entirely on observations of the families' enactments of personal storytelling, not on their expressed ideas about storytelling. To understand these practices more fully, we needed to examine parents' reflections on child-rearing. What was at stake for Longwood parents when they engaged in these narrative practices? What kinds of ideas were informing their child-rearing?

Sequel: Toward Additional Unraveling

To pursue these questions, Mintz (1999) inquired into parents' belief systems about child-rearing, drawing on interviews, the other stock-in-trade ethnographic tool. In-depth interviews with the Longwood mothers revealed that promoting their young children's self-esteem was a matter of the first importance to them. They believed that self-esteem provides the foundation for happiness, inner strength, and moral autonomy. They spoke of the devastating consequences of low self-esteem on children's psychological functioning and success in the world. They tried to support children's self-esteem by praising them, emphasizing their strengths, and avoiding invidious comparisons. When discussing discipline, they made a distinction between "being bad" and "doing bad things," contrasting their child-rearing practices with those of their own parents. They believed that discipline had to be handled with care, lest it undermine children's self-esteem. Like the mothers in Harwood, Miller, and Irizarry (1995), they sought a balance between cultivating self-esteem and respect for others.

These findings shed further light on the Longwood practice of downplaying, laughing about, or simply not narrating young children's transgressions by suggesting that a collective commitment to the goal of supporting children's self-esteem may underlie this practice. Longwood families' reluctance to dwell on young children's past misdeeds is intelligible within a folk theory that valorizes self-esteem, linking it to a host of psychological goods, just as Taipei families' routine narration of child's transgressions is intelligible within a folk theory that is distinctly Confucian, valorizing moral instruction and "opportunity education" (Fung, 1999; Miller et al., 1996; Miller et al., 1997).

Self-Esteem As Folk Theory

In this final section of the chapter, we present a research case by way of illustrating the process of conducting ethnographic research (see Miller, Wang, Sandel, & Cho, 2002, for a detailed report of the methods and results of this study). This case emerged directly out of the line of inquiry described in the preceding section. Our findings from Longwood led us to be interested in American folk theories of self-esteem. By parental folk theories we mean parents' informal, culturally organized understandings about children, child-rearing, and development. These understandings vary within and across cultures, informing and rationalizing child-rearing practices (Bruner, 1990; Goodnow & Collins, 1990; Harkness & Super, 1996).

The Research Problem

The idea that the Longwood mothers articulated—that children's self-esteem should be fostered because it lays the groundwork for a host of psychological strengths—is shared by many American parents, teachers, and psychologists. The ubiquity of reference to self-esteem in both scientific arenas and popular culture naturalizes self-esteem, promoting a kind of invisibleness. This invisibleness is supported, as well, by two striking omissions from the discourse of self-esteem. Rarely is self-esteem and its associated folk theory recognized to be a culture-specific, historically situated discourse. And rarely is the debate about self-esteem informed by the voices of parents as they reflect on these ideas in raising their children. Our study was intended to address these omissions. Its purpose was to examine the meanings and practices associated with self-esteem and the larger folk theory in which it is embedded.

Design and Research Sites

Because other cultures do not necessarily share Americans' preoccupation with self-esteem (see Harwood et al., 1995; Heine, Lehman, Markus, & Kitaymama, 1999; Stevenson et al., 1990) and because perspectives from other cultures can help to expose the cultural specificity of self-esteem, we chose to study this problem comparatively, building on our earlier work with American and Taiwanese families. We wanted to identify the variety of meanings American and Taiwanese caregivers associate with the idea of self-esteem and to delineate the local folk theories that contextualize this idea or that offer alternative understandings of child-rearing. Although we approached this question through participant–observation and interviewing, this question lent itself particularly well to interviewing, and thus we focus on interviewing in this brief sketch.

In choosing research sites, we considered two factors. In recognition of intracultural variability, we wanted to move beyond large urban areas. And because personal contacts facilitate fieldwork, we chose research sites where our research team had preexisting personal networks. We briefly describe some key features of the two research sites.

Chhan-chng (a pseudonym) is a small Taiwanese farming community that embodies a complex mix of old and new cultural practices. The residents speak Taiwanese and Mandarin Chinese and observe traditional religious practices, worshipping their ancestors before the family's ancestral tablets and going to the local temples to ask for peace and prosperity. The grandparents' generation continues to work in the fields, growing rice, sugar cane, fruits, and vegetables. Most families own a motor scooter or automobile and have access to American and Japanese programming on cable television. Although many young families are choosing to have fewer children and some of the mothers work outside the home or even in a nearby city, the traditional three-generation household is still the norm. Like previous generations, children are not segregated from adult activity. They live in a community where homes, farms, shops, and businesses are often joined; children witness and participate in economic activity and they are accustomed to seeing people come and go on a daily basis.

Centerville (a pseudonym) is a small city located in the rural midwest. Although soybeans and corn remain an important part of the county's economic base, Centerville is best known as the home of a major university, which attracts a culturally diverse group of students. Centerville supports a remarkable number of places of worship, including two synagogues, two Buddhist sanghas, a mosque, and more than 100 Christian churches. Because Centerville is much more diverse than Chhan-chng, it is not possible to describe family life in the same sweeping terms. In some families both parents work and young children go to daycare; in others mothers are full-time housewives. Despite these differences, two-generation households are the norm. Contact with grandparents varies widely. Some grandparents provide daily childcare; others live far away and keep in touch through telephone calls and occasional visits. Unlike their counterparts in Chhan-chng, young Centerville children do not have much access to parents' work lives.

The Researchers and Field Entry

In contrast to many classic ethnographic studies, our research team included individuals with varying life experiences in the two cultures. All of us had lived in Centerville for extended periods of time (one to eight years). Miller has been studying American and Taiwanese families with Taiwanese collaborators for many years. Sandel, who speaks Mandarin and some Taiwanese, was born and raised in the United States, but his wife grew up in Chhan-chng and her parents and other relatives still reside there and treat Sandel as kin. Although Chhan-chng was unfamiliar to Wang, she was born and raised in Taiwan and is a native speaker of Taiwanese and Mandarin. Both Wang and Sandel had lived in Centerville for at least a year before we embarked on this study. Sandel has young children, which put him in contact with schools and churches.

These various personal contacts were crucial in allowing the researchers to recruit participants for the study and in easing relationships between researchers and participants. For example, Sandel's mother- and father-in-law helped to explain the study to local families. Beyond the initial phase of field entry, the cultural variability within the research team enabled us to draw on multiple insider–outsider perspectives in conducting the study and interpreting the findings.

The Participants

At each site 16 families participated in the study. The families were chosen to be homogeneous on several demographic variables. Each family had a three-year-old child, who was the focus of the questions about child-rearing. In addition, the families were two-parent families who represented the more highly educated segment of their respective communities. Most of the Centerville mothers had a college degree; most of the Chhan-chng mothers had 14 years of education. The average number of children per family was two for Chhan-chng and three for Centerville families. In both research sites, mothers were either the primary caregivers or shared childcare with a grandmother or a childcare provider.

Conducting/Adapting the Interviews

The researchers talked with the mothers in their homes, using their native language (either English or Mandarin or Taiwanese). The interviews were open-ended, and content areas included child-rearing goals and values, discipline, strategies for promoting development, sources of child-rearing information, shame and pride, and self-esteem. The protocol was intended to provide a rough guideline for conversation. However, the researchers waited until late in the interview to ask questions about self-esteem.

Instead of thinking of interviewing as simply a matter of asking questions and listening to responses, we treated interviewing as an observable social practice that may be more or less familiar to the participants, more or less in need of adaptation to local norms. This perspective owes a great deal to Charles Briggs's book, *Learning How to Ask* (1986). Building on insights from his own extensive ethnographic work, C. Briggs argued that interviews are not transparent windows into informants' beliefs but rather communicative events, analyzable in terms of the metacommunicative features of the talk and nonverbal action that interviewer and interviewee construct together. When these features are addressed, along with other data from local communicative routines, it becomes possible to offer a more precise and well-grounded interpretation than could be achieved through conventional "content" analyses. Like other ethnographers who have written about interviewing (Mishler, 1986; Wolcott, 1995), C. Briggs attends not only to what people say but to when and how they say it, what they convey nonverbally, how silence is patterned. As it applies to comparative research, this approach implies that it will often be necessary to devise different "interview" events, reflecting the different communicative norms of the communities being compared, to yield equivalently meaningful discourse.

In fact, in our study the interview event unfolded in strikingly different ways in the two communities. The Centerville participants seemed to share an interview script that included a particular kind of staging. The mother led the researcher to a table, where she and the researcher sat facing one another. When children were present, mothers would ask them to play with toys or computer games and not interrupt the interview. Although the ethnographers did not request that any special arrangements be made, the Centerville participants established a self-contained time and space for the interview. In addition, although we intended that the interview protocol would be followed loosely, allowing the interviewer to pursue the mother's interests, the researchers found that little alteration was required. The interview script—the researcher asks a question, the interviewee responds—seemed to be taken for granted by these participants. Thus, in Centerville interviewing emerged as a familiar practice shared by both parties.

By contrast, few Chhan-chng participants set up a self-contained time and space for the interviews. Indeed, most interviews took place in the presence of more than one family member. Sometimes even a bypassing neighbor would join in the conversation. Moreover, the protocol had to be altered, as the local women were not in the habit of answering formal questions in the course of everyday life. The researchers tried to find more suitable initial topics that would put people at their ease, and they responded to the participants' curiosity about their lives in the United States. Once the participants felt more comfortable, the researchers retrieved other questions from memory and inserted them into the conversation in as natural a way as possible. They also discovered that talk flowed more freely when they participated in whatever domestic task was underway. In sum, the interview was not a familiar or comfortable speech event to the participants in Chhan-chng. To learn about mothers' child-rearing beliefs, the interviewers had to adapt to local communicative norms, all but abandoning the interview format for a more conversational approach in which participants had significant control over the topics of talk, multiple speakers were accommodated, and everyone got on with the domestic work at hand.

Data Analysis

Our objective in this study was to examine the variety of meanings that Centerville and Chhan-chng caregivers associated with self-esteem and to delineate the local folk theories that contextualize this idea or that offer alternative understandings of child-rearing. It is beyond the scope of this chapter to present the full set of data analyses. Instead, we recap the analytical moves involved in addressing a single subsidiary question: Did self-esteem figure importantly in the mothers' folk theories of child-rearing in the two research sites?

It is necessary first to say a few words about terminology. In the American interviews, the researchers used the term "self-esteem," but the mothers sometimes used such terms as "self-confidence," "self-respect," and "feeling good about oneself," and these were treated as synonyms for self-esteem. There is no term in Mandarin Chinese or Taiwanese that translates directly as "self-esteem." However, there are two terms that approximate some of the meanings associated with self-esteem. One is *zi zun xin* in Mandarin or *chu chun sim* in Taiwanese; the literal English translation is "self-respect-heart/mind." The second term is *zi xin xin* in Mandarin or *chu sin sim* in Taiwanese; the literal translation is "self-confidence-heart/mind."

In ascertaining whether self-esteem figured into the mothers' understandings of child-rearing, we first determined whether the mothers spontaneously mentioned self-esteem before the researcher introduced the term, coding from verbatim transcripts in the original language. We found that the majority of American mothers invoked these terms in response to a whole range of questions. For example, some mothers mentioned self-esteem or self-confidence in response to the initial question, "What are your goals as a parent? What do you hope for your children?" When the self-esteem questions were asked, most of these mothers talked easily and fluently about self-esteem, studding their responses with real-life examples.

By contrast, only a few of the Taiwanese mothers brought up self-respect-heart/mind or self-confidence heart/mind before the researcher's explicit queries, and no one invoked these terms repeatedly. When asked directly about these terms, some of the Chhan-chng women did not seem to find these questions intelligible or meaningful, and no one elaborated on her views in the detail that characterized many of the American responses. However, the Taiwanese mothers did talk at length about other child-rearing issues.

After describing how key terms were used over the course of the interview, we examined all passages in each interview in which the participant talked about self-esteem or related terms. In keeping with the concept of folk theory, which implies that parents hold a set of ideas that are conceptually related, we coded these passages in terms of the ideas that the participant linked to self-esteem. For example, every Centerville mother said that self-esteem was important to children's development and that she actively tries to build, cultivate, or protect her child's self-esteem. They said that self-esteem provides an essential foundation for a wide array of psychological strengths: Children who have high self-esteem are able to learn and grow with ease; they are not afraid to achieve; they interact well with others; and their mental health is good.

The few Taiwanese mothers who spoke about self-respect-heart/mind or self-confidence-heart/mind linked these terms to strikingly different ideas. For example, one mother said that it is best for children to have "normal" self-respect-heart/mind because they will become less frustrated than those whose self-respect-heart/mind is strong. This idea contradicts the American mothers' belief that *high* self-esteem allows children to keep trying in the face of failure. In short, the mothers from Chhan-chng believed that high self-respect-heart/mind creates psychological vulnerabilities, whereas American mothers believed that high self-esteem creates psychological strengths.

This brief sketch of one set of data analyses reveal that self-esteem loomed large in the Centerville mothers' folk theory of child-rearing but not in the Chhan-chng mothers' folk theory. For the Centerville mothers, self-esteem served as a central organizing concept, an idea that came readily to mind when child-rearing was discussed, whether or not the researcher mentioned the term. The Taiwanese mothers' folk theories were just as complex, but they were organized around the ideas that children grow up naturally and that parents are responsible for their moral education. The few Taiwanese mothers who talked about self-respect-heart/mind did so in ways that contradicted the American mothers.

The ethnographic methods used in this research case strengthen the credibility of these findings. First, the intelligibility of the mothers' responses was enhanced by the care that was taken to familiarize the participants with the researcher and to create a communicative event that fit local norms. If we had imposed our conception of interviewing on the Taiwanese women and they had had little to say about self-esteem, we would not have been able to interpret their omission as revealing anything about self-esteem. Second, in analyzing the mothers' talk we sought patterns not only in the content of their talk but in how they expressed themselves. Whether self-esteem was introduced before the researcher mentioned it, how often the term was used, and in which contexts, where there were moments of confusion or unintelligibility—these and other metacommunicative patterns helped us to determine the place of self-esteem in the two folk theories.

In sum, this research case is offered not as a model or a recipe but as one example of how ethnographic work proceeds when addressing a problem in developmental cultural psychology. This case departs from classic ethnographic research in which the ethnographer begins as an outsider, focuses on a single culture, and operates out of an implicitly comparative framework. By contrast, our study was comparative in design and involved a research team that occupied complex insider–outsider positions from the outset. However, like classic ethnographic studies, this case exemplifies the systematic but flexible deployment of method that lies at the heart of ethnographic practice, a flexibility that is disciplined by the goal of understanding meaning from the perspectives of local participants. Sometimes social scientists who have grown up in positivist traditions believe that research cannot be empirical and interpretive at the same time. This case, like much contemporary ethnographic research, demonstrates that this is a misconception.

References

Agar, M. (1980). *The professional stranger: An informal introduction to ethnography.* San Diego, CA: Academic Press.

Basso, K. H. (1996). *Wisdom sits in places: Landscape and language among the Western Apache.* Albuquerque: University of New Mexico Press.

Baym, N. K. (2000). *Tune in, log on: Soaps, fandom, and online community.* Thousand Oaks, CA: Sage.

Becker, H. S. (1996). The epistemology of qualitative research. In R. Jessor, A. Colby, & R. A. Shweder (Eds.), *Ethnography and human development* (pp. 53–71). Chicago: University of Chicago Press.

Behar, R. (1993). *Translated woman.* Boston: Beacon.

Behar, R., & Gordon, D. (Eds.). (1995). *Women writing culture.* Berkeley: University of California Press.

Bloom, L. (1974). Commentary. In F. F. Schachter, K. Kirshner, B. Klips, M. Friedricks, & K. Sanders (Eds.), *Everyday preschool interpersonal speech usage: Methodological, developmental, and sociolinguistic studies. Monographs of the Society for Research in Child Development, 39* (2, Serial No. 156).

Briggs, C. L. (1986). *Learning how to ask: A sociolinguistic appraisal of the role of the interview in social science.* London: Cambridge.

Briggs, J. (1970). *Never in anger: Portrait of an Eskimo family.* Cambridge: Cambridge University Press.

Briggs, J. (1998). *Inuit morality play: The emotional education of a three-year-old.* New Haven, CT: Yale University Press.

Bruner, J. (1972). Nature and uses of immaturity. *American Psychologist, 27,* 687–708.

Bruner, J. (1990). *Acts of meaning.* Cambridge, MA: Harvard University Press.

Cahan, E. D., & White, S. H. (1992). Proposals for a second psychology. *American Psychologist, 47,* 224–235.

Clifford, J., & Marcus, G. E. (1986). *Writing culture: The poetics and politics of ethnography.* Berkeley: University of California Press.

Cochran-Smith, M., & Lytle, S. L. (1993). *Inside/outside: Teacher research and knowledge.* New York: Teachers College Press.

Cohen, D., Nisbett, R. E., Bowdle, B. F., & Schwarz, N. (1996). Insult, aggression, and the southern culture of honor: An "experimental ethnography." *Journal of Personality & Social Psychology, 70,* 945–960.

Cook-Gumperz, J., & Corsaro, W. A. (1986). Introduction. In J. Cook-Gumperz, W. A. Corsaro, & J. Streeck (Eds.), *Children's worlds and children's language* (pp. 1–11). Berlin: Mouton de Gruyter.

Corsaro, W. A. (1985). *Friendship and peer culture in the early years.* Norwood, NJ: Ablex.

Corsaro, W. A. (1988). Routines in the peer culture of American and Italian nursery school children. *Sociology of Education, 61,* 1–14.

Denzin, N. K. (1978). *The research act.* Chicago: Aldine.

Denzin, N. K. (1993). *The alcoholic society: Addiction and recovery of the self.* New Brunswick, NJ: Transaction.

Denzin, N. K. (1996). The epistemological crisis in the human disciplines: Letting the old do the work of the new. In R. Jessor, A. Colby, & R. A. Shweder (Eds.), *Ethnography and human development: Context and meaning in social inquiry* (pp. 127–151). Chicago: University of Chicago Press.

Denzin, N. K., & Lincoln, Y. S. (Eds.). (1994). *Handbook of qualitative research.* Thousand Oaks, CA: Sage.

Emerson, R. M., Fretz, R. I., & Shaw, L. L. (1995). *Writing ethnographic fieldnotes.* Chicago: University of Chicago Press.

Engstrom, Y. (1996). Developmental studies of work as a testbench of activity theory: The case of primary care medical practice. In S. Chaiklin & J. Lave (Eds.), *Understanding practice: Perspectives on activity and context* (pp. 64–103). Cambridge: Cambridge University Press.

Erickson, F. D. (1986). Qualitative methods in research on teaching. In M. C. Wittrock (Ed.), *Handbook of research on teaching* (3rd ed.). New York: Macmillan.

Fung, H. (1999). Becoming a moral child: The socialization of shame among young Chinese children. *Ethos, 27,* 180–209.

Gaskins, S. (1994). Integrating interpretive and quantitative methods in socialization research. *Merrill-Palmer Quarterly, 40,* 313–333.

Gaskins, S. (1996). How Mayan parental theories come into play. In S. Harkness & C. M. Super (Eds.), *Parents' cultural belief systems: Their origins, expressions, and consequences* (pp. 345–363). New York: Guilford Press.

Gaskins, S., Miller, P. J., & Corsaro, W. A. (1992). Theoretical and methodological perspectives in the interpretive study of children. In W. A. Corsaro & P. J. Miller (Eds.), *Interpretive approaches to children's socialization. New directions for child development* (pp. 5–23). New York: Jossey-Bass.

Geertz, C. (1973). *The interpretation of cultures.* New York: Basic Books.

Geertz, C. (1988). *Works and lives: The anthropologist as author.* Stanford, CA: Stanford University Press.

Gergen, K. J. (1985). The social constructionist movement in modern psychology. *American Psychologist, 40,* 266–275.

Giorgio, G. (1999). Living lesbian battering. In N. K. Denzin (Ed.), *Cultural studies: A research annual* (pp. 3–18). Stamford, CT: JAI Press.

Goldman, L. R. (1998). *Child's play: Myth, mimesis, and make-believe.* New York: Oxford.

Goncu, A. (1999). *Children's engagement in the world: Sociocultural perspectives.* Cambridge: Cambridge University Press.

Goodnow, J. J., & Collins, W. A. (1990). *Development according to parents: The nature, sources, and consequences of parents' ideas.* Hillsdale, NJ: Erlbaum.

Gottlieb, A., & Graham, P. (1993). *Parallel worlds.* Chicago: University of Chicago Press.

Grau, M. E., & Walsh, D. J. (1998). *Studying children in context: Theories, methods, and ethics.* Thousand Oaks, CA: Sage.

Harkness, S., & Super, C. M. (1996). *Parents' cultural belief systems: Their origins, expressions, and consequences.* New York: Guilford Press.

Harwood, R. L., Miller, J. G., & Irizarry, N. L. (1995). *Culture and attachment: Perceptions of the child in context.* New York: Guilford Press.

Heath, S. B. (1983). *Ways with words.* New York: Cambridge University Press.

Heine, S. J., Lehman, D. R., Markus, H. R., & Kitayama, S. (1999). Is there a universal need for positive self-regard? *Psychological Review, 106,* 766–794.

Hymes, D. (1982). What is ethnography? In P. Gilmore & A. A. Glatthorn (Eds.), *Children in and out of school: Ethnography and education* (pp. 21–32). Washington DC: Center for Applied Linguistics.

Jahoda, G. (1989). Our forgotten ancestors. In J. J. Berman (Ed.), *Cross-Cultural Perspectives: Nebraska Symposia on Motivation* (pp. 1–40). Lincoln: University of Nebraska Press.

Jahoda, G. (1993). *Crossroads between culture and mind: Continuities and change in theories of human development.* Cambridge, MA: Harvard University Press.

Jessor, R., Colby, A., & Shweder, R. A. (Eds.). (1996). *Ethnography and human development: Context and meaning in social inquiry.* Chicago: University of Chicago Press.

Lancy, D. F. (1996). *Playing on the mother ground: Cultural routines for children's development.* New York: Guilford Press.

Malinowski, B. (1922). *Argonauts of the western pacific.* New York: Dutton.

Markus, H. R., & Kitayama, S. (1991). Culture and the self: Implications for cognition, emotion, and motivation. *Psychological Review, 98,* 224–253.

Marshall, C., & Rossman, G. B. (1995). *Designing qualitative research.* Thousand Oaks, CA: Sage.

Mead, M. (1963). Socialization and enculturation. *Current Anthropology, 4,* 184–188.

Miller, P. J. (2001, April). *New insights from developmental cultural psychology: What the study of intra-cultural variation can contribute.* Paper presented at the biennial meeting of the Society for Research in Child Development, Minneapolis, MN.

Miller, P. J., Fung, H., & Mintz. J. (1996). Self-construction through narrative practices: A Chinese and American comparison of early socialization. *Ethos, 24,* 1–44.

Miller, P. J., Hengst, J. A., Alexander, K., & Sperry, L. (2000). Versions of personal storytelling/versions of experience: Genres as tools for creating alternate realties. In K. S. Rosengren, C. N. Johnson, & P. L. Harris (Eds.), *Imagining the impossible: Magical, scientific, and religious thinking in children* (pp. 212–246). Cambridge: Cambridge University Press.

Miller, P. J., Sandel, T., Liang, C-H., & Fung, H. (2001). Narrating transgressions in Longwood: The discourses, meanings, and paradoxes of an American socializing practice. *Ethos, 29*(2), 159–186.

Miller, P. J., Wang, S., Sandle, T., & Cho, G. E. (2002). Self-esteem as folk theory: A comparison of ethnographic interviews. *Parenting: Science and Practice, 2,* 209–239.

Miller, P. J., Wiley, A. R., Fung, H., & Liang, C-H. (1997). Personal storytelling as a medium of socialization in Chinese and American families. *Child Development, 68,* 557–568.

Mintz, J. (1999). *Self-esteem as ideology and practice: A study of narrative discourse practices among parents and preschool children in a middle-class, European-American community.* Unpublished doctoral dissertation, University of Chicago.

Mishler, E. G. (1986). *Research interviewing: Context and narrative.* Cambridge, MA: Harvard University Press.

Ochs, E. (1988). *Culture and language development: Language acquisition and language socialization in a Samoan village.* Cambridge: Cambridge University Press.

Ochs, E., & Schieffelin, B. B. (1984). Language acquisition and socialization: Three developmental stories and their implications. In R. Shweder & R. LeVine (Eds.), *Culture theory: Essays on mind, self, and emotion* (pp. 276–320). Cambridge: Cambridge University Press.

Philips, S. U. (1983). *The invisible culture: Communication in classroom and community on the Warm Springs Indian reservation.* New York: Longman.

Pike, K. L. (1967). *Language in relation to a unified theory of the structure of human behavior.* The Hague, Netherlands: Mouton.

Prior, P. A. (1998). *Writing/disciplinarity: A sociohistoric account of literate activity in the academy.* Mahwah, NJ: Erlbaum.

Richardson, L. (1997). *Fields of play: Constructing an academic life.* New Brunswick, NJ: Rutgers University Press.

Rizzo, T. A., Corsaro, W. A., & Bates, J. E. (1992). Ethnographic methods and interpretive analysis: Expanding the methodological options of psychologists. *Developmental Review, 12,* 101–123.

Rogoff, B., Mistry, J., Goncu, A., & Mosier, C. (1993). Guided participation in cultural activity by toddlers and caregiver. *Monographs of the Society for Research in Child Development, 58* (Serial No. 8).

Rosaldo, R. (1988). Introduction: Grief and a headhunter's rage. In R. Rosaldo (Ed.), *Culture and truth: The remaking of social analysis* (pp. 1–21). Boston: Beacon.

Scheper-Hughes, N. (1992). *Death without weeping: The violence of everyday life in Brazil.* Berkeley: University of California Press.

Schieffelin, B. B. (1990). *The give and take of everyday life: Language socialization of Kaluli children.* New York: Cambridge University Press.

Seremetakis, C. N. (1991). *The last word: Women, death, and divination in inner Mani.* Chicago: University of Chicago Press.

Shweder, R. A., Goodnow, J., Hatano, G., LeVine, R. A., Markus, H., et al. (1998). The cultural psychology of development: One mind, many mentalities. In W. Damon & R. M. Lerner (Eds.), *Handbook of child psychology, Vol. 1* (5th ed., pp. 865–937). New York: Wiley.

Stevenson, H. W., Lee, S. Y., Chen, C., Stigler, J. W., Hsu, C. C., et al. (1990). Contexts of achievement: A study of American, Chinese, and Japanese children. *Monographs of the Society for Research in Child Development, 55* (1–2, Serial No. 221).

Stewart, E. (2000). Thinking through others: Qualitative research and community psychology. In E. Seidman & J. Rappaport (Eds.), *Handbook of community psychology* (pp. 725–736). New York: Kluwer/Plenum Press.

Strauss, A. L. (1987). *Qualitative analysis for social scientists.* New York: Cambridge University Press.

Taylor, M., & Carlson, S. M. (2000). The influence of religious beliefs on parental attitudes about children's fantasy behavior. In K. S. Rosengren, C. N. Johnson, & P. L. Harris (Eds.), *Imagining the impossible* (pp. 247–268). New York: Cambridge University Press.

Van Maanan, J. (1988). *Tales of the field: On writing ethnography.* Chicago: University of Chicago Press.

Wolcott, H. F. (1994). *Transforming qualitative data: Description, analysis, and interpretation.* Thousand Oaks, CA: Sage.

Wolcott, H. F. (1995). *The art of fieldwork.* Walnut Creek, CA: Altamira.

Wolf, M. (1992). *A thrice told tale: Feminism, postmodernism, and ethnographic responsibility.* Stanford, CA: Stanford University Press.

Wolf, S. N., & Heath, S. B. (1992). *The braid of literature: Children's worlds of reading.* Cambridge, MA: Harvard University Press.

13

The Descriptive Phenomenological Psychological Method

Amedeo P. Giorgi and Barbro M. Giorgi

Phenomenology, as a distinct philosophy in the modern sense, began with the publication of *Logical Investigations* (1900/1970) by Edmund Husserl. Husserl's thought developed continuously, if nonlinearly, over roughly a half century in which he was active as a scholar and thinker. He influenced many of the dominant philosophers of the 20th century who worked in the continental tradition (e.g., Heidegger, 1927/1962; Merleau-Ponty, 1945/1962; Sartre, 1943/1956) and often the thought of those Husserl influenced became more well-known than the thought of Husserl himself, often unfairly so (MacDonald, 2001), especially in the social and human sciences. Speigelberg (1982) has written the classic history of this movement, and the reader is referred to his work for more details concerning philosophical phenomenology and its history.

There was also a grassroots American phenomenological movement in psychology that initiated with the work of Snygg (1935) in the 1930s, especially Snygg and Combs (1949) later. However, this development took place without any influence of continental philosophical phenomenology. In essence, *phenomenology* means for this tradition "from the point of view of the behaving organism itself" (Snygg, 1941, p. 406). The major contribution of this grassroots phenomenological tradition were pulled together and published by Kuenzli (1959). This book contains 14 chapters by the major representatives of this approach, including Snygg, Combs, Rogers, and MacLeod. A check of all the references indicates that no major philosopher of the continental philosophical tradition is referenced in any of the 14 chapters. Only in the selected bibliography section at the end of the book are two of Sartre's smaller works mentioned. Moreover, the idea of a phenomenological method as applied in psychology is not articulated in any of the chapters. Mostly the argument was presented as a need for a phenomenological "approach," "perspective," or "frame of reference." This tradition obviously has interesting aspects but it does not touch on the method to be articulated in this chapter. Neither does the defense of phenomenology by Rogers and MacLeod in the famous debate with behaviorism touch on the manner in which the phenomenological method should be used in psychology (Wann, 1964).

Most of the major philosophers in the continental tradition strongly believed that phenomenological philosophy could help psychology in diverse ways. For example, Husserl (1962/1977) himself, in the summer of 1925, gave a course on phenomenological psychology, but it was clearly a philosophical course on the mind and its activities from a phenomenological perspective (Scanlon, 1977). Husserl believed that his approach could help clarify the fundamental concepts of psychology, and as a consequence, psychologists would be able to use the concepts consistently and more accurately. Merleau-Ponty (1962/1964) also wrote extensively about the relationship between phenomenology and psychology and in ways that were quite sympathetic to the psychologist's perspective. He clarified the ideas of eidetic reduction and eidetic intuition and related the latter to the empirical procedures of induction in penetrating ways. However, these analyses were conceptual and philosophical even though they are very helpful to those psychologists who would adopt a phenomenological perspective. How one would apply the phenomenological method in psychology is not detailed. However, the conceptual clarity Merleau-Ponty gives to certain Husserlian formulae and ideas is well worth the reading. Finally, Sartre (1936/1962, 1939/1962, 1940/1966) in his early works also claimed to have helped psychology, even if via "critique." His two books on imagination and his short essay on the emotions begin with criticisms of the assumptions that traditional psychology brings to its labors, and when he presents the phenomenological alternative Sartre would claim that psychology has been significantly helped. Sartre believed that phenomenological philosophical assumptions help one to interrogate the experiential world far more accurately than either positivistic or logical empiricism would. Although Sartre's insights are unmistakably helpful, just how he achieved what he did is not spoken to—that is, he presented results, not processes.

The previous paragraph illustrates how philosophers familiar with phenomenology touched on the helpful possibilities of phenomenology for psychology. It was inevitable perhaps that the opposite effort should also take place; psychologists familiar with phenomenological philosophy would indicate how phenomenology could help the development of psychology. These two efforts are quite different even if the same philosophy is being tapped by representatives of both disciplines because the sensitivities to the weaknesses of the mainstream paradigm differed. The philosophers concentrated on assumptions and concepts and psychologists looked for methodical help. The American psychologist who attempted a rigorous interpretation of how the phenomenological method as developed within the continental philosophical tradition could be adapted and made useful for psychology was the senior author of this chapter (Amedeo; Giorgi, 1985). Cloonan (1995) has provided an extensive history of this development on the North American continent, so we will be brief.

In the early 1960s the senior author had joined a psychology department that was explicitly existential–phenomenological in orientation and his task was to come up with alternative research strategies consistent with the framework of that approach. Having heard that the phenomenological method was well-developed in Europe, the senior author spent more than a year in the 1960s contacting every phenomenologist he could find, but he was disappointed to discover that none of the workers in the field of phenomenological psychology was actually using an explicit method. They assumed a phenomenological attitude or approach, somewhat like the conceptual work of the continental philosophers quoted earlier, and provided critiques of mainstream psychology (e.g., Graumann, 1960; Linschoten, 1968) but the performance of concrete research with an articulated method that generated data that others could conceivably replicate was not being done. Thus, while Amedeo returned to the United States empty-handed and disappointed, he realized that he would have to take up the task on his own, and in the spring semester of 1970, he introduced a graduate course titled "Qualitative Research: The Phenomenological Method" wherein he put together the experiences he had gained so far in working phenomenologically with psychological data and worked through an interpretation of Husserl's method adapted to scientific psychological interests. The textual bases for the method were Husserl's (1913/1983) *Ideas I* where the method was first formulated and Merleau-Ponty's (1945/1962) preface to *The Phenomenology of Perception*. It should be noted that these texts provided philosophical articulations of the phenomenological method, and the only thing certain was that those descriptions could not be imitated precisely because to do so would have resulted in a philosophical analysis, and what was needed was to apply phenomenology to help enlighten situations from the perspective of scientific psychology.

The latter point is important because very often scientific social science practitioners use Husserl's (or Spiegelberg's, 1982) description of the steps of the method without modification without realizing that such a description is in the service of a philosophical project. Thus, Moustakas (1994) also provided an independent interpretation of Husserl's philosophical method, and he used Husserl's transcendental articulations as a guide. However, our perspective is that the transcendental perspective is wholly philosophical and should not be a guide for psychological analyses. It is psychological subjectivity that interests psychology, not the transcendental one. In any case, there are several other differences between Moustakas's interpretation of the method and our own, but these differences cannot be pursued in this chapter.

Phenomenological Status of the Method

As mentioned, phenomenology in the modern sense of the term is dated from 1900 when Husserl published *Logical Investigations* (1900/1970), although the phenomenological method itself was not explicitly practiced in that work. It was in *Ideas I* (1913/1983) that Husserl made the method explicit. It is important to appreciate that to make phenomenological claims in the strongest sense one would have to use some version of the phenomenological method, along with certain other key procedures. That is why we will first present the philosophical method as articulated by Husserl, and immediately following, we will articulate a scientific version of the phenomenological method.

Husserl's phenomenological method consists of three steps. First, one must assume the attitude of the phenomenological reduction. There seems to be great confusion about the phenomenological reduction, in part because Husserl described several of them and kept clarifying them and in part because many commentators believed that the correct implementation of the reduction was not possible. We will speak only of the two reductions Husserl would want followers to use, either philosophically or scientifically. If one were to perform philosophical phenomenological analyses, then Husserl would want to use the transcendental phenomenological reduction. By the transcendental reduction Husserl means the assumption of an attitude by the researcher whereby the objects and acts of consciousness are considered to belong to any consciousness as such. Specifically, in the interest of the most universal findings possible, Husserl would want to consider the objects and acts under investigation as belonging to any possible consciousness and explicitly as not belonging to a human mode of consciousness. Results of this kind of analysis have universal implications for any imaginable consciousness. That is, a human mode of consciousness is but one type of consciousness: infrahuman organisms or species and imaginably extrahuman species and the way they relate conscious acts to objects would have to be included. It is the essence of "consciousness as such" that Husserl was after.

After assuming the attitude of the transcendental phenomenological reduction, the researcher turns to the object whose essence is to be determined. The object that triggers off the essential search can be a real object or state of affairs or else something fictional. What happens next is that one tries to determine the essence of the "given" object or state of affairs by means of the method of free imaginative variation. The procedure of imaginative variation begins by varying specific dimensions of the given object and one seeks the effect on the object of the removal or variation of the key dimension. If the object "collapses" as a consequence of the removal of the key dimension, then one would have to say that the dimension so varied is essential for the object to appear as whole. If the object is only slightly modified but still recognizable despite the variation of the dimension, then it is considered to be accidental rather than essential.

To take a simple and straightforward example, the essence of a cup determined by means of imaginative variation would be as follows. I can start with a cup with which I am now drinking coffee. It is black, octagonal, and made of ceramic. I then take a certain distance from the specific cup and ask precisely what it is that determines its "cupness." That is, the specific cup that I am using becomes an example of "cupness" as such. But an example, even a good one, does not articulate essentialness. Discovering essentialness requires a process and the process involves imaginative variation. For example, is color—blackness—essential for a cup to be a cup? No, because not only can nonblack cups be remembered by us, but we can also easily imagine many other colors that a cup could be and it would not affect its cupness at all. Changing colors in imagination would be varying the dimension of color, but it does not affect the "cupness" of the cup. How about material? This cup, we said, is ceramic. But one can easily imagine other materials—glass, wood, metal, and so forth. Cupness can be produced by any of the aforementioned. However, materiality does have its limits. A functioning cup cannot be made of porous material (e.g., net). Thus, nonporous material belongs to the essence of a cup, because if it is lacking the very possibility of a cup collapses. Nonporous materiality is essential to it.

One can do the same with any imaginable variable concerning cups: size, strength, aesthetics, and so forth. Whatever a material cup is made of, it would have to be solid enough to hold a moderate amount of liquid and be graspable by an embodied creature with a free hand. Having a handle is not a necessity. Although we used actual experiences and memorable past moments in my example, the whole process could just as easily have been merely imaginative.

The last step of the method is to describe the invariant aspect of the object, or its essence. This we have done by stating that a cup's essence is to be container of liquids manageable by hands.

Now, one difficulty that is frequently not appreciated is that if one followed these procedures exactly as described, one would be doing a philosophical analysis. The same would be true if one followed Spiegelberg's (1982) more extended but essentially similar method. Rather, what is required are changes that will make the method suitable for scientific analyses rather than philosophical ones. Although the fine line between philosophy and science may be hard to draw, the larger sorts of modifications that we have in mind would not be.

First of all, the order of the steps to be followed is not the same as with the philosophical procedure. For the scientific level of analysis, one first obtains descriptions of experiences from others, then one enters into a scientific phenomenological reduction while simultaneously adopting a psychological perspective, then one analyzes the raw data to come up with the essential structure of the experience, which is then carefully described at a level other than that of the original description. We shall now cover each of these points in greater detail.

With the philosophical method, because all of the work is done by the philosopher him- or herself, it is possible to enter into the phenomenological reduction right away. However, within scientific circles such a step would meet with severe criticisms. It is easy to specify the question that would be effectively unanswerable if one were to do a phenomenological analysis of his or her own experiences: How could I prove, the questioner would ask, that my concrete description was not unconsciously selected and construed to prove that my theoretical analysis was correct? One could answer this question philosophically and theoretically from a phenomenological perspective, but it would not necessarily be effective from the perspective of empirical scientists. Moreover, when the method was initially introduced in the early 1970s, the psychological establishment was dead set against qualitative procedures and so it would have been an uphill struggle to try to justify such a procedure even though it was strictly legitimate phenomenologically. As a consequence, to minimize the number of battles to be fought to introduce qualitative research into psychology in a legitimate way, it was decided not to analyze one's own experience even though this step could have threatened the phenomenological claim that we wanted to make for the method. We decided that the only recourse left as scientists inspired by phenomenological philosophy was to analyze the experiences of others, especially those others who had no knowledge of scientific theories and their vicissitudes.

The reason that this step could have threatened the phenomenological status of our method is that within the phenomenological perspective one is meant to analyze only that which appears to one's own stream of consciousness. Insofar as we were requesting descriptions of experiences from others, the raw data of our research comes from the consciousness of others. However, this database is prephenomenological, and insofar as the descriptions are careful and accurate depictions of everyday world events undergone by the participants, it seems to us that there are no rational grounds for rejecting them. After all, even if one were to describe one's own experiences, one would expect that other scientists should accept them as accurate depictions of what the participant lived through. Moreover, because the participants know neither the specific purpose of the research nor the specific mode of analysis, they would not know which way to slant their descriptions. They could possibly cover up or not reveal fully certain aspects of their experiences, but there are interview strategies to help overcome such modes. Ultimately, of course, there are no "perfect" descriptions but only adequate or inadequate ones, the former being usable and the latter not. Adequate descriptions are those that are capable of yielding distinctive structures of the phenomenon from a psychological perspective.

It should be noted that the necessity of including the expressions of the experiences of others within a phenomenological framework has not escaped the attention of all phenomenological philosophers. Spiegelberg (1964) has explicitly argued for this move, claiming that it would be an expansion of phenomenology without dilution, although he argued that the rational justification for the practical steps of such a move would have to be carefully worked out. However, it is apparent that the outcome of the analysis is entirely based on the psychological meaning discriminations performed by the researcher, and these are not explicitly stated as such by the individuals having the experience. Thus a case could be made that the meaningful psychological results are all present to the consciousness of the researcher, fulfilling the phenomenological requirement. This also means that the critical check of the original researcher's procedure can be performed by any competent colleague.

The method is also descriptive in the sense that the end result of the analytical process is a description of the structure of the experience provided by the participants. After using the method of free imaginative variation on the elaborated meanings (see later discussion) that the first part of the analysis produces, the researcher has to describe what the essential constituents of the phenomenon are, just as was done with the cup. Because the description of the structure of an experience almost always includes several key constituents, the description must include the relationships among the constituents as well. This will be discussed later when an example will be provided.

Having obtained a description from a participant, the second step at the scientific level is to enter into the phenomenological reduction. It should be stated at the outset that the phenomenological reduction used at the scientific level is different from the transcendental reduction of the philosophical level. The scientific phenomenological reduction used in this instance Husserl called the psychological phenomenological reduction. What this means is that the objects or states of affairs experienced are reduced, but not the acts of consciousness with which the objects or states of affairs are correlated. To say that the objects toward which the acts of consciousness are correlated are reduced is to say that they are taken exactly as they present themselves except that no existential status is assigned to them. That is, what is experienced is understood to be an experiential given to the person experiencing the object, the person is genuinely experiencing some given phenomenon, but the claim that what is present to the person's consciousness actually exists the way it is given is not affirmed. In other words, in the reduction phenomenologists distinguish between the mode of givenness of an object (its presence) and how it actually exists, which might be determined only after many conscious acts. Phenomenologists recognize that there is a spontaneous positing of the existence of the object that normally takes place in everyday life and in the reduction that positing is withheld. In addition, to use the epoché means to bracket past knowledge about the experienced object to experience this instance of its occurrence freshly. One could say all of this quickly by simply saying that within the scientific phenomenological reduction one takes whatever is given to be a phenomenon, except that we are not sure that the expression would be correctly understood. To be taken as a phenomenon means that everything that is noticed with respect to the given is taken to be worthy precisely as a presence in the manner in which it is present, but one does not have to say that the given *is* the way it presents itself to be. One makes no commitment to the existence of the given within the reduction. This aspect of the reduction is devised to help overcome the natural human bias of stating that things *are* the way we experience them to be without critical evaluation. Often they are, but within scientific circles it is better to be sure, and so the epistemological claim is concerned with what cannot be known in other ways—how things present themselves to persons—but they could exist in other ways. A privileged example of what is referred to would be if one said, "This meal seems salty to me." The person is referring to how the meal presents itself to him or her, but there is awareness that it could be otherwise to others. That is how knowledge claims are to be understood within the reduction.

For the scientific reduction, the acts of consciousness are taken to be acts of human beings who are related to and influenced by the world. The attitude of the transcendental reduction is quite different and that is what prevents it from being immediately useful for human scientific purposes. For this reason, the scientific phenomenological reduction is often understood to be a mixed reduction because the objects or states of affairs are reduced but the acts are not.

When it is said that within the reduction everything that presents itself is to be accounted for precisely as it presents itself, it is a strategy devised to counteract the potentially biasing effects of past experience. When we encounter familiar objects we tend to see them through familiar eyes and thus often miss seeing novel features of familiar situations. Hence, by understanding that the given has to be seen merely as a presentational something rather than the familiar "object that always is there," new dimensions of the total experience are likely to appear. This is what is meant when phenomenologists say that they want to experience things "freshly" or "with disciplined naiveté." Even if objects turn out to be precisely as we first thought, it is more rigorous to give nuances and "taken-for-granted" aspects a chance to show themselves, because phenomenologists do want the totality to be accounted for.

The third step of the procedure is to seek the essence of the phenomenon by means of the method of free imaginative variation, but another difference from the philosophical method is introduced. We are seeking the psychological essence or structure of the phenomenon and not the universal essence or the essence as such. Philosophers tend to seek ultimates and so they always want universal essences. However, universalization often comes at the price of abstraction, but in psychology, the content is as important as the form, and that means that context is also important, so the claim made by the scientific method is only "generality." That is, because of contextual imaginative variation, one can be sure that the findings of the analysis will hold for situations other than the one in which empirical data were collected, but the same contextual imaginative variation teaches us that universality is equally not attainable.

Thus, the very fact that a psychological perspective is declared dominant in these analyses makes the method greatly different from the philosophical method. However, perspective is critical for all science, and psychology is no different. To do a psychological analysis means to adopt a psychological perspective, and this will ultimately lead to a psychological essence, which will be different from a sociological, biological, or historical essence. Each discipline has to come up with essences that are relevant to its perspective, but care also has to be taken that the disciplinary essence (e.g., psychological essence) is not projected beyond its zone of relevancy. A clash of perspectives or essences would have to be resolved on grounds other than those being formulated in this chapter.

A word should also be spoken about the psychological perspective being discussed. What is being recommended is that the psychological perspective of the practitioner be adopted, and not any specific theoretical perspective such as psychoanalytical, cognitive, Gestalt, and so forth, because all of the latter are theoretical perspectives within psychology. What is being advocated is the adoption of a generic psychological perspective rather than that of another discipline such as sociology or anthropology. We are aware, of course, that theoretically speaking, the articulation of a discipline-wide psychological perspective has not yet been formulated or accepted. Nevertheless, thousands of practitioners adopt such a perspective everyday in their concrete work and happily admit that they are theoretically "eclectic" or neutral. That is the position we are advocating. The living of the psychological attitude or perspective is ahead of its theoretical articulation. This is where the general practitioner dwells, except for those who make a point of positing a theoretical position, and the performance of the phenomenological method is a praxis that requires the same general attitude.

Before summarizing the phenomenological status of the method, one other point has to be mentioned even though it is not an explicit step of the method—that is the notion of intentionality, which is, for Husserl, the key feature of consciousness. To say that consciousness is intentional is to say that every object of consciousness transcends the act in which it appears, whether it is a part of consciousness (e.g., a memory) or outside of it (e.g., a table). For those objects, called transcendent, that are actually outside consciousness but related to specific acts that grasp them, the claim can be made that consciousness relates to objects that are not themselves consciousness and yet the acts that grasp them leaves such objects undisturbed. What is important for psychology is the fact that behavior is also intentional—in other words, directed to situations that transcend the behavior itself.

By way of summary, then, the philosophical phenomenological method requires the assumption of the transcendental phenomenological reduction, the search for the essence of the phenomenon by means of the method of free imaginative variation, and, finally, a careful description of the essence so discovered. The scientific phenomenological method also partakes of description, essential determination, and the use of a phenomenological reduction, but with differences with respect to each criterion. The scientific method is descriptive because its point of departure consists of concrete descriptions of experienced events from the perspective of everyday life by participants, and then the end result is a second-order description of the psychological essence or structure of the phenomenon by the scientific researcher. As just stated, essential determination of the phenomenon is sought by means of the method of free imaginative variation, but it is a psychological essence rather than a philosophical one. In addition, the imaginative variation is elaborated on an empirical basis more so than with the philosophical implementation of the method and thus is more contextually limited. Finally, there could be no phenomenological method without some sort of reduction, and with the scientific method, the scientific phenomenological reduction is performed, which is not identical to the transcendental reduction because only the intentional objects of consciousness are reduced, but not the acts. The conscious acts are considered to be acts of a human subject engaged with, and related to, the world.

The Specific Procedures of the Method

Thus far we have been mostly theoretical, explaining the basics of the phenomenological approach. Now we shall list the specific steps to be followed and then we shall provide an example of an analysis.

The research always begins with a description of an experience to be understood psychologically. The description, more often than not, is obtained by means of an interview. The purpose of the interview is to have the participant describe in as faithful and detailed a manner an experience of a situation that the investigator is seeking. Thus, one could be interested in learning, anger, frustration, anxiety, or whatever, and the participant's role as an ordinary person from the everyday world is to describe a situation in which he or she believes such an event took place. The transcription of the interview, precisely as it took place, becomes the raw data of the research. Once the researcher has the description, the following steps constitute the analysis.

Read for a Sense of the Whole

When one has transcribed verbal data, then the data have to be read, of course. The only point to be established is that the entire description has to be read because the phenomenological perspective is a holistic one. One cannot begin an analysis of a description without knowing how it ends. That is the major point of this first step. One does not do anything about what one has read—the subsequent steps take care of that. One simply needs to know the overall sense of the description before embarking on the next step.

Determination of Parts: Establishing Meaning Units

The ultimate outcome of a phenomenological analysis is to determine the meaning(s) of experience. As a consequence, most descriptions within a research context are too long to be capably handled in their entirety, parts have to be established to be able to achieve a more thorough analysis. Moreover, because the disclosure of meaning is the ultimate outcome, the parts that are established are based on meaning discriminations, and the results are called meaning units. Operationally the parts are determined in the following way. The researcher goes back and begins to reread the description from within the perspective of the phenomenological reduction and with a psychological attitude, mindful of the phenomenon being researched, and every time he or she experiences a shift of meaning in the reading of the description, a mark is made in the appropriate place. One continues in such a fashion until the whole description is delineated with such meaning units. That is the termination of the second step. One has to appreciate that there are no "objective" meaning units in the description as such. The meaning units are correlated with the perspective of the researcher. Moreover, the meaning units are not theoretically weighty. That is, they are merely practical outcomes to help the analysis. All researchers would not have to have identical meaning units for the procedure to be valid. The method is judged by its outcome, not by intermediary stages.

Transformation of Meaning Units Into Psychologically Sensitive Expressions

The reader will notice that there is a progressive refinement of the original description with respect to its sense. At first one merely reads what the participant expressed. Then the next step produces meaning discriminations that are meant to be psychologically relevant with respect to the phenomenon being researched. The third step, which is at the heart of the method and where it bottoms out, so to speak, expresses the psychological meaning of the participant's everyday language more directly with the help of free imaginative variation. The whole purpose of the method is to discover and articulate the psychological meanings being lived by the participant that reveal the nature of the phenomenon being researched. The original description is full of "everyday expressions" and it is full of references to the participant's world. The everyday expressions are often idiosyncratic but still rich with meaning. The meanings expressed by the participants have to be made psychologically explicit with regard to the phenomenon that is being researched and not directly as revelatory of the participant in his or her personal existence.

In articulating these psychological meanings, one has to avoid two errors. Clinicians tend to pursue the meanings with respect to the personal lives of the participants to the extent that they are available. That would be pursuing the personal interest of the participant too far. On the other hand, to the extent that contextualized personal meanings reveal something psychologically significant about the phenomenon, they have to be pursued for their relevance for the phenomenon. In other words, personal meanings are pursued not for their own sake but for the value they have for clarifying the context in which psychological phenomena manifest themselves, and therefore, for their role in specifying psychological meanings.

Another potential error one should avoid is the use of psychological jargon as it exists in the literature. It is surely a huge problem to come up with original psychologically sensitive expressions on the spot, but it is more deleterious to try to use already established theory-laden terms. Each established psychological perspective has certain strengths, but also certain limits. Because no theoretical perspective is as broad as the psychological perspective as such one never really knows whether the theory-laden term is being used in an area of strength or not. However difficult, the procedure biases itself toward the perspective that demands a creative use of language to come up with careful descriptions of the invariant psychological meanings of each meaning unit. Ordinary language twisted toward psychologically heightened revelations is the recommended strategy. Mere labeling should also be avoided.

The Determination of the Structure

The third step of the analysis ends with a series of transformed meaning units—that is, meaning units that were originally in the language of the participant are now expressed with heightened psychological sensitivity with respect to the phenomenon under study. One then practices imaginative variation on these transformed meaning units to see what is truly essential about them (like with the cup) and then one carefully describes the most invariant connected meanings belonging to the experience, and that is the general structure. It is quite possible that terms not found in the transformed meaning units are required to describe the structure.

Before turning to the example analyses it may be helpful to the reader to see a flow chart of the scientific method. It may also be helpful to the reader to appreciate that each step of the method is a finer and more particular analysis built on the previous step, until the fourth step, which is once again a holistic articulation of the phenomenon, except that it is done psychologically this time. Exhibit 13.1 summarizes the steps that we have been articulating in this section.

Examples of Phenomenological Analysis of Descriptions

We shall now turn to examples of phenomenological analyses. Readers interested in other examples of analyses or theoretical articulations are referred to the following sources: Giorgi (1985, 1986, 1987a, 1987b, 1989a, 1989b, 1989c, 1992, 1994, 1997). For the example in this chapter, the data will be taken from a master's thesis (Sorenson-Englander, 2000) performed under the senior

Exhibit 13.1. Flowchart Demonstrating the Steps of the Descriptive Phenomenological Psychological Method

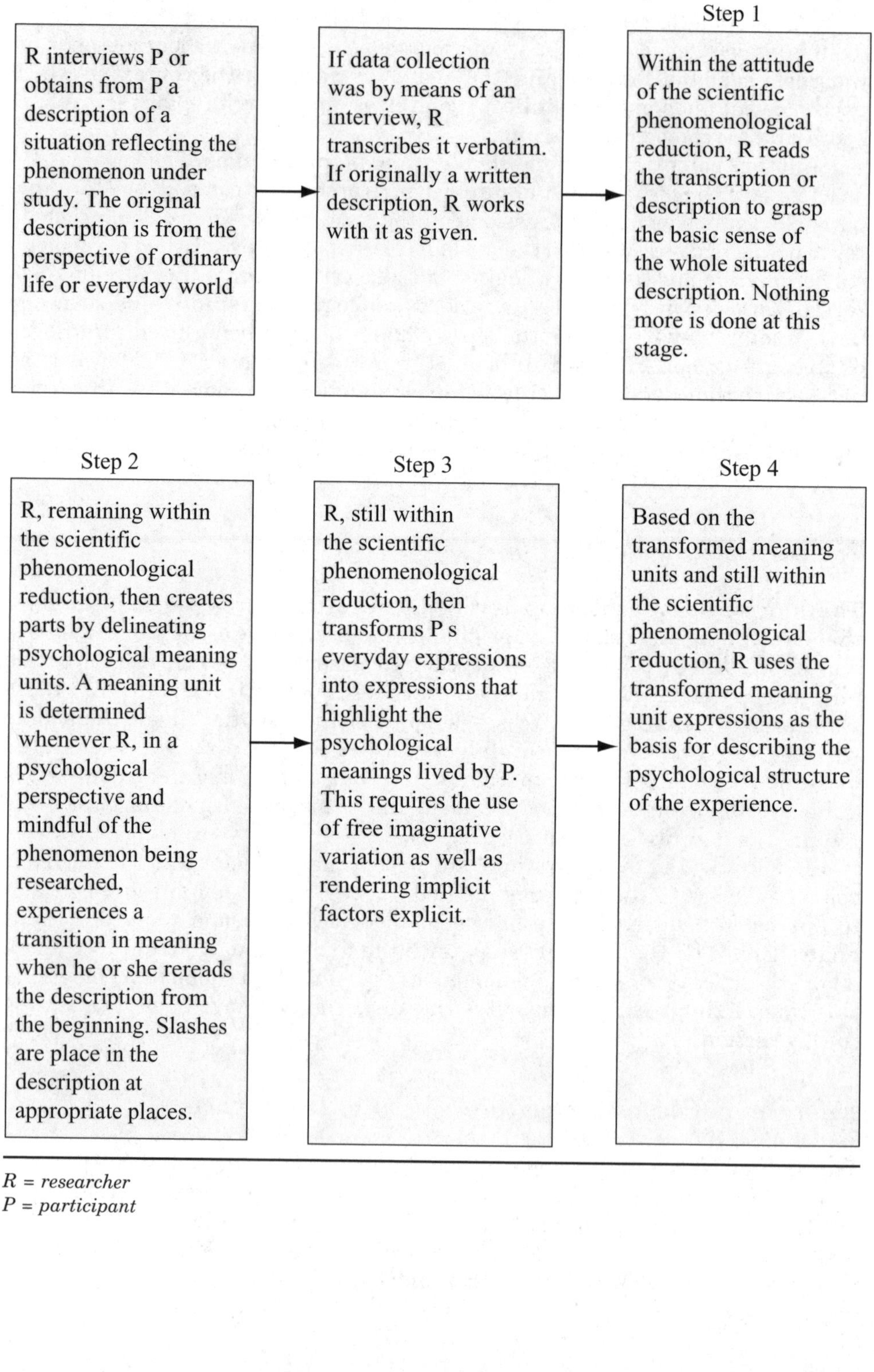

R = researcher
P = participant

author's direction at Saybrook Graduate School. The phenomenon being researched is known as internalized homophobia, although it is not taken for granted that that is what the outcome will be. Two examples of data analysis will be provided because it will help clarify the role of the psychological structure more easily. What follows next are the transcribed interview data. Appendix 13.1 presents the transcripts of the interviews with P^1 and P^2, the participants in this research.

The two sets of data are exact transcriptions of what the participants said. The method begins with a reading of the entire description, but nothing is done except for a first grasp of what the participant said. The second step is the determination of the meaning units, and these are expressed by the slashes in the texts. The third step demands that the language of the participant be expressed in such a way that the psychological meanings within the description be more explicitly stated. Appendix 13.2 highlights the third step. The column on the left shows the participant's words and the column on the right shows the transformations performed by the researcher to highlight psychological insights. Finally, the structure of the experience is determined by means of imaginative variation of the transformed meaning units. Although there is no space to show the process, the structure itself is presented in Appendix 13.3.

Poststructural Analyses

Although the achievement of the structure is an important step of the analytical process, it is not, as some researchers seem to believe, the final step. The purpose of the structure is to help understand the empirical data in a more methodical and systematic way. Again, a full analysis cannot be done, but key constituents of the structure can help understand the variations found in the empirical data.

First of all, we must remember that what stimulated the study was the sense that male homosexuals might be "internalizing" homophobia and thus experiencing negative feelings toward themselves. The participants who responded to the question posed by the interviewer answered from the perspective of everyday life. It is granted beforehand that the everyday life description is richer than any psychological analysis, but it is also true that the psychological dimensions contained within the description have to be highlighted, made explicit, and thematized. That is why the analyses in Appendix 13.2 are presented. They indicate a thematization of the psychological factors whether they were originally explicit or implicit. But precisely because the participants spoke from the perspective of everyday life, it is not a priori certain that the phenomenon they experienced is psychologically equivalent to the everyday understanding of it. As the reader can see, we have labeled the structure differently. We believe that the complexity of the experience calls for some refinement. There are "moments" where one can detect the acceptance of the judgment of the society at large toward homosexuals, but they are only "moments." The total experience is filled with many other meanings, including genuine fear of consequences of being publicly known as gay. The respect for the complexity of the experience and the refinement of psychological understanding are two consequences of the phenomenological analysis.

Table 13.1. Selected Constituents of the Structure Along With Empirical Variations Provided by P^1 and P^2

Constituents	P^1	P^2
Feelings of emotional ambivalence	Some of the people . . . were really effeminate and negative?? . . . maybe this was a good way to let my parents know I was different	I dropped out of the race. Too bad I was ashamed of my decision, but I was more ashamed of being gay.
Feelings of unsafety	My partner and I go to see a therapist to deal with issues like this . . . but it's never going to go away.	I'm still pretty scared of what might happen if I'm really open about being gay, especially with the hate crimes that keep happening.
Curtailing of desires	I couldn't tell my parents that I was gay—not yet at any rate.	I wasn't ready to be openly gay, so I dropped out of the race.
Selective momentary acceptance of judgments of society at large	And shame—at my mother for her reaction—and at myself I guess.	. . . but I was more ashamed of being gay.

Note. Not all constituents are listed because the table is for demonstration purposes only.

Now, if we turn to Table 13.1, a demonstration table, we can see how the delineation of a structure can help deepen the psychological understanding of a situated experience. The first constituent listed is called "feelings of emotional ambivalence." This is a psychological understanding of certain empirical details, which are included in Exhibit 13.1, as well as a generalization of a key psychological factor that belongs to the structure of the experience.

As Table 13.1 shows, empirically P^1 was quite concerned about how to reveal to his mother, who had a negative attitude toward gays, that he himself was gay. P^2 felt ambivalent about becoming class president. He knew that he could do a good job, but was it worth being exposed as gay? He decided that it was not worth it, but not with neutral feelings. He really felt badly that he was not free to use his talents to become a leader of the senior class. Thus, although the empirical details are starkly different for the two participants, they both can be subsumed under the psychological heading "feelings of ambivalence." Thus, the structure generalizes in a psychologically meaningful way and it helps deepen the essential understanding of the experience by reducing myriad details to their essential components.

The reader can examine Table 13.1 to see how the psychological constituents "feelings of unsafety" and "curtailing of desires" are exemplified. Because "internalized homophobia" was the triggering phenomenon of this research, we have included the moments of acceptance of outside attitudes as well. It is interesting to note that there was first, in both cases, feelings of shame directed toward something else before the shame was directed toward oneself. P^1 was ashamed of his mother first, and P^2 was ashamed that he did not continue to run for class president. But why, then, should they be ashamed of themselves simply for being gay? Why is this fact worthy of shame unless, in some measure, they looked at themselves in the same way as they believed the straight world did? However, it is possible that the feeling of shame directed toward themselves might not have arisen if shame for something else did not precede it. In any case, it is clear that the whole experience cannot be primarily called "internalized homophobia." It is even quite possible that without genuine threats from the population at large phobic reactions would also disappear.

More could be said about key psychological constituents and their empirical variations, but because this chapter is primarily methodological, we will move on to other issues.

Some Methodological Clarifications

The first two steps of the method are usually not problematic, but the last two normally require additional comments. Reading a description only to find out what it is about is not difficult nor is the ability to create meaning units once it is understood that anything experienced as a transition even if seemingly arbitrary is a legitimate candidate. Of course, the meaning units have to be large enough to have an explorable significance and small enough to be manageable.

The third step is usually the most problematic because an easily discernible external criterion is lacking. However, this does not mean that no criteria are available. Obviously, persons cannot enter each others' heads to have direct evidence of what is being experienced. That is why the meaning units (parts) are rendered explicit, so that the critical other can know which meaning units are provoking specific forms of psychological explications. However, the meaning units are considered to be constituents that are context-dependent rather than "elements" that stand more or less on their own. This means that there cannot be a rigid one-to-one relationship between meaning units and their transformations. Relevant parts of the context outside the meaning unit can help codetermine the transformation that is articulated.

The purpose of the transformations is to make as explicit as possible the psychological dimensions of the complex concrete experience written from the perspective of everyday life rather than to allow them to remain implicit and inarticulate. As one begins the effort to transform the participant's language, certain intuitions begin to arise in the researcher's consciousness. These first meanings cannot be simply accepted, but they must be critically evaluated by means of free imaginative variation. When the researcher is satisfied that the best articulation has been achieved—phenomenologically speaking, that the fulfilling content matches the emptily presented sense precisely—then that transformation is written down and the researcher proceeds to the next meaning unit and recommences the process.

For example, meaning unit 16 for P^1 is emotionally very powerful. The transformation tries to render explicit in an essential way the network of emotional entanglements that are expressed therein. P^1 observes, but also knew from earlier experience, that his mother reacts and judges negatively to manifest gay postures and gestures. But then P[1] himself says that he does not like such gestures either although he is gay. Is he identifying with his mother's attitude? But he also did not like how his mother was reacting to the gay person, so one cannot say that there is complete identity with the mother's attitude. Psychologically, P[1] says that he wanted to escape the whole situation, but because the whole reception was centered on him, he knew that he could not do so without grave consequences. He would like to leave but he must stay. Once again, like with his homosexuality and with his observation of his mother toward the manifest gay person, P[1] is trapped within a situation that provokes ambivalent feelings. P[1] was also motivated to tell his parents about his sexual preference, but observing his mother's negative, judgmental attitude he realized that she would not be ready to hear this news about himself in a sympathetic and accepting way. Again, ambivalent feelings prevail because P[1] obviously wants his mother's acceptance at some level and he is fearful that it may not be forthcoming. Still, he seems not prepared yet for a radical solution (breaking with his parents entirely) and so he dwells with myriad conflicting feelings. Meaning unit 16 is basically six lines long, yet we were able to unpack all of the above from those six lines, and everything stated is psychologically very important. To leave all of the above implicit makes the psychological analysis obscure and gives the critical reader no chance to double-check precisely what aspects of the analysis he or she might disagree with.

Finally, the structure is meant to convey what is truly psychologically essential about a series of experiences of the same type. Again, the structure is not meant to be universal but only general or typical. Those aspects of the experience that are highly specific or contingent would not be part of the structure. Only those constituents or relationships that are defining for the phenomenon would be included. The criterion is that the structure would be radically altered if a key constituent were to be removed. For example, neither participant that we have presented has declared publicly that he is gay. Can we imagine gays that have publicly declared their homosexuality also experiencing some moments of homophobia? We suppose so, but the dynamics could not be the same as described by these participants. Their lack of public disclosure hovers all around everything they say. That is why the idea of lack of public declaration belongs to the essential description of the phenomenon.

The Scientific Status of the Method

There are still persons today who equate science with quantification rather than with the most precise knowledge possible, which is what science's ideal is. It is true that numbers can provide exactitude, but when the exactness of the means fits oddly with the mode of questioning and the amorphousness of the phenomenon, then one ends up with much less than the apparent exactness that numbers offer. Quantification is a powerful tool when the conditions of research allow it, but it is not the only means of achieving precision.

Rather, for us the criteria of science are met when the knowledge obtained is systematic, methodical, critical, and general. To be systematic means that there is a connection between various subfields within a given discipline—for example, between learning and motivation or anxiety and performance and so on. Of course, at any given time in the history of a discipline these connections may not be well-understood, but at least are recognized as problems to be tackled. To be methodical means that certain basic steps that can be followed by many people to test the knowledge claims that any individual scientist can make are available. To be critical means that the knowledge gained by any method is not simply accepted because it has been gained, but that other experts within the scientific community challenge the procedures or the knowledge, including trying to replicate the findings. It also implies that the scientist who obtained the knowledge also tests it or remains skeptical of it as he or she goes along so that greater confidence in the outcome can be established. Finally, generality means that the knowledge gained is applicable to situations other than the specific one in which the knowledge was obtained. The claim is made that the method described in this chapter meets all four of the scientific criteria just described.

Appendix 13.1. Interviews Concerning the Experience of Internalized Homophobia by Two Male Homosexuals (Raw Data of this Study)[1]

Participant 1:

I: Please describe for me a time in your life when you experienced internalized homophobia.

P¹: It happened after my recital for my Bachelor of Arts degree in music performance./ After the recital, there was a reception which had been arranged by my parents. It was held in a really nice hotel banquet room and everyone from the recital was invited. I didn't know about it until the week before the recital and when I found out, I didn't know if this was a good idea./ My parents didn't know I was gay—and some of the people I knew from the School of Music, who were going to be at the recital, were really effeminate and might give me away. Then I thought maybe this would be a good way of letting my parents know I was different./ But I was really nervous.

I: Can you tell me more about being nervous?

P¹: I had seen the way my mother had acted once before around a gay man. She turned up her nose at him. She said something about him being immoral because what he was doing was unnatural./

I: How did your mother know he was gay?

P¹: Well, she didn't, really. I mean, not too many people were coming out publicly at that time, but he was really swishy and flamboyant. He was what my friends and I refer to as a "Fifi."/ My parents thought that everyone who acted that way was gay. In this case, my mother was right, even though she was making an assumption. I knew he was gay because, well, because he had come onto me./ But I turned him down. Actually, I made a point to get away from him as fast as I could and then I avoided him after that because he was so—so—affected. And I wasn't really sure if I was gay or not—then./

I: What happened next at the party?

P¹: I showed up with my partner, who my parents knew as my roommate from college. We had been living together in a walk-up right next to the campus. A lot of young men shared living quarters without being questioned, and my

[1]The thesis is titled "Alleged 'Internalized Homophobia' as Experienced Among Homosexual Men: A Phenomenological Psychological Analysis" (2000) and it was done by Kristin L. Sorensen-Englander. Data from a master's thesis are being used because doctoral material would be too long for a chapter of this size. Because the method is holistic, it is not possible to use part of the description of any one individual. Normally, special one-page descriptions are used in workshops and demonstrations, but because the descriptions from this thesis are also relatively short, we decided to use them. Two are being presented because the power of the structure of an experience can be more effectively demonstrated with a number beyond one. Although the raw data were taken from Sorenson-Englander's thesis, the analyses and structure contained within this chapter were performed by the authors.

partner and I were not obvious in our behavior or dress./ Most of our gay friends then and now are not obvious. Who would want to draw attention to being a social outcast?/ Anyway, my parents' friends pretty much hung out together by the food, and my colleagues hung out together by the drinks. There wasn't much interaction between the two groups—maybe because of the generational differences—but I think it was mostly because my colleagues made my parents and their friends uncomfortable./

I: Can you tell me more about this—about thinking your colleagues made your parents and their friends uncomfortable?

P[1]: One guy in particular was holding his cigarette like so (participant demonstrates) and he had his legs crossed—not like a man—like a woman./

I: Is there a difference?

P[1]: Oh yes! Men sit like this (demonstrates). and women—and Fifi's—sit like this (demonstrates).

I: I see. So it was the gesture and the posture?

P[1]: (nods). My mom reacted exactly the same way as when she had done before. She was disgusted. And angry that I might have invited someone like that. Or that I would even know someone like that. Or that I might even be like that. My parents sort of prided themselves for not having any gay friends. You know how some people will say "Some of my best friends are gay?" Well, not my parents./ Actually, one of my relatives is gay but no one from my family has associated with him for years./

I: Was it just this one person, or were there others?

P[1]: Oh, ya, I guess—one guy was pretty loud—especially after a few drinks. He giggled a lot. Not laughed—giggled./ But the one who really stood out was the guy with the cigarette and crossed legs. And it gave me the creeps when I saw the say way my mother reacted. I wanted to get out of there as fast as possible. But I was the guest of honor. I realized that I couldn't tell my parents I was gay—not yet, at any rate./

I: Have you since?

P[1]: I waited until I had moved across country with my partner, as far away from them as I could get. It was around my 30th birthday. I wrote them a letter./ At first, my mother pretended she never got the letter. She would call and ask if I'd met any nice women./ My partner and I had a ceremony last year to affirm our commitment to each other, and my mother said I chose to become gay. Both my parents said I should rethink my lifestyle decision. We haven't spoken since./

I: Back to the party—what did you feel when you saw your mother react?

P[1]: Embarrassment—for the way my colleague was acting. And shame—at my mother for her reaction—and at myself, I guess./ You know, I experience internalized homophobia quite often. I can't be around a Fifi. And there are times when I guess that's part of why I continue to see my therapist on a weekly basis. My partner and I go to see a therapist together, but I see one on my own—to deal with issues like this. It's not always there, but it's never going to go away—until other people get over their homophobia./

Interview Participant 2

I was really competitive and successful in high school until I decided to get involved in politics. I was running for senior class president./ I was pretty active in some gay-related activities but didn't openly admit to being gay. Why should I? After all, a lot of people—straight people—were involved in celebrating diversity./

My opponent in the class elections found out I was gay. I can't remember how . . . but he used that to his advantage. He demanded I withdraw from the elections or else he would expose me./ I wasn't ready to be openly gay. So, I dropped out of the race. Too bad./ I know I would have been a good representative for my class. But I couldn't risk being ridiculed or attacked. I was ashamed of my decision, but I was more ashamed of being gay./

I also stopped hanging out with my gay friends from outside the school. I had been active in a gay-friendly group from the Catholic Church, and volunteered once a week at the Food Bank which was specifically for people living with AIDS./ But I stopped going. I made excuses for not showing up. My therapist says it's typical—dropping out in order to hide from exposure. Exposure makes you vulnerable to ridicule and violence./ No one called to follow up. At first I was angry but then I realized the people from the church and from the Food Bank probably understood more than I about respect and confidentiality./

I'm pretty open now, but only in certain situations. I do this volunteer crisis line counseling once a week which, now that I think about it, probably helps me deal with issues of my own that I don't recognize in myself until after I hear about them from someone else who has had a similar experience./ I am grateful to have a committed relationship. We don't go to the bars. We have a few good friends, who are also in committed relationships./ We would like to think we live pretty normal lives—but I don't think we ever will. I guess I'm still pretty scared about what might happen if I'm really open about being gay, especially with the hate crimes that keep happening./

Appendix 13.2. Complete Presentation of the Analysis of the Raw Data of This Research Reflecting the First Three Steps of the Descriptive Phenomenological Psychological Method

Participant 1:

1. **I:** Please describe for me a time in your life when you experienced internalized homophobia.
P^1: It happened after my recital for my bachelor of arts degree in music performance.

1. * P^1 designates a time in his life when he might have experienced "internalized homophobia." He was at a formal social gathering called into being specifically to celebrate his recent achievement (BA degree) and artistic performance (musical recital).

2. After the recital, there was a reception that had been arranged by my parents. It was held in a really nice hotel banquet room and everyone from the recital was invited. I didn't know about it until the week before the recital and when I found out, I didn't know if this was a good idea.

2. P^1 states that the formal social gathering that he attended was arranged by his parents without P^1's prior knowledge until it was too late for him to do anything about it except that it left P^1 in a state of doubt about the worthiness of the idea because he was aware of the mixed values that the people coming together would have. The formality of the occasion was heightened by the nice surroundings in which the gathering was to take place and P1's doubts were in part provoked by the idea that all those who attended his performance were also invited to the celebration afterward.

3. My parents didn't know I was gay—and some of the people I knew from the School of Music, who were going to be at the recital, were really effeminate and might give me away. Then I thought maybe this would be a good way of letting my parents know I was different.

3. P^1 acknowledges that at the time he had not yet revealed his homosexuality to his parents, and yet he was aware that some of the people he knew from his school who would be attending his performance and the celebration following it were blatant in their manifestation of their sexual orientation and he feared that the reading of their behavior by his parents might allow them to infer that he, too, was homosexual. On the one hand this gave rise to the hopeful thought on the part of P^1 that this awkward situation might be the way to inform his parents of his different sexual orientation.

Note. * *indicates that the researcher's question has been incorporated in the transformation.*

4. But I was really nervous. **I:** Can you tell me more about being nervous? **P^1:** I had seen the way my mother had acted once before around a gay man. She turned up her nose at him. She said something about him being immoral because what he was doing was unnatural.	4. *Nevertheless, P^1 asserts that he was nervous about the interactions that might take place at the social gathering because he had observed his mother's reaction to a gay man previously and she treated him with disdain and judged him to be immoral because she assumed the man indulged in unnatural activities.
5. **I:** How did you mother know he was gay? **P^1:** Well, she didn't, really. I mean, not too many people were coming out publicly at that time, but he was really swishy and flamboyant. He was what my friends and I refer to as a "Fifi."	5. * When questioned about how his mother knew that the man she judged negatively was, in fact, gay, P^1 responds by stating that she did not really know. P^1 recalls that not many homosexuals were publicly announcing their sexual orientation at that time, but the man that his mother judged was especially blatant and manifest in behavior so that most people would make the inference that he would want to be known as gay. P^1 states that he and his friends even have a special name for gay men who are as blatant and manifest as the man was.
6. My parents thought that everyone who acted that way was gay. In this case, my mother was right, even though she was making an assumption. I knew he was gay because, well, because he had come onto me.	6. P^1 states that he was aware that his parents shared the stereotypical view that if one portrayed himself as gay, then such a person was gay. P^1 confirms that his parent was correct in this case even though it was an assumption on her part. P^1 states that he did not have to assume that the person being discussed was gay because he had made romantic advances toward P^1.
7. But I turned him down. Actually, I made a point to get away from him as fast as I could and then I avoided him after that because he was so—so affected. And I wasn't really sure if I was gay or not—then.	7. P^1 also states that he had refused the advances of the other man and even with great effort made sure that they did not connect again because P^1 thought that the man was too explicitly manifest in his homosexuality. In addition, P^1 says that he himself was not yet sure about his own sexual orientation at that time.
8. **I:** What happened next at the party? **P^1:** I showed up with my partner, who my parents knew as my roommate from college. We had been living together in a	8. P^1 relates that the next thing about the social gathering that happened was that he arrived with his partner, whom his parents would recognize as his college roommate. They had been living in an apartment next to campus in an area filled with collegians

walk-up right next to the campus. A lot of young men shared living quarters without being questioned, and my partner and I were not obvious in our behavior or dress.	and because neither P^1 nor his partner were obviously homosexual by dress or behavior they were never questioned.
9. Most of our gay friends then and now are not obvious. Who would want to draw attention to being a social outcast?	9. P^1 also states that neither he nor his partner nor most of his gay friends are manifestly homosexual. The motive that P^1 gives is that to do so is to invite social ostracism, thus revealing that P^1 is aware of the general negative attitude toward gays held by the society at large.
10. Anyway, my parents' friends pretty much hung out together by the food, and my colleagues hung out together by the drinks. There wasn't much interaction between the two groups—maybe because of the generational differences—but I think it was mostly because by colleagues made my parents and their friends uncomfortable.	10. P^1 states that there seemed to be a type of segregation at the social gathering because his parents and their friends seemed to congregate in one place (with food) whereas his peers grouped together in another place (with drinks). P^1 was aware that there wasn't much socializing between the two groups and he surmises that perhaps age differences contributed to the segregation, but P^1 believes that another important factor was that his peers made his parents and their friends feel uncomfortable.
11. **I:** Can you tell me more about this—about thinking your colleagues made your parents and their friends uncomfortable? **P^1:** One guy in particular was holding his cigarette like so (participant demonstrates) and he had his legs crossed—not like a man—like a woman.	11. *When asked by the researcher to reflect more on the sense of discomfort P^1 perceived between his parents and their friends and his peers P^1 states that there was one peer in particular who was ostentatious in his postures and gestures so that he clearly manifested feminine characteristics. P^1 was able to demonstrate these differences to the researcher.
12. **I:** Is there a difference? **P^1:** Oh yes! Men sit like this (demonstrates). and women—and Fifi's—sit like this (demonstrates). **I:** I see. So it was the gesture and the posture? **P^1:** (nods).	12. When asked by the researcher whether such a difference was discernible P^1 explicitly answers in the affirmative and demonstrated again to the researcher the differences between masculine and feminine postures and gestures and P^1 affirms that he perceived the gestures and postures to be provocative to his mother.
13. My mom reacted exactly the same way as when she had done	13. P^1 states that he observed that his mother reacted in this situation the same way that

before. She was disgusted. And angry that I might have invited someone like that. Or that I would even know someone like that. Or that I might even be like that. My parents sort of prided themselves for not having any gay friends. You know how some people will say "Some of my best friends are gay?" Well, not my parents.

she had before. He could perceive that she was disgusted and angry that her son might have invited someone to his performance who behaved in such a manner. P^1 then thought that his mother might be upset that he even might know someone with such gestures and postures. Then P^1 intensifies the thought and speculates that his mother might even come to think that he is like that. P^1 was aware that such an identification would violate his parents values because they, on the contrary, would boast that they know no such people. He relates that his parents are the opposite of people who can with confidence say that they are friendly with people who are in some sense socially stigmatized and unlike themselves.

14. Actually, one of my relatives is gay but no one from my family has associated with him for years.

14. P^1 confesses that he is aware that one of his relatives is homosexual but he is also aware of the ostracization status of that individual because no family member has associated with him for years.

15. **I:** Was it just this one person, or were there others?
P^1: Oh, yea, I guess—one guy was pretty loud—especially after a few drinks. He giggled a lot. Not laughed—giggled.

15. P^1 acknowledges that there was also another peer who stood out and was loud and who manifested feminine characteristics after drinking.

16. But the one who really stood out was the guy with the cigarette and crossed legs. And it gave me the creeps when I saw the way my mother reacted. I wanted to get out of there as fast as possible. But I was the guest of honor. I realized that I couldn't tell my parents I was gay—not yet, at any rate.

16. However, P^1 affirms that it was really the first person referred to earlier who stood out at the social gathering with his blatant effeminate gestures and postures. P^1 was upset when he saw how his mother responded to a gay person with exaggerated gestures and postures, no doubt calling to his mind the other instance he had observed. P^1's perception of his mother's response aroused the desire in him to leave the social gathering but P^1 appreciated that the whole gathering was there to honor him and thus conflicted feelings surfaced in him. The major implication for P^1 was that he realized that he could not as yet inform his parents about his sexual orientation.

17. **I:** Have you since?
P^1: I waited until I had moved

17. P^1 states that he has since informed his parents that he was homosexual, but not in

across country with my partner, as far away from them as I could get. It was around my 30th birthday. I wrote them a letter.

a face-to-face setting. P^1 waited until he moved as far away from his parents as he could with his partner, when he was well into his majority, and then he told them by letter.

18. At first, my mother pretended she never got the letter. She would call and ask if I'd met any nice women.

18. P^1 states that his mother seems to choose to deny the knowledge about his homosexuality because she never acknowledged receiving the letter, and even more boldly, she would ask P^1 if he had met any eligible women.

19. My partner and I had a ceremony last year to affirm our commitment to each other, and my mother said I chose to become gay. Both my parents said I should rethink my lifestyle decision. We haven't spoken since.

19. P^1 states that he and his partner confirmed their sexual orientation and relationship with a ceremony the intent of which was to reaffirm their commitment to each other. P^1 then relates that it is his mother's impression that his gay status was a result of a free choice and thus she believes that he can rethink and change his lifestyle decision. P^1 adds that they have not spoken since that discussion.

20. **I:** Back to the party—what did you feel when you saw your mother react?
P^1: Embarrassment—for the way my colleague was acting. And shame—at my mother for her reaction—and at myself, I guess.

20. * In returning to a discussion of the social gathering, P^1 states that when he saw his mother's reaction to the exaggerated gestures and postures, he felt embarrassed as a consequence of the gay man who was behaving that way, especially because it was not P^1's own way of owning homosexual identity. Moreover, he felt shame in front of his mother because he could tell that she was not open to a different way of being sexual. Finally, P^1 expressed some shame with respect to himself, he surmises, perhaps indicating some acceptance of the attitude of society at large with respect to homosexuals.

21. You know, I experience internalized homophobia quite often. I can't be around a Fifi. And there are times when I guess that's part of why I continue to see my therapist on a weekly basis. My partner and I go to see a therapist together, but I see one on my own—to deal with issues like this. It's not always there, but it's never going

21. P^1 verbalizes that he experiences "internalized homophobia" frequently, but that may not be the best expression for his feelings. He gives the example of exaggerated and manifest gays, but it seems to be more the style that is antipathetic to P^1 than the fact of homosexuality. He also admits that there are situations in which he does not reveal his homosexuality, but he does not clarify further.

to go away—until other people get over their homophobia.

22. P^1 states that he hates himself for not always revealing his sexual orientation, but again it is not clear that the lack of revelation constitutes homophobia. P^1 hypothesizes that perhaps those feelings are the reason why he sees a therapist on his own in addition to seeing a therapist with his partner, also on a weekly basis. P^1 claims that his solitary therapeutic appointments are to deal with alleged "internalized homophobia." Still P^1 offers the opinion that although the feeling is not always with him, he guesses that it will never go away until nongays get over their homophobia. This seems to be an acknowledgment that it is not so much a "phobia" that P^1 is responding to as actual feelings of bias against homosexuals by the society at large.

Interview Participant 2

1. I was really competitive and successful in high school until I decided to get involved in politics. I was running for senior class president.

1. P^2 states that in many ways he was a full-fledged successful typical high school student freely participating in high school activities until he decided to enter politics at the high school level by aspiring to become the chief representative for his class. This would be a position in which P^2 would really stand out.

2. I was pretty active in some gay-related activities but didn't openly admit to being gay. Why should I? After all, a lot of people—straight people—were involved in celebrating diversity.

2. P^2 states that at the time he made the decision to become politically active he was involved in some gay-related activities but he did not admit to being gay to the public at large. P^2 did not see any reason why he should divulge his sexual orientation because he was aware that many people were involved in celebrating diversity and his involvement took place under that rubric. That is, P^2 took advantage of a situation that allowed him to keep his sexual identity undisclosed.

3. My opponent in the class elections found out I was gay. I can't remember how. . . but he used that to his advantage. He de-

3. P^2 states that his opponent for the position of chief representative of his class, in a way unknown to him, found out that P^2 was gay and used that information to his (i.e., the

manded I withdraw from the elections or else he would expose me.	opponent's) advantage. The opponent demanded that P^2 drop from the race for chief representative of his class or else he would announce publicly that P^2 was a homosexual. Explicitly or not, the opponent used his awareness of the prejudices against gays by the population at large as a means of gaining unfair advantage over P^2 and the threat was real enough for P^2 to terminate his ambition. It seems that P^2's response was not phobic but realistic.
4. I wasn't ready to be openly gay. So, I dropped out of the race. Too bad.	4. P^2 states that at that time he was not ready to publicly announce his homosexuality so he withdrew from the election race. P^2 expresses disappointing sentiments probably reflecting his own awareness of his competency for the office.
5. I know I would have been a good representative for my class. But I couldn't risk being ridiculed or attacked. I was ashamed of my decision, but I was more ashamed of being gay.	5. P^2 states with some confidence that he knew that he could have been a good representative for his class, but he felt that he could not risk being exposed to psychological or physical harm. P^2 says that he was ashamed of his decision, probably reflecting a disappointment that he would not stand behind his actual identity, but then states that he was more ashamed of being actually identified as gay, possibly because of his awareness of the stereotypical social attitude of the population at large toward gays. This is a possible moment when P^2 is accepting and identifying with the attitudes of the general population toward gays
6. I also stopped hanging out with my gay friends from outside the school. I had been active in a gay-friendly group from the Catholic Church, and volunteered once a week at the Food Bank which was specifically for people living with AIDS.	6. P^2 states that he also ceased associating with his gay friends outside the center of his life space. He had been active with gay-friendly groups related to church and charitable organizations. It seems that the impact of possible exposure had a withdrawal effect on P^2.
7. But I stopped going. I made excuses for not showing up. My therapist says it's typical—dropping out in order to hide from exposure. Exposure makes	7. P^2 reiterates that he stopped all extracurricular gay activity. He did not admit the true reasons for his withdrawal but made excuses for his cessation of helping activity. P^2 relates that his therapist helped P^2 under-

you vulnerable to ridicule and violence.

stand that his withdrawal was a typical strategic response to the risk of exposure of his sexual identity. He was aware that exposure made P^2 vulnerable to possible physical and psychological harm.

8. No one called to follow up. At first I was angry but then I realized the people from the church and from the Food Bank probably understood more than I about respect and confidentiality.

8. P^2 states that no colleague associated with his extracurricular activity called to inquire about his absence. Initially, this angered P^2, but over time it dawned on P^2 that his coworkers probably understood more about the difficulties surrounding being gay and hence they showed greater respect and sensitivity to issues of confidentiality than he at first realized and he came to appreciate their stance.

9. I'm pretty open now, but only in certain situations. I do this volunteer crisis line counseling once a week which, now that I think about it, probably helps me deal with issues of my own that I don't recognize in myself until after I hear about them from someone else who has had a similar experience.

9. P^2 states that he is more open now, but still only in restricted situations. This restriction to partial openness seems to be a reflection of genuine fear on the part of P^2 rather than anything phobic. P^2 now has committed himself to a type of volunteer crisis counseling that he now realizes probably helps him deal with many of his own issues concerning homosexuality. Often P^2 only recognizes the personal relevancy of the issues after talking about them with others who have had a similar experience.

10. I am grateful to have a committed relationship. We don't go to the bars. We have a few good friends, who are also in committed relationships.

10. P^2 states that he is thankful for being in a committed relationship with someone who seems to share his values. P^2 and his partner do not go to bars and they are able to socialize with other gay friends who are also in committed relationships. This type of social life minimizes the threat of exposure to those to whom he does not wish to reveal his genuine sexual orientation.

11. We would like to think we live pretty normal lives—but I don't think we ever will. I guess I'm still pretty scared about what might happen if I'm really open about being gay, especially with the hate crimes that keep happening.

11. P^2 states that he and his partner are aware that they have achieved a relative sense of normal living, but P^2 is skeptical about ever achieving an indistinguishable normalcy. P^2 still harbors genuine fears about a full and open acknowledgment of his homosexuality and he cites as factors for these fears the hate crimes that are still being carried out against homosexuals that often make the news.

Appendix 13.3. The Structure of the Experience of Being the Recipient of Socially Negative Judgments and Consequences on the Part of Nonpublicly Declared Homosexual Males by the Heterosexual World

For P, who is a homosexual who has not publicly declared his true sexual identity, the possibility of being the recipient of socially negative judgments or harmful consequences is experienced as a constant horizonal threat that induces feelings of emotional ambivalence, unsafety, and the curtailing of desires. There is genuine fear of premature and undesired full exposure of one's sexual orientation before significant others as well as a segment of the population at large. The risk of physical or psychological harm as a result of open declaration is also constantly present. Part of the ambivalence that is felt is a result of the participant's recognition that despite potential negative consequences, the person's authentic sexual orientation is homosexual and thus remaining undeclared feels inauthentic. The perceived lack of the possibility of being sexually authentically oneself and yet retain the approval of significant others, the society at large, intimates, seems perennially to place the person at the center of disharmonious feelings, including momentary acceptance of the judgments of the society at large.

References

Cloonan, T. (1995). The early history of phenomenological psychological research in America. *Journal of Phenomenological Psychology, 26,* 46–126.

Giorgi, A. (Ed.). (1985). *Phenomenology and psychological research.* Pittsburgh, PA: Duquesne University Press.

Giorgi, A. (1986). Theoretical justification for the use of descriptions in psychological research. In P. Ashworth, A. Giorgi, & A. deKoning (Eds.), *Qualitative research in psychology* (pp. 3–22). Pittsburgh, PA: Duquesne University Press.

Giorgi, A. (1987a). Problems in self-descriptive research as exemplified in a phenomenological analysis of imaginative experiences. In F. J. van Zuuren, F. Wertz, & B. Mook (Eds.), *Advances in qualitative research* (pp. 41–51). Lisse, Belgium: Swets & Zeitlinger.

Giorgi, A. (1987b). Phenomenology and the research tradition in the psychology of the imagination. In E. L. Murray (Ed.), *Imagination and phenomenological psychology* (pp. 1–47). Pittsburgh, PA: Duquesne University Press.

Giorgi, A. (1989a). An example of harmony between descriptive reports and behavior. *Journal of Phenomenological Psychology, 20,* 60–88.

Giorgi, A. (1989b). One type of analysis of descriptive data: Procedures involved in following a scientific phenomenological method. *Methods, 1*(3), 39–61.

Giorgi, A. (1989c). Some theoretical and practical issues regarding the psychological phenomenological method. *Saybrook Review, 7*(2), 71–85.

Giorgi, A. (1992). Description versus interpretation: Competing alternative strategies for qualitative research. *Journal of Phenomenological Psychology, 23,* 119–135.

Giorgi, A. (1994). A phenomenological perspective on certain qualitative research methods. *Journal of Phenomenological Psychology, 25,* 190–220.

Giorgi, A. (1997). The theory, practice and evaluation of the phenomenological method as a qualitative research procedure. *Journal of Phenomenological Psychology, 28,* 235–260.

Graumann, C. F. (1960). *Grundlagen einer phänomenologie und psychologie der perspektivität* (Foundations of phenomenology and psychology of perspectivity). Berlin: de Gruter.

Heidegger, M. (1962) *Being and time* (Trans. J. Macquarrie & E. Robinson). New York: Harper & Row. (Original published 1927)

Husserl, E. (1970) *Logical investigations I & II* (Trans. J. N. Findlay). New York: Humanities Press. (Original work published 1900)

Husserl, E. (1977). *Phenomenological psychology* (Trans. J. Scanlon). The Hague: Nijhoff. (Original published 1962)

Husserl, E. (1983). *Ideas pertaining to a pure phenomenology and to a phenomenological philosophy I* (Trans. F. Kersten). The Hague: Nijhoff. (Original published 1913)

Kuenzli, A. (Ed.). (1959). *The phenomenological problem.* New York: Harper.

Linschoten, J. (1968). *On the way toward a phenomenological psychology.* Pittsburgh, PA: Duquesne University Press.

MacDonald, P. S. (2001). Husserl's preemptive responses to existentialist critiques. *Indo-Pacific Journal of Phenomenology, 1,* 1–22.

Merleau-Ponty, M. (1962). *The phenomenology of perception* (Trans. C. Smith). New York: Humanities Press. (Original published 1945)

Merleau-Ponty, M. (1964). Phenomenology and the sciences of man (Trans. J. Wild). In J. Edie (Ed.) *The primacy of perception* (pp. 43–95). Evanston, IL: Northwestern University Press. (Original published 1962)

Moustakas, C. (1994). *Phenomenological research methods.* Thousand Oaks, CA: Sage.

Sartre, J-P. (1956). *Being and nothingness* (Trans. H. Barnes). New York: Philosophical Library. (Original published 1943)

Sartre, J-P. (1962). *Sketch for a theory of the emotions* (Trans. P. Mariet). London: Methuen. (Original published 1939)

Sartre, J-P. (1966). *The psychology of imagination.* New York: Citadel Press. (Original work published 1940)

Scanlon, J. (1977). Translator's introduction. In E. Husserl, *Phenomenological psychology* (pp. ix–xv). The Hague: Nijhoff.

Snygg, D. (1935). The relative difficulty of mechanically equivalent tasks: I Human learning. *Journal of Genetic Psychology, 47,* 299–320.

Snygg, D. (1941). The need for a phenomenological system of psychology. *Psychological Review, 48,* 404–424.

Snygg, D., & Combs, A. W. (1949). *Individual behavior.* New York: Harper.

Sorenson-Englander, K. (2000). *Alleged "internalized homophobia" as experienced among homosexual men: A phenomenological psychological analysis.* Unpublished master's thesis, Saybrook Graduate School, San Francisco.

Spiegelberg, H. (1964). Phenomenology through vicarious experience. In E. Straus (Ed.), *Phenomenology: Pure and applied. The first Lexington Conference* (pp. 105–126). Pittsburgh PA: Duquesne University Press.

Spiegelberg, H. (1982). *The phenomenological movement* (3rd ed.). The Hague: Nijhoff.

Wann, T. W. (1964). *Behaviorism and phenomenology: Contrasting bases for modern psychology.* Chicago: University of Chicago Press.

14

The Psychoanalytical Interview as Inspiration for Qualitative Research

Steinar Kvale

A qualitative research wave has swept through the social sciences in the past decades. Interviews, textual analyses, and natural observations have come into widespread use as modes of inquiry. The qualitative research movement is interdisciplinary, and an opening of the social sciences to the humanities has taken place, drawing on hermeneutics as well as narrative, discursive, conversational, and linguistic forms of analysis.

The science of psychology has until recently remained outside the qualitative research movement. This is rather odd, because key modes of qualitative research, such as the interview, work through human interrelationships, which are the subject matter of psychology. In addition, substantial areas of current psychological knowledge were initially brought forth through qualitative interviews. In particular this pertains to Freud's psychoanalytical interview, which has also inspired subsequent interview research. Piaget's interviews of children's thought and Adorno and collegues' interviews about the authoritarian personality illustrate this point. The Hawthorne interviews with industrial workers and the consumer interviews by Dichter were also inspired by the psychoanalytical interview.

In an attempt to advance psychological interview research today, I take these historical interview inquiries as a point of departure. Rather than follow the methodological and paradigmatic direction of the qualitative research wave, I pursue a pragmatic approach, taking the significant knowledge produced by psychoanalytical and other psychological interviews as a basis for this endeavor. Pointing to the paradox that knowledge originally produced by qualitative interviews has become generally accepted but the interview method producing this knowledge has generally been rejected, I also address the methodological marginalization of qualitative research in psychology. In the concluding section I outline two different therapeutic and academic paths of interview research by addressing questions about human interrelations and methodology, about objectivity of knowledge and ethical tensions, which arise when treating therapeutic interviews as research inquiries.

The Psychological Significance of the Psychoanalytical Interview

In this section I shall point out the significance of knowledge produced in psychoanalytical interviews, within psychology as well as in culture at large. I then outline seven key aspects of the psychoanalytical interview, which may contribute to its richness in providing new knowledge. Finally, I mention some problems with psychoanalytical interview research.

The Significance of Psychoanalytically Produced Knowledge

A century after its inception, psychoanalysis still has a professional impact on psychotherapy, continues to be of interest to the general public and to other sciences and to represent a challenge to philosophers. Psychoanalysis has throughout the history of psychology contributed strongly to generating research, and its concepts have been assimilated into the mainstream of psychology and into the larger culture. Central themes in current textbooks of psychology are based on knowledge originally derived from psychoanalytical interviews, for example regarding dreams and neurosis, sexuality, childhood development and personality, anxiety and motivation, defense mechanisms, and unconscious forces. To give a quantitative indication of the pervasive influence of psychoanalysis, it can be pointed out that the *Encyclopedia of Psychology* (Corsini, 1994) contains more than twice as many references to Freud than to any of the other pioneers producing psychological knowledge, such as Wundt, Pavlov, Watson, Piaget, or Skinner.

The significant knowledge generation of psychoanalysis is not confined to Freud's original insights. Later psychoanalysts, such as Jung and Adler, Fromm and Horney, Erickson and Rollo May, continued to produce important knowledge of the human situation through their therapeutic interviews. Also the current focus on a "narcissistic" personality and culture, a clinical term developed theoretically by Freud, originated with clinical descriptions from the psychoanalytical interviews of Kohut, Kernberg, and Mitscherlich in the 1960s.

Key Aspects of Psychoanalytical Interview Research

The psychoanalytical interview is usually treated as a therapeutic method in psychology, and its therapeutic efficiency is a matter of controversy. In this section I address the psychoanalytical therapeutic interview as a method of research.

The focus is on the concrete descriptive and interpretative knowledge derived from the psychoanalytical situation, what Klein (1973) has termed the "clinical theory" of psychoanalysis. The present approach is inspired by the existential and the critical hermeneutic interpretations of psychoanalytical therapy by Boss (1963) and Habermas (1971), respectively. Both scholars analyze the mode of understanding of the psychoanalytical situation while dismissing Freud's speculative metapsychological theories. For sake of simplicity in this chapter, I will disregard other schools in the psychoanalytical tradition, as well as later therapies—such as client-centered therapy, family and system therapy—and limit the discussion to the case of Freud's classical psychoanalysis, as a result of its historical priority and theoretical significance.

To Freud, the psychoanalytical interview was not only a method of treatment for neurotic disorders; it was also "a procedure for the investigation of mental processes which are almost inaccessible in any other way" (1923/1964, p. 235). In psychoanalysis there is an inseparable bond between cure and research: "It is indeed one of the distinctions of psychoanalysis that research and treatment proceed hand in hand" (Freud, 1963, p. 120). In Exhibit 14.1 I outline seven key aspects of the psychoanalytical interview relevant to understanding its potential as a research situation. These key aspects are derived from Freud's writings on therapy and technique (1963), and they have been discussed in an earlier context (Kvale, 1999a).

The seven aspects of the mode of understanding of the psychoanalytical research interview depicted in Exhibit 14.1 have been commonly regarded as merely practical aspects of the therapeutic technique or as sources of error for a scientific research method. The mode of understanding of the psychoanalytical interview falls outside of a conception of psychological science as seeking objective knowledge in the form of unequivocal, immutable, and quantifiable facts through impersonal, standardized, and repeatable observations. From the present perspective it is the very aspects of the psychoanalytical interview depicted earlier that have led to its rejection as a scientific method, that contribute to the significant psychoanalytical knowledge production about the human situation and its philosophical relevance today.

The mode of understanding in the psychoanalytical interview is in important aspects close to conceptions of knowledge developed within existential, hermeneutical, and postmodern philosophy (Kvale, 1999a, 1999b). From these philosophical positions the key human aspects of therapeutic interviews are seen as pivotal for obtaining penetrating knowledge of the human situation, rather than as sources of error in the quest for objective facts. The case study, coming again to the fore in social science research, is congruent with the emphasis on situated knowledge and the philosophical interest in casuistry. Understanding the interview as a mode of research corresponds with the hermeneutical and neopragmatic focus on the conversation as the locus of knowledge. The importance of interpretation of meaning brings psychoanalysis close to the hermeneutical tradition, where it has been addressed as a "depth hermeneutics" and as a "hermeneutics of suspicion." The interrelational base of psychoanalytical knowledge production is congruent with the relational approach of phenomenology and of social constructionism, where the individual is replaced by the relationship as the locus of knowledge. The importance of changing the patient's understanding and behavior corresponds with a dialectical and pragmatic emphasis on the intertwinement of knowing and acting. Knowledge grows out of action and is again validated by its impact on practice. External legitimation of knowledge by appeals to some grand metanarratives is then replaced by a focus on the impact of the knowledge. In colloquial language: The proof of the pudding is in the eating.

Exhibit 14.1. The Mode of Understanding of the Psychoanalytic Research Interview

The individual case study. Psychoanalytical therapy is an intensive case study of individual patients over several years that allows for multiple observations and repeated controls of observations and interpretations of the patients statements and behavior.

The open mode of interviewing. The psychoanalytical interview takes place in the structured setting of the therapeutic hour and proceeds in an open, often indirect, manner. The patients' "free associations" correspond with the therapist's "evenly hovering attention" in which one proceeds "aimlessly, and allows oneself to be overtaken by any surprises, always presenting to them an open mind, free from any expectations" (Freud, 1963, p. 120).

The interpretation of meaning. An essential aspect of psychoanalytical technique is interpretation of the meaning of the patients' statements and behavior. The therapeutic interpretations are open to ambiguity and contradictions, and to the multiple layers of meaning of a dream or a symptom.

The temporal dimension. Psychoanalytical therapy unfolds over several years in a historical dimension. Freud's innovation of seeing neurotic disturbances in a meaningful biographical perspective provided the therapist with a uniquely rich context for interpreting the patients' dreams and their neurotic symptoms.

The human interaction. Psychoanalytical therapy takes place through an emotional human interrelation, with a reciprocal personal involvement. The emotional transference is used by the therapist as a means to overcome the resistance offered to the therapist when attempting to make the patient's unconscious conscious to him or her. The psychoanalysts do not seek to eliminate their own feelings toward their patients but to use this "countertransference" in the therapeutic process as a reflected subjectivity.

Pathology as topic of investigation. The subject matter of psychoanalytical therapy is the abnormal and irrational behavior of patients in crisis. The pathological behavior provides a magnifying glass for the less visible conflicts of average individuals; the neuroses and psychoses are extreme versions of normal behavior, of what has gone wrong in a given culture.

The instigation of change. The mutual interest of patient and therapist is to overcome the patients' suffering from their neurotic symptoms. Despite the patients having sought treatment voluntarily, they exhibit a deeply seated resistance toward changing their self-understanding and behavior. Although understanding may lead to change, the implicit theory of knowledge in psychoanalysis is that a fundamental understanding of a phenomenon is first to be obtained by attempting to change the phenomenon.

Source. Adapted from Kvale (1999a). Copyright © 1999 by Sage Publications. Reprinted by permission of Sage Publications.

Some Problems With Psychoanalytical Research

Pointing out the importance of the knowledge produced by psychoanalytical interviews does not imply a global endorsement of psychoanalytical theory, with its many speculative postulates and trends of individualizing, infantilizing, and sexualizing human activity. Nor does it imply an *in toto* acceptance of psychoanalytical case and interview research, which is beset with a multitude of methodological pitfalls. There are many problems with the private nature of psychoanalytical observations, the lack of systematic recordings, and particularly with overgeneralizations from selected cases. It should, though, be noted that overgeneralizations to normal human behavior in natural settings, whether they come from pathological clinical cases or from artificial laboratory experiments, are inherent dangers for the ecological validity of psychological research. The fact that such overgeneralizations occur does not, however, in general invalidate clinical interviews or laboratory experiments as psychological research methods.

The present analysis suggests that therapists need not always look for other research methods, but may stick to the craft of interviewing, in which they already have expertise with techniques of questioning and interpretation of meaning and use the unique knowledge potentials of the therapeutic situation for research purposes. This does not imply a carte blanche for any therapist to declare oneself a researcher and uncritically produce convincing case stories, a danger that recently has been brought to attention by court cases about therapeutic production of false memories of child abuse (see, e.g., Acocella, 1998). On the contrary, the importance of personal and theoretical training of classical psychoanalysts, as well as knowledge of the methodological pitfalls of the case method and the relevance of linguistic and textual analyses from the humanities all put extra demands on the expertise of therapeutic researchers.

The psychoanalytical case study may today be reappraised in the light of current methodological developments of the case method (see, e.g., Frommer & Rennie, 2001; McCleod, 2001). The psychoanalytical inquiries may also be combined with other modes of inquiry. For instance, the psychoanalyst Stern (1985) has investigated infants' experience of their world by drawing on his direct observations of infant behavior and on therapists' reports of patients' remembrances of their childhood. In addition, therapists may use their own therapeutic cases, for example on anorexia, as research material in combination with the patients' diaries, questionnaires, and research interviews with the patients, conducted by the therapist and by colleagues, and also draw on the cultural attitudes toward eating and fasting as found in literature, painting, and advertisements, and even venture into literary modes of presentation (e.g., Skårderud, 2000). A flexible use of multiple research strategies may contribute to overcome some of the overinterpretations and overgeneralizations from therapeutic case studies.

Few therapists today appear aware of the research potentials of the clinical case study, and in their PhD dissertations they apply statistical and experimental designs to the clinical domain, sometimes with a fervor reminding of an "identification with the aggressor." Recent therapies, such as family therapy, have produced a number of significant and clinically relevant studies for practitioners. However, this therapeutic research has not been widely recognized and tends not to be regarded as "true" research, even by clinicians, as pointed out by Chenail and others (Atkinson, Heath, & Chenail, 1991; Chenail, 1992). The present chapter may be seen as an attempt at self-assertion therapy for the therapeutic researchers' low self-esteem concerning the knowledge potentials of their therapeutic practice.

I shall now turn from the negligence of the research potentials of the therapeutic interview in current clinical psychology to the inspiration the psychoanalytical interview has provided to major investigations within academic and commercial psychology.

Two ways out of this therapeutic research paradox emerge. One solution would be to follow up the methodological censorship of the psychoanalytical research interview to also censor the knowledge it has generated, and ban all psychoanalytically produced knowledge from textbooks of psychological science. An alternative solution, pursued in this chapter, is to regard the psychoanalytical interview as one among many psychological research methods, and investigate its research potentials.

Psychoanalytically Inspired Academic Interview Research

Interview researchers in psychology need not necessarily cross the border to the other social sciences and the humanities and import the latest methods and paradigms of the qualitative wave. By sticking to their own trade, psychologists may find many of the necessary interview tools within their own therapeutic backyard.

The psychoanalytical therapeutic interview has inspired major investigations in the history of academic and commercial psychology. In this section I discuss two academic interview investigations: Piaget's interviews with children and Adorno and colleagues' interviews with authoritarian personalities.

Piaget's Interviews on Children's Thought

Piaget was a trained biologist who was interested in epistemology. As a means of understanding the human acquisition of knowledge he instigated innovative studies of children's thought. He let the children talk spontaneously about the weight and size of objects and noticed the manner in which their thoughts unfolded, using a combination of naturalistic observations, interviews, simple tests, and quasiexperimental designs.

Piaget's early work was inspired by psychoanalysis; he undertook a training analysis, briefly analyzed some patients, and joined the Swiss Psychoanalytic Society (see Litowitz, 1999). His paper on "Symbolic Thought and the Thought of the Child" (1923), presented at the Seventh Congress of Psychoanalysis in Berlin, starts with drawing analogies between the thought of the child and the forms of symbolic thought uncovered by Freud's and Jung's psychoanalysis. In line with the psychoanalytical practice of taking the abnormal behavior of the patients seriously, and searching for the underlying structure of irrational thought, Piaget—working with Simon on the development of intelligence tests—had focused on what the children answered incorrectly and the reasons they gave for the wrong answers, believing that the errors might reveal the underlying structure of children's thought. His "clinical method" was inspired by the psychoanalytical interview:

> If we follow up each of the child's answers, and then, allowing him to take the lead, induce him to talk more and more freely, we shall gradually establish for every department of intelligence a method of clinical analysis analogous to that which has been adopted by psychiatrists as a means of diagnosis. (Piaget, 1923, p. 276; see also the preface by Clarapède in Piaget, 1926/1971)

Piaget became later more critical of psychoanalysis, while continuing to enter into dialogue with psychoanalysts and to write in psychoanalytical journals. In current textbook accounts of Piaget's research, and in the many investigations it has instigated, the experimental aspect has been dominant, whereas the clinical interviewing approach and its psychoanalytical inspiration is rarely mentioned.

The Authoritarian Personality Study by Adorno and Colleagues

Psychoanalytical interviews in Germany in the 1930s had uncovered an authoritarian personality syndrome. In the work by Fromm, Horkheimer, Marcuse, and others (Fromm, Horkheimer, Mayer, & Marcuse, 1936) at the Frankfurt Institute of Social Research this authoritarian syndrome was traced to the social and family structures giving rise to fascism. Adorno and colleagues followed up the German psychoanalytical and Marxist analyses of anti-Semitism in a large-scale research project in the United States on the relationship of personality and prejudice: *The Authoritarian Personality* (Adorno, Frenkel-Brunswick, Levinson, & Sanford, 1950/1993).

The theoretical impetus for the study came from psychoanalysis. Methodologically, the project was an innovative combination of clinical interviews and questionnaires; the inspiration from psychoanalysis appears in the interview chapter of *The Authoritarian Personality.* The best way to approximate an adequate view of the whole person, according to this view, is through the freedom of expression the interview offered, because it permitted inference of the deeper layers of the research participants' personalities underlying an antidemocratic ideology. The indirect interview technique with a flexible interview schedule consisted of "manifest questions" as suggestions for the interviewer to pose to throw light on the "underlying questions," derived from the project's theoretical framework. These underlying questions had to be concealed from the research participant so that undue defenses would not be established through the participants' recognition of the real focus of the interview. The authors emphasized the training of their interviewers; close to half had undergone psychoanalysis. The interviews were analyzed qualitatively in relationship to the theoretical framework of the study and they were used as a basis for individual case studies. The interview results were compared with the findings from the questionnaires, and the interviews also served to check on the validity of the questionnaires.

The quantitative findings and the construction of the questionnaires, in particular the Fascism scale, have dominated the psychological reception of *The Authoritarian Personality.* The extensive interview procedures—in the book treated on an equal level with the questionnaires—have hardly been noted in later psychological reports. A footnote in the concluding chapter, indicating that a sensitive observer of the human situation may arrive at similar results as a large-scale psychological research project, has also gone unnoticed:

> There is a marked similarity between the syndrome which we have labeled the authoritarian personality and "the portrait of the anti-Semite" by Jean-

> Paul Sartre. Sartre's brilliant paper became available to us after all our data had been collected and analyzed. That this phenomenological "portrait" should resemble so closely, both in general structure and in numerous details, the syndrome which slowly emerged from our empirical observations and quantitative analyses, seems to us remarkable. (p. 475; see also Hannush, 1973; Sartre, 1946/1965; note also Sartre's reflections on his method as an existential mediation of psychoanalysis and Marxism: Sartre, 1963)

Psychoanalytically Inspired Commercial Interview Research

I shall now turn to two historical studies of commercial psychology, which were also inspired by the psychoanalytical interview. Their objective was to increase efficiency and profits in the domains of production and consumption—the Hawthorne studies of human relations in industry and the motivational consumer interviews as pioneered by Dichter.

The Hawthorne Interviews on Human Relations in Industry

The investigations at the Hawthorne Chicago plant of the Western Electrical Company in the 1920s have had a major impact on later industrial production by instigating changes from a human engineering to a human relations approach to the control of workers. Experiments on the effects of changes in illumination on production led to unexpected results: Work output and morale improved when the lighting of the production rooms was increased, as well as when it was decreased.

To investigate the reasons for the bewildering experimental findings, the workers were interviewed, and the results suggested that the management's display of human interest to the workers could be a key factor in increasing their morale and industrial output. The unforeseen findings were followed up in what may have been the largest interview inquiry ever conducted: *Management and the Worker* (Roethlisberger & Dickson, 1939/1964). More than 21,000 workers were each interviewed for more than an hour and the interview transcripts analyzed qualitatively and quantitatively. The purpose of the study, which was initiated by the psychologist Mayo, was to improve industrial supervision. In a sophisticated methods chapter, interviewing is presented as a new mode of industrial research, inspired by clinical psychology and anthropology. The authors mention the influence of Janet, Freud, Jung, and in particular Piaget, whose clinical method of interviewing children they found particularly useful.

In their indirect clinical interviews Roethlisberger and Dickson recognized that the social relationship existing between the interviewer and the workers in part determined what was said. The interviewers allowed their workers to speak spontaneously and they did not limit themselves to the manifest content of the intercourse, listened not only to what the workers wanted to say but also to what they did not want to say, and did not treat all that was said as either fact or error. For this type of interviewing Roethlisberger and Dickson regarded several years of training as requisite to become a proficient interviewer. In later psychological accounts of the study's findings about human relations in industrial production, the experimental designs dominate and the study's more than 21,000 interviews are seldom mentioned.

Market Interviews and Focus Groups

The design and advertisements of consumer products are today investigated by quantitative and qualitative approaches, the latter particularly in the form of focus groups. Dichter reported in *The Strategy of Desire* (1960) a pioneer study he conducted in 1939 on consumer motivation for purchasing a car. It was based on case stories, with more than 100 detailed conversational interviews. His indirect interviewing technique encouraged the respondents to talk freely about a subject, rather than to answer "yes" or "no" to a question. He depicted his interview technique as inspired by the investigations of psychoanalysts and termed it a "depth interview," attempting to go beneath the surface and to discover real motivations. According to Dichter, the study's uncovering of the symbolic meanings of cars and the hidden motivations for driving a car decisively changed the marketing of automobiles. Although giving a detailed and sensitive presentation of the depth interview technique, the overall design of Dichter's motivational interviews was less systematic than in the Hawthorne studies.

Today, combinations of qualitative interviews and questionnaires play a major role in the prediction and control of consumer behavior. Probably a major part of qualitative research interviewing today takes place within market research; for example in the year 1990 more than 110,000 focus groups were conducted (Greenbaum, 1998). The extensive use of qualitative research interviews in market psychology today is hardly recognized in textbooks on psychological methodology.

What Can Be Learned From Therapeutic and Therapeutically Inspired Interviews?

The historical interview studies reviewed previously suggest that psychological interview researchers today need not reinvent the wheel but may learn from classic psychological interview inquiries in the therapeutic, academic, and commercial domains. I shall here first summarize some features of these studies in relation to the seven aspects of the psychoanalytical interview outlined in Exhibit 14.1, and thereafter consider the broader style of psychoanalytical research, with an emphasis on the training, the theory, and the culture of the interviewer.

Seven Aspects of Psychoanalytical Interviews Revisited

The psychoanalytical interview has provided direct inspiration for open and indirect interview techniques and for the interpretations of meaning of later interview inquiries. The *open mode of interviewing* was a common characteristic of the four interview studies discussed earlier; it allowed the research participants to talk freely, rather than reacting to predetermined standard questions. (When *Time* magazine selected for their 2000 anniversary issue the "top 20 scientists and thinkers" influencing the culture of the 20th century, two psychologists were included—Freud [featured on the cover with Einstein, surrounded by Milton Keynes, Jonas Salk, and Rachel Carson] and Piaget. In the biographical text Freud's and Piaget's ability to patiently listen to and observe their clients' behavior was emphasized as essential traits of their research.) The mode of questioning was not totally nondirective; the manifest questions posed to the interviewees could be derived from underlying theoretical questions.

The interview inquiries were directed toward the *interpretation of meaning,* unfolding the complexities of the participants' answers, and not forging them into predetermined categories for subsequent quantification. The studies entailed a tolerance for ambiguity; rather than seeking unequivocal facts, they listened not only to what a person manifestly said but also to what a person did not want to say. However, it should be noted that, in these classical psychological studies, little was reported about the methods used for analyzing the interviews.

Psychological interview researchers may in this respect learn from the methods of textual analysis of the humanities, as these are now being applied in the qualitative research of the other social sciences (see, e.g., Denzin & Lincoln, 2000).

With regard to *pathology,* though this was not the topic of the four interview studies, they were all open to the nonrational elements of their participants' answers. Piaget thus directed his interviews toward the errors in the children's thought, and the Adorno group addressed the unconscious defenses of the authoritarian personalities interviewed. The Hawthorne investigators refrained from treating all that was said as either fact or error, and Dichter studied unconscious and irrational motives of consumer behavior.

We thus find a direct inspiration from psychoanalysis in the four interview inquiries discussed regarding the open and indirect mode of interviewing, the interpretation of meaning, and of taking apparently irrational interview answers seriously—"If this is madness, there is method in it."

Psychoanalytical research is predominantly based on therapeutic interview *case studies.* The four later interview inquiries discussed were to a considerable extent case studies, characterized by a methodological eclecticism in which interviews were applied as one among several methods used—including natural observations, experiments, tests, and questionnaires—to unravel the meaning of the phenomena investigated. The studies went beyond the single-subject case to encompass a larger number of interviewees; Freud and Piaget reported observations from multiple patients and children, both the authoritarian personality study and the Dichter's motivational consumer study included more than 100 interviews, and the Hawthorne study more than 21,000 interviews.

It may be noted that in the light of these historical interview studies some dichotomies—such as quantitative versus qualitative, and exploratory versus hypothesis testing—of current paradigmatic debates dissolve into pseudo issues. Thus neither quantitative nor qualitative techniques were treated as more scientific or more legitimate; they rather served as different and supplementary tools to obtain different forms of knowledge about the phenomena of interest. The other current dichotomy also absent in these studies was the conception of qualitative inquiries as merely an exploratory prelude to subsequent scientific questionnaire and experimental investigations. In the authoritarian personality study one of the uses of the qualitative interviews was to validate the findings from the questionnaires. The many interviews of the Hawthorne study were conducted *after* the original experiments, to explain the unexpected experimental findings about the effects of illumination on work.

Some of the key aspects of the psychoanalytical interview outlined earlier were not transferable to the academic and commercial interview inquiries discussed, such as the extended *temporal dimension* of several years with the intense emotional *human interaction* of the psychoanalytical interview and the *instigation of changes* in the persons interviewed. Ethical dilemmas involved by a transfer of such aspects of the psychoanalytical interview to research settings is addressed in the concluding section of this chapter.

It is paradoxical that, within the discipline of psychology, some of the most lasting and penetrating knowledge of the human situation has been produced as a side-effect of therapeutically helping patients to change their lives. One implication of the knowledge potentials of the therapeutic situation may be a move from treating professional practice merely as the application of scientific theories toward also regarding professional practice as a powerful site for producing knowledge of the human situation. There are scholars today who take practitioners' knowledge serious in its own right, often inspired by postmodern and pragmatic philosophy (e.g., Fishman, 1999; Gergen, 1994; Polkinghorne, 1992; Schön, 1987). A rehabilitation of professional practice as a site of psychological knowledge production need not necessarily lead to an unreflective practicism devoid of theory; the history of psychoanalysis testifies to the possibility of theorizing from the therapeutic situation.

The Training, the Theory, and the Culture of the Interviewer

Psychoanalytical research goes beyond the seven aspects of the psychoanalytical interview situation discussed in this chapter. They are subordinate to a general style of research, which puts a strong emphasis on the training, theory, and culture of the interviewer.

The experience and the *training* of the interviewer are central for the interview studies discussed. The academic and personal training of the therapist over several years is a prerequisite for conducting psychoanalytical therapy and research. Piaget had undertaken a psychoanalytical training and analysis and followed psychoanalytical seminars—in the authoritarian personality study close to half of the interviewers had undergone psychoanalysis, and in the Hawthorne study several years of training at actual interviewing was considered necessary to become a proficient interviewer. The extensive training of the interviewers in the classical studies discussed is in stark contrast to the novice interviewing in much qualitative research today.

The psychoanalyst seeks during the therapeutic hour to listen with an evenly hovering attention to what the patient tells, and the subsequent interpretations draw on psychoanalytical *theory*. Piaget's studies of children's thought were based on his epistemological conceptions of the general development of human thought. The authoritarian personality study by Adorno and colleagues was inspired by psychoanalytical theory regarding personality formation and defense mechanisms. The extensive theoretical basis of these investigations contrasts with the atheoretical empiricism of many current qualitative interview studies.

The early psychoanalytical inquiries, in particular of Freud and Jung, were informed by an extensive knowledge of human *culture*—the knowledge of the human situation recorded in classical myths, literature, and art. In academic and commercial interview studies inspired by psychoanalysis, it has mainly been the interview technique, rather than the openness to human culture, which has been appropriated from psychoanalysis. Within the psychoanalytical tradition an academic formalization has taken place during the 20th century, whereby a theoretical focus on internal ego mechanisms, and of therapy as the repair of ego functions, became stronger than a focus on cultural changes and their impact on human behavior. It may be noted that anthropological research, which today provides provoking insights into our culture, comes in some respects close to psychoanalytical research, with their different subject matter of the individual and the culture taken into account, respectively. This concerns the use of case studies taking place over extended periods of time, the care to establish rapport with the research participants, the open mode of observing and interviewing, and the interpretation of multiple layers of meaning. The cultural orientation of classical psychoanalysis contrasts with a cultural abstinence of academic psychological research, where human civilization is often ignored or treated as a source of error in a modern quest for universal cognitive mechanisms or laws of human behavior.

Psychological Marginalization of Qualitative Research

We may ask why not only the psychoanalytical interview, but qualitative research in general, until now has been methodologically marginalized within a psychological science. Perhaps quantitative methods in psychology have, beyond their scientific value in obtaining knowledge of the human situation, also served as a scientific legitimation of a new science. Externally, the dominance of quantitative methodology may have provided the discipline of psychology with a line of demarcation to competing professions in the market of human relations—historically from theology, and today from the many competitors on the therapeutic market (Kvale, 2002). Internally, for a discipline today characterized by a Babelian theoretical fragmentation, the monopoly of quantitative methodology may have served as a unifying force. Thus in *The International Handbook of Psychology* (Pawlik & Rosenzweig, 2000), published under the auspices of *The International Union of Psychological Science,* therapeutic and research interviews are hardly mentioned; they do not enter the book's chapter by Estes on *Basic Methods of Psychological Science.* The quantitative unification of psychology may today be threatened by qualitative dissidents. Such concerns appear supported in the chapter on *Theoretical Psychology* where the present fragmentation of psychology is addressed: "What has remained is a theoretically de-centered discipline that nevertheless is still methodologically uniform, despite the rising pressure from what is broadly (but somewhat misleadingly) labeled as qualitative psychology" (Stam, 2000, p. 556).

It remains a paradox that major parts of psychological knowledge have been generated by a qualitative method that does not exist in psychological methodology. General textbooks of scientific psychology today survive parasitically on knowledge produced by a psychoanalytical method denied a scientific status.

The Two Paths of Therapeutic and Academic Interview Research

In this final section I return to key aspects of the psychoanalytical interview, particularly the extended temporal and emotional interaction and the instigation of personal changes, and discuss some implications for interview research today. Although academic interview researchers may learn from therapeutic interviews, they should not try to imitate them. By taking account of the ethical differences between a therapeutic and a research relationship, two different paths for interview research emerge. The first *therapeutic interview path* departs from the standpoint that key aspects of the psychoanalytical interview, which aims at helping the interviewees change through an intensive emotional interaction, are ethically out of bounds for academic interview research. The therapeutic interview as such should therefore be reflected on and refined as a research procedure. The second *academic interview path* departs from the standpoint that although the strong emotional interaction of the therapeutic interview is ethically out of bounds for academic interview inquiries, these may nevertheless have much to learn about modes of questioning and the interpretation of meaning from the psychoanalytical interview and classical interview inquiries inspired by psychoanalysis.

The two paths of therapeutic and academic interview research involve different rules of the game, different methodological and ethical issues, and they entail different crafts to be learned. The following discussion may highlight both some of the knowledge potentials and the hazards when moving into the field between therapeutic and academic interviews. It will not result in any step-by-step procedures for therapeutic and academic interview research, but may point out some fruitful directions for pursuing interview research in psychology.

Psychological Research as Human Interaction

The psychoanalytical interview is part of a personal relationship lasting over several years, and it goes beyond the verbal dimension to include intuitive and bodily knowledge. For a psychological science that is based on eliminating the human factor from methods of investigating the human situation, the psychoanalytical interview, which is based on this very human interaction, must be dismissed as unscientific. Psychoanalytic inquiry deliberately furthers an intense human interrelationship, provoking strong feelings of transference and countertransference. The slow pace of the therapeutic conversation, with the trust established through a long-term personal interrelationship, opens up opportunities for layers of self-disclosure not accessible in brief research interviews.

Academic psychology is today essentially a psychology of strangers, a psychology that constructs knowledge of human experience and behavior on the basis of brief random encounters. In psychological experiments and tests, and often in qualitative interviews, the researcher meets the anonymous research participants for a short period, rarely for longer than an hour. Academic psychology has largely remained a tourist psychology, constructing a short-term knowledge of the human situation based on snapshots.

The knowledge obtained in a therapeutic interview also goes beyond the verbal dimension to also encompass tacit and bodily modes of knowing. Much of the therapists' knowledge is based on an intuitive listening to what goes on in the therapeutic relationship. Freud (1963) thus recommended that the therapists aimlessly listen to their patients with an evenly hovering attention, and therefore refrained from taking notes during the therapeutic session, because it might interfere with an attitude of open listening.

Therapeutic researchers may today enrich their interpretations by drawing on linguistic and narrative modes of analysis. It should nevertheless not be forgotten that the observational basis of therapeutical interpretations encompasses the lived human relation of the therapy encounter, including the bodily presence of the patient. In the therapeutic situation, the wealth of information provided by facial gestures and bodily postures is essential and has been systematically used within psychoanalytical character analysis and the vegetotherapy developed by Wilhelm Reich.

The therapeutic attention to the personal interaction in the interview, the open listening and observing, the focus on a bodily human being may also be of value to academic interview research. Linguistic modes of analysis are restricted to an impoverished, disembodied material, desituated from the human presence of the interview interaction. Current interview research may be subject to the tyranny of verbatim transcripts and formalized methods of analysis. One may speculate that if tape recorders had been available in Vienna in Freud's time, there would have existed no powerful psychoanalytical theory today; instead there might perhaps remain a small sect of psychoanalytical researchers reading and categorizing their transcripts, and discussing their reliability, rather than attentively listening to the multiple layers of meaning revealed in their embodied therapeutic interactions.

Qualitative Research as Methodology or as Craftsmanship

When the human relationship of the patient and the therapist are decisive for the generation of psychoanalytical knowledge, the question of the methodological basis of this knowledge becomes critical. The psychoanalytical interview falls outside strict conceptions of method by analytical philosophers, such as: "A method is a set of rules which can be used in a mechanical way to realize a given aim. The mechanical element is important: a method shall not presuppose judgement, artistic or other creative abilities" (Elster, 1980, p. 295).

When qualitative interviews eventually enter psychological methodology we may perhaps come to encounter a new qualitative positivism. This may be in the form of attempts to overstep human judgment by the interpretation of meaning with a quest for mechanical methods of formalized step-by-step rules and a heavy reliance on computer programs for the interpretation of interview texts. I will instead, following the Dreyfus model of skill learning, regard research interviewing as a skill, where context-free rules characterize novice behavior, whereas experts increasingly rely on situated emotionally involved intuitive judgments (Dreyfus & Dreyfus, 1986).

Rather than searching for a methodology free of human judgment, I understand qualitative interviewing as a human interaction, and as suggested by Mishler (1990), as a *craft*. The quality of the knowledge produced in an interview depends on the craftsmanship of the researcher. As a craft, interviewing does not follow content- and context-free rules of method, but rests on the technical mastery and the reasoned judgments of a qualified researcher, acquired through accumulated experiences of longer periods of training. The emphasis on the interviewer as a craftsperson does not accredit the interviewer a mystical infallible status of "the big interpreter." The interpretations and knowledge claims put forward by the interview researcher need to be documented and argued, as in any scientific endeavor, with the ideal of making the line of reasoning transparent for the reader to follow and evaluate critically.

In contrast to an analytical positivist ideal of psychological research, devoid of human judgment, the flexibility of approach and the importance of well-reasoned judgments put a heavy emphasis on the training of the therapist and on his or her expertise and maturity (e.g., see the chapter "Learning the Artistry of Psychoanalytical Practice" by Schön, 1987). The level of expertise required to make psychoanalytical observations and interpretations, particularly the timing of the interpretations, makes this form of research unavailable for novice researchers following a standard method.

Learning the craft of research takes place through practice and through the study of good exemplars of research practice. Interviews with, and biographies of, Nobel laureates in the natural sciences document how they learned research in practice through the personal relationships of apprenticeship within strong research communities. Rather than teaching transferable knowledge, rules, and techniques, these relationships promote an attitude and a vision, a gut feeling of what makes good science—a style of thinking encompassing not only the cognitive skills but also the values and norms of the science (see Kvale, 1997).

Eisner (1991) has gone beyond a craft approach to research by arguing for *art* as a model for educational research, which involves a connoisseurship regarding the subject matter of inquiry. In interviews with social scientists at the Center for Advanced Study in the Behavioral Sciences in Stanford, Eisner and Powell (in press) found five pervasive themes throughout the interviews that also mark artistic modes of thought and aesthetic forms of experience: imagination, somatic knowledge, empathic knowledge, a sense of place, and social–cultural influences on motivation. Again, we encounter a discrepancy between the demands of a scientific methodology devoid of human judgment and empirical studies of elite scientific behavior.

I have earlier attempted to spell out techniques and procedures of conducting and analyzing interviews and came to the conclusion that tentative rules of procedure may be helpful at initial stages, whereas the decisive factor remained the researcher's judgments, based on the application of rules according to the content and context of the interview (Kvale, 1996). When the researcher is regarded as a craftsperson or an artist, rather than a methodologist, the importance of studying textbooks on methodology recedes in relation to training the craft in research practice. It is thought-provoking—with the widespread use of psychoanalytical knowledge in the social sciences and the humanities today—that hardly any textbooks on psychoanalytical research methodology exists. Perhaps we encounter, in some cases, an inverse relationship between an emphasis on research methodology and the significance of the knowledge produced.

The Objectivity of Knowledge Produced in Interviews

When the person of the interviewer, with his or her craftsmanship, is essential to obtaining knowledge, the objectivity of the knowledge gets called into question. Qualitative interviews, and in particular therapeutic interviews, have been criticized for being subjective. An interview inquiry is admittedly subjective in the sense that the person who is the interviewer is the central research instrument and the knowledge is produced through the inter-subjective relation of the interview. The key issue is whether the intrinsic subjectivity of therapeutic and academic interviews precludes the production of objective knowledge, which I will discuss with regard to four meanings of objectivity.

First, objectivity in the sense of *free from partisan bias* is a general aim of research, and distortion by personal or professional bias and prejudice is always a danger in research. Bias is reduced by the craftsmanship of the researcher, by his or her systematic cross-checks and verifications of the quality and reliability of the knowledge generated. Intensive training of therapists and interviewers can make them aware of their personal influence on the interaction.

Second, objectivity, in the sense of *intersubjective agreement,* is a common requirement of research. Intersubjectivity in the form of "member checks" is possible when the therapeutic or the academic interviewer checks his or her interpretations with the interviewee. Intersubjectivity in the form of "peer checks" may be obtained when recordings from interviews allow colleagues to inspect, categorize, and evaluate interview interaction and interpretations. In a dialogical conception of intersubjectivity, the interview attains a privileged position, with a conversation and negotiation of meaning between the interviewers and their subjects. We may speak of *communicative validity,* in the sense of testing observations and interpretations in a dialogue—that is, testing the validity of knowledge claims together with the subjects investigated, as well as with the interpretative community of colleagues.

Third, objectivity may mean being adequate to the object investigated, letting the object speak, *reflecting the nature of the object researched.* The objectivity of a method then rests on its relation to its object and depends on the nature of the object investigated. With the object of the interview understood as a conversational subject in an intersubjectively negotiated social world, the interview as a conversational and intersubjective production of knowledge obtains a privileged objectivity regarding the human domain. The interview is sensitive to and reflects the nature of the object investigated—in the interview the "object" speaks.

Fourth, objectivity may also mean pragmatically *allowing the object to object.* Latour (2000) draws on this meaning of objectivity in the sense of giving the objects of the natural sciences an opportunity to object to what is told about them. He dismisses the social scientists' images of the natural sciences as "physics envy"; from the perspective of empirical studies of natural science research, "The imitation of the natural sciences by the social sciences has so far been a comedy of errors" (p. 114). Contrary to social scientists' belief in imitating the objectivity of the natural sciences by impartiality and complete mastery of the laboratory set-ups, Latour maintains that

> if social scientists wanted to become objective, they would have to find the very rare, costly, local, miraculous situation where they can render their subject of study as much as possible able to object to what is said about them, to be as disobedient as possible to the protocol, and to be as capable to raise their own questions in their own terms and *not* in those of the scientists whose interests they do not have to share! Then, humans would start to behave in the hands of the social scientists as *interestingly* as natural objects in the hands of natural scientists. (p. 116)

Latour pointed to the way in which the social science literature on housewives and gender roles has changed after feminism has rendered recalcitrant most of the potential interviewees. This opened for objectivity in the sense of "ability to propel novel entities on the scene, to raise new questions in their own terms and to force the social and natural scientists to retool the whole of their intellectual equipment" (p. 116).

We may add that an interview, in principle, allows "the objects to object." Throughout a century of psychological science, the therapeutic interview has been one of the rare research situations in which subjects could talk at length in their own terms, raise new questions, and also resist and object to the psychologist's interpretations of their behavior. The openness of the classical psychoanalytical situation—letting the patient talk while the therapist offers occasional interpretations—gives ample room for the patient's objections and resistance toward the therapist's interventions. Classical psychoanalysis deliberately follows the path of maximum resistance in treating the patients' objections. According to Freud, "The whole theory of psychoanalysis is . . . in fact built up on the perception of the resistance offered to us by the patient when we attempt to make his unconscious conscious to him" (1923/1964, p. 68).

In his article—*Constructions in Analysis*—Freud (1937/1964) addressed some common objections about the validity of the psychoanalyst's interpretations, in particular regarding the patients' objections to the therapist's interpretations. The therapist makes constructions about the forgotten past of the patient, and he or she conveys those constructions to the patient. Freud acknowledged that the patients' ability to object to what the therapist says about them may be counteracted by the therapist's authority and suggestive influence.

Freud drew on what may be termed communicative and pragmatic validation of interpretations. He did not rely entirely on the patients' self-understanding and verbal communication. He did not treat either the patient's direct "yes" or "no" to his constructions at face value as sufficient confirmation or disconfirmation, because they were both ambiguous and could be results of suggestion, as well as of resistance. He went beyond merely verbal "member checks" and recommended more indirect forms of validation, inferring from the patient's reactions after he had offered an interpretative construction. Acknowledging that a patient's reactions to the therapist's constructions may be the expression of legitimate dissent as well as of unconscious resistance evoked by the subject matter of the construction, Freud would carefully observe the patient's subsequent behavior for indirect forms of confirmation, such as changes in the patient's free associations, dreams, the recollection of forgotten memories, and alteration of neurotic symptoms. We may speak of a *pragmatic validation,* which goes further than verbal communication; it represents a stronger knowledge claim than an agreement through a dialogue—"Actions speak louder than words."

I have discussed a common objection to interview inquiries as lacking objectivity by drawing on four conceptions of objectivity: freedom from bias, intersubjective agreement, reflecting the nature of the object investigated, and allowing the object to object. An interview inquiry may, in principle, produce objective knowledge in all four senses, allowing for communicative and pragmatic validation of knowledge claims. With the conceptions of objectivity outlined, the psychoanalytical interview, rather than lacking objectivity, pushes the limits of objectivity in social science research, allowing the objects investigated emotionally and verbally to object to what the researcher says about them, thus being one of the rare psychological research situations in which the research objects' objections to the researcher's interpretations may be taken into account.

Ethical Tensions in Therapeutic and Research Interviews

Therapeutic and academic interviews aim respectively to help patients change and to produce knowledge. They are different ethical situations, precluding any simple transferal of therapeutic techniques to research situations. The provocation of strong emotional objections from the subjects investigated, thereby obtaining objective knowledge in the sense of allowing the object to object as discussed earlier, is thus part of an implicit contract for the therapeutic interview, but is ethically out of bounds for academic research interviews.

Ethics becomes as important as methodology when pursuing the two paths of therapeutic and academic interviewing. This relates to the dilemma of mixing therapeutic and research interests in the same interview situation, the possibilities and rights of the interviewees to object to what is said about them, the effects of the interpretations given on the self-understanding of the subjects interpreted, as well as on the broader culture and the use of indirect questioning modes in a larger social context.

In therapy the main goal is a change in the patient; in research it is the advancement of knowledge. A therapist needs to consider the ethical tensions by bringing the role of the therapist and the researcher closer together, particularly where a strong research interest may interfere with the therapeutic process. Freud thus warned against formulating a case scientifically while treatment is proceeding, because it could interfere with the therapist's ability to listen to the patient with an open mind (1963, p. 120). On the other hand, an academic interviewer's ability to listen attentively may in some cases lead to quasi-therapeutic relationships, which most interviewers have neither the training nor the time to enter into. In particular, long-lasting and repeated research interviews on sensitive personal themes may lead the interviewee into a therapy-like relationship. The creation of close therapeutic interrelationships over several years, which may be required for obtaining insight into the deeper layers of personality, are ethically out of bounds for academic interviews.

Objectivity, in the sense of creating extreme situations in which the objects are maximally provoked to object to the interviewer's interpretations, is likewise ethically out of limits for academic research interviews. The provocation of extreme patient reactions and taking the resistance and objections of the patients seriously may be one reason for the contributions of psychoanalysis in raising new questions and bringing forth new understandings of the human condition. A therapeutic ethical license with regard to academic ethical codes permits the creation of extreme situations of inquiry that open up possibilities for objectivity in the sense of allowing "the object to object," in word and in body. Thus, rather than treating therapy as merely a practical application of theoretical knowledge, we may regard the therapeutic relationship, with its unique intertwinement of ethics and objectivity, as one privileged production site for knowledge of the human situation.

The possibilities for giving interpretations and for the validation of interpretations differ in therapeutic and academic interviews. When an academic interviewer makes interpretations that go beyond the self-understanding of an interviewee, several ethical issues are raised: Should subjects be confronted with the new interpretations of themselves that they may not have asked for? And what should be done about disagreements between the subject's and the researcher's interpretations of a theme? In research interviews, which the interviewees themselves have not sought, it may be unethical to instigate new self-interpretations or emotional changes. In therapy it may, in contrast, be unethical if the therapeutic conversations the patients have sought, and often paid highly for, do not lead to new insights or emotional changes. The penetrating interpretations and repeated critical checks of the subjects' statements, which may instigate deep changes in their self-understanding and personality, are a part of the therapeutic contract, but out of reach for research purposes.

An inherent contradiction in pursuing scientific knowledge and ethically respecting the integrity of the interviewee has been discussed by Fog (1992). As a therapist also conducting separate research interviews, she addressed the dilemma of the researcher wanting the interview to be as deep and probing as possible even at the risk of trespassing the person, and at the same time wanting to be as respectful of the interview person as much as possible, at the risk of getting empirical material that only scratches the surface. She reported the example of a woman who repeatedly and energetically tells the interviewer how happy she is in her marriage. The woman also gives many verbal and nonverbal signals denying the happiness, and reports situations in which she is angry about the marriage. The information obtained by the interview is thus ambiguous and puts the interviewer in a conflict between scientific and ethical considerations. Should she accept at face value the woman's version, or should she follow her hunch that the woman is denying the realities of the marriage and probe further and point out to her the many inconsistencies and contradictions in what she tells about her marriage? A consequence of the latter could be a radical challenge to the woman's understanding of herself and her marriage. This would have been part of an implicit contract of a therapeutic interview, but is definitely beyond the contract of a normal research interview—and in fact was not attempted in this case.

The ethical issue of the impact of the therapist's interpretations goes beyond the therapeutic relationship. In line with trends in psychoanalytical theory, the patients' narratives have often been reported within a perspective of a therapeutizing individualization, infantilization, and sexualization of human activity. With the compelling force of therapeutic narratives based on a unique access to the biographies and the daily lives, to the dreams and the fantasies of the patients, a one-sided therapeutizing perspective on human activity has had a strong impact on the self-understanding of men and women in Western culture throughout the 20th century. The individualizing perspective of psychoanalytical interpretations reflected a modernist culture, an individualistic culture toward which psychoanalysis has itself contributed.

Ethical issues of the interaction within therapeutic, academic, and commercial interviews are situated in a broader social context. Within a therapeutic relationship it is ethical to "by indirections find directions out"—here exists a common interest of both therapist and patient to promote change, and indirect forms of questioning and validation can be necessary parts of the joint venture of helping the patient change. In academic research, however, indirect interviewing to get beyond the research participant's defenses violates an ethical requirement of informed consent. In the authoritarian personality study an indirect interview technique was deliberately applied to get beyond the research participants' defenses and obtain knowledge about their reasons for anti-Semitism. Concealed modes of questioning become ethically more questionable in commercial interviews, with opposing interests of the parties involved. The Hawthorne interviews served the management interest in increasing the workers' morale and productive output, and motivational market interviews serve to manipulate the behavior of consumers without their knowledge.

Although qualitative interviews within humanistic and feminist psychology sometimes are viewed as in themselves a progressive alternative to behaviorist experimentation, we should not forget that historically, as well as today, a large part of psychological qualitative interviewing takes place in the interest of management control of workers and in particular by the manipulation of consumer behavior. Interview interventions, which can be ethically desirable within a joint therapeutic venture of helping a person change, may become ethically questionable in academic settings and unethical in larger social contexts with opposing economic and political interests, such as between management and workers. Although the vested and conflicting interests and power contexts of commercial interview research are rather visible, potentially less obvious partisan interests and power contexts of apparently impartial academic interview research need as well be taken in account.

Conclusion

Knowledge originally generated in psychoanalytical interviews has changed the ways we understand our selves and our world, and today it belongs to the core of the psychological discipline. I have attempted to spell out some aspects of the mode of understanding of the psychoanalytical interview and also documented how it has inspired classical interview studies within academic and commercial psychology.

Two different paths for pursuing interview inquiries in current psychology have emerged. On the first path, therapists, rather than being hampered by low research self-esteem, may conduct research by sticking to their trade, and develop its unique potentials for obtaining knowledge of the human situation, following Freud's approach of letting research and treatment proceed hand in hand. On the second path, academic interview researchers may today learn from the knowledge potentialities and intricacies of the human interaction in therapeutic interviews, taking account of the differences of ethics and objectivity in the therapeutic and the research interview.

No straightforward transfer of psychoanalytical interview techniques to academic research interviews has been proposed or any simple step-by-step procedures for conducting academic interviews. The psychoanalytical interview raises principal challenges to established conceptions of psychological knowledge and methodology. The therapeutic aim of helping persons change allows for therapeutic interventions that are ethically out of bounds for academic purposes of knowledge production; differences that make the therapeutic situation one extreme and privileged site for generating objective psychological knowledge. A focus on therapeutic interviews as research situations highlights tensions in the use of human relationships for research purposes, which in less visible forms also pertain to academic interview research—tensions between methodology, ethics, and politics in producing of knowledge of the human situation.

References

Acocella, J. (1998, April). The politics of hysteria. *The New Yorker, 6,* 64–79.

Adorno, T. W., Frenkel-Brunswik, E., Levinson, D. J., & Sanford, R. N. (1993). *The authoritarian personality.* New York: Norton. (Original published 1950)

Atkinson, B., Heath, A., & Chenail, R. (1991). Qualitative research and the legitimation of knowledge. *Journal of Marital and Family Therapy, 17,* 175–180.

Boss, M. (1963). *Psychoanalysis and daseinsanalysis.* New York: Basic Books.

Chenail, R. (1992). A case for clinical qualitative research. *The Qualitative Report, 1*(1), 1–7.

Corsini, J. R. (Ed.). (1994). *Encyclopedia of psychology* (2nd ed.). New York: Wiley.

Denzin, N., & Lincoln, Y. (Eds.). (2000). *Handbook of qualitative research.* Thousand Oaks, CA: Sage.

Dichter, E. (1960). *The strategy of desire.* New York: Doubleday.

Dreyfus, H. L., & Dreyfus, S. E. (1986). *Mind over machine.* New York: Free Press.

Eisner, E. W. (1991). *The enlightened eye—Qualitative inquiry and the enhancement of educational practice.* New York: Macmillan.

Eisner, E. W., & Powell, K. (in press). Art in science. *Curriculum Inquiry.*

Elster, J. (1980). Metode (Method). *PaxLeksikon IV.* Oslo: Pax.

Fishman, D. B. (1999). *The case for pragmatic psychology.* New York: New York University Press.

Fog, J. (1992). Den moralske grund i det kvalitative forskningsinterview (The moral ground in the qualitative research interview). *Nordisk Psykologi, 44,* 212–229.

Freud, S. (1963). *Therapy and technique.* New York: Collier.

Freud, S. (1964). Two encyclopedia articles. In *Standard edition of the complete psychological works of Sigmund Freud* (Vol. 18, pp. 235–259). London: Hogart. (Original published 1923)

Freud, S. (1964). Constructions in analysis. In *Standard edition of the complete psychological works of Sigmund Freud* (Vol. 23, pp. 1–182). London: Hogart. (Original published 1923)

Fromm, E., Horkheimer, M., Mayer, E., & Marcuse, H. (1936). *Autorität und Familie* (Authority and family). Paris: Alcan.

Frommer, J., & Rennie, D. (Eds.). (2001). *The methodology of qualitative psychotherapy research.* Engele: Pabst.

Gergen, K. J. (1994). *Realities and relationships. Soundings in social constructionism.* Cambridge, MA: Harvard University Press.

Greenbaum, T. L. (1998). *The handbook of focus group research.* Thousand Oaks, CA: Sage.

Habermas, J. (1971). *Knowledge and human interests.* Boston: Beacon.

Hannush, M. J. (1973). Adorno and Sartre: A convergence of two methodological approaches. *Journal of Phenomenological Psychology, 3,* 297–313.

Klein, G. S. (1973). Two theories or one? *Bulletin of the Menninger Clinic, 37,* 102–132.

Kvale, S. (1996). *InterViews—An introduction to qualitative research interviewing.* Thousand Oaks, CA: Sage.

Kvale, S. (1997). Research apprenticeship. *Nordisk Pedagogik—Nordic Journal of Educational Research, 17,* 186–194.

Kvale, S. (1999a). The psychoanalytic interview as qualitative research. *Qualitative Inquiry, 5*(1), 87–113.

Kvale, S. (1999b). Constructing knowledge through inter views. In W. Maiers, B. Bayer, B. Duarte Esgalhdo, R. Jorna, & E. Schraube (Eds.), *Challenges to theoretical psychology* (pp. 50–59). New York: Captus Press.

Kvale, S. (2002). The church, the factory and the market as metaphors for psychology—Scenarios for psychology in the postmodern age. In C. V. Hofsten & L. Bäckman (Eds.), *Psychology at the turn of the millenium, Vol. 2: Social, developmental, and clinical perspectives* (pp. 409–436). Hove, UK: Psychology Press.

Latour, B. (2000). When things strike back—A possible contribution of 'science studies' to the social sciences. *British Journal of Sociology, 51,* 107–123.

Litowitz, B. E. (1999). Freud and Piaget: Une fois de plus (Freud and Piaget: One More time). Retrieved Sept. 22, 2002, at http://www.piaget.org/GE/1999/GE-27-4

McLeod, J. (2001). *Qualitative research in counseling and psychotherapy.* London: Sage.

Mishler, E. G. (1990). Validation in inquiry-guided research: The role of exemplars in narrative studies. *Harvard Educational Review, 60,* 415–442.

Pawlik, K., & Rosenzweig, M. R. (Eds.). (2000). *The international handbook of psychology.* Thousand Oaks, CA: Sage.

Piaget, J. (1923). La pensée symbolique et la pensée de l'enfant (Symbolic thought and the thought of the child). *Archives de Psychologie, 18,* 273–304.

Piaget, J. (1971). *The language and the thought of the child.* London: Routledge and Kegan Paul.

Polkinghorne, D. (1992). Postmodern epistemology of practice. In S. Kvale (Ed.), *Psychology and postmodernism* (pp. 146–165). London: Sage.

Roethlisberger, F. J., & Dickson, W. J. (1964). *Management and the worker.* New York: Wiley. (Original published 1939)

Sartre, J.-P. (1963). *The problem of method.* London: Methuen.

Sartre, J.-P. (1965). *Anti-Semite and Jew.* New York: Schocken. (Original published 1946)

Schön, D. (1987). *Educating the reflective practitioner.* London: Jossey-Bass.

Skårderud, F. (2000). *Unruhe—Eine Reise in das Selbst (Unrest—A Journey in the self).* Hamburg: Rogner & Bernhard.

Stam, H. J. (2000). Theoretical psychology. In K. Pawlik & M. R. Rosenzweig (Eds.), *The international handbook of psychology* (pp. 551–569). Thousand Oaks, CA: Sage.

Stern, D. N. (1985). *The interpersonal world of the infant.* New York: Basic Books.

Time, March 29, 1999.

Author Index

Numbers in italics refer to listings in reference sections.

Subject Index

About the Editors

Paul M. Camic, PhD, is professor of psychology and cultural studies at the Department of Liberal Education, Columbia College Chicago. He was formerly on the faculty at the University of Chicago and Northwestern University. He completed his doctoral work at Loyola University and took undergraduate and master's degrees from Clark and Tufts Universities, respectively. Both his internship and postdoctoral fellowship were at the University of Chicago. He is author and coeditor of *Assessing Chronic Pain: A Multidisciplinary Clinic Approach* and *Clinical Handbook of Health Psychology*. He has also published numerous articles and chapters. He has taught qualitative research methods to graduate and undergraduate students for more than a decade, and is co-investigator, along with Jean E. Rhodes, in a multiple-site, five-year funded study that examines the social and emotional climate of academically excelling middle schools using qualitative and quantitative methodologies.

Jean E. Rhodes, PhD, is professor of psychology at the University of Massachusetts, Boston. She took her undergraduate degree at the University of Vermont, did her graduate work in clinical–community psychology at DePaul University, and completed her internship at the University of Chicago. She was previously on the faculty at the University of Chicago Medical School and the University of Illinois. She has conducted extensive research on the topic of youth mentoring, including an analysis of the Big Brothers Big Sisters national impact study. She has published more than 20 articles and chapters on the topic of mentoring as well as the book *Stand by Me: The Risks and Rewards of Youth Mentoring* and the edited volume *On Second Glance: Critical Perspective on Youth Development.*

Lucy Yardley, PhD, is professor of health psychology and head of the Department of Psychology at the University of Southampton in the United Kingdom. She is editor of two books, *Material Discourses in Health Psychology* and *Research Methods in Clinical and Health Psychology,* and has a long-standing interest in combining the insights from qualitative and quantitative research. Her program of empirical research on the experience of chronic illness and treatment integrates findings from discourse and phenomenological analysis with the results of psychophysiological experiments and clinical trials. She has published extensively in both health psychology and qualitative methodology.